Sex
Variant Woman

Sex Variant Woman

⚛ THE LIFE OF ⚛
Jeannette Howard Foster

JOANNE PASSET

Da Capo Press
A Member of the Perseus Books Group

Designed by Brent Wilcox
Set in 11 point Goudy by the Perseus Books Group

Cataloging-in-Publication data for this book is available from the Library of Congress.

First Da Capo Press edition 2008
ISBN: 978-0-7867-1822-1

Published by Da Capo Press
A Member of the Perseus Books Group
www.dacapopress.com

Da Capo Press books are available at special discounts for bulk purchases in the United States by corporations, institutions, and other organizations. For more information, please contact the Special Markets Department at the Perseus Books Group, 2300 Chestnut Street, Suite 200, Philadelphia, PA 19103, or call (800) 810-4145, extension 5000, or e-mail special.markets@perseusbooks.com.

1 2 3 4 5 6 7 8 9

For those who treasured Foster's work.

Contents

List of Illustrations

FOREWORD

I'm twenty-two years old and the year is 1962. I've just been admitted to UCLA as a graduate student in English. McCarthyism isn't over, and before I'm permitted to become a teaching assistant in the English Department—a glorious honor—I have to sign a loyalty oath that promises that I'm not subversive. I sign the oath without a qualm because I know I'll be too busy studying English literature and teaching English 1A to think about overturning the government. Yet I am indeed subversive—my sexuality is certainly subversive. And I'm sure that if it should come to be known by the authorities, whoever they are, I'll be booted out of UCLA—denied a place on that enchanting campus, with its grand old buildings and stellar faculty and its promise that if I behave myself I'll be credentialed into a career of scholarship for which I yearn. So I watch where I step and look over my shoulder a lot. As far as I know, I'm the only homosexual at UCLA, and I have to make sure that no one suspects.

But something very confusing happens to me during my first few weeks on campus. I get seduced. By a book. I've made it a habit already in between my classes to go study in the English Reading Room, a small, comfortable retreat for graduate students and faculty. The English Reading Room has a pretty good little library that includes most of the books that are assigned in the graduate classes. Today I'm after an E. M. Forster book—*Passage to India* or *Howards End*, perhaps—certainly not *Maurice*, a novel about Forster's own homosexual desires, which he wrote in 1913, in between those other two novels, but of which I'd never heard, because it was not to be published until 1971, a year after he was safely dead, and almost a decade after my story. Clearly my Brit Lit prof had never heard of *Maurice* either, or if he had, he wasn't telling. Just as he wasn't telling other things that would have interested me passionately about the writers we read for his course, things such as the fact that Forster was a homosexual, and that most of his Bloomsbury friends—Lytton Strachey, Virginia Woolf, and a slew of others—shared his gay proclivities. Nor were the biographies I read in 1962 telling. As far as I knew, the Bloomsbury writers were eccentric bachelors or proper married ladies, quite without frightening, dark secrets such as my own. I was virtually alone in my scary subversion, and the fact that no one ever said the word "homosexual" at UCLA—unless perhaps you were in an abnormal psych class—was proof of my aloneness.

But I digress. So I'm in the stacks of the English Reading Room about to be seduced. I'm looking for a novel by E. M. Forster, and it's not there. Someone else from my class must already have taken it off the shelf. But in the spot where the book is supposed to be sitting is another book, not by Forster, but by Foster. Jeannette Foster. With the title *Sex Variant Women in Literature*. Sex Variant. Could it be? Surely not. Not in the UCLA English Reading Room. I look to my right and to my left to make sure no one is coming, and I hurriedly take it from the shelf—that book, and then E. M. Forster's *Where Angels Fear to Tread*, to serve as a cover, so that if someone should happen by they'd see me with two books in my hand, but they'd only be able to read the title of the Forster book. Is "Sex Variant Women" really a euphemism for what I think it is?

It is! And that spectacular revelation knocks the breath out of me. I can see from a cursory look that *Sex Variant Women in Literature* is a remarkable book-length bibliography in which the author presents 2500 years worth of writings about love and sex between women, literature especially from America, England, France, and Germany, literature especially from the seventeenth and eighteenth and nineteenth centuries, as well as the first half of the twentieth century. All of it about female same-sex relationships! Standing there in the stacks, I devour the opening section, even forgetting to look over my shoulder to see if I'm being observed. I read for twenty minutes or half an hour, and no one comes by to frighten me away. But I mustn't press my luck. I place the book back in its slot, vowing to visit it again as soon as I can, praying I'll have no rival for my devoted attention to it. What will I do if I come back to find that someone has snatched it away?

I think about the book constantly when I can't be holding it in my hands and losing myself in the guilty pleasures of it there in the dim lit Reading Room stacks.

It had been published in 1956. I'd never heard of the publisher, Vantage Press. A so-called vanity press, I was sure. But it did not surprise me that no real publisher would take a risk on so subversive a book. Paperback publishers were still bringing out pulps about Odd Girls or Twilight Lovers, in which young women like me invariably ended badly—but who in the 1950s and even in 1962 would want to read this erudite bibliographic study of literature that dealt with a subject no respectable person ever seemed to want to talk about?

Who except me? My secret love sat waiting for me always, revealing beauties and wonders whenever I could pay a visit. It took me the whole semester to finish *Sex Variant Women in Literature*, ten or so pages at a time, standing in the stacks, never daring to take the book out to a soft chair in the Reading Room, where I would be so much more comfortable.

Despite my romance with Foster's book, I couldn't imagine in those days how profoundly it would affect my life. I went on to finish graduate school with a Ph.D., never once in my years at UCLA hearing a word such as "homosexual" from my professors, though we read Walt Whitman and Emily Dickinson and W. H. Auden and Stephen Spender and Carson McCullers and James Baldwin and . . . the list is endless. Though I would have loved to have done my dissertation on one of the women authors about whom Jeannette Foster wrote in *Sex Variant Women in Literature*, it was still the mid-1960s, and I wasn't crazy. With my advisor's blessings, I wrote my dissertation on the stirring topic of B. L. Farjeon and the Popular Victorian Novel. My passion for Foster's book remained my secret.

Until the glorious revolutions of the late 1960s and the 1970s. In 1976 a Women in Print conference brought together lesbians and feminists who were interested in all aspects of publishing and selling literature by and about lesbians. Soon women's bookstores were proliferating all over the country—literally hundreds of them—and Jeannette Foster, whose *Sex Variant Women in Literature* had long been out of print, came back into print with two other books—a collection of her poems and a translation of a Renee Vivien novel.

By then I no longer felt that I had to read her work standing in dimly lit library stacks. I found a used copy of *Sex Variant Women in Literature* in a women's bookstore, and I reread it, devouring it once again, so cognizant this time of the changes for the better that had taken place since I'd first found Foster's book almost fifteen years earlier. It was the inspiration of that book that made me begin in 1976 the study that would eventually be published in 1981 as *Surpassing the Love of Men: Romantic Friendship and Love between Women from the Renaissance to the Present.* As I say on the acknowledgement page of that book, Foster's work was indispensable to my own, and it was my fondest wish that what I wrote would be as helpful to future scholars as *Sex Variant Women in Literature* was to me. That was an extremely ambitious wish because I think that no serious scholar of lesbian literature to this day can do without Foster's wonderful book.

I find her contribution all the more remarkable because she was writing in what were truly the dark ages for lesbians and gays—and readers (if I, myself, am any example) had to read her book in the near dark. I really wonder if my own career as a lesbian writer would have been possible had it not been for all the work that Foster did before me, all the leads she gave me for my own research—and the deep inspiration she made me feel by virtue of her own pure and driven commitment to create a work about the lesbian past, even when no one seemed interested.

Jeannette Foster died in 1981, the same year that *Surpassing the Love of Men* was published. I never had the privilege of meeting Foster, to my very great regret. But Joanne Passet's thorough, probing, and fascinating biography makes me feel that I now know well not only Jean-nette Foster's indispensable work but also the life that was behind that work and that made the work possible. *Sex Variant Woman* is a book for which any reader interested in the history of women or lesbians—or in the stirring story of how one woman led her life usefully and bravely—will be very grateful.

Lillian Faderman

Lillian Faderman has published numerous books about lesbian history and literature, including *Surpassing the Love of Men: Romantic Friendship and Love Between Women from the Renaissance to the Present, Odd Girls and Twilight Lovers: A History of Lesbian Life in Twentieth Century America,* and *To Believe in Women: What Lesbians Have Done for America—A History.*

ACKNOWLEDGMENTS

This book had its origins in a conversation with my colleague, Indiana University historian James H. Madison. Since my last book was about nineteenth-century free lovers, he suggested that I consider doing a project based on materials housed in the Kinsey Institute for Research in Sex, Gender, and Reproduction. Intrigued by his suggestion, I met with Liana Zhou, director of collections at the institute, and after reviewing several possible research topics with her, I decided to write an article about Jeannette Howard Foster, Kinsey's first professionally trained librarian. As a historian of women who also has a doctorate in library and information science, I considered myself uniquely qualified to explore her life. Since Jeannette Foster did not leave her papers to any one institution, it became necessary to reconstruct her life through her publications, the people who knew her, and the correspondence and other records that survive in the manuscript collections of people she knew and archival collections of places where she studied and worked. During my search for these records, the intended article expanded into a book!

In the process of researching Foster's life, I met many warm, generous, and fascinating people. I am deeply indebted to Jeannette's niece and nephew, Alison Cope Puffer and Winslow Howard Cope, for sharing their family's history with me. Their enthusiasm for the project and their willingness to share family photos, diaries, and correspondence have immeasurably enriched the story of Jeannette's early years. I appreciate Alison's enthusiasm and energy and Win's patience and willingness to answer endless questions. They, along with their spouses Richard Puffer and Alora Cope, also made me feel at home in the Hamlin Lake cottage where Jeannette summered with her family. I hope this book will give them a deeper understanding of their aunt.

I was fortunate, early in the project, to discover Barbara Grier, a close friend of Jeannette's beginning in the 1950s. Since our first conversation by phone, Barbara has patiently and with good humor answered numerous email messages, identified people in photographs, shed light on the world of publishing, helped me locate people related to Jeannette's story, and read and commented upon drafts of the book. Through countless anecdotes she has breathed life into the Jeannette I only knew on paper, illuminating her attitudes, outlook, relationships, sense of humor, and most of all, passion for lesbian literature. Barbara's enthusiasm for the project has been infectious and during the final days of writing her well-timed words of encouragement and feedback have proven invaluable.

I also wish to acknowledge the assistance of a number of other individuals who knew and/or corresponded with Jeannette Foster. I am thankful to Marie J. Kuda for so generously sharing her personal archives and vast store of knowledge of Chicago gay and lesbian history with me, for reading and commenting on drafts of the manuscript, for helping me connect with others, and for patiently responding to numerous questions via email. Karla Jay shared her impressions of Jeannette with me and I benefited greatly from reading her correspondence with Foster and listening to the oral history she conducted in 1975, now housed at the New York Public Library. In preserving Jeannette's voice on tape, Karla allowed me to appreciate her expressiveness and articulateness as well as to gain a deeper understanding of the impact aging had on her indomitable spirit. The late Tee Corinne generously shared Jeannette's correspondence with Valerie Taylor along with images she took of Jeannette in 1977. Most delightful of all are the eloquent memories of her visits with Jeannette that she sent me months before her death. Others who knew

Jeannette and have answered many questions and provided invaluable advice and guidance include the late Barbara Gittings, Jonathan N. Katz, and the late Anyda Marchant. I also am thankful to Ann Bannon, Hazel Barnes, B. J. Bruther, Robin Cohen, Katherine V. Forrest, Bill Kelley, Lee Lynch, Christine Pattee, Maida Tilchen, and Susan Wiseheart for sharing memories of encounters with Jeannette or her printed works, and to Katherine Czarnik for providing information about Diana Press.

Writing this biography has been a collaborative venture, and I have benefited from the substantive support of friends and colleagues. My good friend Carol McCafferty, who is a librarian, has selflessly and enthusiastically tackled numerous challenging research questions, read and commented on the entire manuscript, and prepared the photographs for publication. I also appreciated her willingness to listen to me talk endlessly about the many details that I found fascinating throughout this project. Lillian Faderman generously gave of her time to read drafts of the manuscript and pushed me to see Jeannette's life in the larger historical context. I also am grateful to her for writing the foreword to this edition. James V. Carmichael Jr. also read and commented on drafts and opened doors for me to helpful people in the library world. Others who have read portions or all of the text and provided feedback include Donna McBride, Frances Peacock, Lynn Gorchov, Laverne Nishihara, and Maida Tilchen. Dozens of additional people have provided research assistance and advice, but I would like to single out Denise Bullock, John D'Emilio, Marcia Gallo, Guy Garrison, Julie Golia, James H. Jones, Judith Serebnick, and Mary White. I also am grateful to Dorothy Collins, Paul Gebhard, Barbara Grier, Marie J. Kuda, Donna McBride, and Henry Remak for granting oral interviews.

In Jeannette's lifetime, the gay and lesbian archives that have been so helpful to this project did not exist. I would like to thank Frank Gagliardi, of Gender Equity Collections, Central Connecticut State University; Karen Sendiak, at Gerber/Hart Library; Jacob and Terrence at the Gay, Lesbian, Bisexual, Transgender Historical Society, San Francisco; volunteers at the June L. Mazer Lesbian Archives; Deborah Edel, at the Lesbian Herstory Archives; the staff of ONE Institute and Archives; and Tim Wilson, of the James C. Hormel Gay and Lesbian Center, San Francisco Public Library. Several librarians and archivists have gone the extra mile in helping me to understand specific aspects of Jeannette's life and career. These include Ginger Cain, at Emory University Archives; Stuart Campbell, at Chicago State University Archives; George Franchois, at the U.S. Department of Interior Library; Dina Kellams, at Indiana University Archives; David Kuzma, at Rutgers University Archives; Kevin Martin, at Drexel University Archives; David Pavelich, at the University of Chicago Archives; Mary Pryor, at Rockford College; Alice Taylor-Colbert, at Shorter College; Shawn Wilson, of the Kinsey Institute for Research in Sex, Gender, and Reproduction; and Melanie Yolles, of the New York Public Library.

I also would like to acknowledge the helpful and knowledgeable assistance of librarians and archivists at the American Library Association Archives; Antioch College; Atlanta History Center; Beinecke Library, Yale University; Buncombe County Public Library, Ashville, North Carolina; Central Missouri State University, Columbia University Archives; Cordele Crisp Carnegie Library, Cordele, Georgia; Cornell University Division of Rare and Manuscript Collections; Decatur (Georgia) Public Library; Cowles Library, Drake University; Franklin D. Roosevelt Presidential Library; Hamline University Archives; Hedburg Library, Janesville, Wisconsin; Hollins University Archives; Indiana University Reference Department; Indiana University East Interlibrary Loan Department; Lindenwood University Archives; Mason County Library, Ludington, Michigan; Medical Center Archives of New York; Milwaukee Public Library; Missouri State Historical Society; Northwestern University Archives; Oberlin College Archives; Randolph County (Arkansas) Public Library; St. Charles City-County Library District, St. Charles, Missouri; St. Charles (Missouri) County Historical Society; Smith College Archives; Special Collections Department, University of Arkansas; University of Illinois Archives; University of Iowa Libraries; Special Collections Department, University of Missouri, Kansas City; University of

Pennsylvania Archives; St. Louis Public Library; Wellesley College Archives; and Winnetka-Northfield Library Reference Department.

Photographs add immeasurably to Jeannette's story. I am grateful to Winslow Howard Cope, the late Tee Corinne, Rose Fortier, Lisa Gensel, Stephanie Giordano, Barbara Grier, Lesli Larson, Linda Long, Donna McBride, Carol McCafferty, Debra Oswald, Alison Cope Puffer, Saskia Scheffer, Bart Schmidt, and Wanda Taylor for their assistance in making these images available.

I am indebted to the women and men who have been involved in the editing and production of this book. From the first time he heard about my research, Don Weise has been enthusiastic and supportive of the project. I am very grateful to have him as an editor, and appreciate his thoughtful and knowledgeable feedback. Renee Sedliar, senior editor at Da Capo Press, has been a joy to work with and I appreciate her enthusiasm and guidance during the final stages of the project. I also would like to thank literary agent Frances Goldin for her helpful advice when I was deciding where to place the book. Others, too numerous to name, have assisted in the production process, and I appreciate their contributions.

Friends have provided love, support, and understanding throughout this process, and their help, even if indirect, has made my load lighter and more enjoyable. Thank you to Anne and Sharon at Carefree, Carole Bailey, Jill Butcher, Damiana Chavez, Mary Fell, Susan Haswell, Nancy Lair, Barbara Orbach Natanson, Judy Serebnick, and Julie Snyder for answering and asking questions, assisting with research, and sharing their perspectives on my discoveries. Finally, I can never find enough words to thank Deb Wehman for being my muse, sounding board, and best friend, for chauffeuring me to many of the places where Jeannette lived and enjoying the journey! Through it all she has been patient, encouraging, genuinely interested, and a good listener. Many times her perceptive observations have led me to a deeper understanding of Jeannette's world. She has been supportive throughout the project, but during the final months of writing and editing she found many loving and thoughtful ways to lighten my load.

In the process of doing the research for this book, I had the great fortune to interact with many kind and wonderful people who were touched by Jeannette's scholarship and approach to life. Learning about Jeannette Foster's life has helped me grow in my historical knowledge and self-understanding, and my life has been enriched beyond my wildest expectations. I am grateful to Jeannette for giving me this opportunity.

Joanne Passet
Richmond, Indiana

INTRODUCTION

In the early 1950s, Alfred Kinsey's Institute for Sex Research received an enormous donation of anonymous erotic manuscripts. Working on the campus of Indiana University, Kinsey's librarian Jeannette Howard Foster sorted them into piles on two long library tables in the basement of Wylie Hall. Since such works could not be organized by author, she decided to catalog them by subject matter—were they heterosexual or homosexual? Was the theme sadistic or was it about a particular type of fetish? Fortunately for her, these anonymous authors got down to business in the first page or two.[1]

Jeannette looked like a typical grandmother of the time in her prim Nelly Don dresses and sensible ground-gripper shoes and seemed on the surface the caricature of an old-fashioned librarian. She did not appear to be the type of woman who would deign to touch pornography, let alone read it, nor did she look like someone who would comb seedy bookstores searching out lesbian paperbacks. But looks belied her identity. Beneath the prim and proper demeanor, Jeannette was a woman driven by her passion to root out examples of lesbians, bisexuals, and crossdressers in literature and to document their presence in a book so countless others could find validation of their sexual identity in print. In 1948 this lifelong quest led her to the Institute for Sex Research (ISR), with its extensive library of erotic fiction and works on sexuality. She had to know if she had overlooked any elusive yet critical works,

and the ISR—the largest collection of its kind in the United States—
was the place to do this.

For Jeannette Foster, organizing pornographic works was boring, and
sorting it hour after hour was as tedious and tiring as the yard work she
had done as a young girl with her father. During her four years at the Institute, the strong-minded and opinionated woman grew weary of Kinsey's dictatorial ways. She also became convinced that he would prevent
her from publishing a book about sex variants because he did not want
her work on homosexuality linked to the Institute. Breaking away from
Kinsey, she boldly self-published *Sex Variant Women in Literature* in 1956,
a time when many viewed being gay as sinful, sick, and criminal. Indeed,
homosexuals were routinely institutionalized, fired from their jobs, and
imprisoned, simply for being gay. Jeannette's pioneering book played a
pivotal role in raising awareness for the first time of the lesbian presence
in literature and history, provided subsequent scholars of lesbian literature with the cornerstone for their research, and served as a source of validation and inspiration for generations of women who went on to
become activists, publishers, and scholars. Its republication in 1976 and
1985 kept her work alive and ensured that new generations of readers
would be influenced by her scholarship.

The life of the lesbian author, educator, librarian, poet, and scholar
Jeannette Howard Foster spans from the late-nineteenth century, an era
that historian Carroll Smith-Rosenberg has labeled "the female world of
love and ritual," to the rise of the gay liberation movement of the 1970s;
from an era of alienation and isolation to one of collective consciousness. As the oldest of three children in an upwardly mobile middle-class
family, Jeannette acquired important tools during her childhood that ensured her success in the coming decades. Her father, lacking a son, had
high expectations for his first-born child's academic performance. Raising her with the expectation that she would attend college, he pointed
with great pride to educated women in the family's past, among them
Ada Howard, who had served as the first president of Wellesley College.
A controlling man, Jeannette's father admonished his daughters to keep

detailed journals and to write letters to their parents weekly. It was this letter-writing habit that empowered Jeannette to cultivate the web of lesbian friendships that sustained her throughout a life that was indelibly conditioned and shaped by her social class. Jeannette's mother, who regretted her inability to pursue a musical career, broke with convention by encouraging her daughters to aspire to college. It was important to her that they had a choice between marriage and self-sufficiency. Her mother also endowed her with impeccable manners and social skills, which she later used to her advantage. Both parents personified the Puritan work ethic and instilled this trait in Jeannette, along with a love of reading and an appreciation for the fine arts, history, and nature.

The story of Jeannette's life is a study of lesbian struggle, empowerment, and triumph amid the persistent hostilities of twentieth-century America. From an early age, Jeannette knew that she was attracted to women and felt comfortable with her identity, in part because her father was often absent from home, and she grew up in a homosocial environment populated by her sisters, mother, aunt, and female schoolmates. Even though her friends sometimes felt uncomfortable with her intense fondness for them, no one explicitly told her there was anything wrong with her feelings or behavior—but she soon began to intuit this from the society at large. Her study of science at the University of Chicago provided her with an objective, matter-of-fact approach to life and led her to become a freethinker, minimizing any struggle with the Judeo-Christian concept of homosexuality as an abomination. In her lifetime, Jeannette had many loves—some of them characterized by deep emotional bonds, others by physical intimacy. The seemingly unrequited love that inspired her best poetry in the 1920s trumped them all and set the standard for all of her subsequent relationships.

The printed word played a critical role in the positive construction of sexual identity for many twentieth-century women. Jeannette's discovery of same-sex romantic friendship in books sparked a burning desire to find other examples in literature and history, and for the remainder of her reading life she would take delight in detecting them despite the difficulties inherent in the task. In the 1920s and 1930s, some gays and lesbians internalized the condemnation of their sexual orientation by the church, the courts, and the medical community's pronouncement of homosexuality as a disease. Social purity advocates pushed the censorship of books and plays with gay and lesbian content and the Catholic Church's National Office for Decent Literature added homosexual literature to its list of condemned books; as a result, mainstream publishers often engaged in self-censorship in order to avoid prosecution, and some librarians restricted access to books on homosexuality. Undaunted by the social forces that collaborated to render the gay world invisible, Jeannette learned to decode the references to lesbianism that in spite of prohibitions continued to appear in stories, novels, and poems and fed her insatiable desire to find validation of her identity.

Living in relative isolation, lesbians of the pre–World War II era searched for one another in homosocial environments, for instance, women's colleges, the Women's Army Auxiliary Corps (later called the Women's Army Corps), or in female-intensive occupations. In Jeannette's case, the protective cover of women's college campuses and library schools provided her with space in which she could court women intensely without attracting undue attention. A passionate romantic, she showered the objects of her affection with candy, flowers, and poems, and on at least one occasion was willing to change employment and move across several states in order to be near her beloved. With few exceptions, however, Jeannette's loves were unrequited or short-term relationships, governed by passion, pragmatism, and unfulfilled expectations, and her search for the girlfriend of her dreams contributed to her persistent restlessness. While working for sex researcher Alfred C. Kinsey, Jeannette met Hazel Toliver, the woman who would become her companion for the final three decades of her life. Theirs was a caring yet unconventional relationship that defied definition even among lesbians, one that provided each of them with emotional and intellectual sustenance.

During her lifetime Jeannette, like many other gays and lesbians, used a variety of terms to describe her sexual identity. In 1915, after first read-

ing the work of sexologist Havelock Ellis, she began to think of herself as
a homosexual. Having felt same-sex attraction as a young girl, she therefore considered her homosexuality to be innate and—like literary critic
F. O. Matthiessen, who encountered Ellis's *Sexual Inversion* nine years
later—attributed her identity to nature, not immorality.[2] In poetry written as early as 1916, she used the word *gay*, but it clearly referred to people who were full of joy or mirth. A little later in life, when reflecting on
her relationships, she described them as *homosexual*, but during her years
at Kinsey's Institute for Sex Research, she came to associate that term
with male behavior and began referring to herself as a *lesbian*, a woman
who loved women. Under ideal circumstances, she believed, that type of
love was expressed emotionally and physically. When searching for a
title for her book, however, she chose the label *sex variant* because she
believed it to be less stigmatized than *gay*, *homosexual*, or *lesbian*. Only
late in her life did she use the labels *gay* or *queer* when speaking about
her sexuality.

At a time when most gays and lesbians felt compelled to conceal their
sexual identity, Jeannette systematically located, confidently requested,
and defiantly examined volumes of variant literature at libraries from
Chicago to Boston to Atlanta. Under the mantle of scholarship and
armed with her doctorate in library science, she unabashedly pursued her
passion for lesbian literature because she recognized the writing of fiction
as an essential vehicle for lesbian self-expression, identification, and resistance. As a librarian, she insisted on her right to examine books, no
matter what the subject matter. Jeannette even cultivated personal
friendships in order to gain access to many obscure and difficult-to-access
materials, though it took her years. Proud of her scholarship, she published *Sex Variant Women in Literature* under her given name, at a time
when many gays and lesbians felt compelled to hide their identities behind pseudonyms. When her lesbian short fiction appeared in *The Ladder* in the late 1950s and throughout the 1960s, she began using not
one but several pseudonyms, mainly because she wanted her real name
associated with her scholarly work. Near the end of her life, however, as

she contemplated the possible publication of one of her novels, she debated which pseudonym to use and then wrote her editor, "Oh, go on & use 'Jeannette Foster' if you think it has any sales value! I'll be buried soon enough to make no matter."[3]

As she pursued life, love, and lesbian literature, Jeannette lived and worked in seventeen states. Driven by her desire to ferret out works of lesbian literature, she changed locations and positions frequently in order to gain greater access to public and private library collections. Like many other middle-class lesbians of her generation, Jeannette gravitated toward New York City, a city she dearly loved, and she frequently summered there. As with many middle-class professional women, she did not seek out the bar culture, but instead socialized with other professional women in private settings. She had a knack for making friends wherever she lived, and they became part of a lifelong support network sustained by correspondence. Her family tacitly acknowledged her sexual identity, but because she felt they did not approve of sexual expression, let alone her preference, she was not comfortable sharing some of the most important aspects of her life with them. As a result, they could never fully appreciate her accomplishments, warmth, and wit, and she therefore turned to her lesbian friends for the validation she would have received from her family.

During her four years as the librarian of the Institute for Sex Research, Jeannette became desensitized to the discussion of sexual topics. As someone who had been out to herself since the 1910s, out to other gays and lesbians, and out to sympathetic employers and coworkers, she was generally more comfortable with her sexuality than many of her friends. It was this openness that enabled an aging Jeannette to share freely about her sexuality and personality with younger gays and lesbians, among them Barbara Grier, Karla Jay, and Jonathan Katz. The correspondence and conversations she had with them in the 1970s provide rare and intimate glimpses into her life story.

Living much of her life during a time when it was unwise, even risky, to have incriminating evidence like letters and homosexual literature in one's possession, Jeannette nevertheless amassed a large collection of lesbian fiction and medical works about homosexuality. Some of her books—the lesbian pulp fiction in particular—survive today in the Christine Pattee Lesbiana collection at Central Connecticut State University. She also maintained an extensive correspondence with lesbians around the globe. Their letters to her evidently have not survived, in part because of her desire to protect their identities, but her correspondence with such activists and writers as Margaret Anderson, Elsa Gidlow, Marie Kuda, and May Sarton exists in archival and manuscript repositories across the nation. Many of Jeannette's poems, lovingly typed by her friend the author Valerie Taylor, survive in the Valerie Taylor Papers at Cornell University, and her unpublished novels, *Home Is the Hunter* and *Death Under Duress*, are housed along with typed copies of short stories and novellas in the Barbara Grier and Donna McBride Collection at the San Francisco Public Library.

One of the challenges in telling Jeannette's story stems from the need to reconcile contradictory information found in letters, diaries, oral histories, published accounts, and memories of friends into a coherent whole. Jeannette was unabashedly lesbian when it came to her wide circle of friends, but she led a pragmatically closeted life with employers and coworkers until she came to trust them. On occasion, she self-censored or erected smokescreens in an attempt to protect the privacy and wishes of some of her more closeted friends. She occasionally was prone to exaggeration, and as age began to affect her memory, some errors crept into the accounts of her life that she shared with others. In such instances, the historian and biographer must become a detective, seeking to confirm, deny, and correct the story, based on surviving historical evidence.

Jeannette Foster's lesbianism was central to her identity. It governed her course of study, where she chose to live and work, the focus of her research and writing, and who she wanted to be near. It shaped her creative output: her poetry and prose were expressions of her emotional desire, and *Sex Variant Women in Literature* was the product of her intellectually curious and daring mind. Jeannette Foster's journey from childhood in Oak

Park, Illinois, to a retirement home in Pocahontas, Arkansas, is punctuated by such flashpoints as encounters with the journalist Janet Flanner, the novelist Glenway Wescott, sex researcher Alfred Kinsey, and psychiatrist George Henry. Consequently, her life illuminates lesbian history at several critical junctures: the waning of romantic friendship, the sexually charged 1920s, the pre–World War II era of invisibility, the repressive 1950s, and the 1970s movement culture that emerged in the wake of the civil rights, feminist, and gay rights movements. Hers is the story of an isolated individual who, in looking for positive validation of her identity, opened the closet door for lesbian literature. It is the narrative of a fearless and passionate trailblazer who claimed life for herself and on her own terms. Finally, it is the account of a brilliant scholar who lived long enough to see her pioneering work embraced by her intellectual heirs who, in turn, smashed stereotypes that had plagued and suppressed lesbians and gays for generations.

One

Early Years

VALENTINES
When I was seven, it lay
Between the covers of a green-gold book;
At twelve, in the rippling tongue of a girl
With auburn braids.
Later, in a notebook, worn,
Be-pencilled with my soul's outpouring.
And now, within your far gray eyes
It lies—
Enchantment!
— JEANNETTE HOWARD FOSTER, 1916[1]

"To begin with," remembered Jeannette Howard Foster in her eightieth year, "I was born in Oak Park, Ill., in Nov. 1895, when *it* was still one of a string of suburbs on the West side 'El,' outside the city limits [of Chicago]. . . . *That* was where I first fell in love—with the Sunday School teacher who taught, *not* my beginner's class, but a neighboring group, probably about 2d graders."[2] Over the course of the next seventy-five years, the irrepressible Foster would have many loves, some of them grand passions, others brief encounters, but all of them female. While each left an imprint on the life of this indomitable force, Foster's courage to claim the life she wished to live can be traced to her New England ancestry.

1

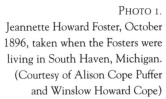

PHOTO 1.
Jeannette Howard Foster, October
1896, taken when the Fosters were
living in South Haven, Michigan.
(Courtesy of Alison Cope Puffer
and Winslow Howard Cope)

New England Heritage

As a child, Jeannette Foster was reminded that she came from solid
New England stock, with ancestors "reared on stern and rockbound
coasts." Her mother's flat Boston accent and thriftiness, her father's tireless work ethic, and the thin ginger cookies she and her sisters consumed served as daily reminders of the family's Yankee heritage. Because
Jeannette's father and paternal grandfather devoted long hours to ge-
nealogical research, she grew up knowing that ancestors on both her
maternal and paternal sides of the family had settled in New England in
the 1600s, and that their number included lawyers, merchants, inven-
tors, teachers, and farmers.[3]

Jeannette's family tree also offered her numerous examples of well-
educated, accomplished, independent, and freethinking women who in
the late-twentieth century would have been known as feminists. Ada L.
Howard, a cousin on her father's side of the family, grew up in a home
that valued education, and was sent to the New Ipswich Academy, the
Lowell High School, and the Mount Holyoke Seminary, from which she

graduated in 1853. Founded in 1837 by Mary Lyon, Mount Holyoke prepared women "to be serious scholars and independent beings." Howard's distinguished career as an educator included teaching at Mount Holyoke before the Civil War, and at the Western College for Women (Oxford, Ohio) and Knox College (Galesburg, Illinois). She was teaching at the Ivy Hall Seminary in Bridgeton, New Jersey, when Wellesley College tapped her to become its first president in 1875.[4]

It would be anachronistic to label Jeannette's female ancestors as feminists; however, she came from a line of strong-minded independent thinkers whose behavior sometimes resulted in persecution. According to historians of American witchcraft, accusers often targeted older women who owned property and as widows or spinsters lacked men to protect them. In 1692 Jeannette's seventh great-grandmother, Ann Foster (1617–1693), was condemned as a witch during the Salem, Massachusetts, witch-trial hysteria but died in jail before she could be executed. Authorities also condemned and hanged two eighth–great aunts as witches—Rebecca Towne Nurse (1621–1692) and Mary Towne Estey (1634–1692)—and a third, Sarah Towne Cloyce (1639–1703), was tried but not convicted. In the twentieth century Sarah would serve as the inspiration for the film *Three Sovereigns for Sarah*.[5] Jeannette's genealogist father shared his findings about these illustrious forebears with her, so she grew up knowing that that she came from a long line of resolute and capable women.

New Englanders led the nation in recognizing the beneficial consequences of educating their young women, who would in turn educate the nation's future citizens, and that region led the nation with 75.7 percent of its young white women attending school by the mid-nineteenth century. Because of the increasing feminization of teaching in the two decades prior to the Civil War, many of them would enter that field, if briefly.[6] Jeannette's paternal grandmother, Susan Morton Houghton Foster, embodies this pattern. The daughter of a tanner and farmer named Stedman Houghton, she grew up outside of New Ipswich, New Hampshire, an early mill town. She graduated at twenty from the Appleton

Photo 2.
Jeannette's paternal grandfather, Dr.
Addison Howard Foster (1838–1906),
demonstrated his support of women's
education by affiliating with the
Chicago Hospital for Women and
Children and by serving as one of the
original faculty members of the
Woman's Hospital Medical College of
Chicago. (Courtesy of Alison Cope
Puffer and Winslow Howard Cope)

Academy (established 1789) after absorbing lessons in such subjects as anatomy, geology, botany, and a special course for training teachers. Capable, energetic, and well-read, she put her education to use by traveling west to teach school in Cincinnati. She was in her late twenties when she married Addison Howard Foster in 1866.[7]

Like his wife, Addison Howard Foster grew up in a farming family. The oldest of eight children, he had to decide between having a share in the family farm or attending college. Choosing the latter, he took a college preparatory course at the Appleton Academy before enrolling at Dartmouth College in 1859, where he played football and sang in church and chapel choirs. After earning a BA degree in 1863, Foster continued his study of medicine, earning an MD degree from the New York College of Physicians in March 1866. Setting up practice in Lawrence, Massachusetts, he and Susan moved west to Chicago two years later with their firstborn son, Fred. Opening an office on Madison Street, Addison installed his family on the southwest corner of Halsted Street, less than a mile north of the Hull mansion that social reformer Jane Addams would transform into her famous settlement later in the century. In 1869 they moved a short distance west to a two-story frame house on the northwest corner of Monroe and Hoyne streets. A respectable residential district, there were so few neighbors that the family could see easily through to the western horizon. Remaining there until 1879, they added two sons, Winslow (born in 1869) and Charles (born in 1874), to their family while burying a daughter, Louisa (born in 1870).[8]

Shortly after arriving in Chicago, Addison Howard Foster demonstrated his support of women's education by becoming affiliated with the Chicago Hospital for Women and Children, founded in 1865 by Dr. Mary Harris Thompson. A graduate of the New England Female Medical College in Boston and a supporter of woman suffrage, she established the hospital to provide medical care for impoverished women and children at a time when only two of the city's three hospitals accepted women patients. To succeed in this venture, Thompson needed the support of consulting physicians like Foster to give her hospital the stamp of medical approval and to counter the prevailing prejudice against women physicians. In the fall of 1870, she and Dr. William H. Byford founded the Woman's Hospital Medical College with Foster as one of the original nine physicians on the faculty. After a successful first year, the college moved to its own quarters in October 1871, but only four days later the great Chicago Fire consumed the college and hospital buildings. Undeterred, Thompson reopened the hospital to care for victims of the fire, and it ultimately became the Northwestern University Woman's Medical School. During the early years when Foster held the chair of Surgical Anatomy (from 1870 to 1873) and chair of Surgery (from 1873 to 1875), the school faced significant financial challenges, which faculty members helped offset.[9]

After Susan Houghton Foster suffered a crippling spinal injury in the mid-1880s, Addison Foster buried himself in work, spending sixteen-hour days, seven days a week with his patients or at his office. Making gynecology his specialty, he became president of the Chicago Gynecological Society in 1896. He also contributed to Chicago's medical community through his leadership in the Chicago Medical Press Association and by serving on the advisory board of the Cook County Hospital and several privately funded children's homes. Despite the hard work that ultimately took a toll on his health, Foster remained a jovial man and many of his patients said his cheerfulness did them as much good as his medicine. At six feet tall and weighing more than two hundred pounds, he would also be remembered by his granddaughter Jeannette as a cheerful man who looked like a giant.[10] To others, however, he simply appeared to be the epitome of success—confident and dedicated to improving the quality of medical care for Chicago's women and children.

During his years as a student at Dartmouth, Addison Foster became good friends with Sanford Burr, the charismatic and gregarious man with a gift for oratory who would become Jeannette's maternal grandfather. Born on a farm near Foxboro, Massachusetts, he was well-dressed and popular. Indeed, during the Civil War, Burr raised a company of eighty-three students from Dartmouth College and Norwich University (in Vermont) to fight for the Union cause. Rejected by the governors of New Hampshire, Massachusetts, and Maine, Burr and his colleagues persisted and mustered in as the Dartmouth Cavalry Company B, Seventh Squadron of the Rhode Island Volunteer Cavalry.[11] Burr, who served as captain of the unit, subsequently studied to be a lawyer and was admitted to the Massachusetts Bar in 1866, but his penchant for mechanical inventions led him in another direction. During the next seventeen years he would file sixteen patents, but patented folding beds would become his specialty. In 1863 he married Eliza Jane Osgood, known for her "sunny, happy disposition." In the years to come, however, her life would be filled with many trials because marriage to an inventor, especially one unskilled in the management of investments, was not easy. Compounding those challenges were the mental and physical ailments that afflicted their children: their eldest, Carrie, born in 1865, had a cleft palate and spinal problems; Herman, born in 1866, would spend a number of years in the Eastern Illinois Hospital for the Insane; Frank, born in 1869, was a deaf mute; and two sons and a daughter would either die in infancy or be still-

PHOTO 3.
Jeannette's maternal grandfather,
Sanford Smith Burr (1838–1901),
was an inventor of folding beds,
tables, and other household
articles. (Courtesy of the
Winnetka Historical Society)

born. Childbearing in this family was problematic, at best: only Jeannette's mother Anna Mabel, born in 1868, appeared to be completely
healthy. Exposure to her siblings' health problems may have contributed
to her disinterest in maternity and her desire to delay motherhood.[12]

Perhaps Jeannette acquired some of her willingness to take risks from
the entrepreneurial and energetic Sanford Burr, who heard good reports
about the rapidly growing metropolis of Chicago from his classmate Addison Foster and decided to market his folding beds there. In 1879 the
Burrs moved to Winnetka, Illinois, a suburb located sixteen miles north
of the Loop. Becoming a civic leader by virtue of his personality and social class, Sanford Burr served as president of the village for four years.
Progressive-minded, Burr worked for the construction of city waterworks, a sewer system, and an electric plant. Jeannette also may have observed Sanford Burr's love of reading. A voracious consumer of prose and
poetry, he helped establish the Winnetka Public Library and served as
first president of the public library board from 1885 until his death. Burr's
folding beds became phenomenally popular because of the need for
sleeping spaces during Chicago's Columbian Exposition of 1893, which

drew 27.5 million visitors to the city, but unfortunately his company failed during the economic depression that followed the Panic of 1893. Retreating with his family to the South Haven, Michigan, fruit farm he had purchased in 1891, Burr continued to tinker with inventions and added several more patents to his name.[13]

The friendship between Addison Foster and Sanford Burr spilled over to the next generation as the two families summered together, attended concerts and plays, celebrated holidays and birthdays together, and helped each another in times of need.[14] Eventually they became more formally linked when Sanford's daughter Anna Mabel married Addison's son, Winslow. Born in Dedham, Massachusetts, on July 1, 1868, Mabel (as she was called) spent her youth enjoying Boston's rich cultural heritage and nurturing dreams of becoming a singer. Jeannette undoubtedly acquired her appreciation for music from her mother and grandmother, who had been a church organist. After the family moved to Winnetka, Mabel became known for her sweet and beautiful soprano voice, which soared above those of other parishioners in the Winnetka Congregational Church. A bit of a dilettante, she studied voice in Chicago, sang at club meetings and church functions, and was a member of Chicago's famed Apollo Club, a choral group that first admitted women as full members in 1885. As the daughter of one of Winnetka's leading families, she enjoyed shopping downtown at the Carson & Pirie and Marshall Field & Co. department stores and going to concerts and plays with her friends. Cultivating the social graces, she strived to appear cultured and well-mannered.[15]

During the early 1890s, Sanford and Eliza Burr spent months at a time in Michigan trying to improve their South Haven property. Carrie Burr Prouty, an invalid, could not supervise her younger sister, but the Fosters made a point of inviting her to their home and on outings. Like many others of their class and status, the Fosters had a cottage on the east shore of Long Lake, just south of the Wisconsin border, and retreated there in the heat of summer. Mabel enjoyed becoming part of the "Long Lake Crowd" and partaking in canoeing, hikes, and amateur dramatics.

In contrast, she dreaded her brother Herman's visits home from the Eastern Illinois Insane Asylum and dutifully went to rural South Haven to help her mother cope with her "cross and contrary" brother Frank, who sometimes tore the Burr home apart when he had tantrums. Spoiled by the convenience of city life, she longed to return to Winnetka and like many women of her era contemplated marriage as a way to realize her dream. At twenty-five, her best prospect appeared to be one of Addison Foster's sons.[16]

Growing up in the shadow of his father's success, Winslow Howard Foster felt pressured to succeed. As a child, he grew to love the outdoors and became a collector—of butterflies, wild flowers, and stamps—hobbies that he pursued for the remainder of his days. After entering the University of Illinois in 1888, a bout of malaria left him thirty pounds lighter and plagued by migraine headaches for the next quarter century. Winslow wanted to study civil engineering but changed his plans when his invalid and protective mother expressed a desire for him to become a mechanical engineer, because it would mean less exposure to workplace hazards and the weather. After graduating with a BS degree in 1892, he secured a position as chief draftsman and estimator for the Shiffler Bridge Company's Chicago office, headed by Winsell Morava. Foster's education completed and a good job in hand, he asked Mabel Burr to marry him and they were wed on September 20, 1894.[17]

From Jeannette's perspective, her parents did not have a harmonious marriage. Her father's nervous temperament, combined with her mother's regret that she could not pursue a musical career, created tension and resentment. Heavy responsibilities and long hours at the Bridge Company proved overwhelming and in 1896, when Jeannette was not yet one year old, her father suffered his first "nervous letdown." Leaving his position, he took his family to South Haven, bought ten acres from his father-in-law, and spent the next year working outdoors and building a cottage. Mabel enjoyed being reunited with her mother, who shared her love of music, but also felt wary about exposing her daughter to her brother Frank's fits. Pictures of Jeannette during this year show an alert, brown-haired toddler

Photo 4.   Winslow Howard Foster (1869–1942) and Anna Mabel
Burr Foster (1868–1943), circa 1908–1910. Jeannette adored her father,
who encouraged her to excel academically and professionally. Her
mother nurtured dreams of a musical career and as a wife and mother
was known for her thrift and industry. (Courtesy of Alison Cope Puffer
and Winslow Howard Cope)

with dark eyes and a look of willful determination.[18] After a year in the
fresh air, Winslow felt well enough to return to his job with Morava. He
appeared healthy and stable but Mabel—whose awareness of mental illness had been heightened because of her brothers—remained keenly sen-
sitive to fluctuations in his emotional state.

Jeannette's earliest memories date to her fourth year when the Fosters
lived on the first floor of a wood-frame two-flat built in 1894 by Addison
Howard Foster for his sons Fred and Winslow, who both married that
year. Winslow's books adorned the glass-fronted secretary in a parlor fur-
nished with wicker furniture and art prints. Empty fields surrounded two
sides of the home. Located at 216 Harvey Street in Cicero Township,
(Oak Park was a community within the township and would separate
from it and incorporate as a village in 1901), it stood a few blocks from
the boyhood home of Ernest Hemingway. Like Mabel, his mother, Grace

Hall Hemingway, had yearned to be an opera singer and both women were Congregationalists. At that time Oak Park seemed to be a peaceful haven on the Illinois prairie, and a place where villagers lived at a slower pace than in Chicago. Their activities revolved around church and family, yet the community was not completely idyllic: smoke from the burning of soft coal polluted the air and, Jeannette later believed, left her with mild yet chronic emphysema. Like other middle-class households in the community, the Fosters engaged a servant to help Mabel with household duties and Winslow joined the army of Oak Park husbands who commuted to and from their jobs in the city by train.[19]

In the spring of 1899, Sanford Burr suffered a severely debilitating stroke and his wife died a few months later, in May. Calling upon her internal strength, Mabel struggled to nurse her once jovial but now uncooperative and obstinate father while raising a precocious child and trying to stabilize her moody husband. After becoming pregnant with a second child, she had no recourse but to commit her father to the National Soldiers' Home in Milwaukee.[20] A precocious Jeannette, intuiting that "Mother wanted me out from underfoot at any price," spent many weekday mornings on the front stairs of their Oak Park home inventing physically daring games "like climbing the stairs on the outside of the railing, thrusting my feet between the spokes." Even though she viewed it as "perfectly safe," her mother "didn't think so when she found me at it, so I was *sat* down with *Mother Goose* or *The Three Little Kittens*, from which I taught myself to read long before I went to school."[21] Earlier experiences with books, when Mabel and Winslow read stories to her, combined with her curious mind and tendency to ask questions about the words and pictures, in all likelihood meant that she did teach herself to read. In books she found a welcome escape, a way to vicariously have adventures, and later, keys to understanding herself.

To further occupy his energetic and inquisitive daughter, Winslow enrolled four-year-old Jeannette in a Sunday School at a local Congregational Church. Almost immediately the little girl who yearned for a mother's love developed a crush on "Miss Helen," who "looked at me with the first look of *love* I had ever seen on a woman's face." Heartbroken not to be in Miss Helen's circle of little red chairs, Jeannette spent the next hour twisting around to look at her. Each night thereafter, she later recalled, she had "imagined her just as I was falling asleep, and 'dreamed' she was in bed beside me."[22] Later in life she would always recall this incident as the first time she had felt love for another woman, and her tendency thereafter would be to fall in love with older women.

Years later Jeannette remembered her mother as frustrated, overworked, cold, and unloving, someone who resented her first-born daughter and had little time to spend with her. She "never showed any tenderness whatever toward me," she later reflected, but was instead a "sexually cold New England *puritan* . . . not given to any form of petting or caressing." Mabel wanted, as her daughter came to realize, "a singing career, not a child, and resented that her gynecologist father-in-law "would not assist her in her efforts at birth-control." Jeannette was convinced that her mother also resented the fact that Winslow, a genealogist like his father, had given his firstborn "all the hereditary family names on *his* side."[23] When Mabel gave birth to a second daughter on June 12, 1900, she named her Anna Burr Foster in honor of herself and her father.

The spring of 1901 brought new challenges for the Foster family when the Shiffler Bridge Company merged with the American Bridge Company and made Winslow Foster's future uncertain. In a bold move, Winsell Morava decided to separate from American Bridge and incorporate the Morava Construction Company with Winslow Foster as vice president and chief engineer. Determined to make a success of the venture, Morava and Foster devoted long hours to cultivating contracts for building projects. For Winslow, the increased responsibilities meant travel and more time away from his family as he supervised the construction of bridges, schools, and public buildings around the country. When he was at home, he had a longer daily commute from Oak Park to the new large structural steel plant which was located "way to hell-and-gone out on the 'South Side.'" Therefore, on May 1, the day that leases customarily expired in turn-of-the-century Chicago, the Fosters exchanged their Oak Park two-flat for one in Normal Park so Winslow would have an easier commute to the plant on the Rock Island Railroad.[24]

In the fall of 1901 Jeannette entered the Parker Practice School, a cadet school conducted by the Chicago Normal School at Sixty-eighth Street and Stewart, near Normal Park. In addition to being conveniently located near their home, Winslow believed the school would offer Jeannette the foundation she needed for future success. Named for Francis Wayland Parker, a progressive educator who used the classroom as "a laboratory for the testing of his social and educational concepts," the school's curriculum was structured "to develop students with democratic attitudes and commitment to democratic values."[25] Advocating freedom of movement, Parker refused to impose external restraints on children; consequently, outside observers thought the school disorderly and the children boisterous. Jeannette flourished in this environment. Advancing quickly because of her self-taught reading ability and an excellent memory, she entered second grade at midyear. Almost immediately she fell in love with her teacher, Miss Leubrie, a twenty-seven-year-old dress-reform enthusiast in the days when most women wore long skirts and tight corsets. Jeannette adored the soft woolen jumpers that she wore over white silk blouses, and the fact that she "looked—and incidentally moved—like a human being."[26] Hungry for maternal affection, Jeannette responded eagerly to the praise Miss Leubrie lavished on her star pupil. Unfortunately, this crush was short-lived because in May 1902 the Fosters withdrew Jeannette from school when they moved further south to the suburb of Beverly Hills.

Situated twelve miles south of Chicago's Loop on a terminal moraine known as the Blue Island Ridge, Beverly Hills appealed to Jeannette's parents because it reminded them of New England's terrain. Their building site, located at 9238 Pleasant Avenue, Jeannette remembered, was in "the only part of Chicago that wasn't as flat as a table top." The move from a rented flat to a spacious home in the suburbs also signified a shift in social status. Built by the Morava Construction Company, their two-story frame house cost approximately $2,500. When the Fosters looked out of the second story window of their new home, they saw a tree-lined street filled with grand homes on large lots. Their neighbors included industrialists and professionals: a chewing-gum manufacturer, a bank vice president, a real estate broker, an attorney, contractors, and even an instructor at the Art Institute of Chicago. Most, befitting their socioeconomic class, had servants, and many sent their children east to boarding schools.[27]

Because the Fosters moved before the end of the school year, Jeannette still had two months of second grade to complete. She mourned the loss of her beloved Miss Leubrie and languished in a classroom at the nearby Alice L. Barnard School until the close of the school year. The following fall, two months shy of her seventh birthday, Jeannette entered third grade. Winslow Foster took great delight in her academic precociousness, which he encouraged by talking with her about books and by playing games requiring strategy. When Jeannette shocked him by bringing home an F in arithmetic, he quickly remedied the situation through tutoring, and she never again had academic difficulty. Naturally gifted, she wanted to excel in order to please him.[28]

That year Mabel Foster's third pregnancy was less stressful than her previous one because her husband now had steady employment, she no longer had to care for her father, and she had a lovely new home. Her older sister visited regularly, providing companionship as well as help with sewing, baking, and caring for the children. Aunt Carrie, as the children called her, was childless and enjoyed spending time with her nieces. On January 12, 1903, the Fosters welcomed their third daughter and final child, Helen Houghton Foster, into the world. Named for her paternal grandmother, she would become the artist of the family. Steeped in an appreciation for the finer things in life, all three girls grew up with an appreciation for art, music, and literature. In addition to dance and piano lessons, they studied drawing and painting at the Art Institute of Chicago. In the summertime, Mabel and Carrie frequently took the three girls to Ravinia Park, where after 1911 they attended concerts and operas. In the winter they traveled to downtown Chicago to attend plays and other performances.[29]

PHOTO 5.
Carrie Burr Prouty (1865–1945)
After Jeannette's breakdown in
1914, she stayed with her
mother's older sister, who
arranged for her niece to enroll
at Rockford College. (Courtesy
of Alison Cope Puffer and
Winslow Howard Cope)

Even though they now lived in the affluent suburb of Beverly Hills, Winslow and Mabel Foster remained exceedingly protective of their children. Their father built a tree house so Jeannette, Anna, and Helen would stay in their backyard under parental supervision, and seldom allowed them to play with neighborhood children, fearing that the girls might acquire bad habits or be exposed to profanity. During her childhood, Jeannette concluded, she had been "practically under a bell jar as far as Protection Against Bad Influences went. I really wonder *how* I ever grew up! . . . *One* good thing—it kept away *boys*, horrid beasts! Oddly enough," she paused to reflect, "both my sisters (some years younger), got married! So maybe something about *me* was 'queer.'"[30]

Jeannette's early years had been driven by a search for love. Her preoccupied and aloof mother raised her to be a proper, well-mannered, and cultured young woman, but etiquette lessons were no substitute for the intimacy Jeannette craved. Additionally, as she entered adolescence, Jeannette began to see her mother as a negative role model, an unhappily married woman who resented her children and regretted that she had not been able to pursue a career. Consumed by her own disappointment and unable to realize her dreams vicariously through her rebellious oldest daughter, she remained incapable of demonstrating love. Thus, Jeannette looked elsewhere—to Sunday and public-school teachers—for maternal affection, but their warm looks and smiles, while satisfying,

PHOTO 6.   9238 Pleasant Avenue, circa 1906. The Foster family residence in Beverly Hills, a community annexed by Chicago in 1890. (Courtesy of Alison Cope Puffer and Winslow Howard Cope)

could not fill the void. Five years older than her next younger sister, Jeannette also failed to find the closeness she so desperately sought in her siblings. Asked to help care for Anna and Helen when Mabel became ill, she developed a deeply engrained sense of responsibility for her sisters, one that inhibited the sharing of confidences and the intimacy she might have cultivated under different circumstances.[31]

Despite his work-related absences from the home, Winslow Howard Foster became a significant influence in his oldest daughter's life. In contrast with her duty-bound and pragmatic mother, Jeannette's father represented action, learning, and worldliness. He entertained the family with stories of travel, adventure, and accomplishment. His daughters took pride in being Winslow Foster's children, pointing out to others that their father had supervised construction of the Twelfth Street station of the Illinois Central Railroad in Chicago, the Evanston High School, and the indoor pool at the Manitowoc, Wisconsin, high school.[32] Jeannette admired his passion for life, the vigor with which he tackled any project, and his willingness to take risks. From him she learned to hold herself to a high standard, and she learned a meticulousness that would serve her well in the future.

Jeannette also had difficulty making friends at school because she was so much younger than her classmates. Boys undoubtedly teased her because she lagged behind in physical maturity and she had little in common with adolescent girls because she did not share their budding interest in boys. "I was," she remembered, "a mere babe when my classmates were beginning to get boy-crazy, and I was *colossally* unpopular with the boys in dancing school, etc., and began to think 'all right, the dickens with you!'"[33] Her ability to make friends also suffered because her status-conscious parents encouraged her to view public-school classmates as socially inferior.

During the early-twentieth century, members of the educated class and especially those in medical families were becoming aware of the signs of sexual inversion. Havelock Ellis, in his volume on sexual inversion (*Studies in the Psychology of Sex* Volume II), presented case studies that sounded very similar to Jeannette's childhood. Even if her mother had not read Ellis, she might have read articles about his work in popular magazines of the day. Mabel, increasingly aware of her daughter's tomboyish tendencies and her penchant for developing crushes on other girls, futilely struggled to keep Jeannette a proper young lady. She also dressed her in elaborate white dresses with matching hair bows and plied her with dolls, but without much success. When the Fosters posed for a family picture on the steps of their Pleasant Avenue home in 1904, Mabel sat primly in the center while a scowling Jeannette defiantly assumed an unladylike pose.[34] When she was a nine-year-old seventh-grader, Jeannette finally found two like-minded girls for companions and with them formed a group known as the "Great Triumvirate." Together, she recalled, they raised "all the mild hell we could in and out of classes. . . . Individually we were Ted, Pete, and Hector—why, I do *not* remember, but I was Pete."[35]

Jeannette matured in the midst of an onslaught of publications about masturbation, and an ever-concerned Mabel became so watchful of her

PHOTO 7.   Winslow and Mabel Foster with Jeannette (seated next to her mother), Anna (middle), and Helen (bottom) on the steps of their Beverly Hills Home, circa 1904. (Courtesy of Alison Cope Puffer and Winslow Howard Cope)

daughter's behavior that she "hardly allowed" Jeannette to wash her genitals. Her caution extended to Jeannette's relationships with other girls, and she monitored their activities closely in order to keep them from spending time together behind closed doors. Her mother very likely read about masturbation and homosexuality in popular literature of the day, and something in Jeannette's behavior triggered Mabel's proactive stance. Later in life, Jeannette speculated about her mother's "adolescent history," hinting that her preoccupation with sexual behavior might have stemmed from her own youthful experiences.[36]

Despite her mother's best efforts, Jeannette formed an attachment to a "*very* good girl-friend" during her seventh- and eighth-grade years, and they "spent a number of nights in the same bed." Reflecting on this friendship later in life, Jeannette recalled feeling "the same imaginative craving" for her classmate that she had previously felt for her Sunday School teacher. Each time Jeannette tried to hug her friend, "she would shrink off & say 'ooh, doesn't it make you feel *funny* to get so close?'"

Disappointed, Jeannette simply knew that she loved the young girl, wanted to be close, and did not associate that desire with anything negative. Her friend's mother, however, may have shared Mabel Foster's concern about the two girls' close friendship because after they graduated from eighth grade, she took her daughter abroad for a year, thus terminating the friendship.[37]

A voracious reader from childhood, Jeannette escaped into fiction and had the good fortune to come of age at a time when authors still depicted female friendship in a positive light. Within a few years, however, attitudes would begin to change as Freudianism permeated popular culture and people began to emphasize the erotic aspects of same-sex love. By the 1920s, love between women would be portrayed as an illness.[38] In 1908 and 1909, however, Jeannette discovered a charming portrayal of female friendship in *St. Nicholas Magazine* when she read a serialized story entitled "The Lass of the Silver Sword." Written by Mary Constance DuBois, the tale, which told of a boarding-school girl (whose name coincidentally was Jean) who had a serious crush on an older female student, made a significant impression on her because it validated some of her yearnings. It was, she later recalled, her earliest print-based encounter with lesbianism, though not by that name. A second story, Josephine Dodge Daskam's "A Case of Interference," from *Smith College Stories*, described an upperclasswoman's efforts to keep a gifted but unpopular underclasswoman from leaving school. In both instances, "the female character was emotionally touched by another female." Finding validation for her feelings in print, Jeannette was from that point forward "on a sharp lookout, largely fruitless, for the subject."[39]

During elementary school, Jeannette viewed her friendships with other girls and crushes on teachers as positive and natural, but Mabel's suspicious reaction planted seeds of doubt in her mind. "My mother," she remembered, "used to gossip occasionally about a couple of the most 'elite' married women—mothers of my schoolmates—as being noticeably attached to one another . . . (I suspect my Mother was a good deal more 'hip' to such situations than I ever suspected)."[40] Her mother's obsession with women

PHOTO 8.
Jeannette (left) with an unidentified
school friend, circa 1909, one of
several images taken in a five-and-
dime-store type of photo booth.
(Courtesy of Alison Cope Puffer and
Winslow Howard Cope)

who were "too fond" of each other and her efforts to discourage Jeannette's crushes on other girls and teachers heightened her awareness of same-sex relationships. At the time she had no label for it but increasingly was on the watch for it. "I lived within walking distance of a big Catholic convent in grade-school days," she recalled in a 1975 interview, "and a few parents with fairly 'mature' [physically] and unruly daughters sent them there to keep them away from boys! . . . I never caught a *hint* of any lesbian attachments developing in the convent crowd. . . . *That* aspect of life I observed, on my own, in our mixed grade-school and *never* thought of it as lesbian— nor I am sure, did anyone else."[41]

Winslow Foster's fluctuating financial position made it impossible to send Jeannette to a private high school, so she entered Calumet High School in the fall of 1907, just a few months short of her twelfth birthday. Many of the Fosters' neighbors sent their daughters away to boarding schools, so Jeannette did not know many of her classmates, and since she was younger and had been taught to regard students at Calumet as socially inferior, she made few friends. Instead, she became obsessed with one of her younger high-school teachers. As a thirteen-year-old sophomore, Jeannette developed a "violent crush" on a biology and chemistry teacher named Nell Jackson. "I wasn't taking the subject," she remembered, but she had a number of study halls with Miss Jackson in a large hall on the school's top floor. Jeannette's attraction led her to sign up for Jackson's biology class the following year. An early riser, she normally prepared box lunches for herself, her father, and her sister Anna and practiced the piano each day for forty-five minutes before taking the Rock Island Suburban to the Auburn Park station, from which she walked a short distance to the school. So smitten was she with Miss Jackson that she took the 8:00 a.m. train rather than the 8:14, "in order to sneak flowers in season (from violets to nasturtiums) into 'Nell's' office without being seen and ridiculed by my pals, who *all* went on the 8:14!" Upon learning of her daughter's crush, Mabel became quite angry. "I remember only her *fury* at my attachment to the H.S. teacher who was my first serious love!" she remembered. "And a fine, distinctly scornful, practically contemptuous fury it was."[42] Rejecting her homebound and morally restrictive mother's example, Jeannette's feelings for independent and intellectual women like Jackson grew even deeper.

As the historian Martha Vicinis has written, adolescent crushes filled an important need for young girls during the late-nineteenth and early-twentieth centuries. Coming of age at a time of modernization and change, they looked to women who pioneered in new roles as models, and this tendency "encouraged an idealized love for an older, publicly successful woman."[43] Such crushes often were not seen as unhealthy or immoral because they were regarded as asexual. In Jeannette's case, such women not only became romantic interests but also provided positive role models of self-supporting single women. Jeannette's mother, however, must have had some medical or pseudoscientific understanding of homosexuality because she felt uncomfortable with her daughter's emotional demonstrativeness and unsuccessfully attempted to quash her outward display of affection for female friends and teachers. As a result, the two would never have an emotionally satisfying relationship.

In the spring of 1909, Mabel Foster had a new cause for concern when Jeannette contracted diphtheria. The family blamed a Christian Science classmate whose locker adjoined hers for spreading the disease. Eager to spare Jeannette's sisters, her parents sent Anna and Helen to stay with Aunt Carrie in Winnetka, but a week later Anna also developed symptoms. Winslow retrieved Helen and left Anna quarantined with her aunt for several weeks. Miraculously, all three girls survived the deadly disease, but according to family accounts, Jeannette had lingering aftereffects because the family doctor had given her an overdose of newly developed antitoxins. By the following July she seemed well enough to take a short trip with her parents, but ultimately the illness would have significant consequences socially and academically, as well as physically.[44]

Jeannette began her junior year at Calumet High School in the fall of 1909 by taking a full load of courses there as well as classes at the Art Institute of Chicago. Like many other girls her age, she also attended dances and concerts with friends. In November, shortly after her fourteenth birthday, she became ill and missed more than a month of school. Her menstrual cycle became irregular, her waist-length hair fell out and would never again grow more than shoulder length, and she suffered a series of minor maladies.[45] The family, believing that she had not fully recovered from diphtheria, decided that the best course of action was rest.

Meanwhile, the year proved difficult for other reasons. Jeannette's father had a serious disagreement with Winsell Morava in November 1909 when he discovered an underling at the Morava Construction Company scheming to get his position through unethical means. Foster succeeded in clearing his name, but broke down from the strain of it all and on December 31 submitted his resignation. As the eldest daughter, Jeannette observed the problems facing her distraught mother and depressed father. Early in January, Winslow left for San Diego, California, in hopes of improving his situation. In March he purchased acreage near Grants Pass, Oregon, and by late April 1910 had set himself up as a fruit farmer, living and working with Ernest R. Jeffries, a twenty-four-year-old native of Illinois.[46] Perhaps he expected to regain his health in a western climate, or he saw the fruit farm as an investment opportunity. Either way, it meant leaving his family behind. When Carrie Burr Prouty came to visit her sister on February 22, she found Mabel "half sick" in a house as cold as a barn. Seeking to alleviate her sister's despair, she began visiting on an almost weekly basis to help with sewing, washing, baking, and caring for the children. As the weeks passed, Mabel grew increasingly despondent. The children's illnesses and the responsibilities of managing the household without a reliable income seemed daunting. As the oldest child, Jeannette took responsibility for cooking the family meals while her mother, suffering from ulcers, spent a great deal of time resting on a downstairs couch.[47]

That summer, Carrie Burr Prouty's long-unfaithful husband of twenty-four years informed his wife that their marriage was over. In August a demoralized Carrie moved her possessions from Winnetka to the Foster home in Beverly Hills until she could make other arrangements. It must have been a very unhappy time in the house as the two sisters commiserated with one another about their marriages. Even the joy from Winslow's return on September 10 was short-lived because he spent most of his time embroiled in negotiations with Morava about the conditions under which he would return to work for him. At the same time, he attempted to manage the Oregon fruit farm from afar. Aware that they needed time together as a family, Carrie moved into a rented room in Winnetka.[48]

If she had stayed on schedule, Jeannette would have graduated from high school in 1911, but because of illness and the continued family drama she remained in high school for what she later called "a wretched fifth year." It turned into "a disguised blessing," she recalled, because it kept her from going to college at fifteen and enabled her to spend more time near Miss Jackson.[49] At a time when her family seemed to be falling apart and she felt unloved, Jeannette felt joy and happiness whenever she was in Miss Jackson's presence. Even though chemistry was not her favorite subject, she signed up for chemistry classes because Jackson taught them. As she discovered the following year, this decision had a significant impact on her choice of major in college.

Meanwhile, Mabel was consumed by worry about her husband's seeming mental instability and financial problems. Growing steadily thinner as the winter advanced, she was "flat on her back" with worry about the lack of money by December 1911. In March 1912, when Aunt Carrie came to cook and clean, she found that Winslow had fallen "all to pieces" and the following month the Fosters had to withdraw their two younger children from private school because they could no longer afford the tuition. Unable to find any other employment, a desperate Winslow sold his much-prized stamp collection in July.[50]

Winslow and Mabel Foster valued education and believed that it was a key to anchoring their family to a modestly wealthy middle-class existence. Additionally, both parents wanted their daughters to have the option of being self-sufficient should they prefer a career over marriage. Mabel's regret over her unrealized musical career and the example of several self-supporting single women in the family's past informed their decision. At the same time, however, they wanted their daughters to choose fields of study in keeping with their social class. While higher education or the arts would be acceptable, they could not condescend to let their girls enter such service professions as nursing and social work. Aware of their connection to Wellesley College through president Ada Howard, Winslow and Mabel raised their oldest daughter with the expectation that she would go East for college.[51] When her father's unemployment shattered that dream in the spring of 1912, Jeannette's excellent academic record at Calumet High School—she graduated as salutatorian—served her well. As all hope of a college education appeared to vanish, she learned that the boy ahead of her in the class had declined a scholarship automatically awarded by the University of Chicago to valedictorians at area high schools, making her the recipient by default. Delighted by the news, her overly protective parents campaigned to keep their daughter at home and commuting to campus, but the family's physician—the same one who had urged her to take a fifth year of high school—convinced them to let her live on campus. With her delicate health, he urged, she needed to avoid the strain of a daily commute by suburban train and street car.[52]

Relations between Jeannette and her envious mother remained tense, and in the summer of 1912 Aunt Carrie and Winslow made every effort to avoid confrontations. Jeannette spent extended visits in Winnetka with her aunt, who allowed her to sleep until noon and distracted her with games of tennis, introductions to young girls in the neighborhood, and concerts at Ravinia. Winslow played his part by taking Jeannette for a two-week vacation at the resort community of Hamlin Lake, located approximately ten miles north of Ludington. She must have felt very favored, especially since her sisters remained at home with their mother. When Winslow and Jeannette returned in mid-September she was rested, refreshed, and ready to start the next chapter of her life.[53]

Two

Romantic Friendship and Voiceless Longing

A Song Unuttered

Ever returning it rises and surges within me,
Passionate, prisoned song of the love I bear you;
Need to wear for your eyes the treasures you bring me.
Light of my morning.
Beauty and suffering, peace, and the wisdom of ages—
But ah, Very Dear, the words are like threads that tangle.
How bind the width of a soul in the chain of a sonnet;
How hold a brimming heart within stanza and couplet—
How more than "I was a child, and now am a woman,
Eyes that see and are glad, heart knowing and fearless"—
These are but wing beats of song that is prisoned within me,
Star of my evening.

—JEANNETTE HOWARD FOSTER, 1918[1]

Artists, writers, and editors flocked to Chicago in the early 1900s, among them Carl Sandburg, Sherwood Anderson, and Margaret Anderson, editor of the *Little Review*.[2] A city of great cultural institutions, it offered the Art Institute of Chicago, the Field Museum of Natural History, the Chicago Symphony Orchestra, the Newberry Library, and much more. Scholars like John Dewey, George Herbert Mead, and Robert Herrick built their careers at the University of Chicago where, in the fall of 1912, the freshman class included two lesbians who later would gain fame for their writing—Janet Flanner (1892–1978) and Jeannette Howard Foster. Flanner, who wrote under the pen name Genet, earned national and international prominence as a journalist and essayist for her weekly "Letter from Paris," which appeared in the *New Yorker* from 1925 to 1975.[3] Jeannette Foster's work would not be recognized until much later. In 1912, however, the two young women lived in adjacent dormitories, commiserated with one another about their troubled families, and developed a friendship that would span decades.

The University of Chicago was entering its third decade when Jeannette arrived at the Hyde Park campus on October 1, 1912. As she walked the grounds of the Gothic revival campus, with its enclosed quadrangles reminiscent of Oxford or Cambridge, she dreamed of becoming a writer. Upon registering, however, her hopes were dashed by a university requirement stipulating that freshmen must major in a subject they had studied during their final year of high school. Since she had filled her senior year in high school with chemistry courses taught by Nell Jackson (in order to be near her), Jeannette had to choose between chemistry and Latin. As Jeannette later recalled, "I knew damn well I didn't want to major in Latin!"[4] Her decision to major in chemistry, with an accompanying minor in physics, was the first instance, she later noted, when homosexuality had a significant impact on her life. If she had not had a crush on her high school chemistry teacher, her senior year probably would have been filled with courses in English and American literature.

A nonsectarian school, the University of Chicago promoted modern scientific research and provided an excellent foundation for Jeannette's later research on homosexuality and lesbian literature. The knowledge she acquired while studying chemistry and physics sharpened her analytical ability and problem-solving skills, and whetted her appetite for research. The study of new scientific thought prompted religious crises in students of her generation, but Jeannette, the daughter of nominally Congregational parents who had long been irregular in church attendance, did not feel especially bound by her religious beliefs. Encouraged by professors to think independently, she became an agnostic sometime during her first two years of college. An excerpt from her poem "Alone" (1917) captures Jeannette's feelings as she reordered her world according to science. Although she did not know it at the time, her repudiation of religion freed her from the struggle that so many homosexuals of her era experienced when confronted with Judeo-Christian beliefs condemning their sexual orientation as a sin.

> Out the warm, narrow doors of childhood fell
> Into the far cold space where God is not,
> A question—nor found I love nor peace, nor aught
> But law—and knew my soul an aimless wraith.[5]

Jeannette belonged to a generation of college women that combined old and new values. Her pioneering predecessors, the privileged white women who attended college from the 1860s to the 1890s, sought knowledge but defined it according to the tenets of true womanhood and tended to move into female-intensive fields. In contrast, the modern college woman of the 1910s increasingly gravitated to a world dominated by men. For these forerunners of flappers, a college education increasingly led to a heightened sense of individualism, economic independence, and social mobility. Even though men tended to dominate faculties numerically, female undergraduates nonetheless took inspiration from the single professional women who held appointments as lecturers, professors, and librarians on many college campuses. As "new women," Jeannette's generation was responsive to Progressive era causes yet delighted in flouting conventional mores. They attended college in pursuit of both knowledge and personal happiness. As residents in women's dormitories, they had ample opportunities to develop close friendships and at times "primary sexual relationships" with other women. Before World War I, such romantic friendships still were seen as part of the growing-up process and hence lacked the negative stigma they would acquire in the 1920s.[6]

Coeducational from its beginning in 1892, the University of Chicago had so many female undergraduate and graduate students in the early-twentieth century that some alarmists believed that female admissions should be restricted. Jeannette appreciated the presence of so many intelligent and talented women on the faculty and in them found models of what a single professional woman could do with her life. She observed Marion Talbot, who would serve for more than three decades as a department chair and dean at the University of Chicago, urge female students to take full advantage of academic and cultural opportunities. She admired women like assistant dean of women Sophonisba Breckinridge, who in 1901 had become the first woman to earn a doctorate in political science from the University of Chicago, and had subsequently become active in city-, state-, and federal-level reform. Because of her courses in physical culture, she also came to know Gertrude Dudley, who served as director of women's athletics (known at the time as physical culture) from 1898 to 1935 and, in that capacity, encouraged interclass and, later, intercollegiate competition. As she looked to these women as role models, she observed the deep friendship and professional collaboration that characterized their interactions with one another.[7]

The word *lesbian* (when referring to women having sexual interest in other women) appeared in such medical writings as Richard von Krafft-Ebing's *Psychopathia Sexualis* and John S. Billings's *The National Medical Dictionary* since the 1890s, but would have been an unfamiliar term to Jeannette and her peers. They might have witnessed women living in Boston marriages—for instance, Jane Addams and Mary Rozet Smith—but, like the Victorians, tended to view them as nonsexual romantic friendships. As historian Lillian Faderman has found, most lesbians of this era did not regard themselves as immoral; instead, they "simply loved a particular female, or they preferred to make their life with another woman because it was a more viable arrangement if one were going to pursue a career, or they did not think about it at all."[8]

In the early 1910s, it was not uncommon for female college students to have crushes on older students and faculty. As an undergraduate, Jeannette (the veteran of a number of earlier crushes on teachers and friends) witnessed some female faculty members and students in her dormitory who had crushes on one another or openly expressed affection. Through dormitory gossip she also became aware of "a couple of gals who dressed & acted out the butch-femme bit to the limit."[9] Perhaps she may have heard students talk about a romantic friendship between Gertrude Dudley and Frances Kellor, a graduate student in sociology who supplemented her income by serving as an instructor in physical culture. Letters do not exist to document the nature of the relationship between the two women, but according to Faderman "it appears likely that the two women were lovers while Kellor studied and taught at the University of Chicago."[10]

Jeannette selected Beecher Hall, one of the university's five dormitories for women, because it was the least expensive, offering room, board, and laundry for only $225 per year, less than half that charged to residents of the best quarters. The women's dormitories overlooked a sheltered quadrangle, an arrangement that fostered an insular, tight-knit community of scholars. Home to eighteen undergraduates and twenty-four graduate students—most of them the daughters of professionals and small businessmen—Beecher Hall offered Jeannette a welcome respite from living under her mother's watchful supervision. Like many college freshmen, she threw herself into extracurricular activities. "It was so *wonderful* to be free of parental requirements of 'in bed by 10,'" she later recalled, "that I never counted the physical cost of my activities." According to an entry in Aunt Carrie's diary, Jeannette found life in the dormitory "very satisfactory" and very much enjoyed being at the university.[11]

It is difficult to reconstruct the extent to which she formed lasting friendships with other students during her time at the University of Chicago. Dormitory residents typically built a sense of community by observing and establishing traditions. Most of the young women living in Beecher Hall, for example, had single rooms but gathered in the dining room or sitting rooms when they wished to socialize. A fall beach party broke down barriers between the old and new girls, and upperclassmen who served as counselors adopted freshmen and entertained them at parties throughout the year. Halloween brought a masquerade, with girls dressing as Swedes, Chinese, Vandals, gypsies, witches, and farmers. Sings, the ritual "cozy Sunday evening hour around the fire," and "informal spreads and gatherings" in each other's rooms further contributed to the hall's sociability.[12]

In later life Jeannette remembered her freshman self as a bookishly precocious, "timorous, impoverished and repressed little nonentity."[13] Consumed by her studies, which included rhetoric and composition, elementary physics, and general inorganic chemistry, she made only occasional visits home. Unlike many of her classmates, Jeannette did not join in the Young Women's Christian League, the Neighborhood Club, the Dramatic Club, various language clubs, or any other formal organizations available to female students. Despite her literary aspirations, she put them aside and instead devoted herself to time-intensive laboratory courses. She did find time to make friends with an older, more confident, and energetic Janet Flanner, who immersed herself in many extracurricular activities, including the German Club, the *Chicago Literary Monthly* (for which she was associate editor), and amateur dramatics. Jeannette admired Janet's disaffected attitude and spirited personality, which manifested itself in late-night dances and the flaunting of middle-class social conventions. As the two women began what would become a lifelong friendship, they shared confidences and on one occasion Janet even showed Jeannette the "bean-shooter" [pistol] that she claimed her father had used to commit suicide. Flanner's career at the university was short-lived, however, and in March 1914 university authorities dismissed her as a "rebellious influence."[14]

Theodora Burnham and Aesthetic Dance

Jeannette balanced her academic work by fulfilling the university's physical culture requirement with aesthetic dancing, a craze that was sweep-

PHOTO 9.
Jeannette's love for aesthetic
dance blossomed during her
undergraduate years at the
University of Chicago when she
studied with Theodora Burnham.
(Courtesy of Alison Cope Puffer
and Winslow Howard Cope)

ing the nation in the early 1910s. Popular among middle-and upper-middle-class white women, this alternative form of dance expression ultimately evolved into the modern dance movement associated with Isadora Duncan, Chicagoan Loie Fuller, and Ruth St. Denis. The artist Paul Swan compared it to sculpture in motion. At the University of Chicago in the fall of 1912, however, young women like Jeannette donned dark tights, bloomers, and white middy blouses, formed straight lines, and made synchronous movements to music. In time, some of them exchanged this durable wear for translucent dresses that looked as though they had been sewn out of gossamer. The following spring, Jeannette and her dance classmates performed for the fourth annual spring athletic carnival, along with students from Mary Wood Hinman's School of Gymnastic and Folk Dancing.[15]

In short order, Jeannette developed a crush on one of the aesthetic dance instructors, Theodora Burnham, with her lovely tall, slim figure, and exquisite grace. Fourteen years her senior, Burnham hailed from Waltham, Massachusetts, and "had a beautiful eastern accent" much like Jeannette's mother. A 1903 graduate of the Sargent Normal School of

Physical Education in Cambridge, Massachusetts, she had studied under its founder, Dudley Allen Sargent (1849–1924), an early innovator in physical education. After teaching one year at Havergal College, a women's school in Toronto, she joined the faculty of the all-female Rockford College in 1904 as director of the college gymnasium. Devoted to the study of physical education, Burnham returned to Cambridge, Massachusetts, in the summer for further work with Sargent at the Harvard Summer School of Physical Education, another school he founded. She also studied in Boston at the Gilbert Normal School for Teachers of Dancing during the summer of 1909. With these credentials, she was well prepared to serve as director of the Rockford College Gymnasium from 1904 to 1910, and physical director at the college from 1906 to 1910. In the fall of 1912, she became an assistant in the Department of Physical Culture and Athletics at the University of Chicago, working under the direction of Gertrude Dudley.[16]

Jeannette found "physical satisfaction" in watching Burnham dance and took great delight "in her very occasional signs of approval, e.g., laying a hand on my shoulders when I had done something especially satisfactorily." There is no evidence that Burnham returned her student's feelings or even knew of Jeannette's admiration for her. Eager to learn more about this much-adored teacher, Jeannette lay in wait, scanning the brick-walled gym yard from her fourth-floor dorm window for extra glimpses of her as she walked the campus. While watching for Burnham, she happened to notice Janet Flanner's courtship of another dancing instructor—Winifred Pearce—in the courtyard beneath their adjoining dormitories.[17]

Jeannette had much to ponder when she returned home at the end of the fall quarter for Christmas break. She was pleased with her first semester's excellent performance at the university, but there was little time to dwell on her achievement or to dream about Miss Burnham. Instead, she found her mother "utterly worn out, body & mind," her father "wretched" from a case of grippe, and Aunt Carrie morose and depressed over Carlton Prouty's remarriage. After exchanging gifts on Christmas,

Jeannette and her sisters spent much of the day outdoors. Unable to remedy family problems, she immersed herself in household chores and socialized with high school friends.[18]

Jeannette eagerly returned to the university on January 2, 1913, for the beginning of winter quarter. Taking a rigorous course load that included plane trigonometry, general inorganic chemistry, and a second quarter of elementary physics, she spent long hours in science labs, but found time to end her day at the gymnasium, taking more courses in aesthetic dancing from her beloved Theodora Burnham. Aware that she needed to retain the honor scholarship if she wished to continue at the university the following year, Jeannette worked diligently to earn good grades. At the end of the winter and spring quarters she felt some satisfaction after earning A's in all but one course. Excelling in inorganic chemistry and molecular physics, she earned her lowest marks, somewhat surprisingly, in English literature, perhaps because they studied so few women writers.[19]

Family Drama

Carrie Burr Prouty quite likely regarded her eldest niece's studies and activities as a diversion from the ugliness in her own life. The nation's rising divorce rate notwithstanding, most middle- and upper-middle-class families looked askance at divorced women, and regarded them as morally suspect. In addition to the sting of rejection, Carrie felt humiliated when Carlton Prouty defied an Illinois state law prohibiting remarriage within one year after divorcing. Only four days after his divorce became final, he drove to LaPorte, Indiana, to marry his redheaded stenographer. Ten years his junior, Mary B. also may have been the mother of his children, having given birth to twins in 1911. Concerned about what people in Winnetka must think, Carrie confided to her journal, "Feel like *Godiva* everywhere I go."[20]

Carrie coped by spending time with her sister and nieces, visiting Jeannette on campus and sewing all kinds of clothing—silk shirts, voile dresses, underwear, and even slippers—for her. She filled her days by going to the Art Institute of Chicago to see "incredibly ugly!" cubist paintings and by listening to people like Jacob Riis speak at Hull House. On a November evening in 1912, she attended vespers and heard Chicago psychoanalyst Dr. William Sadler speak. The son-in-law of Dr. John Harvey Kellogg of Battle Creek, Michigan, he had traveled to Europe in 1911 to study with Sigmund Freud, who believed that a patient's problems stemmed from the repression of socially unacceptable ideas or traumatic memories, many of them sexual. While Sadler did not accept all of Freud's teachings, he did find his system helpful in dealing with the patient who had sexual problems. He refused, however, to believe that all nervous disorders stemmed from sexual origins. Inspired by his message of health and healing, Carrie turned to his book, *Physiology of Faith and Fear* (1912), and became a firm supporter of his ideas, which she shared with the Fosters.[21]

Meanwhile, after drifting from late 1909 until 1912, Winslow Foster returned to work at the Morava Construction Company and drove himself hard in an attempt to make up for lost time. Traveling throughout the Midwest, he supervised a variety of structural engineering projects, ranging from bridges to schools. The stress of his unstable job situation and his frequent trips away from home had taken a toll on Mabel, who felt ill-equipped to manage the family's business in her husband's absence, but her condition improved somewhat during the summer of 1913 when the Fosters, like many privileged Chicago families, fled the city's sweltering summer heat and retreated to their summer cottage at Hamlin Lake, Michigan.[22] Despite improved family finances, Jeannette's return to the University of Chicago for her second year remained questionable until late July when the family learned that she had earned one of the twenty honor scholarships awarded to students who had demonstrated exceptional ability during their first year of study.[23]

As a nineteen-year-old sophomore in the fall of 1913, Jeannette appeared more confident, outgoing, and active. In addition to maintaining a rigorous course of study, she filled her schedule with outings to football games, operas, and concerts, and visits home. Once again she signed up for aesthetic dancing, perhaps because she wanted to be near instructor Theodora Burnham, but she had left the university's employ at the end of the previous academic year.[24] Jeannette soon filled that void when she "entered on a really *serious* passion" for a new Beecher Hall resident. Repeating a familiar pattern, she chose an older woman as the object of her affection: a thirty-year-old graduate student in English named Edna Grace Taylor.[25] Born in 1883, this Harlan, Iowa, farmer's daughter shared Jeannette's sense of imagination and love of books. As a child she and her brother Carl "rode Taranus and Tircuus [sic] through the African wilds hunting lions," hung imaginary foes for piracy, and wished for "a mountain of rice, a river of custard and a hog that was all liver." After graduating from Drake University in 1902, Grace (as she was known) had taught high school for several years before deciding to pursue graduate work. A serious-looking young woman with striking eyes and a Grecian nose, she wore her brunette hair upswept in the style of the era.[26]

Planning her days so she could spend every possible waking moment with Grace, Jeannette rose at 5 a.m. and played a set of tennis with her before breakfast. Since Beecher Hall housed both undergraduate and graduate students, Jeannette benefited from laxer rules governing residents' hours. After long hours of study, she savored leisurely twilight walks she took with Grace along Lake Michigan's shore. The older woman found Jeannette to be an enthusiastic conversationalist and a warm and attentive friend. As the year progressed, Jeannette grew hopelessly enamored with Grace, and "completely aroused emotionally."[27] Yearning to stir similar emotions in her friend, Jeannette plied Grace with candy, flowers, and poems left on the floor outside her door, but with limited success.

Throughout her life, Jeannette would fall for women who, as she later reflected, remained "safely out of my reach (for them) for social or psychological reasons."[28] Grace was no exception. She treasured Jeannette as a friend and enjoyed their cerebral connection, but at the same time felt uneasy about the intensity of the younger woman's affection. Coming from a deeply religious family, Grace repressed the feelings of attraction she had for Jeannette. From Jeannette's perspective she remained "pretty cold sexually" and their relationship "never went beyond my kissing her goodnight (her return was sisterly cool)." Years later, Grace would make her home with a female companion, but in the spring of 1914 she chose to keep whatever feelings she had for Jeannette in check.[29]

Seeking an outlet for the passion evoked by her love for Grace, Jeannette poured her feelings into poetry. Her earliest surviving love poem, "White Night" (1914), tells of watching from her Beecher Hall window for glimpses of Grace. Revealing her romanticism and love of nature, this excerpt also suggests that Jeannette had a preference for slim, boyish women (like Theodora Burnham) and a fascination with eyes:

> My window, there above me in the wall—
> One little spot of bright against the gray
> Of age-stained pine; the others smile and say
> "But such a little window." That is all.
> They have not watched the gem-clear bit of blue
> That, like your eyes, smiles on me where I lie
> Nor, slim and brave and straight against the sky,
> The young pine's tip that somehow seems like you.

Other stanzas contain hints of Jeannette's sensual side, referring to "the afterglow, rose-fair," the "soft touch of your hair," and "the first faint gold of dawn—your smile."[30]

Breakdown

As the year came to a close, Grace made plans to join her brother, a missionary teacher in Nanking, China. Perhaps the intensity of Jeannette's feelings had convinced Grace of the need for physical distance between them, or she may have felt a familial sense of duty beckoning. Either way, Jeannette dreaded the prospective loss of her "adored amour" to a place halfway around the globe, one to which communication would be unreliable at best. On June 15, 1914, however, she put on her best face and accompanied Grace to the Englewood train station to say goodbye. "Of course," she remembered later, "I thought I'd die after I'd seen the suburban train taking her away—but I didn't! I merely started menstruating." Taking the long Sixty-third Street streetcar ride back to her dormitory room, an exhausted and devastated Jeannette collapsed into bed and could not summon enough energy to rise the next morning.[31]

The Fosters, who blamed their daughter's breakdown on overwork and a rigorous course of study, soon arrived to move Jeannette back to Beverly Hills. When she failed to show signs of improvement they took her to their Hamlin Lake cottage, hoping that rest and relaxation in this beautiful natural setting would restore her to health. Despite her mother's watchful eye, she tried to hoard a sedative until she "had enough for suicide," but weakened before making a successful attempt. Jeannette could not confide in her mother, who had responded furiously to Jeannette's adolescent crushes, and she no longer had faith in religion. When she hinted to her female physician why she felt so despondent, the woman soundly boxed her ears. At the time, adults would have given young girls like Jeannette such publications as Dr. Irving D. Steinhardt's *Ten Sex Talks to Girls (14 Years and Older)*, which advised young women to avoid "girls who are too affectionate and demonstrative" and to remember that "beds are sleeping places" and that young girls should resist bodily contact.[32] Increasingly aware that she must hide her feelings for women, Jeannette found solace in the writing of poetry, which seemed to be an acceptable emotional outlet.

Try as they might, Jeannette's parents could not persuade their oldest daughter to return to the University of Chicago for her junior year. Despairing, they raised the possibility of a transfer to Wellesley (believing their family connection to its first president Ada Howard might warrant special treatment), but Jeannette would have none of it. As weeks passed and her condition showed no sign of improvement, she later noted, "My mother grew so over-conscious of my moods that it became advisable for me to go for a protracted visit to her elder sister in Winnetka."[33] Aunt

Carrie, who felt genuine affection for her oldest niece, delighted at the chance to demonstrate her usefulness to the family. If anyone had reason to be depressed and discouraged, it was Aunt Carrie, who had lost her comfortable home and now lived in the same town as her former husband and his new wife. Undaunted, she held her head high and immersed herself in church and volunteer work, and served as president of the library board for a number of years.[34] Jeannette benefited from her positive example, and soon found herself taking renewed interest in the world around her.

Whether or not Aunt Carrie knew the source of Jeannette's depression and lethargy, she nonetheless believed that the newly popular field of psychoanalysis could help. Sharing an article about psychoanalysis with Jeannette during the summer of 1914, she convinced her niece, for the first time, that "there was *any* help [to be had] from learned circles." With Carrie's assistance, Jeannette began seeing Dr. William Sadler, the psychoanalysist whom her aunt had heard lecture two years earlier. Later in life Jeannette pointed to her psychoanalysis by Sadler as a critical turning point, a time when she grew in understanding and acceptance of herself and her sexual desires. Even though Sadler believed that there was "no grander, more noble, or higher calling for a healthy, sound-minded woman than to become the mother of children," it is unlikely that he attempted to persuade her to embrace a heterosexual lifestyle.[35] In addition to viewing homoeroticism as a stage through which most young women and men passed, he did not view those who failed to develop into heterosexuals as perverts, diseased, or abnormal. Instead, he regarded them, much like Havelock Ellis, as victims of a congenital condition. Calling for toleration rather than censure, he believed that the "full-fledged homoerotic" was "not responsible for his condition." Arguing that it was "high time that such wide-spread and common-place attractions should no longer be regarded as vices requiring punishment or diseases calling for treatment," his attitude, combined with her study of science, laid the foundation for Jeannette's acceptance of her sexuality as an inborn trait.[36]

Rockford College

A few months after she had begun psychoanalysis with Dr. Sadler, Jeannette heard a young Winnetka woman's enthusiastic account of the school from which she had recently graduated—Rockford College, known for its most famous alumna Jane Addams. Located ninety miles northwest of Chicago, Rockford College was easily accessible by rail. Set on ten acres "of undulating and wooded land, situated on a bluff which commands a beautiful view of the Rock River," the campus had a secluded feel yet stood only ten minutes' walk from the city center. The main building housed recitation rooms, biology labs, the library, and chapel, and advertisements for the college boasted that typical student rooms featured hot as well as cold water.[37]

Jeannette had visited Rockford College during her senior year of high school, but had ruled it out after the University of Chicago offered her an honor scholarship. Sometime during the fall of 1915, she returned to the campus accompanied by Aunt Carrie, who informed a friend on the faculty about Jeannette's breakdown and refusal to return to the University of Chicago. As a result, she received permission to become a part-time student even though the quarter had already begun.[38] If she succeeded, then they would consider letting Jeannette enroll for her junior year.

Rockford College proved to be an ideal environment for Jeannette, who would flourish in the women's college campus setting. In contrast with her experience at a coeducational university, female faculty were more accessible to students and had greater opportunities for informal communication with them because they often resided in dormitories. Aware of the obstacles confronting women in higher education, they often identified and made great effort to encourage talented young women in their charge. As feminist historian Barbara Solomon observed, such attention could set the fortunate student "on an intellectual course for life." Given the intimacy of these relationships, with faculty teaching and socializing with students, the latter often developed crushes on their mentors. Additionally, Solomon notes, "pairing among women professors also became a familiar pattern."[39]

Since her appointment as Rockford College president in 1902, Julia Gulliver had assembled a faculty that included many talented women with PhD degrees from such schools as Cornell, the University of Pennsylvania, and Johns Hopkins University. In addition to being committed to scholarship, they instilled in their students a love for learning and an ethos of caring. Living and studying together in close proximity, they cultivated a close sense of community by going for walks and on picnics with students and by celebrating festive occasions with them in their rooms. Students also absorbed Gulliver's feminist perspective. When speaking to the Chicago College Club in December 1913, she reiterated the school's intent: "'To increase women's power by making her fitter for power,' is at the heart of the feminist movement, according to W. L. George. This is also at the heart of our effort at Rockford to enable woman to attain the freedom for which she is so restlessly seeking."[40] In this context, Jeannette began to tap her creative abilities and to grow confident in her ability to succeed as a single professional woman.

Despite her excellent academic preparation at the University of Chicago, Jeannette's transition to Rockford proved difficult both academically and socially. The once-excellent grades plummeted in the fall of 1915 to an unprecedented C in history and a B in English. By spring, fortunately, her ability to concentrate improved and she regained some enthusiasm for learning as she studied English, history, and the Bible. The summer of 1916, her parents hoped, would contribute further to their daughter's emotional recovery. An emergency appendectomy in early July, however, meant that she had to remain at home with her mother while the rest of the family went to Hamlin Lake for vacation. Her spirits soon lifted, however, when she learned that Rockford College had awarded her a service scholarship for the 1916 to 1917 academic year.[41]

After losing a year to illness in high school, and over a year of college due to her breakdown, Jeannette's age finally matched that of her classmates when she returned to Rockford College in the fall of 1916. Evaluation of her transcript revealed that she only needed one more course for a major in chemistry. Choosing a second major in English and

American literature, she began pursuing a deep-seated love for literature and writing.

Blossoming as a full-fledged junior studying a subject she enjoyed,
Jeannette joined the college creative-writing club, served as literary edi-
tor for the school's yearbook (the *Cupola*), was elected president of the
English Club, joined the Tolo Council, and served on the House Com-
mittee. Soon some of her poems and short stories began appearing in *The
T̲a̲p̲e̲r̲*

about what you know, many of
utobiographical elements. The
nce, appeared in *The Taper* in
:o societal expectations of the
'een a young boy and girl, but
:mistry teacher Nell Jackson.
s for Jackson, the story's pro-
chocolates anonymously to a
also used the poetry she had
blication of Radclyffe Hall's
quited love she harbored for
:ms from 1916 is one entitled
ion and sense of loneliness

; *gay,*

'ing—

ſe

ʌ̲nu̲ *so there came my little gleam—I knew*
No world could be quite worthless, that held you.

Many of her other poems also contained references to Grace, describing a "pensive backward glance and farewell smile" as she left Jeannette at the train station, and such physical characteristics as Grace's "curling knot of dusky hair" and her "voice all cello tones/That stirred me once to madness." The poem "Ashes" suggests that Jeannette was in the process of coming to terms with the death of her youthful, innocent, and naïve self while evolving into a resolute, courageous, and passionate woman.[44]

> *Nay, 'tis a grown-eyed child with flushing cheek*
> *And eager parted lips and hurried breathing,*
> *Shaken at your mere glance with pulsing rapture.*
> *But she is dead, I think.*
> *I know it is not I that you desire.*

Lillian Faderman argues that education, especially in women's colleges, was responsible for contributing to the spread of lesbianism among middle-class women. In these supportive settings, young women observed faculty role models in Boston marriages, where two women lived together independent of male support. Coined in the nineteenth century, the term suggested intimacy and commitment, and sometimes included a sexual dimension.[45] Sheltered and idealistic, Jeannette slowly comprehended the significance of shifting attitudes toward same-sex intimacy.

As a Rockford College undergraduate, Jeannette acquired a heightened awareness of the onus attached to same-sex relationships when one of her close friends who sat on a student council told her about two students who were brought before a review board and expelled from college for suspected lesbian behavior: they had locked themselves in their room for several hours at a time. Nearly forty years later a modified version of this incident would appear in the preface to her *Sex Variant Women in Literature*. As a young woman, however, it piqued her curiosity about homosexuality and sent her to the well-stocked Rockford College Library for information. Her generation, she later explained, had not been well-educated about sexuality. As she browsed the thousands of volumes on the library's shelves, her eyes happened upon a brown buckram volume by British sexologist Havelock Ellis entitled *Studies in the Psychology of Sex*, Volume II. Taking the work to a secluded table and chair in the stacks, she began reading the case studies of sexual inversion in women (or lesbianism) for hours at a time. A number of passages from chapter IV would have struck a chord with Jeannette, including, "The inverted woman is an enthusiastic admirer of feminine beauty"; she is known for cherishing "lofty ideals of love"; and "the congenital anomaly occurs with special frequency in women of high intelligence." If she had seen the 1913 edition of this 1901 work, with its new preface, she would have read about the new "knowledge of the physiological mechanism of the sexual instinct," which supported the idea of nature, not nurture.[46] Several days later, after finishing the book, she had found the answers to some of her questions, as well as a label for herself—homosexual.

With the exception of the physician who had boxed her ears a year earlier, Jeannette's formal introduction to homosexuality occurred in a neutral, if not positive, context. According to Ellis, homosexuality was inborn rather than a disease, and therefore was not immoral. Moreover, Ellis noted, many homosexuals had made significant contributions to society. "I was very, very much interested and relieved," Jeannette remembered, "to learn that I was not an isolated specimen, but that I was a pretty good copy."[47] After reading Ellis, Jeannette was eager to locate other books containing insights into homosexuality. Covertly scanning both nonfiction and fiction titles, she began to keep a list of works and purchased them whenever the opportunity arose.

In later life Jeannette downplayed any struggle she endured while coming to terms with her sexual identity, but the poem "Resolve" (1916), preserves a counter narrative.[48]

> Clear-eyed I made my choice:
> Life a calm stagnant thing,
> Or glad—with suffering;

Urged by no outer voice,
Clear-eyed I made my choice.
Free-will I chose my way,
Counting both cost and gain.
Now that I pay with pain
It shall be valiantly,
Silently, gallantly.
Free-will I chose my way.

Like many homosexuals at that time, Jeannette felt isolated and alone. The decision to live life fully rather than to stifle her urges came, she recognized, at a cost and required her to "pay with pain." She could have repressed her desire for women, but when she thought of Grace Taylor "some buried voice began to sing/Of a great strength that once had touched my life." Reassured by the positive power of the love she felt for Grace, she knew that "no world could be quite worthless, that held you." Choosing her path, she did not look back.[49]

With her newfound knowledge and awareness of homosexuality, Jeannette began to notice that "plenty of the faculty at the college were in the know." She studied human physiology with Dr. Mabel Bishop, whom Jeannette described as "a butch for sure." Bishop made much of the fact that she had once studied with Anna Howard Shaw, the noted clergywoman and suffragist who had a number of relationships with women. Once, Jeannette recalled, she asked "if I knew what 'the French way' meant, or if I'd ever heard of 'going down on' anyone—and I *hadn't.*"[50] Even though Jeannette was not familiar with the concept, it is noteworthy that Bishop, who undoubtedly recognized Jeannette's lesbian tendencies, raised the subject with her. The presence on the faculty of well-educated and highly accomplished homosexual women like Bishop and Clara Louise Thompson provided Jeannette with positive role models, and she began to see the viability of a future for herself as a single professional woman, or as one who found domestic happiness with another woman. In the nineteenth century, such relationships had become so commonplace at Wellesley and other women's colleges that they were known as Wellesley marriages.[51]

Clara Louise

Jeannette's second homosexual attachment (she discounted the crushes she had on women before her first emotional attachment to Grace Taylor) and her "first experience of physical intimacy of any sort" occurred at Rockford College. As was the case with her previous crushes, the object of her affection was an older woman, the lovely and feminine classics professor, Clara Louise Thompson. Jeannette's academic work showed marked improvement after she began studying Greek with her, and taking part in weekend canoe trips with her and students on the Rock River. Born in 1884, Thompson had a privileged childhood in St. Louis, Missouri. Her father, a successful mining engineer, sent his first-born child to Washington University, from which she graduated with a BA degree in 1906. After earning her master's degree from the University of Pennsylvania in 1908, Clara Louise won a fellowship at the American School of Classical Studies in Rome, where she studied for one year before beginning doctoral work at the University of Pennsylvania in 1909.[52]

Early in 1910, Clara Louise met Alice Paul, recently returned from England and radicalized by her work with the British suffragist Emmeline Pankhurst. Becoming friends, the two young women decided to share a pension near the campus and during that year Alice infused Clara Louise with her passion for the suffrage movement. Despite her intense involvement in the suffrage movement, Paul made an effort to remain friends with Thompson, who went to Washington, D.C., in the summer of 1913 to help Alice with the campaign for woman suffrage and remained until the following summer. She joined the faculty of Rockford College in the fall of 1914, yet remained devoted to the suffrage cause and in the spring of 1915 became a member of the advisory council of the Congressional Union for Woman Suffrage.[53] Even in later years, after both women moved on to other causes, their paths continued to cross.

Eleven years Jeannette's senior, Thompson was the epitome of femininity with her golden-brown hair and delicate features. A Phi Beta Kappa scholar of the classics, she possessed the cultural and intellectual traits, passionate devotion to a cause, and cosmopolitan experience that Jeannette found so attractive. Like Jeannette, Thompson also poured her emotions into poems, which appeared in the college literary magazine *The Taper* under such titles as "Courage" and "Defeat."[54] Students would have been impressed by her feminism and knowledge of her work with the Congressional Union as it campaigned for woman suffrage. The poem "Désirée" (1916) captures Jeannette's admiration for Thompson during the early days of this love.[55]

> *In your black gown, you are so far away*
> *Not as the high white stars I have adored,*
> *But human, thrilling, near, and yet withdrawn*
> *Subtly, some lovely stranger that I yearn—*
> *But all in vain—to reach. I know the pain*
> *Of voiceless longing . . .*

Jeannette's crush on Thompson deepened when the instructor invited a handful of "intimates . . . to visit her in her room late in the evening, and to go a certain distance with physical caresses." Sometimes they danced with each other, or expressed affection by exchanging caresses, cuddling, or kissing. Their behavior was innocent, yet intimate, in keeping with the times. When Thompson roomed with Alice Paul and worked with Congressional Union supporters in Washington, D.C., she had known a number of women in lesbian relationships. Recalling their relationship in later years, Jeannette noted that Thompson tended to stop intimacy "short of any 'completeness'—(occasionally, I am sure, worse for our nerves than going the whole way would have been)." Those experiences inspired her to write the poem "A Flash" (1916).[56]

> *Your kiss upon my hand!*
> *How I am lifted to a queenly place*

Among the singing stars! My soul is shaken!
The whole of me knows ecstasy turned pain,
So small a thing—yet I have wept for it—
Your lips against my fingers.

Obsessed with her instructor, Jeannette showed her love by leaving candy, flowers, and poems outside Thompson's door, just as she had done earlier for Nell Jackson and Grace Taylor. A dreamer, she yearned for the day when the barriers would fall, the time when they could be together.

Jeannette's affection for Thompson deepened during the summer of 1917 when Clara Louise and her sister Alice summered at Hamlin Lake with the Fosters. There is no evidence that Mabel objected to the budding friendship and her daughter's obvious devotion to the older woman. Together day in and day out, the Thompson sisters shared many intimate moments with Jeannette, Anna, and Helen Foster—washing each other's hair, swimming in their teddies, canoeing home by moonlight, and sharing hot chocolate before drifting off to sleep. Jeannette preserved her memories of these golden days of summer in this excerpt from "Chains" (1917).[57]

And once a year has sped, and twice, and never years more sweet,
Nor have I dearer blessing craved than sitting at her feet.
And times have been she set me free, but ne'er would I depart
For summer breeze has all my soul, and hers is all my heart.

Jeannette's deepening sense of her sexuality and her proximity to Thompson inspired other poems, including "Platonics" (1917), which appeared in an anthology of work gathered from college newspapers.[58] More sexualized than any of her previous works, its lines spoke of passion and restraint:

Dear, dearest,
Why do the arms of me yearn?

Dear, dearest
Why do the lips of me burn?
I, who have trained my mind in an austere school,
Why do I quiver because your brow is cool?
I, who have vowed that Minerva alone is fair,
Why is my world ablaze at the touch of your hair?
I, who have scorned things sensuous under my feet,
Why do I freeze and burn if your lips are sweet?
I, who know I must be as steel, and forget,
Why does the soul in me faint when your eyes are wet?

Her father, who intercepted the gratis copy sent to her home address, praised the poem "as entirely pleasant," she recalled, but observed that "it sounded as if I knew what I was talking about." How could she, a sheltered young woman, understand the meaning of such phrases? Her mother, he felt certain, could not have shared these sentiments with Jeannette because, he explained, she was "the coldest woman he had ever known."[59] At that point Winslow Foster began suspecting the nature of his daughter's fondness for women.

Senior Year

In September 1917, Jeannette's younger sister Anna joined her at Rockford College and the senior and freshman became roommates. A diligent diarist, Anna captured the many times that school year she, Jeannette, and Clara shared meals and went for walks, picnics, and weekend canoe trips. In the fall, for example, they went upriver to Professor J. Gardner Goodwin's picnic place nearly every other weekend until the weather turned too cold for such outings. A senior, Jeannette led an active social life, singing first alto in the Glee Club, serving as literary editor of the *Taper*, and playing as a substitute on the field hockey team. She and other members of the English Club volunteered for the Red Cross and studied Russian life and literature. Jeannette also participated in meet-

PHOTO 10.   Mock Prom, Rockford College, January 19, 1918.
Jeannette's sister Anna (at right) wore white duck trousers and a dress
uniform coat. According to her diary entry for the evening, she enjoyed
a "very nice dance" and a table party with Clara Louise Thompson,
Louise Hannum, Florence Bleecker, and Jeannette. (Courtesy of Alison
Cope Puffer and Winslow Howard Cope)

ings of the Classical Club because it provided another opportunity to be
near Clara Louise Thompson, the club's advisor. In addition to attending
the mock prom, where some of the girls dressed as men, she donned a period costume and danced for the Washington party.[60]

Jeannette displayed no interest in dating young men, but her younger
sister Anna felt differently. During the war years, college officials tried to
shelter students from the presence of thousands of soldiers at Camp Grant,
located on the southern edge of town. Some of the dance class students
performed there during the 1917 to 1918 academic year, but the college
made Monday its weekly holiday instead of Saturday so the students
wouldn't be "contaminated" by the soldiers walking along State Street during the weekend. Anna expressed great excitement when soldiers sta-
tioned at the camp asked her out on dates, while Jeannette remained
disinterested. On one occasion, however, Anna became ill and Jeannette
dutifully served as a substitute, but with markedly little enthusiasm. If
given a choice, she preferred going to Chicago with Clara Louise and other

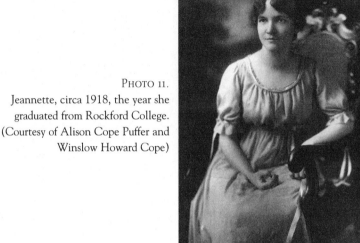

PHOTO 11.
Jeannette, circa 1918, the year she
graduated from Rockford College.
(Courtesy of Alison Cope Puffer and
Winslow Howard Cope)

friends. After dining at the Russian Tea Room and seeing a film or play, they often stayed overnight at the Foster home in Beverly Hills before returning to campus.[61]

Jeannette's grades steadily improved from a B average for the 1915–1916 school year to an A average during her senior year. As her time at Rockford College drew to a close, she participated in a number of college rituals, including giving flowers to friends, hosting table parties, and participating in processions around the campus. To commemorate her final days as a student, she swam in a nearby fountain and shared her special homemade watered fudge and ice cream with friends. The Fosters and their youngest daughter, Helen, traveled to Rockford to attend some of the week's festivities. On her sister Anna's birthday, Jeannette and the other graduates listened to the Reverend C. W. Gilkey, pastor of the Hyde Park Baptist church, deliver a "wonderful" commencement address in honor of the Rockford College class of 1918.[62]

By the time she graduated with a BA degree from Rockford College, Jeannette and her family fully expected that she would become a self-sufficient career woman. Unlike her sister Anna, she had shown no interest in dating men and the family did not pressure her to look for a husband. Jeannette would miss the regular contact with Clara Louise, but she had come to terms with her sexuality even though her experience with love remained unrequited. Only two days after receiving her BA degree in chemistry and American and English literature, Jeannette informed her family that she had accepted a position at the prestigious Science Hill Preparatory School for Young Ladies in Shelbyville, Kentucky.[63]

The Summer of 1918

In anticipation of his family's annual Hamlin Lake vacation in the summer of 1918, Winslow Foster bought his daughters a bright blue canoe and then surprised everyone by purchasing an automobile. His financial situation had improved during the war years, in part because of his new position at Chicago's National Malleable & Steel Castings Company, which had been converted into a defense plant.[64] As a sign that Jeannette's parents recognized her growing maturity, Winslow and Mabel went ahead to the lake on July 14, leaving their oldest daughter, now twenty-two, and Anna at home for an additional two weeks. That summer Winslow further demonstrated his confidence in his daughter's capabilities by teaching her to drive the car and shoot and clean a pistol. Unlike some fathers of this era, he did not attempt to keep her under his roof until marriage. He fully expected Jeannette to have a career and recognized that she might need to protect herself. She named the gun that he gave her Ignatz after a popular cartoon mouse appearing in George Herriman's "Krazy Kat" cartoon strip, and spent many hours that summer target shooting.[65]

As in previous summers, the Foster sisters spent many treasured hours in the company of friends. With her newly acquired driving skill, Jeannette took her sisters, a college friend Florence Bleecker who summered at the lake that year, and the Thompson sisters—Clara Louise and Alice—for lectures, concerts, and dances in Ludington.[66] Unlike previous summers, however, Clara Louise kept Jeannette at a distance, and when people paired off to go for walks or canoe rides she often accompanied one of the other women. Outwardly resigned to the new parameters of their relationship, Jeannette poured her feelings into poems such as "A Song Unuttered," which contained references to the "Passionate, prisoned song of the love I bear you." She also consoled herself by doing things with Florence. The daughter of a salesman, she had graduated from Morgan Park High School the same year as Anna and had gone to Rockford College. Jeannette enjoyed the fact that she was a talented debater who could converse on a wide range of subjects.[67]

As the end of summer neared, Jeannette grew eager to begin her position as a teacher of chemistry and science at the Science Hill School. For the past two and a half years she had enjoyed the homosocial environment of Rockford College, and she fully expected to flourish in her new position. Returning to Chicago in late August with her youngest sister Helen, she spent the next few weeks in a flurry of preparations before boarding a train on September 10, the day that marked the beginning of her life as an independent woman. While pragmatism would govern some of her future decisions, Jeannette at last felt in charge of her destiny, and she expected great things.[68]

Science Hill School

Located between Louisville and Lexington in the small community of Shelbyville, the Science Hill School prepared young women from privileged Kentucky families for admission to such eastern women's colleges as Bryn Mawr, Vassar, and Wellesley. As she first approached the community, Jeannette took in the rolling hills, golden leaves of tobacco, and Baptist churches dotting the landscape. The school occupied an impressive two-story brick structure dating to 1790.[69] She felt awed by the school and its impressive reputation, but also experienced a bit of culture shock after living for so many years in Chicago. Who would she socialize with in this rural community? Would she feel culturally and socially isolated in this sleepy little town? Would she find female friends?

Established in 1825 by Julia Ann Hieronymus Tevis, the Science Hill School was unlike many girls' academies and seminaries of the era. Its curriculum emphasized chemistry rather than embroidery, and mathematics rather than sewing. After changing hands in 1879, its new head, Dr. Wiley Taut Poynter, remained loyal to its founder's creed: "Woman's mind is limitless. Help it to grow." Both the genteel elegance of the grounds and Science Hill's emphasis on women's minds would have appealed to Jeannette. As a college preparatory school, it attracted the daughters of prominent families in Lexington, Harrodsville, Louisville, and other nearby communities. Nominally Methodist, the school held chapel every day and instilled in students a strong sense of social obligation. As a part of a lyceum lecture circuit, Science Hill hosted famous speakers, writers, and educators of the day. In addition to high academic standards, it offered students a rich athletic program.

Jeannette began the school year optimistically, expecting to share her knowledge of science with highly motivated students. She enjoyed the open-air courtyard, the well-stocked library, and the elegance of the school's formal dining room. According to her sister Anna, Jeannette flourished in her new environment, throwing herself into activities much as she had at Rockford. When some Mississippi schoolgirls challenged the Science Hill girls in a game of basketball, for instance, she good-naturedly served as a cheerleader. In retrospect, however, Jeannette dismissed the school as archaic and lamented the fact that fear of losing her job had prevented her from helping girls who, like herself at a younger age, sought information about their sexual identity.[70]

Rather than cultivate friendships in Shelbyville, Jeannette maintained close and regular contact with her sister Anna and their mutual friends at Rockford College. Throughout the fall she mailed Anna packages—decorations for her room and treats to share with classmates—and returned to Rockford as often as her schedule permitted. When the tragic influenza epidemic of 1918 and 1919 closed Science Hill in late November, Jeannette returned home to Beverly Hills and then traveled on to Rockford for several days of fun and relaxation. Once again, she thrilled to be in Clara Louise Thompson's presence even though the prospect of a relationship with her remained dim.[71]

The Goodwin Scandal

Because of regular correspondence with Anna, and her occasional visits to Rockford College, Jeannette heard all about a scandal that was rocking the campus in early 1919. According to her sister, chemistry professor J. Gardner Goodwin had been dismissed because of his alleged homosexual tendencies. As she explained in her diary: "He has been taking young boys up the river & learning masterbation [sic]." Rumors abounded, with someone even declaring that Goodwin was a hermaphrodite, a person with both male and female genitalia. The accusation would have been shocking to Anna because she and Jeannette had been close enough to "Goody" to use his picnic place up the river.[72]

Julia Gulliver held the respect of trustees, faculty, students, and alumni from her appointment as Rockford College president in 1902 until the winter of 1918, but her handling of the Goodwin incident led to the irreparable creation of factions on campus. Descended from Plymouth Colony founder William Bradford, Gulliver had come to Rockford with impeccable cultural and educational credentials, including a PhD from Smith College earned in 1888 and membership in Phi Beta Kappa. Appointed head of the Department of Philosophy and Biblical Literature in 1890, she spent her entire career at Rockford with the exception of one year's study in Germany at Leipzig University. Inspired by the example of Jane Addams, who spoke at her inauguration, Gulliver worked diligently and tirelessly during her seventeen years as president to increase the school's enrollment from 105 students in 1902 to 216 by 1919. Her success in increasing the endowment was even more remarkable: it grew from $28,595 to $243,620 during her administration.[73] All of these achievements, however, seemed moot in the spring of 1919.

When Anna Foster returned to campus from Christmas break, she learned that a handsome, about-to-be-married male teacher had replaced

Goodwin in the chemistry classroom, but the incident was far from over. By February, twenty-one Rockford College professors—more than two-thirds of the faculty—had called for President Gulliver's resignation and threatened to withdraw from the school if she did not leave. Gulliver's opponents, led in part by professor of history Edith Bramhall, objected to the fact that she had provided a letter of recommendation for Professor Goodwin, who sought another position after his dismissal. Defending her actions, Gulliver explained that she "wanted to keep all this filth [reports about Goodwin's activities with young boys] away from the girls." She believed that in helping Goodwin quietly find another position, she could save the college from unwanted publicity, which, she believed, would lead parents to withdraw their daughters from the school and would hurt enrollments for the coming year. It was hopeless. Goodwin's career was over and he became a traveling salesman.[74]

In an effort to protect her reputation, Clara Louise Thompson sided with the majority. Late one night she even dragged students into the fray when she awakened Anna Foster and her friends, urging them to circulate a petition stating that students would leave the college unless Gulliver stepped down. Believing it to be in the best interest of the school, Gulliver went on a leave of absence effective February 20. Remaining devoted to the college she had helped build, she advised the trustees to appoint a man—William Arthur Maddox—as her successor in order to quell student and teacher unrest. A professor at the Teacher's College of Columbia University, he became the first male to head the school in its seventy-two year history.[75]

As this crisis unfolded, the post–World War I Red Scare also threatened to dampen student enrollment. In the anticommunist hysteria surrounding the arrest of one hundred Rockford residents as alleged members and supporters of the Communist party, rumors circulated that there were a number of communist sympathizers on the campus. After the negative publicity surrounding Goodwin's dismissal, gossips also could have suggested that the college was a hotbed of homosexuals, an allegation that would not have been taken lightly. The earlier open attitude toward women's romantic friendships had faded away by the late 1910s, a casualty of the new era. As faculty took sides in the Goodwin-Gulliver controversy, students began referring to those who opposed Gulliver's efforts to cover up the scandal as the "Reds" and to those who supported her as the "Whites." "In a dim way," Gulliver wrote to Maddox in March 1919, "the students are recognizing the facts in the case, namely that we have an outbreak of bolshevism here."[76]

In one of his first acts as president, Maddox asked all faculty members to submit their resignations. After reviewing faculty members' records, he reappointed only the ones he considered loyal, above suspicion, and unlikely to make trouble. Despite efforts to distance herself from this anticommunist and homophobic panic, Clara Louise Thompson found herself among the dismissed, which included Julia Gulliver's sister Mary (a professor of art), Edith Bramhall (who had instigated the call for Gulliver's resignation), Jeannette's French professor Helen Epler, home economics professor Rose Baird, mathematics instructor Marie Allen, physiology professor Mabel Bishop, professor of English Louise Hannum, and six others. Jeannette was firmly convinced that Bishop, Hannum, and Allen had lost their positions because of their homosexual tendencies. Indeed, Allen moved to Champaign, Illinois, with one of Jeannette's classmates, Mabel Lindop, where the two opened a tearoom.[77] Jeannette and Anna were upset by the dismissal of some of their favorite professors, but they refused to distance themselves from the women they had grown to regard as friends. Anna continued to picnic and canoe with Clara Louise during the spring of 1919, and she in turn visited the Foster sisters in their home and at Hamlin Lake during the summer. During the Christmas holidays, the Fosters spent time with Marie Allen and Mabel Lindop when they visited from Champaign.[78]

The "Goodwin Affair" signified a turning point at Rockford College and nationally in tolerance for gays and lesbians. With the popularization of Freudian theories about sexuality and the rise of the flapper, post–World War I Americans developed a heightened awareness of the female sex drive and ceased to regard same-sex intimacies as innocent behaviors. Societal changes, among them the growth of coeducational high schools and the commercialization of recreation, promoted heterosocial mixing and cast homosocial intimacy in a suspicious light. As a result, "serious love relationships between women could no longer be highly regarded since they would interfere with companionate heterosexual relationships." Some of the women who persisted in defying gendered expectations of women found themselves branded as lesbians. Alarmed by the presence of militant suffragists picketing the White House during World War I, physicians and sexologists attempted to contain their influence by equating independent women and their defiant gestures with mannishness, maladjustment, deviance, and psychological illness. Not everyone would succumb to this pressure—lesbianism would, if anything, become more evident among artists, writers, and musicians during the 1920s—but middle-class lesbians knew that outward manifestations of their sexual identity could have serious consequences. With the onset of the economic depression of the 1930s, lesbianism clearly was "not a choice for the fainthearted" as Americans embraced the idea of men as wage earners and became more vocal in expressing hostility toward economically independent females.[79] If the prospect of losing one's job was not enough, others increasingly found themselves struggling with feelings of doubt and self-hatred.[80]

As a well-read individual, Jeannette was aware of the medical and scientific stigmatization of homosexuality, but her freethinking outlook and indomitable spirit kept her from internalizing negative messages about her sexuality. The fallout from the Goodwin scandal, however, reinforced the necessity of judiciously camouflaging her true identity and of taking care to eschew masculine behaviors and appearance. As she had learned by watching Clara Louise Thompson, Mabel Bishop, and others, homosexual faculty members could not risk public disclosure. Admittedly, most of them found other employment following the scandal, but as a single woman who would have to rely on herself for financial support, Jeannette knew that she could not risk losing a position.[81]

E.G.T.

While the Goodwin scandal was unfolding in late 1918 and early 1919, Jeannette had her mind on another matter: her first serious love, Edna Grace Taylor, had returned to the United States from China on August 13, 1918.[82] During her four years away, Jeannette had recognized her feelings for Grace (as she called her) as sexual, and she had discovered a label for those feelings—homosexual. She also had been a devoted correspondent, sending detailed letters and possibly poems to her friend in China. An excerpt from Jeannette's poem, "Mail" (1918), captures the anticipation she felt upon awakening in the morning when waiting for the postman to deliver one of Grace's letters, and the exhilaration she felt upon its arrival.[83]

> But there—
> There it is, on top.
> I take it coolly—I do not even close my hands about it
> Because once
> Long ago,
> So long that it was someone else's letter I waited for,
> My mother saw me kiss an envelope—
> And commented!
> But I go in
> And sit down
> And tear it—and read—
> And while I read, even,
> (Dizzy a little with joy)
> Already my heart is whispering
> How long it is
> Before I can look
> For another.

Once she learned of Grace's return to the United States, Jeannette could not help but allow herself to hope that their relationship would evolve beyond platonic friendship. The exact details of her reunion with Grace remain a mystery, but on Saturday, December 28, Anna returned to the family's Pleasant Avenue home after doing errands to find Grace there. She had, Anna learned, decided to continue her graduate work in English at the University of Chicago. The two friends had much to talk about, so the following day Jeannette traveled with Grace to her home in Harlan, Iowa, before returning to her position in Kentucky.[84]

In her eagerness to be closer to Grace, Jeannette grew increasingly restless at Science Hill and began contemplating a change in position or a return to school for a graduate degree. Later in life she would attribute her resignation to the realization that "I couldn't stand that age group," but when she returned to her family home for Easter 1919 and announced that she had decided to leave her position at Science Hill, Anna believed it was because of Grace. She would, Jeannette told her family, either study for her master's degree or take a position closer to home paying a better salary than she currently earned. Anna, aware of the depth of Jeannette's attachment to Grace, predicted that she would choose the former option. After a perfunctory overnight visit with the family, Jeannette rose early Easter morning, went to visit Grace (presumably in Iowa), and then returned to Shelbyville to complete the remainder of the school year.[85]

The intensity of Jeannette's feelings, along with her stubborn devotion, proved overwhelming to Grace who, like a number of other women who would enter Jeannette's life in years to come, could not openly enter into a lesbian relationship due to personal inhibitions, emotional barriers, and fear of reprisals from her family. At the end of the spring quarter she left the university without earning her degree and accepted a high school teaching position in her hometown of Harlan, Iowa. After living with her family for several years, Grace moved to Council Bluffs and became a teacher at Abraham Lincoln High School (where she stayed until her retirement in 1954), and in time made her home with a female companion. Jeannette remained in correspondence with Grace throughout the remainder of her life, but respectfully protected her first love's identity by using only the initials E.G.T. when speaking of her to others.[86]

With Grace's departure, Jeannette became less certain that she wanted to pursue graduate work in the fall of 1919. Working with a teacher's agency in Chicago, she instead secured a position teaching science in the Janesville, Wisconsin, high school. Her time at the Science Hill School had been short, but nonetheless beneficial. First, it had given her a glimpse of southern culture, and an introduction to the region that she would grow to love later in life. Second, it had given her an opportunity to try on a new role—that of teacher. While she did not especially enjoy teaching science to high school girls, she did like the authority and respect her position provided. Third, she realized that she did not want to sever her ties to Rockford College because of its comfort, familiarity, and warm female-centered environment. Fourth, her exposure to the Goodwin scandal and the dismissal of several of her beloved Rockford College instructors heightened her awareness of society's negative attitudes about homosexuality and the impact her sexual identity could have on her future. Finally, after two experiences of unrequited love she came to distrust romance. Wanting to protect herself in the future, she resolved (albeit unsuccessfully) to rein in her feelings and "put glamour and romance away."[87] Lacking other confidantes, she once again turned to Dr. Sadler for psychoanalysis in the hopes that it would lead to clarity and understanding. No record of their conversations survives, but Sadler must have been an important outlet for a young woman who felt she could not freely discuss her sexual desires with her convention-bound parents, her devout aunt Carrie, her younger sisters, or the objects of her love.[88]

Life in Janesville

After returning from her annual vacation with the family at their Hamlin Lake cottage, Jeannette prepared for her new position as a public-school teacher in Janesville, Wisconsin. While teaching at the Science Hill School she had begun to have doubts about her future as a high school teacher. Her year in Janesville verified her hunch, though it provided her with a much-needed income while she reconsidered her future. She arrived in Janesville on September 4, 1919, an interesting period in the city's history. General Motors Corporation was just beginning operations in the community, and it was something of a boomtown due to the influx of many new workers. It was a time when most of the streets were unpaved, there was no municipal garbage service, housing stock was old and overcrowded due to the new workers' arrival, outhouses were prevalent even in town, and horse-drawn carriages were still the primary mode of transportation—with many flies drawn to the manure left in the streets. Pure milk was difficult to obtain, and cholera and dysentery were frequent summer visitors.[89]

Like many other single women teachers across the nation, Jeannette found lodging at a nearby boardinghouse and made friends with two women, Della E. Hairgrove, a teacher of English, and Leila F. Venable, who taught domestic science. Both were in their twenties and had studied at the University of Chicago. By the time Anna Foster came to visit in the fall, she found the three attending vaudeville shows, dining in restaurants, and holding parties for one another in their boardinghouse rooms. Because teachers were expected to be of good moral character, Jeannette attended a local Congregational church and took part in the Loani Band of the King's Daughters, a church-affiliated club that ate meals together and acted out plays.[90]

When she reported to work in the fall of 1919, Jeannette found Janesville High School located in a large Romanesque brick building overflowing with nearly six hundred students, over two hundred of them freshmen who needed to take science. Teaching at Janesville was like living in a fishbowl because the local paper reported the smallest details in its "High School Notes," even her absence from school for an illness. In addition to classroom instruction, she joined other faculty in judging oratorical contests and escorting students on field trips. On one level she appeared conventional, but the fact that students poked good-natured fun at Miss Foster suggests that something about her manner or her directness may have led them to suspect that she was gay. Ironically, in one

performance she played an impassioned lover of a female American missionary, a role reminiscent of her relationship with Grace Taylor, and in
the 1921 yearbook student editors included a picture showing Jeannette
with a woman on bended knee before her with the caption "Her thrilling
moment."[91] Evidently Jeannette was comfortable enough to be "outed"
in jest because her appearance as a conventional young professional
woman seemed to belie the fact.

Jeannette made friends with boardinghouse mates Della and Leila, but
she missed the companionship of the intelligent and sociable women she
had known at Rockford College. With Rockford only thirty-five miles
away by the Beloit–Janesville interurban train, it was relatively easy to
visit her younger sister Anna, now in her junior year, and Florence
Bleecker, of whom she had grown quite fond. Since nothing in her experience since graduation could measure up to the happiness and comfort she had known there, she traveled to Rockford frequently for
weekend visits, which often were occasions for table parties held in the
dining hall. Although a day early, the three celebrated Jeannette's birthday on November 2, 1919, with a white cake decorated with twenty-four
candles.[92]

Jeannette's visits to Beverly Hills usually coincided with Anna's, with
both young women returning home for the holidays. Christmas day 1919
was more festive than in previous years because of the family's renewed
prosperity, and the sisters lavished numerous presents on one another.
With their father often traveling on business, the house had become a
very female-centered place with visits from Aunt Carrie, Jeannette, her
sisters, and their many female friends. Anna had ample opportunity during summers at the lake and Jeannette's senior year at Rockford to ob-
serve her older sister's fondness for women. She had thought nothing of
dressing as a male for the mock prom, but after the Goodwin scandal her
awareness of homosexuality had opened Anna's eyes to the stigma associated with her sister's sexual preference.[93] In time, the closeness they
shared during childhood and college years would fade as their interests
took them in different directions.

Restless in her Janesville position, Jeannette turned once again to the comforting homosocial environment of Rockford College. While visiting her sister and other friends there she pondered the future as they went shopping and to silent movies like *Haunted Spooks* and *The Imp*. In nice weather she joined them for overnight canoe trips up the Rock River, and in mid-May she arrived in time to help decorate the gymnasium for the next day's May Party.[94] By that time she had decided to make a change. Since her days as an undergraduate at the University of Chicago, she had harbored a desire to become a writer, and she believed she had to potential to excel in graduate work. Upon learning that she had been accepted as a graduate student in English at the University of Chicago, and that she had won an honor scholarship reserved for graduates of Rockford College, she took the plunge and resigned her teaching position.[95] At long last she would be able to devote herself to subjects that she truly loved—literature and creative writing.

With her plans for the fall in place, Jeannette sent her belongings home to Beverly Hills before spending a month in Oberlin, Ohio, with friends. She arrived at Hamlin Lake in mid-July, having missed her mother's birthday celebration for the second year in a row. Perhaps she was asserting her independence, albeit in a small and subtle way. After more than a month at the lake, filled with fresh air and favorite activities, a reinvigorated Jeannette returned to Chicago on September 2, eager to begin graduate school.[96]

ᘓᘓᘓ *Three* ᘓᘓᘓ

Unrequited Love

WISDOM

I have swallowed bitter truth at last; I know
All that for many a month I would not learn:
What spark I might awake in you would burn
A little moment darkly, and then go
Sullenly out . . . You will not have it so,
And you are wise. But . . . now, you say, you turn
Away from all flame together, nor still yearn
Once and again with bitterness for its glow.
This I believed awhile; but as I see
You fluttering helpless near another flame,
Counting peace empty, wisdom but a name,
Wooing it to consume you utterly—
So am I driven to wonder who is wise,
What heart beside my own has fed on lies.

JEANNETTE HOWARD FOSTER, 1928[1]

In 1960 Margaret Anderson sought Jeannette Foster's advice about publishing the manuscript of her lesbian novel entitled *Forbidden Fires*.[2] The woman who had founded and edited *The Little Review* and who had earned a literary reputation for her memoir, *My Thirty Years' War* (1930), could find no one willing to publish this particular piece of fiction because it did not conform to the 1950s standards for pulps, in which lesbian characters must suffer or pay a price for their love. Mild and a bit old-fashioned, it told the story of a college student named Margaret, who fell in love at first sight with a charming, worldly, older woman named Audrey Leigh. During an enforced separation, the innocent and pure Margaret has a "substitute experience" that, while pleasant, never compared with the depth of her feelings for Audrey. By the time they meet again, Margaret has grown to understand the unique sense of connection they share. Unfortunately, Audrey is unable to respond in a satisfactory way because organized religion and society have damned up her physical and emotional energies. Margaret's love for Audrey thrives on the anguish caused by this obstruction because, she reflects, "being loved isn't what matters most to me; *to love* is what matters."[3]

Anderson's story, inspired by events from an earlier era, resonated with Jeannette because it reminded her of the years she had spent on college campuses in the Midwest and South during the 1920s. "I am," Jeannette explained to the author, "of an age to have been steeped in Romantic Love myself; you capture its essence to perfection, as also the truth that it can survive long only through unfulfillment, whether through separation or imposed 'restriction.'"[4] The period that most mirrored Anderson's story had been spent at Shorter College near the object of her love, professor Clara Louise Thompson. Jeannette's love for Thompson had an ending, but it never came to an end. Even though it never became a full-blown lesbian relationship, it remained the one by which she measured all subsequent relationships and found them wanting.

The University of Chicago

When Jeannette matriculated at the University of Chicago in the autumn quarter of 1920, she took great delight at finally beginning formal study in her "proper" field of interest. Yearning to become a writer, she pragmatically knew that a master's degree in English would prepare her to become a college professor, a career her class-conscious parents held in high esteem. Even though her father was once again working for the Morava Construction Company, her parents remained concerned about the family's financial condition because they would soon have three daughters in college. Everyone rejoiced to learn that Jeannette had received a scholarship reserved for graduates of Rockford College who chose to pursue graduate work at the University of Chicago. Painfully aware of the financial constraints that governed her life, an economically prudent Jeannette chose to board with her parents, and to commute from their Beverly Hills suburb to the university by suburban train and streetcar.[5]

Living at home after several years of relative freedom from parental supervision proved challenging for Jeannette, who possessed a newfound sense of her identity. While she did not flaunt her sexuality, she nonetheless strived to remain true to herself. It was easy enough to slip back into a routine of lunching with friends at Marshall Field's tearoom, visiting her sister Anna at Rockford College, and attending the theater or concerts with her youngest sister Helen. Her mother's awareness of lesbians had not lessened in the intervening years. A devoted reader, she would have seen the increased coverage devoted to homosexuality in popular magazines and fiction. She might have noted lesbian characters or themes in Sherwood Anderson's *Poor White* (1920), James Huneker's *Painted Veils* (1920), or Henry Gribble's play *March Hares* (1921). Later in the decade she may well have seen her former Oak Park neighbor's treatment of lesbianism in *The Sun Also Rises* (1926) and *A Farewell to Arms* (1929).[6] She also must have noted Jeannette's failure to date, especially when contrasted with Anna's growing interest in men, but since she herself had been slow to wed, she could not say too much. Efforts to control Jeannette proved futile as she consciously asserted her independence by maintaining her own schedule, inviting female friends home for weekend visits and going to their homes for overnight visits. When questioned, she could attribute her comings and goings at all hours to the demands of university studies and the necessity of using the library.[7]

Despite her pragmatism in daily life, Jeannette remained idealistic when it came to the life of the mind. In the winter quarter 1920–1921, she earned an uncharacteristic B minus in a course on contemporary literature taken with the novelist Robert Herrick. As part of a new generation of American realists who saw the world through critical eyes, he required the class to read authors who depicted contemporary life and American society as it really was, rather than the romanticized portrayals that it superceded. Steeped in romanticism, Jeannette had a difficult time relating to those grittier and more realistic works. Herrick also lectured to his students about the uproar surrounding the serialized publication of James Joyce's *Ulysses* in *The Little Review* (from March 1918 to December 1920), but they were more interested in another cause célèbre. In 1919 the New York Society for the Suppression of Vice failed in its efforts to suppress James Branch Cabell's fantasy novel, *Jurgen, A Comedy of Justice* (1919). John Gunther, who later would be known for his classic memoir *Death Be Not Proud,* loaned his copy of the book to Jeannette and her friends, who devoured it because of the mild eroticism, time travel, and urbane vocabulary it contained.[8]

As Jeannette quickly discovered, graduate coursework in English language and literature required a substantial commitment of her time. The basic requirements for a master's degree in English included eight seminars of graduate work (at least one of which was in Old or Middle English), a reading knowledge of at least one modern language other than English, and three or four courses in a special field of study which would determine her thesis topic.[9] During the 1920–1921 academic year, she took nine courses that gave her a solid grounding in Chaucer, nineteenth-century English poetry and prose, nineteenth- and twentieth-century American literature, and contemporary literature. Eager to absorb as much knowledge as possible, Jeannette also audited a course in Southern and Western literature and signed up to take physical culture (physical education), a course she had loved as an undergraduate. Always conscious of her weight, she may have wanted a reason to include exercise in her schedule. With the exception of the grades earned from

Herrick in two quarters of Contemporary Literature, she performed well, earning all A's.

While at the University of Chicago, Jeannette had the opportunity to study with a number of distinguished scholars who taught her to be a critical reader and thinker. The brilliant John Matthews Manly chaired the department and strived to build his reputation as a Chaucer scholar. James Weber Linn, a nephew and biographer of Jane Addams, taught nineteenth-century English prose. Jeannette also studied with George Wiley Sherburn, who specialized in Alexander Pope, Chaucer scholar James R. Hulbert, and Carl Henry Grabo, perhaps best known for his work on Percy Bysshe Shelley. Her New England heritage may have influenced Jeannette's decision to take three courses from the renowned scholar Percy Holmes Boynton, a specialist in New England poets and essayists. He made Ralph Waldo Emerson a particular specialty.

Jeannette produced some of her best poetry during these two years at the University of Chicago. That she benefited from formal study and exposure to hundreds of volumes of poetry in the university library is evident in comments by the poet Elsa Gidlow, who considered her poetry written after this time, especially "Sapphics to One Called Helen," to be "carefully crafted" and far superior to Jeannette's earlier poems, which were "sentimental" and "too content with clichés of the period."[10] Her inspiration for this Sapphic poem undoubtedly had several roots. While combing the stacks of the university library, Jeannette may have discovered the published fragments of the lesbian poet Sappho's works, or perhaps she encountered Sapphic stanza, a poetic form spanning four lines, when she read the work of the English poet Algernon Charles Swinburne. Although the first volume of poetry written by the lesbian poet H. D. (Hilda Doolittle) appeared in 1916, it does not appear that Jeannette discovered her work until later in life. Other lesbian poets of the era, for instance Amy Lowell, often turned to Sappho as a source of inspiration.[11] Whatever the source of her literary technique, those close to Jeannette knew that the poem's emotional power derived from her unrequited love for Clara Louise Thompson.

Long ago it must be she knew Athéne,
Wandered Grecian hills, heard the Lesbian singer,
For so gravely straight is she made and lovely,
Walking like music.
Bronze for hair, a coronal proudly lying
Smooth as folded wings across brow and temple,
Ivory her flesh like the cool of peonies
Opened in April.   .
Wind-cleared eyes that suddenly warm to amber
Measured voice, with pulsing of prisoned fire;
All of her an echo from halcyon hillsides
Anciently vanished.

Summer and Fall of 1921

After a full year of academic work and family responsibilities, Jeannette welcomed her annual visit to Hamlin Lake. This summer, however, chaos replaced tranquility when her father decided to undertake a major renovation of the family's cottage. Jeannette's relationship with her parents was mediated by the presence of her sister Anna, who had returned home to live after graduating from Rockford College. Taking a position at the Marshall Field department store, she commuted downtown each day with Jeannette and sometimes on weekends for shows and shopping.[12]

The following fall, Jeannette immersed herself in academic pursuits. Like many graduate students, she gained college teaching experience by serving as the instructor for two sections of freshman composition. Preparation for those classes consumed so much of her time that she took only one course, Early American Literature.[13] The novelty of teaching in her chosen field quickly wore off as she graded dozens of uninspired undergraduate compositions while struggling to keep up in her studies. Yearning to produce her own creative works, she resented the energy and time that grading required.

Intent on pursuing subjects of her own choosing, Jeannette informed the department's all-male faculty that she would write her master's thesis on the literary allusions contained in the work of the famous nineteenth-century transcendentalist, feminist, and journalist Margaret Fuller, best known for her *Woman in the Nineteenth Century* (1845). Jeannette would have been drawn to Fuller for several reasons. In addition to sharing her New England roots, she admired Fuller as a woman ahead of her time, an intellectual who refused to be confined by stereotyped gender roles. Fuller had married at thirty-four, but Jeannette detected a hint of sexual variance (which she defined as being conscious of a passion for one's own sex) prior to that point in her life. At the age of thirteen Fuller had fallen deeply if briefly in love with an Englishwoman, then had become smitten with a sympathetic teacher, and finally had developed strong emotional connections with women who participated in her famous "Conversations." Perhaps Jeannette saw parallels in their love lives: after Fuller's adored departed, she succumbed to melancholy, could not eat, and declined in health. Unable to find companionship her own age, Fuller remained devoted to her love and corresponded with her for years. In the process of doing this research, Jeannette also became increasingly cognizant of the powerful role female-centered environments like Fuller's literary salon could play in nurturing a woman's emotional development and creative energy.[14]

Professor Boynton would have supported Jeannette's choice of Fuller, despite her minor status as an author and essayist, because a study of her life might shed additional light on Emerson. In her thesis, entitled "Literary Allusions in the Works of Margaret Fuller," Jeannette systematically and thoroughly reviewed the influence of classical, Spanish, French, Italian, German, and English literature on Fuller's use of literary allusions. As an undergraduate, she had studied both German and Latin, which she used as a foundation for her reading knowledge of several romance languages. She sought "to discover the extent and nature of her reading, and where possible its occasion and its effect upon her."[15] Bringing her own experiences to bear on her examination of Fuller's life, she

PHOTO 12.
Clara Louise Thompson
(1884–1963), circa 1915.
Active in the suffrage
movement and a professor of
classics at Rockford College
and Shorter College, she
inspired much of the poetry
Jeannette wrote during the
1920s. (Courtesy of the
Library of Congress)

included references to psychoanalysis and emotional intensity. Most striking is Jeannette's emphasis on Fuller's struggle to balance her passionate nature with her Puritan inheritance and "love of self-control which bound her so strongly to the ancient Romans." Perhaps it is no coincidence that in Jeannette's lifetime she fell in love with several women who made the study of ancient Rome their specialty. She did not broach the subject of sexual variance in her thesis, yet the project confirms that by the early 1920s Jeannette had begun seeking out the presence of lesbians in literature—a task that would consume her for three decades to come.[16]

Laboring diligently on her thesis throughout the summer of 1922, Jeannette paused briefly to visit with friends in Rockford and Janesville, and practiced driving the family's Buick. Her long hours of study paid off on July 20, when she passed the final exam for her master's degree, and on September 1, when she earned her MA degree in English and American literature.[17] By the fall of 1922, the pieces of Jeannette's life seemingly had fallen into place. She had proven herself as a scholar, had written some of her finest poetry, and had been exposed to feminist ideas—in part because of her exposure to Clara Louise Thompson and also because of her graduate study of one of the nineteenth century's preeminent feminists. She felt comfortable with her sexual identity, and optimistic about her future as a professor and writer.

Hamline University

In the years following World War I, female college graduates entered the job market with a sense of optimism, and as historian Barbara Solomon writes, believed "that there were no limits to what they could do."[18] Jeannette, along with many others, bobbed her hair, listened to jazz, and felt a newfound sense of freedom. Using a teacher's agency, she secured her first college teaching position at the highly regarded Hamline University in the fall of 1922. Located in St. Paul, Minnesota, the coeducational liberal-arts college had been founded by the Methodist Church in 1854, and seventy years later enrolled approximately six hundred students. Upon her arrival, Jeannette found herself in a minority: only a handful of the faculty—approximately five out of forty-four— were female. In her photo in the *1924 Hamline Liner,* Jeannette appears both sweet (because of the smile about to erupt from her lips) and serious (because of her intent gaze into the camera). Her clothes—especially the Peter Pan collar on her blouse—convey a sense of innocence and youth, and their classic lines suggest that she is a woman with discriminating taste.[19]

Always diligent, Jeannette devoted many hours to preparing lessons for her freshman composition and English literature classes and helping the English Club plan programs for the year. In 1922 and 1923, for instance, they chose an ambitious reading list that included such works as Homer's *Odyssey,* H. G. Wells's *Outline of History,* and Dostoevsky's *The Idiot.*[20] Even though she was an agnostic, Jeannette attended the Hamline Methodist Church because it was expected of faculty to have a church affiliation. Like other single female faculty members, she settled into her quarters in the Manor House, a woman's dormitory completed earlier that year, and played a dual role as instructor and counselor. Residence in a women's dormitory meant that her social life primarily revolved around school functions, undergraduate student activities, and interactions with female faculty members. The contrast with Rockford College was striking. As one of few women on the faculty, she had no status and was cast in a supporting role, teaching only English Composition and the basic survey of English literature. The coeds were polite, but she missed the homosocial warmth of an all-female college. A poem she published in the November 1923 *Hamline Review* spoke of homesickness for "dear old places" and "vivid-coated homing girls" and longing for "the old loved faces" that were "camp-fire flushed" and "eager-eyed with grave talk, or tender after song."[21]

After years of being infatuated with others, Jeannette found herself confronted with a new experience when a thin bespectacled English instructor named Mary Shirley began courting her. She easily recognized the signs—the knowing looks and extra attention—but Shirley lacked the classic feminine beauty that Jeannette preferred. Four years her junior, she wore her red hair drawn back into a bun and was a serious midwestern woman whose aspirations would take her far from her hometown of Orleans, Indiana. Graduating Phi Beta Kappa from Indiana University in 1922 with a BA in psychology and a minor in Latin, she began teaching at Hamline University the following fall while simultaneously pursuing graduate work in psychology, physiology, and physiological chemistry at the University of Minnesota. The two shared several things in common: both were trained in the sciences, were nonnatives of Minnesota, and were lesbians. Others would not have realized it, but Mary could tell that Jeannette was a lesbian, in part because of the confident way she carried herself and the direct and knowing way she looked into her eyes. When Mary began to share stories from her active lesbian history, it became evident to Jeannette that she was "badly disillusioned over a just-past experience." Likewise, Jeannette's emotional attachment to Clara Louise made it difficult for her to consider a romantic relationship with Mary. Instead, the two cultivated a warm friendship, going to movies, attending concerts, and spending many hours talking about mutual interests. After Jeannette left Hamline in 1924, they remained in contact for many years, and eventually came to share several friends.[22]

Mabel Foster found her home much quieter that fall than in previous years with Jeannette in Minnesota and Winslow at the University of Illinois, where he had enrolled in engineering classes. Anna accompanied her father, serving as his housekeeper and filling her extra time by working as private secretary to a faculty member. With the family scattered in different directions, Winslow expected each daughter to write a detailed weekly letter, with carbon copies for their mother, Aunt Carrie, and sisters. In these typed, single-spaced letters that often ran two to three pages in length, Jeannette constructed an image of herself as a confident and hard-working young career woman who seldom took time for pleasure. She matter-of-factly mentioned female friends and activities enjoyed with them, but for the most part emphasized the work that she was doing and books that she had read.[23]

In the early 1920s, Jeannette felt closest to Anna, in part because of their shared experiences at Rockford College. Indeed, when they were roommates, Anna may have observed her sister's fondness for Clara Louise Thompson and Florence Bleecker, but because many women formed close friendships in this homosocial environment, Jeannette's homosexuality may not have been obvious to her. Jeannette appears to have taken a genuine interest in Anna's dates and offered advice about suitors and marriage. In a letter written in early 1924, she expressed hope that Anna would be happily married before she turned twenty-seven, noting without elaborating that it had been "such a messy age" for her.[24]

During two bitterly cold St. Paul winters, Jeannette's respiratory problems—the ones caused by her exposure to bituminous coal smoke during her childhood—surfaced. When a nose and throat specialist advised her to move to a warmer climate she determined that from thenceforth she would "work permanently in the South." After putting out the word to her growing network of friends and colleagues that she sustained through correspondence, she learned from Clara Louise Thompson of a vacancy in the English department at Shorter College. Thompson had secured a position at this Rome, Georgia, women's college after losing her position at Rockford College. Since her graduation from Rockford, Jeannette had remained in regular correspondence with Clara Louise. Perhaps she had hidden the emotional distress she felt as a result of the unrequited love for her beloved instructor, and instead emphasized her academic successes and achievements. It is difficult to assess Clara Louise's motivations for informing Jeannette about the position because no correspondence survives from this time. A strong feminist, Clara Louise recognized the necessity of career women helping one another, and there is no doubt that she felt a genuine fondness for Jeannette and respected her intelligence. Perhaps she believed that Jeannette, now a mature young woman, had moved beyond youthful crushes, but it also is possible that she did not know what kind of relationship she wanted to have with Jeannette.

Thrilled at the prospect of moving to the South, returning to a women's college environment, and being near her beloved teacher, Jeannette successfully applied for the Shorter College position, then tendered her resignation at the end of the 1923–1924 academic year and said farewell to her friend Mary Shirley. Adjourning to Hamlin Lake for her annual summer vacation, Jeannette allowed her hopes to soar as she contemplated the move to Georgia and a renewed hope that this time Clara Louise would return her love.[25]

Shorter College

Jeannette's love for the South took root as she approached Rome and the verdant hills of northwestern Georgia in the autumn of 1924. Located at the center of a triangle formed by the cities of Atlanta, Birmingham, and Chattanooga, Rome had many historic houses and broad streets that conveyed an atmosphere of grace, charm, and tranquility. Formerly home to such noted Cherokee leaders as Major Ridge and Chief John Ross, this Floyd County seat acquired its name because the area's topography was reminiscent of the seven hills of ancient Rome. Noted for mineral wealth, it had become a major hub for transportation because it was there that the confluence of the Oostanaula and Etowah rivers formed the mighty Coosa River. It is quite possible that Jeannette, raised with an appreciation for history, would have visited the town's famed Myrtle Hill cemetery, final resting place for President Woodrow Wilson's first wife, Ellen. From its vantage point, she would have had an unimpeded view of Rome's downtown, as well as of the Etowah Valley to the east and the Appalachian foothills to the south.[26]

If Jeannette had looked toward Shelton Hill, she would have seen Shorter College standing amid a grove of ancient oaks, just two miles from the center of the city. Founded in 1873 by the Baptists as a finishing school for females, Shorter College had evolved into an accredited women's college attracting nearly three hundred students from the southeastern United States. From campus, Jeannette would have enjoyed a panoramic view of wooded ridges, wide valleys, and distant mountains. In the early morning she would have seen mist arising from the Coosa River and she would have inhaled the scent of evergreens, dying leaves, and grasses.[27] What a contrast from the urban settings she had known for most of her twenty-eight years.

In later life Jeannette irreverently referred to Shorter as "a fancy-assed girl's school," but in the 1920s the protective cover it provided offered an ideal environment for a budding lesbian. By 1923, when the school gained membership in the Southern Association of Colleges and Secondary Schools, its mission was "to furnish a thorough well rounded education for young women; to prepare them for greater activity and service in life; to endow them with higher ideals; to build character, body and mind together."[28] During a decade known for sexual experimentation, however, Jeannette's students would have been far less sheltered than her own generation had been. Freudian psychology and the fiction of the era, including works by Ernest Hemingway and Sherwood Anderson, Radclyffe Hall's *The Well of Loneliness* (1928), and a host of less-publicized novelists, increasingly referred to the sexualized nature of love between women. Nonetheless, middle-class college women continued to enjoy many of the same-sex activities and intimacy they had known during the pre–World War I years. At Shorter, for instance, they defied gender stereotypes by holding mock weddings (women played the roles of clergyman, bride, groom, and attendants), mock proms, and a variety of holiday-related dances, all of which provided them with ample opportunities to form lifelong friendships and sometimes lesbian relationships. In this supportive setting, Jeannette searched for emotional and sexual fulfillment.

Jeannette arrived on campus at the beginning of a new era in higher education. Following World War I, men began to displace women in administrative and faculty positions, and students began to press for greater freedom by testing the limits of curfews and other rules intended to preserve order and decorum. During her first year at Shorter, the board of trustees appointed a new president, William D. Furry, and under his leadership the school's enrollment grew steadily, buildings underwent renovation, and the grounds became increasingly more beautiful. At Shorter in the early 1920s, women constituted half of the faculty, but President Furry wanted to enhance the college's reputation by increasing the number of male instructors, especially those possessing doctoral degrees. On several occasions he arranged for the school to loan faculty members money to work on their doctorates if they promised to return after earning the degree. Jeannette took graduate coursework in English at the University of Chicago twice during the six years she spent at Shorter, but there is no evidence that the college helped her finance it or that she officially had enrolled in a doctoral program.[29]

Jeannette loved the life she carved out for herself at Shorter College and did not feel cultural isolation because President Furry worked to establish the college as a cultural center for the community of Rome. Shorter's lyceum series hosted such distinguished visitors as the Russian novelist Count A. N. Tolstoy, American poet Carl Sandburg, Nellie Tayloe Ross (who in 1925 became the first woman governor in the United States when she assumed office in Wyoming), and lecturers from many countries around the world. As an English faculty member, Jeannette worked closely with student editors of the bimonthly *Periscope* and the college literary magazine *Chimes*, and she also advised the Phi Kappa Alpha Study Club (for English majors) and the Omicron chapter of Chi Phi Delta (an honorary literary society). As someone who loved music, she joined faculty and students in the McDowell Choral Society, activities that made her feel a part of the campus community.

Like the other unmarried women or widows who taught at Shorter, Jeannette's residence in a dormitory reinforced her role as an adviser, confidante, and authority figure. Her suite in Van Hoose Hall featured a large living room where she entertained small groups of students on social occasions. Bells regulated her life, beginning with one for rising at 7 a.m. and concluding with one for retiring at 10:30 p.m., although she did not feel compelled to abide by them. Classes and work with students filled her days Tuesday through Saturday and obligatory church attendance consumed a portion of Sunday, leaving Monday free for such activities as taking in a picture show, going to town, or taking a hike.[30]

Clara Louise

A gracious Clara Louise, now forty years old, would have welcomed her former student warmly, showing her around campus, helping her settle into her quarters, and familiarizing her with college requirements and expectations. One can imagine the thrill and delight Jeannette felt at being in her presence once again. The two undoubtedly spoke eagerly as they compared notes about music, books, and plays "with the eagerness of old friends who have not for a long time had the chance to compare impressions."[31] Thompson, a feminine beauty whose image could draw "strangers hypnotically across a room," appreciated Jeannette's sharp wit and enjoyed her intellectual companionship. Living in daily proximity of one another in dormitory suites fostered a sense of intimacy and fueled Jeannette's romantic yearnings. Ever the romantic, she courted Clara Louise with flowers, candy, and lines of verse left outside her door. She expected that they would spend intimate time together as they had at Rockford College and even Hamlin Lake. Clara Louise, however, preferred to hold Jeannette at arm's length, as Jeannette's poem "Aftermath" (1924) suggests.[32]

> I should have known, my friend; indeed—I knew.
> For under velvet of your touch there lay
> Steel; and past the warm and changing gray,
> The sea that made your eyes—slate-cliffs' cold blue.
> The clear deliberate rill of speech flowed, too,
> From hidden snows, and all the lovely sway
> With which you moved, and swept my heart like spray,
> Was chill and distant like the rest of you.
> But still at twilight when your windows lure
> Gold through the dusk, and all your portico
> Sleeps in clear ivory shadow—still, unsure,
> Unwilling, up the rosy walk I go,
> To knock—the old quick signal knock of yore—
> To knock, and wait unanswered at your door.

Emboldened, or perhaps frustrated by Clara Louise's imposed distance, Jeannette published three poems in the December 1924 issues of *Chimes*. The first, her Sapphic poem inspired by Clara Louise, was simply entitled "To One Called Helen." Students familiar with the classics might have made the connection between Helen of Troy and their Greek professor. The second, which bore the title "Lady Elusive," and the third, "Survival," contained physical descriptions of a woman whose hair was like "Ripe wheat in summer sun" and whose eyes were the "blue of twilight when stars wake." As difficult as it is to keep secrets on a small college campus, the object of Jeannette's love may have been tellingly obvious. According to Lillian Faderman, an increasingly sophisticated generation of college women grew wary of same-sex attraction because of its association with sexual pathology.[33] Given the climate of the times, when only the boldest women risked betraying their lesbianism, Clara Louise may have been disturbed and perhaps angered by her former student's indiscreet behavior.

As sociologist Katharine Bement Davis discovered in her nationwide study, *The Factors in the Sex Life of Twenty-two Hundred Women* (1929), more than half (50.4 percent) had experienced "intense emotional relations with other women," and about half considered those experiences as "sexual in character." Jeannette and Clara Louise clearly had developed an intense emotional bond during their time together at Rockford. Clara Louise, however, suffered from internalized homophobia. According to Jeannette, she "boasted of many overt affairs with girls and women of all ages," but "would not allow the words 'homosexual' or 'lesbian' to be uttered in her presence."[34] Like the women in Davis's study who engaged in homosexual behavior, Thompson did not wish to identify herself as a lesbian, perhaps because she was well-read enough to know that popular images of lesbians—the man trapped in a woman's body, the pervert, or the Greenwich Village bohemian—did not apply to her. The flirtations she had had with undergraduate women were casual and easily terminated if they threatened to become too involved. As a single woman who had carved out a career for herself in academia, one who strived for professional advancement, she believed it necessary to hold Jeannette at a distance even if she felt drawn to her.

Steeped in romantic imagery from an earlier generation, Jeannette was irresistibly and at times perilously captivated by Clara Louise. Despite good intentions, she found herself repeatedly yielding to her emotions because whenever she was in her beloved's presence she felt alive and energized. It was so "sweet and easy," she wrote in "A Lovely Lapse" (1924), "To rise and follow after/A cool lifted shoulder/And gray-eyed laughter!" During many long and lonely nights, however, she realized the folly of her dreams and captured her despair in such aptly titled poems as "Desolate" (1924).[35] After giving her feelings free reign, Jeannette now found herself in a vulnerable position.

Might only the pale stillness possess my eyelids,
the fluid air cool an aching throat,
the little stars touch my heart
with their ancient quiet . . .
But outside a night hawk
swoops and shrills, swoops and shrills,
craving, questing, beating at the calm of the small hours
with a shattering cry—
to him my heart makes answer.

In later life Jeannette spoke freely about every decade of her life except for the years she spent at Shorter College. One might speculate that
there was nothing of significance to record, or that the time there was so
sacred that she could not bear discussing it with others. Letters from or
about this period may not have survived, but short fiction, especially a
novella entitled "Temple of Athéne," sheds some light on these years.[36]
In this story, which was not published until it appeared in serialized form
in *The Ladder* (one of the first lesbian publications in the United States)
in late 1967 and early 1968, an assistant professor of anthropology,
Theodora Hart (named for Jeannette's aesthetic dance instructor at the
University of Chicago) falls in love with Radnor College president
Lenox Van Tuyl. All too quickly, Theodora discovers that Van Tuyl's earlier romantic relationship with a female artist still consumed her, and she
is offered an ultimatum: either take a leave of absence from her position
at the college or contain her feelings and live as if no attraction existed
between them. In such a public environment, it was too risky to do otherwise, especially in an increasingly homophobic world. In the novella,
as in the 1920s, college discipline committees expelled students and dismissed teachers who succumbed to same-sex attractions.

According to Jeannette, she was a "latecomer" when it came to sexual
experience. Twenty-eight when she arrived on the Shorter campus, her
cumulative lesbian sexual experience consisted of kisses, cuddling, and
caresses, and she was eager to experience "completeness." As the charac-

ter Theodora, in "Temple of Athéne," explained to the object of her love, "[a]bstention is very well for you, you had fulfillment before you chose it. But not for me who have never known fulfillment wholly."[37] In the poem "Anniversary" (1925), Jeannette describes a woman—perhaps herself—waiting "in silk and fragrant hair," glowing in anticipation of the time she would experience intimacy with her beloved. Rejected, she found herself walking "through the empty chambers of my heart—Door broken and ajar."[38]

Clara Louise valued Jeannette as a friend and colleague and had an emotional bond to her, but she used silence, coolness, and distance to keep her at arm's length. Perhaps she enjoyed the opportunity to play a cat-and-mouse game with the younger woman, or it may be that she did not find her physically attractive. When pressed to explain why, Thompson informed Jeannette that she "didn't know what she wanted and there were plenty of these college kids who did." Clara Louise may also have enjoyed the power dynamic and her ability to manipulate a jealous Jeannette, who, in "The Final Mutiny" (1926), captures powerful feelings provoked by knowing that her love "will lie with another" and bestow caresses upon her "in the May Darkness."[39]

> Drifting along the edges of sleep
> you will know the touch of small soft limbs;
> bronze hair will lie like silk
> across your face,
> and your lips press warm
> frail eyelids . . .
> All this I can endure.
> But your hands—
> your hands!
> . . . how can I yield her your hands?

Spending the decade on an emotional roller coaster, Jeannette alternated between refusing to give up hope and resigning herself to the fact that

Clara Louise could not be compelled to love her. Her alternatives seemed limited: either she could seek another position or she could mask her feelings in order to remain in Clara Louise's presence. If the poem "Bluff" (1925) is any indication, Jeannette became very skilled at camouflaging her feelings, but ultimately this practice proved tiring and frustrating.[40]

> And now the shining mask I wear
> Is so much mine that you can say—
> Even with your keen eyes—
> "How well
> You look today!"

Weary from a year of crushed hopes and the reality of "proud lips that will not love at all," Jeannette yearned for the respite and peace that summer would bring when "I can no more from morn to noon/Listen for her swift step, nor longer hear/Her lilting voice, nor feel her distance near."[41] If she found peace that summer, it was only temporary.

Rewarded with a promotion to associate professor, Jeannette returned to Shorter College in the fall of 1925 for a second year. Seemingly resigned to the fact that Clara Louise would not return her love, she immersed herself in work. Even though she knew that it was futile to pursue Thompson, it proved difficult for such a romantically inclined person to relinquish all hope. One day, while teaching poetry to a composition class, she penned a sonnet "To be put up with others from the class," but refrained because her references to Clara Louise were so obvious that the others would have known the source of her inspiration. In a poem entitled "Foreword" (1925), she explained:

> Now, if My Love were but more pale, more—tame,
> Such could be published wide and make no matter,
> But in this milieu there is but one name
> To match my song, and they're all looking at her.[42]

Lenore

Eventually, Jeannette found herself warming to the admiring glances and overtures of an English major named Lenore Ward as they interacted in class, school clubs, and when working on school publications.[43] Eleven years her junior, the thin brunette stood in marked contrast to Clara Louise Thompson's elegant femininity. Dark and plainer, the athletic, bookish, literary, and witty Lenore wore an intense look under her bobbed hair. The daughter of the sheriff of Crisp County, Georgia, she dreamed of traveling the world. She also loved cats because "they are able to be what I would like to be myself . . . selfish." A bright young woman with a sarcastic wit, she must have admired her professor's seemingly endless knowledge of literature, her confidence and energy. Jeannette, in turn, would have found her quiet admiration a welcome respite from Clara Louise's self-imposed distance. As the poem "Dear Hands" (1925) suggests, Lenore offered Jeannette understanding, compassion, and love.[44]

> *Other hands I loved once*
> *Proudly tense and white.*
> *But those hungry fingers*
> *Would tear my heart tonight.*
> *On all its empty aching*
> *Falls your still touch.*
> *You who, understanding, never*
> *Ask too much.*

That Foster later renamed this poem "Healing" is significant, because the love she experienced with Lenore represents a first step in healing the pain of the unrequited love she had for so long harbored for Clara Louise. Jeannette and Lenore had a number of opportunities to grow closer during Lenore's junior and senior years. As editor of the school's literary magazine, Lenore naturally would have consulted her English professor and adviser about its contents. Ironically, Lenore also was an active member of Thompson's Classical Club, and in the spring of 1926 was chosen to serve as vice president for the coming year. What did Clara Louise think when she witnessed one of her pet students gazing admiringly at the lover she herself had spurned?

During her second and third years at Shorter, Jeannette became more involved in student clubs, especially those emphasizing the arts. In addition to carrying on her regular load of teaching and study, punctuated by walks in the woods and countryside for exercise, she joined with students in campus social activities. In March 1926 she gave an illustrated lecture about works of art dealing with music and musical instruments. In November 1926, the campus was all abuzz as faculty and students prepared for a visit from the poet Carl Sandburg. Jeannette, who claimed to know him personally, spoke to the Phi Kappa Alpha Study Club about his life, read several of his poems from "Smoke and Steel," and played two of his records on the Victrola. When Sandburg arrived on campus the following February, however, English professor Paul Cousins usurped Jeannette's claim to familiarity with the poet and escorted him around campus. Undeterred, she next spoke to the club in March, taking as her topic the Irish literary renaissance. The culmination of her social life at Shorter may have been the dinner party she hosted for the Chi Delta Phi literary society on May 2, 1927. As befitting a book lover, Foster presented each guest with a copy of the *New York Times Book Review* and held a contest in which participants had to identify authors mentioned in the *Review*. In keeping with her love of reading, Jeannette chose a book (whose title is unknown) as the prize given to the student who recognized the most authors.[45]

Summer in Europe

In 1926, Shorter College French professor J. N. Ware had led a small group of Shorter College faculty, students, and alumni on a two-month tour of Europe. When he announced plans to conduct a similar trip in the summer of 1927, Jeannette and Lenore decided to take part. Traveling with a student, especially a recent graduate, would not have raised eyebrows in 1927. Indeed, other Shorter faculty, including Clara Louise Thompson, had set a precedent for traveling with former students.[46] On the Shorter campus, as at Rockford College, female faculty not only taught but also lived and socialized with their students. In the days before awareness of sexual harassment became a concern, they cultivated warm, and sometimes intimate, relationships with one another. Jeannette, who was relatively close in age to the young women she taught, would have enjoyed canoeing, hiking, and other outings with them. Even though knowledge of female sexuality had increased during the decade, the protective cover of women's college campuses meant that a professor and student of the same sex could travel together without raising eyebrows.

Jeannette's parents, on the other hand, had grown in their awareness of her homosexuality during the 1920s and sensed that her relationship with Lenore might be something deeper than platonic friendship. Now in her early thirties, Jeannette had never dated men. As early as 1914, Winslow and Mabel had suspected that a crush on Edna Taylor had precipitated their daughter's emotional breakdown, and in subsequent years they had witnessed her deepening fondness for Clara Louise Thompson. Jeannette's father, who had read her love poetry, questioned how she could express such emotions without first having experienced them. Despite their tacit realization, Jeannette and her parents never openly discussed the subject of her sexual orientation. Her mother found references to any kind of sexuality, not just lesbianism, disconcerting, but as time passed, Jeannette began writing home about her female friends and roommates.

Shortly after Lenore graduated with honors on June 7, 1927, she and Jeannette traveled by train to New York City, where they boarded a Holland America Line steamer, the *Veendam*, for England. The trip's itinerary included travel in a tourist-class cabin to Plymouth, England. From there they boarded a train to London, where they spent two weeks taking excursions to Warwick Castle, Canterbury, Oxford, and Shakespeare country. In Holland for three days, they visited the Hague, Amsterdam, Edam, and Marken before journeying on to Germany. There they spent five days taking in the Cologne Cathedral, cruising up the Rhine River on a day trip, and visiting Mainz, old Heidelberg, and Brünen. During their week in Switzerland, Jeannette and Lenore traveled William Tell country, admiring the lions and glacial gardens of Lucerne before traveling over the Brunig Pass to the spectacular views of Interlaken and an ascension up the Jungfrau. Three weeks in Italy flew by as the group toured Baveno on Lake Maggiore, Milan, Venice, Florence, the nearby Leaning Tower of Pisa, Naples, and Pompeii. They saw spectacular views along the Amalfi coast, and stopped in Sorrento, Capri, and the Blue Grotto before visiting Rome, where they saw Da Vinci's *Last Supper* and many cathedrals. Their travels concluded in France, where they stopped in Nice, and saw the French Riviera and the Papal Palace at Avignon. The organized portion of their tour concluded after two weeks in Paris, with opportunities to take day trips to Versailles, Fontainebleau, Reims, and the site of World War I battlefields.[47]

Jeannette would have viewed Paris through a romantic lens, in part because of its expatriate community of women and writers living on the Left Bank. Imagine her enchantment as she and Lenore lunched at sidewalk cafes and strolled through busy outdoor markets and past intriguing bookstalls along the Seine. No letters or diary entries survive to document their time in Paris, the people they met, or the place they visited. A number of expatriate writers, among them Natalie Clifford Barney, Gertrude Stein, and Alice B. Toklas, lived in the city but Jeannette would have regarded them as being in a class apart from, and superior, to her own. Perhaps Jeannette and Lenore visited the famed Shakespeare and Company bookstore, operated by Sylvia Beach and Adrienne Monnier, and delighted at the sense of freedom they felt while walking the streets of a city where lesbians could be more open about their sexuality. After two wonderful months together, it was time to return home.[48]

Jeannette returned to Rome for her fourth year of teaching at Shorter College, while Lenore moved some seventy miles away to Atlanta, where she enrolled in a business course. In her memories of this period, Jeannette was explicit in indicating that Lenore was the woman with whom she first experienced sexual intimacy; however, she was vague about when this occurred. As significant as the occasion was for her, she maintained a discreet silence about the specifics of the occasion. Nonetheless, her poem "Morning After" (written sometime between 1925 and 1930) appears to capture the euphoria she felt upon experiencing the "completeness" for which she had yearned.[49]

> *For already love had torn me,*
> *Left a heart stripped, quivering,*
> *Bare of its last defenses.*
> *And then*
> *Came song . . . Beautiful, terrible beautiful*
> *Unspeakable . . .*
> *Where are words to tell of*
> *A sudden divine ravisher?*

The love she felt for Lenore differed significantly from the tempestuousness of her relationship with Clara Louise. Lenore, she explained, had given her strength, joy, rest, and peace. Nineteen of Jeannette's poems survive from the period between 1924 and 1926, with more than half of them written in 1925, when she was in agony because of her unrequited love for Clara Louise. Only a handful remain from the years 1927 to 1929. Contented, and feeling more serene than she had in years, Jeannette experienced fewer of the emotions that had driven her to verse, a fact she explains in the poem "Sonnet out of Serenity" (1928).[50]

> *True, you have had no verse of me, my dear;*
> *And since my verses are of love, so you,*
> *Lacking them, seem unloved. It is not true.*

You have freed me from old pain and fear—
Verse being wrung from me in hard distress

Author

In her newfound state of tranquility, Jeannette turned to writing fiction, and was rewarded in the fall of 1927 when a story entitled "Lucky Star" appeared in *Harper's Magazine*. As she had done in stories written during her undergraduate years at Rockford College, Jeannette wrote about heterosexual relationships, but based them on her experiences with women. Set in a southern community much like Rome, filled with "ancient mansions and wide, deep-shaded streets," "Lucky Star" tells the story of a gracious, intelligent, and privileged woman named Nancy Wayne Graham who is "caught in a constricted if exquisite cage"—an unsatisfactory marriage to a prosperous man. A visiting novelist named Hamilton North becomes smitten with Graham, argues that she is not really living life fully, and invites her to spend a season with him in New York City. Even though she loves him, Nancy chooses to remain in the comfort of her secluded community, informing the novelist that he doesn't understand them "at all."[51] Nancy could well represent Clara Louise Thompson, willing to sacrifice the fullness of life for the comfort of a cage.

When Jeannette left Rome for the summer of 1928, she did not know if Clara Louise would be there when she returned the following fall. After nine years on this rural Southern college campus, Thompson yearned to be at a larger university where she would have greater access to books and could interact with other scholars who shared her interests. When filing her application with the University of Pennsylvania placement service, she explained that Shorter had been good to her, but her desire to leave stemmed from the difficulty she experienced in building up a department with so few students interested in the classical languages. By 1928 it would have been difficult to place Thompson, then forty-four and earning $3,000 per year, despite her excellent credentials. As the historian Lynn Gordon has found, higher education began to restrict women's entry and advancement despite the more socially liberal atmosphere of the 1920s. When the economic hard times of the 1930s hit, Thompson's mobility decreased even further, and she remained on the faculty of Shorter College until her retirement in 1953.[52]

Eager for advancement and self-improvement, Jeannette returned to the University of Chicago in the summer of 1928 for additional graduate coursework in English. As a teacher of college writing classes, she also thought it wise to audit Advanced English Composition. If she had paid attention to trends on college campuses in the late 1920s, she would have realized that it would have been more advantageous to enroll in a doctoral program than to take postgraduate courses. She also would have seen that male faculty earned more than women whether they taught in the sciences or the humanities. While Jeannette studied at Chicago, her colleague Paul Cousins used the $1,500 advance given him by Shorter College to fund his doctoral study in English at Columbia University. When he returned the following fall without having completed his degree, the college nonetheless advanced his salary to $3,000 while hers lagged behind at $2,250. Confident in her intellectual abilities, she resented being treated as an "inferior" to Cousins.[53]

Meanwhile, Jeannette's father, who previously had speculated on land in Oregon, impressed upon her the desirability of acquiring property. With $400 in hand, she went to the Floyd County courthouse on October 20, 1928, and purchased a wooded lot a short distance from the campus on Oakland Avenue. She may have coordinated this purchase with Clara Louise, who just three days later acquired an adjacent lot twice the size of Jeannette's.[54] It appeared that they would one day grow old side-by-side, if not together. By the following spring, however, the idea of building a permanent home in Rome had lost some of its appeal. Perhaps her growing fondness for Lenore had loosened some of the bonds that tied her to Clara Louise and Shorter College. On May 31, 1929, Jeannette sold the plot to Clara Louise before departing for the summer.[55]

Jeannette returned to Shorter College in the fall of 1929 with a determination that it would be her last year there. Her relationship with

Lenore, her graduate study at the University of Chicago, and her travel to Europe made her experiences at Shorter pale by comparison. She had tired of grading freshman compositions and felt undervalued by the college administration. Additionally, the pre–World War I climate on women's college campuses had yielded to a modern age, one characterized by frivolity and heterosexuality. Working with a teachers' agency, she began the job search process with renewed zeal, but at the same time contemplated the possibility of returning to school for a doctorate in English or a degree in librarianship.

Visits with Lenore, now working for a government agency in Atlanta, brightened her days, as did warm friendships she cultivated with several other Shorter College English major students who shared her interests and possibly her sexual orientation. One, a Chicago native named Lenore Harvey, transferred to Shorter from Baylor University in the fall of 1929 as a junior. Known for her extensive vocabulary, she enjoyed writing for school publications and was intellectually compatible with Jeannette. Another, Lillian Lee, became editor of *The Periscope*. These friendships, forged during her final years at Shorter, remained intact and spanned five decades, ending only in death.[56]

The crash of the stock market in October 1929 played a critical role in shaping Jeannette's immediate plans. When her father lost his position at Porkins, Follows, and Hamilton that year she, as the oldest daughter, felt an obligation to help her family financially. Pursuing another degree, whether it be a doctorate in English or a degree in librarianship, did not appear viable. When unexpected surgery for a uterine fibroid on May 7, 1930, depleted her savings, her fate seemed sealed— she needed to continue teaching.[57] Given the circumstances, it would have been pragmatic to remain at Shorter, yet a newly appointed chair of the English department so clearly favored her colleague Paul Cousins that she knew her chances of advancement were nil. Restless and frustrated, she put out the word to her network of friends and worked with teacher placement agencies until she located a new position as an assistant professor at Hollins College, located in Roanoke, Virginia. The position was a demotion in rank, but it enabled her to remain in the South and on a women's college campus.

As her time at Shorter College came to an end, Jeannette reflected on the six pivotal years she had spent there. Arriving as an emotionally immature twenty-eight-year-old, she had grown stronger and her understanding of relationships and their complexity had deepened. She still felt drawn to Clara Louise Thompson, but now recognized the futility of the relationship and had taken steps to transform it into a warm and collegial friendship. In time, Jeannette reasoned, she would learn to think of Clara Louise's beauty as she did the beauty of northwest Georgia's hills and sky—something she could always claim, at least in her memories. She preserved these sentiments in the poem "Song" (1929).[58]

> *Those remembered cannot be lost hereafter,*
> *Nor can flame be darkened within my shrine;*
> *Your lilting step, your throbbing voice and laughter,*
> *Delicious jesting, tenderness divine—*
> *Let who will claim you—these are forever mine.*

Shorter College provided Jeannette with the protective cover she needed to pursue the object of her love and to continue constructing her identity as a lesbian and a feminist. As her relationship with Lenore Ward reveals, she matured emotionally during the 1920s, moving beyond the romantic dreams of her youth and the unrequited love for Clara Louise to an emotionally healthy, reciprocal relationship. As she would discover, however, no subsequent loves could compare to the power of unfulfilled romantic love, and for the remainder of her life, Jeannette could not help but hold all other loves to this standard. Yet Ward and other friends made during the 1920s formed the foundation of a vital lesbian network that would provide support to Jeannette for the remainder of her life. Much like Natalie Clifford Barney, she put enormous effort into maintaining friendships, turning nearly every ex-lover (or would-be lover) into a lifelong friend.[59]

˙ Intellectually, Jeannette indulged her passion for writing poetry and short fiction during the 1920s. While one story did appear in *Harper's* in 1927, affirming her talent, she knew full well that writing was not a viable option for a self-supporting career woman. While she would continue to write verse in the years to come, the 1920s clearly constituted her most prolific outpouring, stemming as it did from the unrequited love for Clara Louise Thompson. Since there was virtually no market for lesbian poetry, it would remain unpublished for another three decades. An emotional and passionate dreamer, she remained realistic when it came to her career and by the late 1930s had begun to recognize the limitations of her gender and her MA degree in English.

Four

Libraries and Loves During the Great Depression

THE WAVE
Beloved, the whole night sky
looks down with your gray eyes;
night wind lays upon me
your cool thrilling fingers;
all waking April calls in your poignant voice.
And I wait—
ah Beloved, in the face of all wisdom
I wait. . .

JEANNETTE HOWARD FOSTER, 1932[1]

As the nation's worst economic depression settled over the country-side in 1930, Jeannette Foster joined the faculty of the all-female Hollins College, located in Roanoke, Virginia. Hired to teach English by seventy-four-year-old Matty Cocke, president of the college since 1901, Jeannette arrived at a time when campuses everywhere contended with declining enrollments and revenues. Hollins was no exception, with enrollment sinking from 352 students for academic year 1930–1931 to 239 two years later.[2] Still, Jeannette's one year at Hollins provided her with financial solvency as she reevaluated her personal and professional goals. Unable to envision a future as a cash-poor professional woman teaching composition to lackluster undergraduates year after year, she contemplated the possibility of returning to school for a doctorate in English, but the window of opportunity for women in higher education had begun to close and she doubted there would be many opportunities to advance in that field during the coming years. She also lacked the financial resources to remain out of the workforce for the several years that doctoral study would require.

Reviewing her options, Jeannette considered the more pragmatic possibility of a career in the female-intensive profession of librarianship. Her interest in that field had grown gradually since holding a service scholarship in the University of Chicago library in the early 1920s. She loved books and was a consummate user of academic and public libraries. In later life, she also attributed this decision to her experience as a summer substitute at the New York Public Library, but no record of that employment survives. To all appearances, a career in librarianship seemed more conducive to her temperament and talent and had, as she observed, "all the attraction of teaching without the onus of grading papers."[3] It was a wise choice. As a librarian and library educator, she would acquire the tools, make the connections, and build a professional reputation that one day would enable her to research and boldly publish, under her own name, a monograph exploring literary examples of sex variant women. In 1931, however, she simply wanted to find a more suitable and satisfying occupation.

Emory University Library School

Wasting no time in planning her future, Jeannette did research to determine where she could earn a degree in librarianship and in January 1931 sent a letter to the Emory University Library School, in Atlanta, requesting information about its requirements, cost of the degree, and opportunities for part-time work. Informing the school's dean Clara E.

Howard that she liked Georgia "better than any other part of the country I have ever known," she spoke of settling permanently in that state upon completion of the degree. Graduation from a Southern school, Jeannette anticipated, would increase her chances of finding a permanent position in that region, so appealing because Lenore and several other former Shorter College favorites had settled there. Emory also offered another advantage: students could complete the BLS (Bachelor of Library Science) degree in only one year.[4]

The Emory University Library School had begun as the Southern Library School in 1905 with a gift from industrialist Andrew Carnegie. A subvention from the Carnegie Corporation (known for library philanthropy) and the Julius Rosenwald Fund led to the school's affiliation with Emory University in 1925. The move from public library to university campus brought significant change to the school, including raised entrance requirements. Limiting enrollment in each year's class to fifty, the school required students to be at least twenty and discouraged individuals over thirty-five from making application unless they had prior experience in libraries or comparable intellectual activity. Emory was not alone in imposing age limits. Library-school directors throughout the nation served as gatekeepers to the profession and knew from experience that it was easier to mold younger students who were less set in their ways into library professionals and to place them in positions, especially if the candidates were female.[5]

When considering the possibility of becoming a librarian, Jeannette had to confront the realities of her situation: she could not expect financial assistance from her parents because of their Depression-related losses, and her savings had been depleted the previous summer by the cost of surgery and the inability to work during her recuperation. Her concerns prompted Jeannette to inquire about such pragmatic matters as the cost of tuition, the possibility of loans and part-time work to offset the cost of schooling, and placement rates. While it was reassuring to know that only six of thirty-eight graduates from the previous year's class lacked library positions, it was disappointing to learn that Emory graduates could expect to earn an average salary of $1,500 per annum, less than half of what Jeannette had earned at Shorter College. Dean Howard also quashed Jeannette's plan to work part-time, informing her that most library schools expected students to devote themselves full time to their studies. "The work given here is intensive," she explained, "and we do not allow any of our students to engage in part time work.[6]

Undeterred upon learning about salaries and placement rates, Jeannette submitted her application and applied for a loan. She hoped that her many assets would offset her age—she would turn thirty-six in the fall of 1931. In an application submitted in mid-February, she portrayed herself as a well-educated and cultured middle-class woman who had studied enough German and French to "get along easily in traveling abroad." Her recent reading included books by H. G. Wells, Bertrand Russell, Joseph Priestly, Joseph Krutch, John Galsworthy, and Rebecca West, as well as such periodicals as *Literary Digest, New Republic, New York Times Book Review, New Yorker,* and *International Studies.* In her role as a professor of English she had managed college magazines, written and staged amateur theatricals and pageants, sung in choruses, and participated in the American Association of University Women. Letters of reference arrived from several Shorter College colleagues, including her "intimate friend" Clara Louise Thompson, who commended Jeannette's "intelligence, appearance, interest in people & books, and social gifts," concluding that she was "eminently suited" for library work. Mathematics Professor Ruby Hightower noted that "few of my acquaintances equal her" fondness for books, and former English department colleague Paul Cousins pronounced her "exceptional," because of her "keenness of mind, training, experience, natural fondness for books, and general ability."[7]

Confident that she would be admitted, Jeannette next fired off a series of letters to library school officials about options for room and board. Her limited resources weighed heavily on her mind, and by her calculations, she could only risk attending Emory if she limited her living expenses to $45 per month. Indicating that she had a friend doing graduate work at Emory in another department, she inquired if there would be an opportunity to room with her in a university dormitory. This woman's identity is unknown, but she may have been one of Jeannette's former students from Shorter College. Upon learning that the university had limited dormitory housing for graduate students, Jeannette quickly realized that it would be best to seek lodging in one of the area's many rooming houses. More than half of the students in the current class, she learned, lived in such homes and took midday meals either in local tearooms or in the university cafeteria.[8]

Jeannette received notification of her acceptance in late May, shortly after an unexpected tonsillectomy. After nine years of teaching English and composition to undergraduates, she welcomed the prospect of working among books and with people who appreciated culture. She did not yet fully appreciate the extent to which librarianship would prove to be a gay-friendly profession, one in which she would thrive. Tendering her resignation at Hollins College, she visited Clara Louise, Lenore, and a few other friends in Georgia, and while in Atlanta made arrangements to lodge in a boardinghouse on Clifton Road, in the historic Druid Hills suburb. Planned by the eminent landscape architect Frederick Law Olmstead, who designed New York City's Central Park, and his successors, the Olmsted Brothers, Druid Hills was home to many important political, financial, commercial, professional, and cultural figures in early-twentieth-century Atlanta history. Well-suited to a woman of her social class and taste, it was only two miles from Lenore's residence on Amsterdam Avenue and conveniently located a few blocks from the Emory University campus.[9]

When Jeannette reported to the library school's quarters on the upper floor of the university library (named for Coca-Cola Company founder Asa Griggs Candler) in late 1931, she immediately noted that her class of forty-five contained only six men. Since the inception of professional education for librarians at Columbia University in 1887, library schools had attracted a far larger number of female than male students. Men who wished to have careers as librarians often did not need the professional degree because they could rise to executive positions by virtue of their previous experience. The profession's low salaries and lack of prestige compounded the difficulty library schools faced when trying to recruit men. Prospective candidates also were put off by the stereotype of male librarians as introverts or men who had failed in other lines of work. Five of the six men in the Emory class of 1931 to 1932 had enrolled because of a Julius Rosenwald scholarship fund that encouraged men to enter the southern library field.[10] Several men and women in Jeannette's class would go on to have distinguished careers, including William C. Haygood (program administrator for the Rosenwald Fund and U.S. Information Librarian in Madrid), hospital librarian Albert M. Johnson, and Sarah Lewis Jones (later head of the Textbook and Library Division of the Georgia Board of Education and longtime partner of Lucille Nix). Diligent and intelligent, Jeannette performed well, prompting Library School dean Clara Howard to pronounce her "undoubtedly the most intellectual member of the class, combining a fine mind with a splendid background."[11]

As one of the older students in the program and as someone with college teaching experience, Jeannette found that she had more in common with the all-female library school faculty than with her classmates. Once again, she found herself falling in love, this time with her book selection professor Miriam Tompkins. Just three years her senior, the Montana native had earned a bachelors degree (1916) and master's degree (1917) from the University of Wisconsin. A highly capable woman, she had served on the faculty of the Wisconsin State Teachers College and the Milwaukee Public Library's Training Class for Library Workers before becoming chief of that library's newly established division of adult education in 1923. Six years later a Carnegie fellowship enabled her to study at the University of Chicago's Graduate Library School, but she left after only one year to become an associate professor at the Emory University library school.[12]

As Miriam and Jeannette began discussing their shared love of literature, art, and music, Jeannette felt her senses awaken. Like Clara Louise, Miriam had the combination of intelligence, physical beauty, and refinement that she found so compelling. Committing her feelings to poetry, she wrote in "The Wave" (1932) of "learning to leave unstirred the imperious need of you" as she struggled to quiet the "hot sudden clamors of the flesh." She attempted to shut out the "Beauty of great music" and kept "lovely words shut between their pages" for fear that they would trigger uncontrollable emotional responses.[13] In an unprecedented move, Jeannette included Miriam's name as the last line of "Sketch for a Portrait," which contained lines comparing her black hair to the mane of a stallion and describing her "Olive face all firm curves, sound as ripe fruit; lips burning crimson with life, eager, masterful, melting-tender." If the final lines are any indication, Miriam resembled Clara Louise in demeanor, if not appearance: "passion schooled with power, tenderness more strong than sweet."[14] Whether the two women had a sexual relationship or it was a one-sided passion on Jeannette's part is unknown, but the quality of the poetry written that year is similar to her anguished output from the mid-1920s. The five that survive from this year preserve sensuous impressions of stolen moments with a beloved under "dark starred nights" infused with "the perfume of new life." In "Leap Year Night" (1932), for instance, she conveyed a fierce optimism.[15]

> Beloved—
> Come, let us live high and gallant days together;
> For life has not downed us until we say so
> (And it will never down you!)
> Side by side to work fiercely till we fall
> And in an hour be up again . . .
> But coming back is quicker with an arm
> Over shoulders,
> And lips near whispering
> Courage.

Jeannette had much in common with Miriam, ranging from their shared Midwestern background to their familiarity with the University of Chicago campus, and soon she came to share her professor's passion for the emergent field of adult education. In the 1930s and 1940s, Miriam's teaching in this field would become one of the greatest single influences in the creation of a "cadre of adult services specialists" in America's public libraries.[16] Founded in 1876, the American Library Association had long been known for emphasizing the positive power of good literature, but in the 1920s librarians and educators made a systematic effort to promote adult education. In 1924, the year the National Education Association established a Department of Adult Education, the American Library Association established a Commission on the Library and Adult Education. Readers' advisory work, an outgrowth of this mission, grew popular in the 1920s and 1930s as public libraries transitioned from being book-centered to reader-centered institutions. In theory, specially prepared librarians, known as readers' advisers, would guide independent adult learners in developing informal reading programs by creating bibliographies for patrons and counseling them on the selection of reading matter.

Jeannette may not have realized it at the time, but studying under Tompkins gave her important knowledge that would enable her to ferret out works of literature containing references to lesbians. Later that decade, when Jeannette began the systematic research that would culminate in *Sex Variant Women in Literature*, she recalled Tompkins's lectures on trade bibliographies and how to search *Publishers' Weekly* and a host of other selection aids for books on specific themes. Tompkins also gave her students extensive practice in creating annotated bibliographies, another useful skill, especially since Jeannette initially envisioned disseminating her research on lesbian literature in that format. Miriam also introduced Jeannette to the work of Dr. Douglas Waples, a professor in the Graduate Library School at the University of Chicago, whose research focused on reading interests, encouraged her to become professionally active, and appointed her to the American Library Association's Readable Books Sub-Committee, which she chaired.

Jeannette flourished in Tompkins's courses but had little patience for some other aspects of the library-science curriculum. As someone with high self-esteem who was accustomed to the rigors of studying chemistry, physics, and graduate courses in English, Jeannette found it dull and tedious to study the technical and mechanical preparation of books for use in libraries. Miriam, aware of the difficulty older students faced when adjusting to student life after many years of teaching, lent a sympathetic ear when she became frustrated by seemingly trivial assignments. When the library school students had to complete five supervised practicums in Atlanta's Carnegie Public Library and in various departments of the Emory University Library, Jeannette's supervisors praised her enthusiasm for the work but expressed concern about her reaction to suggestions for improvement. She insisted, they reported, on her own point of view and was not a good team worker. Her inflexibility when asked to use an unfamiliar typewriter reinforced their belief that older students could be difficult to shape into library workers.[17]

At the conclusion of her year of study Jeannette stood ready to receive the BLS degree.[18] When Dean Howard reviewed her performance she rated Jeannette as excellent in many categories, including editorial ability, originality, executive ability, scholarship, and industriousness. She was, Howard asserted, "one of the brightest members of her graduating class when it came to book learning." In contrast, she earned only fair marks in adaptability, common sense, judgment, disposition, and tact. "Personally," Howard wrote, "she sometimes proves a trial, being fussy about details and hypercritical of other people, and not always a good team worker." In other words, Jeannette did not suffer fools gladly.[19]

Librarianship

Jeannette began the arduous process of searching for a job in the spring of 1932, one of the two worst years of the Great Depression. As unemployment rose to nearly 24 percent and libraries cut costs in order to remain open, she filed applications with numerous teachers' and librarians' agencies. Clara Howard, eager to place Emory graduates, emphasized

Jeannette's "fine mind" and "exceptional background" when writing letters of reference, but to no avail: in the pragmatic 1930s her lack of practical library experience posed a daunting challenge.

Eager to help her protégée, Miriam Tompkins contacted Hazel Timmerman, executive assistant for the American Library Association Board on Personnel Administration. "As is the case with hundreds of other librarians at this time," she wrote, "Miss Foster is very badly in need of a position, and both because of her real ability and my own personal interest in her I am anxious to do all that I can to help her." Tompkins, who knew that Jeannette could give the impression of being impatient and intimidating, noted that she would be very effective if working with other intellectuals, but cautioned that she lacked "appreciation of the needs of the non-intellectuals which a readers' adviser has to meet."[20] The solution, she believed, would be to have her work under the direction of an experienced person or to have her work independently.

Following graduation in the summer of 1932, Jeannette spent nearly two weeks with Clara Louise Thompson in Rome before returning to the invigorating hustle and bustle of Chicago, where she began putting her networking skills to work. Visiting the American Library Association headquarters on Huron Street, she introduced herself to officials Carl Milam (executive secretary of the American Library Association from 1920–1948) and Hazel Timmerman. She next visited the Graduate Library School, where she met with Professor Douglas Waples and doctoral student Errett W. McDiarmid, an Emory University Library School graduate in the class of 1930.[21] She found the school's environment and its emphasis on research so invigorating that for a moment she felt tempted to begin work on a doctorate.

Established in 1926 with support from the Carnegie Corporation, the University of Chicago Graduate Library School was the first in the nation to offer a doctorate in library science. By the early 1930s, it had built a national reputation for sociologically oriented studies of reading and library use. Using social-science techniques, the scholars there had begun to systematically construct a philosophy of librarianship based on verifiable data. Jeannette's visit to the school left her infused with the "infectious enthusiasm . . . which runs one's professional temperature up at once." As much as she yearned to pursue a doctorate in library science, she knew it would be wiser to gain practical library experience first.[22]

Jeannette's difficulty in finding a library position was not for lack of trying. Depression-era employers were so inundated with applications for positions paying from $1,600 to $1,800 per year that they could not respond in a timely manner. After making numerous unsuccessful applications to Chicago-area libraries, Jeannette began to comprehend the bleakness of the job market: "Northwestern [University] is turning down a half-dozen experienced applicants a day." Her dual background in science and librarianship made her a natural for the famed John Crerar Library, a research library for the natural and social sciences, but after interviewing there her hopes sagged: "I shall have to *wait* for my spirit to revive a bit before I even try the others." She found prospects at the Newberry Library, a research library concentrating on history and the humanities, "as hopeless as Crerar." Casting her net further, she applied for jobs in New York, Louisiana, Iowa, Illinois, and elsewhere, trying to put herself "in the way of every possible chance at the very scarce vacancies the season offers." Upon learning of a position at the State Teachers' College in Fredericksburg, Virginia, for instance, Jeannette immediately wrote the president indicating that she would enroll in the College of Education at the University of Chicago, if needed, to make up any deficiency she had in formal courses in pedagogy. Increasingly desperate by late August, she concluded that she would be "very glad to hear of any vacancies, at any salary no matter how low" and that she was willing to "go anywhere on twelve hours' notice at any time during the year." She was, she confided in a dramatic tone to Dean Howard, at the end of her resources.[23]

As the summer neared an end, Jeannette developed a contingency plan: if she could not secure a position by late August, she would move in with her sister Anna Foster Cope, now married, and the mother of Alison, two years old, and Winslow, born earlier that month. Since their

PHOTO 13.   Left: Anna (8), Helen (5), and Jeannette (13) Foster, May 1908. Right: Jeannette, Helen, and Anna, with Anna's dog Skeeks, Champaign, Illinois, September 1930. (Courtesy of Alison Cope Puffer and Winslow Howard Cope)

home was in Champaign, Illinois, she pragmatically reasoned, it would be possible to take a second year of library training at the University of Illinois Library School and earn her MLS degree. Emory's Dean Clara Howard had no reservations about recommending Foster to the school, but she still hoped that Jeannette would land in a college library or a reference department "where her cultural background and appreciation of the finer things would be an asset."[24]

Jeannette's persistence yielded results in September 1932 when Antioch College, a small liberal-arts school located in the village of Yellow Springs, Ohio, responded to her application for the position of science librarian. It was with exhilaration that she wrote Dean Howard on September 13 to announce her appointment as science librarian at a salary of $1,500. After an additional year of study, she was taking a significant pay cut, but it was, she exclaimed, "a matter for devout Thanksgiving."

Jeannette had not been able to secure a position in her beloved South, but after five months of searching for a position she realistically accepted this "less desirable certainty."[25]

Coeducational from its establishment, Antioch College first opened its doors in 1852 under the direction of Horace Mann. Beginning in the 1920s, under the leadership of President Arthur E. Morgan, the school modified its liberal arts approach to education by adopting the concept of cooperative education. From that time forward, students combined classroom learning with practical experience, or on-the-job training. The college, situated on 80 acres of ground, stood near an 850-acre glen featuring "picturesque slopes, natural forests, and wild scenery," and Jeannette liked the New England flavor of the community of Yellow Springs. When she desired a change of scenery, it would be easy to travel the short distance to Springfield or Xenia by car or to Dayton, Cincinnati, or Chicago by train. Unlike her previous positions at Hamline College and Shorter College, she was not required to profess a church affiliation at Antioch; indeed, the school catered to freethinking young men and women. Jeannette, who had by this time abandoned her faith, would have enjoyed the school's liberal environment.[26]

The enthusiastic newly minted librarian reported to work on September 16 and spent two weeks familiarizing herself with the science library, located on the third floor of the recently constructed and well-equipped science hall. Writing from her boardinghouse at 616 Xenia Avenue, she sent a progress report to Dean Howard the following month: "I'm thoroughly enthusiastic about the work," she declared, and "never expected in my life to like what I was forced to do for a living so well." There were several reasons why the position of science librarian suited her. First, Jeannette, who enjoyed having control of her surroundings, was in sole charge of the science library. It provided her with more autonomy than if she had worked inside the campus library, which was directed by Guy R. Lyle. "My student assistant and I," she boasted, "do everything except actually order new books and handle periodical subscriptions and binding." The students who worked with her were part of Antioch's cooperative-learning program, where each girl worked five weeks, then devoted herself to study for five weeks. As much as she had detested the technical aspects of library work while in library school, Jeannette threw herself into the circulation of reserves and the processing of overdue notices. She was eager to answer reference questions so she could demonstrate her knowledge of science, but she also found great satisfaction in the detailed work of taking inventory, creating a cross reference index for the vertical file, and putting a wealth of uncataloged government documents into better order. As she worked with more than one hundred science periodicals, Jeannette refreshed her knowledge of French and German and taught herself enough Spanish to work with other materials.[27]

When she was not working, Jeannette continued to devour books and undertook an assignment from the *Journal of Adult Education* to translate a document into Basic English, a system developed in the late 1920s by English scholar Charles K. Ogden. Adherents argued that 850 words were sufficient for ordinary communication and could be used internationally for general and technical communication. For a wordsmith like Jeannette, who enjoyed the beauty of language, such a task must have represented a challenge. Never one to lead the life of an introvert, she also participated in campus activities, including the local chapter of the American Association of University Women. It was at one of those meetings, only a month after her arrival in Yellow Springs, that she met her next love.[28]

Jennie Gregory

Jeannette first encountered the enigmatic Jennie Gregory at a meeting of faculty women held in the home of Mrs. Jessie Armstrong, a member of the Antioch College Board of Trustees from 1927 to 1945. While other women discussed "a group of Negro plays," Jeannette became captivated by the young woman who served refreshments. The "image of a handsome boy in drag," Jennie wore "barber-clipped patent-leather hair and a poker-face above an Irish-green chiffon afternoon frock, nylon full length hose

PHOTO 14.
Jennie Eliza Gregory (1908–1978).
Jeannette met Jennie Gregory at
Antioch College in 1931 (Courtesy
of the Axel Bahnsen negative
collection, Antiochiana Collections,
Antioch College)

& patent-leather slippers with heels." Later in her life Jeannette would
compare Jennie's dark-eyed, slender good looks to that of the American
painter Romaine Brooks. Evidently Jennie also noticed Jeannette. Within
the first two glances, Jeannette later recalled, "we'd got each other's
number—my first experience of that instant telepathic certainty."[29]

Thirteen years younger than Jeannette, Jennie Gregory had grown up
on a farm near Elmira, New York, where her androgynous appearance and
nonconformist behavior had garnered much unwanted attention for the
family. With her close-cropped hair and stubborn refusal to wear female
clothing, she created disturbances when walking into the girls' restrooms.
By virtue of her aunt Armstrong's influence, Jennie had enrolled as a
graduate student in science at Antioch. She was, Jeannette snobbishly recalled, "no intellectual giant," yet her wild streak appealed to the seemingly "proper" librarian. Standing in stark contrast to her widowed aunt's
unpretentious dignity, Jennie was bisexual, promiscuous, and had already
had an abortion by the age of twenty-four.[30]

During the next few weeks, Jay (as Jeannette came to call her) began
studying in the science library and the two women quickly became close

friends. With the "very free use of her aunt's venerable but handsome Franklin," she drove Jeannette to Springfield, Dayton, and other nearby towns "for larks." Despite prohibition, Jay had cultivated a taste for liquor and, as Jeannette recalled, "we drank an awful lot of beer!" A canny Jessie Armstrong, recognizing her niece's proclivities, attempted to keep her on a small cash allowance, and encouraged Jay to invite guests to the house for dinner and an occasional overnight. Little did she realize that Jay and Jeannette retired to the family's well-stocked cellar where they "sneaked nightcaps" and soon began having sex.

Jeannette at first demurred, claiming to be in love with someone else (perhaps Miriam Tompkins), but Jay, who at the time was involved with a male chemistry assistant, dismissively replied, "Does it really matter?" This instance was Jeannette's initiation to "sex-for-release," as she called it, but appeared to be routine behavior for Jay. The relationship with Jay proved to be a breakthrough for Jeannette, whose earlier love life had been characterized by romantic pining. In contrast, the relationship with Jay was casual and careless, providing excitement and adventure while generating much grist for the short fiction Jeannette would write in the future. The affair may have lacked depth, but it persisted intermittently for a few years before evolving into a friendship that endured until Jay's death in 1978.[31]

Despite the relief of having a paying position, Jeannette felt "as home-sick for Georgia climate as one gets for a person" and she hoped there would be an opportunity to return there one day. Georgia, of course, of-fered more than a compatible climate: several of her former loves all resided there. Driven by her persistent restlessness and Antioch College's fiscal uncertainties, Jeannette decided to seek another position. In Janu-ary 1933 she steeled herself to inform Dean Howard of her plans, fully aware that her desire for change in the midst of the Depression would be regarded as yet another indicator of her poor judgment. "It will seem the height of folly," she wrote, "to suggest that I shall be looking for another position next year," but Antioch had left her with no other choice when it announced that she would only receive $952 of her $1,500 salary for the year. Like many employers across the nation, Antioch did not recognize that the Depression had rendered it necessary for single working women like Jeannette to "send something home each month" to help their families.[32]

Library school deans and directors of this era, many of them women, felt an almost maternal responsibility for placing their students and monitoring their careers. Consequently, Clara Howard expressed her disappointment two weeks later, urging Jeannette to hold on to her position if at all possible because she had not heard of a position paying as much as $1,500 "for some time." If Foster's ears had been burning, she continued, it was because faculty at Emory had been discussing what to do with her. It is quite likely that her mentor and friend Miriam Tompkins interceded on her behalf, because Howard mentioned that the faculty had recommended her for one of the doctoral fellowships offered by the Graduate Library School at Chicago. "We thought," she concluded, "there might be a chance for you."[33]

Jeannette agonized for nearly two weeks about her plans for the coming year and had endless discussions with family and friends, who assured her that giving up her position, no matter how little it paid, was "nothing short of madness" given present economic conditions. Writing to Dean Howard in late February 1933, she cited Antioch's anticipated 30 percent "cut in 'drawing allowances'" for the coming year as the deciding factor, explaining that "the immediate profit seems too great not to win against the more distant risk." She had decided to apply for one of the Chicago fellowships. In typical Jeannette Foster fashion, she assumed that one would be awarded to her and began making plans for the move. Finding her attitude more than a little presumptuous, Dean Howard admonished her to remember that there were only three scholarships and many applicants. "I should not sever connections," she emphasized, "until you are assured of something better."[34]

While Howard questioned Jeannette's judgment, she respected her intellect and conveyed a high opinion of her academic potential to the Graduate Library School faculty. Calling her an "exceptional" student and potential scholar, she indicated that Jeannette had "real capacity" as an investigator, was "very critical" of conventional procedures, "very original," and "decidedly" self-propelled. Without a doubt, Howard elaborated, she was industrious, "exceptionally" well-read, possessed "unusual" good judgment and skill in evaluating books, "reads widely in many fields," and was "keenly interested in literature of science." Jeannette was far and away "one of the best students" Howard had ever taught.[35]

In late December, the Graduate Library School (GLS) had mailed 750 placards announcing fellowships for the following academic year, and at subsequent GLS committee meetings they agreed that each would review and vote for twenty applicants, and that people receiving the most votes would receive the awards, used to attract the top students. According to historian John V. Richardson Jr., women were less likely than men to receive fellowships at Chicago because the assumption was that top scholars would be male. By late March, the faculty had reached an agreement: the three GLS fellowships would go to Jeannette H. Foster, Errett W. McDiarmid, Jr., and Lewis F. Stieg, while six others, among them J. Perriam Danton and Carlton B. Joeckel, would receive ALA Fellowships. It truly was a distinguished group of students: Errett McDiarmid would one day become president of the American Library Association, Lewis F. Stieg would distinguish himself in the field of international librarianship, J. Perriam Danton would become dean of the School of Librarianship at the University of California–Berkeley, and Carlton B. Joeckel would craft the first national plan for U.S. libraries that led to the passage of the Library Services Act of 1956.[36] The letter informing Jeannette of her fellowship arrived at an opportune time on April 1, 1933, the same day that Antioch College sent letters to faculty notifying them that it could "pay but 55% of stated salaries as drawing allowance next year." Outwardly relieved, Jeannette could hardly believe her good fortune. "A year without constant financial worry is going to be an inexpressible boon, aside from the wonderful chance for study."[37]

The GLS (Graduate Library School)

As the first school in the nation to offer a doctorate in library science, the GLS was an exciting place to be in the 1930s. Under the leadership of Dean Louis Round Wilson, a spirit of inquiry prevailed as students and faculty conducted systematic survey research and statistical analysis and published path-breaking results. When Jeannette matriculated in the autumn of 1933, the faculty offered such wide-ranging courses as Methods of Investigation, Studies in Adult Reading, Popular Reading in Europe, Community Analysis, and courses in the administration of different types of libraries. Jeannette, as a first-year student, took a rigorous load including Librarianship as a Field of Research, Library Trends with Dean Wilson, a course in statistics from the psychology department, and a sociology course, Social Trends. Later in her life she would remember these two years as a time when she "worked harder than ever before and accomplished more, including acquaintance with quantitative methods applied to non-quantitative material."[38]

When Jeannette moved back to Chicago for graduate school, the most pragmatic arrangement was to live with her parents and pay them board. One way of asserting her independence was by spending long hours on campus in the Harper Library, a building that had been inspired by such examples of English Gothic architecture as King's College Chapel in Cambridge and Christ Church at Oxford. She especially loved working in the Harper reading room, which with its thirty-nine-foot-high ceiling was one of the most beautiful and awe-inspiring spaces on campus. In addition to immersing herself in reading for courses on research methods, book selection, adult reading interests, financial management of libraries, and the statistical analysis for which the GLS would become famous, Jeannette joined a team of student researchers tabulating data about readers and their books.[39]

Despite living under her parents' roof, Jeannette was determined to assert her independence personally as well as professionally. In the autumn of 1933, just a few months short of her thirty-eighth birthday, she briefly resumed her casual affair with Jennie (Jay) Gregory, who soon after moved to New York City's Greenwich Village. When Jeannette learned that Mary Shirley, her redheaded admirer and colleague from Hamline University, had received a fellowship at the National Council of Parent Education and also would be moving to New York, she decided to introduce the two women. Jay could, she anticipated, keep a watchful eye on the younger, less-cosmopolitan woman as she adjusted to the city.[40]

When Jeannette entered the GLS in 1933, she anticipated devoting the next two to three years to her doctoral study, but events in early 1934 proved challenging. First, Depression-era realities forced GLS faculty to announce a reduction in GLS fellowship stipends from $1,500 to $1,000 for the 1934–1935 academic year. Deciding that "it was necessary to go out after bigger game," she immediately applied for a fellowship from the Carnegie foundation, but was not successful. At the same time, her parents, now in their mid-sixties, decided to leave Chicago. Selling their home in Beverly Hills, Winslow and Mabel Foster purchased a ten-room house at 109 Pine Street, in Ludington, Michigan, and moved there in the summer of 1934.[41] The daughter of a thrifty and resourceful woman, Jeannette knew how to economize in order to remain at the university so she could complete her degree.

By Easter 1934, Jeannette was ready for a break, so she traveled to New York City to visit Jay, who had settled into the Village "with a jolly Greek gal" whose father had an under-the-counter business providing abortions. Together, they "did the town" with some of Jay's friends and, as Jeannette recalled, "I had lots of fun & liquor & very little sleep." The Village, she explained, "was only *just* declining from its really historic E. V. Millay–Elinor Wylie days," and was still quite exhilarating, much like the Left Bank of Paris in the 1920s. She loved the bohemian sensibility and secluded, picturesque side streets filled with small presses, avant-garde art galleries, experimental theater companies, and the inevitable speakeasies. After an intense few days there, she fell ill on her return trip to Chicago, and had to stop in Cleveland "in a $1.00/night flop house" before she could continue home. Fearing the possibility of pneumonia, she went immediately to the University Hospital when she arrived in Chicago, but only a few days later she was once again manning her statistical calculator in the library school rooms.[42] In the ensuing years, she gravitated to New York in the summers, justifying her presence there by jobs that sounded impressive to her family but which barely covered the cost of room and board. She felt alive and at home in the world as she walked the streets, pausing in doorways to listen to music.

In the summer of 1934, Jeannette moved into a dormitory, enrolled in a course in advanced reference work, and began the research that would culminate in her doctorate. Despite the many hours devoted to study, Jeannette did not lack for sexual companionship. After she moved into the dormitory, Gertrude Dudley (head of the physical education department) approached and requested her assistance in dealing with a young female graduate student. Dudley, who may have remembered Jeannette from her aesthetic dancing days as an undergraduate, explained that the student in question had become hopelessly infatuated with a male classmate and had begun making a display of herself on campus. Taking a page from Jennie Gregory's life, Jeannette contacted the young woman, "gave her a lecture on Sex & What To Do About It, and ended by taking her quite coolly to bed with me." The single rooms in her graduate dormitory proved conducive to such liaisons; indeed, she noted, "several other women were doing likewise." During the next year and a half, the young woman became "a good deal fonder of me than I could be of her," Jeannette remembered, "but no damage was done; we parted friends."[43]

During this time, Jeannette supplemented her GLS fellowship by working four evenings a week in the library of the International House, a home for foreign students erected with funds given by John D. Rockefeller Jr. Boasting that she could eat for seventy-five cents a day, she fixed breakfast in her dorm room each morning and took her two remaining meals in the university cafeteria. Limiting herself to meat only once a week, she further economized by adopting a diet of protein-rich vegetables and eggs "in any & every form!" Jeannette seemed to flourish under this regimen, and that fall passed her German proficiency exam while continuing to take courses, among them College Libraries, Elementary Social Psychology, and Popular Reading in Europe, while increasingly devoting herself to thesis research.[44]

For decades American librarians had been concerned with the American reading public's preference for fiction, and librarians had striven to guide people from novels to non-fiction works, which they considered more uplifting. By the 1930s, however, it had become evident that readers would not be swayed; therefore, librarians decided to provide a different kind of guidance, one that made distinctions in the quality of fiction available to readers.[45]

Under the guidance of Douglas Waples, Jeannette decided to undertake an alternative approach; instead of classifying fiction, she proposed analyzing the groups who read fiction. Initially, she planned to conduct her study of reading in Knoxville because the findings could potentially have relevance for all of the Rosenwald libraries in the South.[46] Working there, she also hoped, would give her opportunities to steal away for weekend visits with friends in Atlanta. When that project proved too costly and time consuming to undertake, she drew upon the reading records of more than fifteen thousand people that students and faculty of the school had collected between November 1933 and January 1935. Using the techniques of statistical analysis she had learned from sociology professor William Fielding Ogburn, she identified a list of 254 authors who had been read by a minimum of ten readers each. Then she prepared a demographic analysis for each author-group as well as extensive analysis of the works they read. Jeannette defended her thesis, "An Experiment in Classifying Fiction Based on the Characteristics of Its Readers," on August 20, 1935, and received her doctorate ten days later. A condensed version of her findings appeared in *The Library Quarterly* in April 1936, confirming trends that librarians instinctively knew: male readers tended to prefer works of adventure, humor, and history, while housewives tended to select books on the family, psychology, and love. Fascinated with why people read what they did, Jeannette believed that her study would enable librarians to one day say to patrons: "Tell me what you read and I will tell you what you are."[47]

PHOTO 15.
Dr. Jeannette Howard Foster, circa
1935, the year she earned her PhD
from the University of Chicago's
Graduate Library School.
(Courtesy of Alison Cope Puffer
and Winslow Howard Cope)

To celebrate her achievement, Jeannette planned to spend a few
weeks with Jay at the Foster family cottage on Hamlin Lake. The day before she was scheduled to arrive at the Michigan Transit dock in Ludington, however, Jay sent Jeannette a wire: "Am going to Boston to live
with Mary [Shirley]." Evidently the two women had grown close during
Mary's year in New York, and when she received a research fellowship at
the Harvard School of Public Health, Jay decided to accompany her. It
came as a blow, but "not a complete surprise, knowing Jay," who had led
an increasingly promiscuous lifestyle since Jeannette first met her.[48] Instead of spending two weeks alone at the lake, she decided to go early to
Roanoke, Virginia, and her next assignment.

When Jeannette had begun the arduous task of searching for a position
earlier in the year, she felt drained from the effort of completing her doctorate in two rather than the customary three years. Refusing to consider
the directorship of the Simmons Library School, she instead announced
her decision to return to Hollins College (where she had taught several
years earlier), which now had a new president, a new head of the English
department, "and many other wholesome changes in personnel." Because
the GLS groomed students for research, teaching, and leadership positions in the profession, her professors expressed disappointment at her

choice, which paid only $1,600 per annum plus board. "I had infuriated my Library School dean by accepting the head librarianship in the Virginia College," Jeannette remembered a number of years later, but she had had enough of "overwork, undernourishment, and the sheer nervous strain of 8 Univ. of Chi. 'quarters' with no real rest," and felt "*absolutely* unequal to coping with an *absolutely* strange place."⁴⁹

Jeannette returned to Hollins College determined to avoid emotional entanglements with faculty and students. Moving into a much better room than she had occupied during her year as an assistant professor of English, there were "no more epoch-making emotional experiences than a devotion-at-a-distance to a quite remarkable senior girl . . . and a bothersome attachment by a hysterical colleague." Before the end of two years there, the colleague had gone "psychotic" and eventually was committed to an institution. "Fortunately," Jeannette recalled, "I wasn't the primary object of her obsession—only the catch-all for her wilder overflows." According to Jeannette, she began sharing apartments with female roommates in 1936, and in early April her parents mailed her sheets, pillowcases, a quilt, and several other items that could be construed as a housewarming gift. The following December she took a vacation to Florida, the first of many to come, quite possibly with her companion from that time.⁵⁰

After two years of rigorous and intellectually stimulating work at the Graduate Library School, Jeannette found her position at Hollins College comfortable yet anticlimactic. Slipping easily into the role of head librarian, she supervised the other library staff and student assistants, and under her direction the library grew at a rate of over a thousand books per year despite Depression-related cutbacks. In her spare time she read voraciously (as was her habit), revised portions of her dissertation for publication, and wrote short stories.⁵¹

Jeannette, like many lesbians of her era, gravitated to New York City during summer months when her services were not needed at the library. In 1936 a library degree combined with GLS connections helped her land a summer substitute position at the New York Public Library, one of the nation's greatest research libraries and an excellent place to continue the search for examples of sex variance in literature that she had begun during her undergraduate years at Rockford College. Assigned to the Readers' Advisory Department when she reported to work on June 24, she took great pleasure at the opportunity of working with Jennie Maas Flexner, a pioneer in that field. In addition to preparing bibliographies for library users, members of the department counseled individuals on the selection of reading material.[52] While in New York, Jeannette socialized with her friend Jay (who had by then moved to New Jersey where she took a position with Hoffman-LaRoche Pharmaceuticals, Inc.) and Miriam Tompkins, who had taken a position at the Columbia University School of Library Service the previous year. She spent as much free time as she could manage searching texts for references to lesbians and browsing bookstores for items to add to her personal library, among them William Stekel's *The Homosexual Neurosis*.[53]

Jeannette had begun collecting books with lesbian themes in the 1920s, and by the early 1930s had decided to write her own book about women who loved women. The bibliographic knowledge she gained during her year of study at Emory University proved invaluable and conversations with Miriam Tompkins may have spurred her to action. As a scholar and a writer, the desire to produce such a book would dictate her research focus for more than three decades. Access to library collections dictated what jobs and summer employment she accepted. With the book as her all-consuming passion, she had little time to pursue love interests, at least not the kind requiring a deep emotional attachment.

Determined to ferret out even the most elusive printed references to lesbians, bisexuals, and crossdressers, Jeannette quickly discovered that many of the books she needed to consult were housed in noncirculating collections. She could find plausible excuses for requesting some of these works, but the content of others prompted curators to raise their eyebrows. Using her scholarly credentials to advantage, Jeannette remained cautious about spelling out her goals to librarians when she requested the books because she knew that some would disapprove on moral grounds while others would look contemptuously upon the topic of her research. Librarians who were in the know, however, would have guessed the subject of her research when she requested the works of Renée Vivien or Colette, and it was even more difficult to camouflage her intent when paging such scientific and psychiatric titles as *The Invert and His Social Adjustment,* and *Female Sex Perversion.* Compulsive and a perfectionist, Jeannette did not waiver.

Jeannette returned to Hollins for the 1936–1937 academic year, fully aware that she should be doing more with her doctorate than directing a small college library. Her love for the South and her friends there clashed with her desire for advancement and her need to be in a larger city where she could continue doing research for the book. Ultimately the latter triumphed. Writing to Tommie Dora Barker, Clara Howard's successor as dean of the Emory University Library School, she confided, "I would rather work in Atlanta than anywhere I have ever been." Barker, less nurturing than Howard, simply replied that she had nothing to offer her at Emory.[54] At that, she turned for assistance to her mentors at the GLS, knowing that they would like to see her placed in a more prestigious institution.

Jeannette was immediately receptive when Marie Hamilton Law, dean of the Library School at the Drexel Institute of Technology, contacted her about the possibility of joining the faculty of the Philadelphia school. The position offered a number of advantages, including approximately one-fourth more in salary than she earned at Hollins, the strong possibility of increases in the future, access to major research libraries, and the cultural amenities of living in a city. When the offer arrived, however, it posed a dilemma for the woman who hated winter weather, wanted to live in the South, and had deliberately left teaching for library work because she had little patience with the pedestrian abilities of the majority of college students. Pushed to make a decision by mid-April 1937, Jeannette recalled, "I locked myself in my office, laid my head on my 'private' desk, and spoiled a new blotter with a copious shower of silent tears. Then I 'hushed' my nonsense and typed my acceptance."[55]

❦ *Five* ❦

Another Philadelphia Story (1937–1948)

It had happened. . . . Within a matter of minutes she was in love. . . .
Oh, she had been ripe for it, months over-ripe, and this woman had
power for any audience, but knowing all that didn't lessen the impact.
She was gone beyond help, . . . , shivering, a little sick, and happier than
she had remembered for five years one could be. Well, meet it open-
armed, make the most of it!

—JEANNETTE HOWARD FOSTER,
"ANOTHER PHILADELPHIA STORY"[1]

On June 8, 1937, Winslow and Mabel Foster made the sixty-mile trek from their home in Ludington, Michigan, to the Muskegon County Airport to meet their oldest daughter's plane. For a woman whose main mode of transportation had for many years been Greyhound Bus and trains, her arrival by air seemed in keeping with her recent appointment as librarian to President Franklin D. Roosevelt's Advisory Committee on Education (ACE). She had applied unsuccessfully for a permanent position, but felt thrilled to serve in this capacity for the summer. Still a novelty, commercial air transportation had become increasingly popular during the 1930s. As he watched the plane land, Winslow Foster felt a heightened sense of pride in Jeannette's accomplishments: a doctorate from the University of Chicago, publications, a federal appointment, and at summer's end, an associate professorship at the Drexel Institute of Technology in Philadelphia.[2]

Summer in Washington, D.C.

Jeannette packed her summer vacation full of catching up and sharing the exciting news in her life. Saying farewell twelve days later, she flew to Washington, D.C., and reported for work on June 21, 1937, at the ACE offices, housed in the North Interior Building. Initially known as the President's Committee on Vocational Education, the ACE had been established in 1936 to study the existing level of federal aid for vocational education and the relationship of aid programs to current conditions. Enlarged in the spring of 1937 to include the problems of education in general, the committee soon needed a professional librarian to acquire data and resources for committee members' research projects.[3]

Jeannette learned an important lesson about flexibility that summer. As soon as she arrived, ACE secretary Paul T. David informed her that the library was being moved downstairs and consolidated with the National Resources Committee (NRC) Library, and she would be responsible for both. Established by Executive Order no. 7065 in June 1935, the NRC was to study and make recommendations to President Roosevelt for the planned development and use of natural resources. Key members included the secretary of the interior, the secretary of war, the secretary of agriculture, the secretary of commerce, the secretary of labor, and the federal emergency relief administrator.[4]

Setting to work in her characteristic efficient and diligent fashion, Jeannette and the small library staff under her supervision spent long hours each day fulfilling committee members' requests for data and publications. In an era before computers, they made fifty to seventy-five phone calls and typed dozens of letters each day as they tracked down the needed information and arranged for its delivery to their ACE/NRC offices. Jeannette loved the art of detection, and delighted in impressing people with her ability to retrieve elusive material. Refining her bibliographic skills and expanding her range of professional contacts, she and her staff processed an amazing 1,256 interlibrary loan requests in only ten weeks. They also purchased new materials for the library's permanent collections, but ran out of time to catalog them according to the Library of Congress system.[5]

A consummate networker, Jeannette knew or had something in common with several of the ACE and NRC research consultants. Her ACE coworker Paul David had graduated from Antioch College in 1928, and Carlton B. Joeckel, a Graduate Library School classmate, prepared reports on libraries and education. She took special delight in discovering her former University of Chicago professor, the eminent sociologist William Fielding Ogburn, serving as an NRC research consultant in a suite of offices across the hall. Heading up a Technology and Social Trends project, he remembered Jeannette from an advanced statistics class she had taken with him four years earlier and gave her an autographed copy of his two-volume *Recent Social Trends* (1933). Later, however, she jokingly referred to "the damn thing" as being as "big & heavy as the D.C. phone book."[6]

Jeannette's summer in the nation's capital was much like a Turkish bath, a time of sweltering heat and humidity, and it was a time devoid of emotional entanglements. Other than her carefree relationship with Jennie Gregory, she had not had a serious crush on anyone since she studied with Miriam Thompson at Emory University. Instead, she took vicarious pleasure in watching a thin and rather intense secretary from another floor do an "assiduous courting job" on Ogburn's secretary, a handsome married woman who Jeannette regarded as "a Dish." Serving as "an interested audience of *one*," she found it amusing to watch the younger woman's futile efforts because they reminded her of times when she had made a fool of herself over someone. "It got so," she later recalled, that "the pore gal hated to meet me in the washroom, tho I wore a good poker face."[7]

During her limited free time, Jeannette was a woman on a mission, doing research for her book at the Library of Congress, canvassing area bookstores for works with lesbian content, and penning a few lesbian-themed stories of her own. The surrounding Virginia countryside provided her with the setting for a piece of short fiction entitled "A Man's World." In it, an aristocratic lesbian named Paige Courtney invites the artist Jerry Ashburn to a Virginia estate to paint her and a companion, Miss Wylie Cooper. He finds Paige easier to capture on canvas, but is intrigued by Wylie, who volunteers to pose nude for him. During their time together, Jerry has sexual relations with Wylie, but then overhears her telling Paige that the experience was horrible because she prefers being with her. Time passes, Wylie gives birth to a girl, and it becomes clear that the two women had duped Jerry into becoming a sperm donor. When Jerry finally meets his daughter (whom Paige and Wylie have raised) she tells him that she never knew anything could be so beautiful as the kind of love her two mothers share. Ahead of its time, the story presented lesbian love in a compassionate and positive light, much like Jeannette regarded her own homosexuality, and remained unpublished until its appearance in *The Ladder* in July 1968.[8]

Drexel Institute of Technology

By summer's end, Jeannette had grown anxious to begin her new position as an associate professor of library science at the Drexel Institute of Technology. On an uncomfortably hot Labor Day weekend, her friend Jennie Gregory drove to Washington, helped Jeannette pack, and moved her to Philadelphia. Known for American history, Quakers, and publishing, it was the nation's third-largest city in 1937 and an important shipbuilding, railroad, and publishing center. Jeannette had intentionally chosen the position in Philadelphia because of the access it would provide to library collections and because of its proximity by rail to New York City, New Haven (Yale), and numerous college collections (for instance, Bryn Mawr, Swarthmore, and Wellesley) in the surrounding environs. Jeannette eagerly anticipated visiting them as she continued on her quest to locate books containing literary and historical references to lesbians.[9]

Her search for housing close to campus led Jeannette to the Tracy Hotel, a seven-story brick structure conveniently located on Thirty-sixth Street, just four blocks from Drexel and a short walk to the University of Pennsylvania campus. Shabby but respectable, her rooms there overlooked the noisy Market Street El, with trains running every ten minutes between 6 a.m. and midnight. "My reason for submitting to the inconvenience," she later explained, "was that my prospective Dean of the Lib. School had written asking me to share her apt. in Germantown—and I had *no* idea of becoming my boss's roommate!" Jeannette's initial impression of Marie Hamilton Law had not been positive. Describing the Dean as a "big, *soft*-fleshed, whiney-voiced woman," she complained that Law had left her "more than cold." Convinced that she had offended her employer by refusing the invitation, she believed she was beginning the job "with a mild count" against her.[10] In reality, the two women had much in common—graduate study in English, doctorates, careers in librarianship, and New England roots, and once on the scene, Jeannette quickly overcame her initial discomfort and the two worked together quite effectively for the next decade. Appointed dean in 1936, Law continued the genteel tradition established by her predecessor, Anne Wallace Howland, yet would move the school in new directions during her tenure, which coincided with Jeannette's, by opening doors to part-time students and developing courses in the field of special librarianship.

An urban technical school, Drexel Institute's imposing building covered one acre and stood on the corner of Thirty-second Street and Chestnut, just two blocks from the lines of the Pennsylvania Railroad. With her awareness of the finer things in life, Jeannette would have noted the building's classical ornamentation and its light-filled, multi-story arcaded space that resembled the courtyard of an Italian palazzo. Standing in the entrance, she could have appreciated the library to her left, the museum to her right, and the thousand-seat auditorium that made it possible to bring great speakers and artists to the Institute. As she walked up the grand staircase that led to the library school, classrooms, laboratories, and studios, she would have taken in the classical statuary, especially

William Wetmore Story's marble of Sappho, the Greek poetess from the island of Lesbos.[11]

Jeannette arrived at Drexel at a time when the institute's administration, desiring to upgrade the school's status and reputation, placed great value on doctorally prepared faculty. In the library school, which never had more than six faculty during her tenure there, only Dean Law and she possessed the precious degree. Jeannette enjoyed the institute's recognition of her academic achievement, but some of the students perceived her as formal and stuffy because of the expectation that they refer to her as Dr. Foster. In contrast with the women's colleges where she had previously taught, Drexel was predominantly a commuter campus, and most of Jeannette's students lived in the Philadelphia area. The institute also had a strong male presence: only one-fourth of the its approximately five thousand day students were female. In keeping with the times, the school's degrees in engineering and business administration and its evening diploma program tended to attract men, whereas women gravitated to the programs in home economics and library science. During the war years, however, change began to occur and the first woman enrolled in the School of Engineering in 1943.[12]

Entering into her new responsibilities enthusiastically, energetically, and with high expectations, Jeannette filled lengthy letters to her parents with details about her classes, colleagues, and quarters at the Tracy Hotel. With her previous experience in readers' advisory work and her research skills, it was logical for her to assume responsibility for teaching courses in book selection, reference materials, and subject bibliography. During these years Jeannette consciously constructed an image of herself as scholarly, businesslike, and professional, seldom letting students see her more personable side. She was so focused on filling them with bibliographic knowledge that one student described her as "stern, without humor, but well-prepared," her courses "dull but useful."[13] How ironic for a woman whose friends cherished her wit and sardonic sense of humor.

Jeannette's sense of professional achievement heightened during her years at Drexel as she found opportunities to share her expertise in numerous settings. She and her colleagues led their students on field trips to some of the area's outstanding libraries, among them the Free Library of Philadelphia, the Library Company of Philadelphia, and the Philadelphia Museum of Art. When they traveled to New York City to tour the H. W. Wilson plant (producer of such important reference resources as *Readers' Guide to Periodical Literature* and *Book Review Digest*), they met with company founder Halsey Wilson, who, with characteristic warm hospitality, provided lunch in the company cafeteria for his hungry visitors from Drexel. At faculty meetings she recommended books for her colleagues to read, reviewed titles she had recently finished, and conducted an analysis of the students' extracurricular reading interests. Drawing on her experience with the University of Chicago's International House library, which she described in an article written for Drexel's alumni magazine, she selected titles for a newly established dormitory library. She also capitalized on her acquaintance with such prominent librarians as Louis Round Wilson, Jennie Maas Flexner, and Miriam Tompkins, offering to help secure them as guest speakers for Drexel and local library programs.[14]

Searching for Love

In the late 1930s and 1940s, Jeannette devoted nearly all of her spare time to research for her book. Consumed by that passion, she did not attempt to have a full-blown romance but instead had casual sexual encounters and short-lived relationships with several women who she met in the female-intensive world of the library-school setting. None of those liaisons proved emotionally satisfying because they could never equal the exquisite love she had felt for the elusive Clara Louise. Looking back fondly to the age of romantic love, a Janus-faced Jeannette at the same time searched for the modern woman who would fill the empty space in her heart. Increasingly, the young lesbians Jeannette met in her classroom had come of age in the 1920s and were more forthright and open when it came to their sexuality, and she had no qualms about becoming involved with her students who, for the most part, were adults already in possession of a baccalaureate degree.

Tish

During her first semester at Drexel, Jeannette's class included a "French-Irish gal" living alone in Philadelphia's equivalent of the Village. "She had no real appeal for me," Jeannette remembered, but "she got my number on right and made definite advances." Based on her recounting of this incident, Jeannette was not the initiator; once or twice the student caught her in a weak moment in her hotel room and they had sex, but it was à la Jennie Gregory—casual and without any sense of obligation. Soon thereafter, one of Jeannette's colleagues began pursuing her. Late on Friday afternoons students from each of the institute's schools opened their doors, turned their radios on loudly, and danced in the school's Great Court. One week, Jeannette recalled, a cataloger from the main library named Letitia Pool "caught me in a vacant corner of 'the stacks,' & we danced together for quite awhile before anyone saw us."[15] It had been five long years since Jeannette had fallen in love with Miriam Tompkins, and her casual affair with Jennie Gregory had long since evolved into platonic friendship. An incurable romantic, Jeannette missed the exhilaration that accompanies new love, yet as her relationship with the cataloger confirms, she was not yet ready for another emotional attachment. Born in 1901, Letitia Evans Pool (or Tish, as she preferred to be called) grew up on a farm near Middleton, Delaware. Fair complected, with golden brown hair and full lips, she had a fun-loving spirit but at times could be temperamental. Shortly before meeting Jeannette, she had broken off her lesbian relationship with a cataloger at the Philadelphia Public Library. The two women soon discovered that they had several things in common: during her college days Tish had earned a reputation as a "brick presser" with few equals, and she loved to eat. That fall the two women took many long brisk walks and ate lavish meals together.[16]

In December 1937 Jeannette and Tish traveled to Lake Worth, Florida, for some much-needed vacation. Jeannette, who saw herself as a

PHOTO 16.
Jeannette's loves included
Edna Grace Taylor (upper left,
courtesy of Special Collections-
Cowles Library, Drake
University Library), Leonore
Ward (upper right, courtesy of
Shorter College), Miriam D.
Tompkins (lower left, courtesy
of the Milwaukee Public
Library), and Letitia Pool (lower
right, courtesy of the University
of Delaware Archives)

migratory bird, enjoyed going north to Ludington in the summers and south to Georgia and Florida during winter and spring breaks. Whether it was the frugal New Englander in her or necessity wrought by living through the Great Depression, Jeannette traveled economy-style, staying in Lake Worth, Jacksonville, or the *un*stylish part of Miami Beach, south of Lincoln Road "in the little places where the 'help' from the hotels north of Lincoln holed up." Exhausted by a mad rush of grading, Christmas shopping, mailing packages, and the twenty-five- to thirty-hour train ride from Philadelphia to Florida, she often spent her first day there sleeping before commencing a routine of bicycling (a habit she had acquired from her Aunt Carrie), walking on the beach, and dining in restaurants. Wherever she went, she took something to read and stationery for the detailed letters she would write to friends and family. Jeannette enjoyed these winter sojourns but remained incapable of revealing to her family just how much fun she had; instead, she sent missives describing rain, humidity, and ailments.[17]

Deciding that they were compatible, Tish and Jeannette began talking about moving in together. As she contemplated that possibility, Jeannette's Yankee thriftiness shone through: as a single working woman she appreciated the economic benefit of shared housing. She also welcomed the prospect of companionship and a more convivial atmosphere than she had at the Tracy Hotel. Love does not appear to have been an overriding factor in her decision. Her move was delayed until mid-April because the movers went on strike, so the two had barely settled into a routine when the school year came to a close.[18]

Jeannette did not let her arrangement with Tish interfere with the professional and personal agenda she had planned for the summer of 1938. Drawing upon her network of professional contacts, she landed a position at Columbia University working in the library school's library. It paid very little, but she did not care because work was simply an excuse to justify spending part of the summer in New York City. Jeannette loved to walk the city streets after dark, listening to music through doorways. She had a penchant for the romantic torchy ballads of the era, like "Lady Be Good," "The Touch of Your Hand," and "The Very Thought of You." She also loved to walk into the lobbies of New York's fine hotels, where she liked to find a cozy lounge where she could hole up for an afternoon of reading. She did it all with an attitude of confidence and assurance, as though she belonged there.[19]

Spending six weeks at Columbia, Jeannette audited classes taught by her former love, Miriam Tompkins, who had moved there from Emory in the fall of 1935.[20] Whether or not they had a physical relationship, the two women connected well on a cerebral level and had a powerful emotional bond. Miriam's interest in adult education had shaped the direction of Jeannette's doctoral research. Jeannette also spent as many of her waking hours as possible in the reading room of the New York Public Library examining books for sex variant content, doing biographical research on authors she had "long suspected" of being lesbians, and reading scientific and psychiatric works on homosexuality.[21]

As her younger sister Anna once observed, Jeannette made friends wherever she went, and Philadelphia and New York were no exceptions to the rule. She never enjoyed the bar scene, although she had gone to a few in the Village with her friend Jennie Gregory; instead, she preferred socializing with friends in their apartments. In Philadelphia, she gravitated to intelligent professional women like Dr. Ella Roberts, medical director of Children's Heart Hospital, and when in New York, Jeannette visited Miriam Tompkins and Jennie Gregory and also renewed her friendship with childhood friend Dr. Phyllis Greenacre, who had moved to New York in the 1930s after divorcing her husband. A noted psychoanalyst, she directed the outpatient unit of the Payne Whitney Psychiatric Clinic at the New York Hospital. Jeannette also may have reconnected with a former Rockford College classmate, Grace Hall Woolley, who worked in the hotel business on West Fifty-seventh Street.[22]

Even though Jeannette was driven by her research for the book, she remained susceptible to women with a particular look, especially slim, boyish-looking females like Jennie Gregory (butches) or ultrafeminine beauties like Clara Louise Thompson. During the summer of 1938 she found herself becoming infatuated with Harriet MacPherson, a professor of cataloging and classification. Jeannette, who described her as "thin, tall, at times brusque and inclined to be a drill master," felt an instantaneous attraction to the intelligent brunette with bushy eyebrows and direct gaze. In addition to intellectual compatibility, the two shared interests in travel, reading, and mystery novels, which MacPherson wrote under a pseudonym. If it had not been for a scheduled vacation with her family, Jeannette later recalled, she might easily have made a fool of herself over this woman.[23]

As much as Jeannette loved Hamlin Lake's clean air, towering trees, shimmering water, and night sounds, her first few days there always seemed a bit surreal because of the contrast with her life in Philadelphia. Operating on the premise of "don't ask, don't tell," Jeannette sometimes invited women to the lake, but they stayed at the Stearns Motor Hotel in Ludington rather than at the lake cottage or in her parents' home. In addition to reading and corresponding with distant friends, Jeannette passed her days helping her father with outside work. Winslow Foster

took a great interest in her professional accomplishments, dutifully reading and commenting on the articles she published in professional journals and even asking her to recite some of her poems. In contrast,
Jeannette and her mother maintained a cordial yet distant relationship.
Perhaps Mabel envied her career or was concerned by the fact that she
had never married. Spending her days doing endless housework, Mabel
watched disapprovingly as her increasingly cosmopolitan daughter went
to movies, ate in restaurants, shopped, and had her hair done at the
beauty salon, a luxury her other daughters eschewed.[24]

Jeannette sensed that something had changed when she returned in
the fall of 1938 to the apartment she shared with Tish. Caught up in the
flurry of activities that accompany each new school year, she did not immediately realize that her companion had fallen in love with another
woman, Ruth Harry, a twenty-three-year-old library school graduate who
had joined the Drexel Institute library staff in July.[25] That fall, Tish's attraction for Ruth grew increasingly obvious to Jeannette, who recognized
but wished to delay the inevitable disruption it would mean for her living
arrangement. Immersing herself in state and local professional activities,
she made plans to attend the midwinter meeting of the American Library
Association in Chicago and took great pride in the fact that Dean Law,
vice president of the American Association of Library Schools (AALS),
had asked Jeannette to serve as her substitute. Making an unprecedented
Christmas visit to Ludington before she traveled on to Chicago and the
conference, she arrived home with bundles of luxurious presents, perhaps
hoping to demonstrate her professional success in a concrete way.
Winslow, delighted by his daughter's presence, even bought a small tree
for her to decorate. During her three-day visit the Fosters confined their
conversation to such safe topics as the state of affairs in Europe.[26]

Jeannette's participation in the ALA and AALS conferences reinforced her already healthy sense of professional self-esteem. As one of a
small number of women in the nation to possess a doctorate in library
science, she felt empowered to offer her opinions and to share her expertise with others. After returning to Philadelphia in January 1939, she de-

voted long hours to planning a district meeting of librarians to be held at Drexel on February 8. Under her direction, the planning committee selected adult education (one of Jeannette's pet topics) as the meeting's focus, and Jeannette invited Miriam Tompkins to serve as keynote speaker. The following fall she took part in a meeting to establish a Philadelphia Adult Education Council.[27]

By mid-February 1939, Jeannette could no longer ignore the fact that she had become a "fifth wheel" in her relationship with Tish. Ever the pragmatist, she moved into an efficiency apartment in the same building so Tish could live in the larger unit with Ruth. Writing off the relationship as one of "no Grand Passion on either side, just a damned convenient arrangement and less boring than being alone," she nonetheless declared that she would "*never* see anything faintly appealing about my successor," conceding that "one seldom does." Her heart had suffered no injury, but she found the new apartment "dark & inconvenient." In letters to her family, Jeannette presented the move in an upbeat tone, emphasizing its cost effectiveness and sending drawings of the new layout. Since she remained formally closeted with her parents, they, in customary fashion, they did not acknowledge that Tish had ever been anything more than a roommate.[28]

After breaking up her relationship with Tish, Jeannette had an opportunity to re-evaluate her situation. That March she traveled south by train to Georgia during spring break weak, visiting Clara Louise in Rome and Lenore Ward in Atlanta. Swayed by the first glimpses of spring blooms and the agreeable climate (especially when contrasted with the recent Philadelphia winter), Jeannette realized that she must act if her dream of living in the South was to come true. Since her last visit, Lenore had purchased a new Chevy coupe and took great pleasure in driving Jeannette around the outskirts of Atlanta. It was during these drives that Jeannette saw the hillside lot she would purchase a month later, the plot of ground where she one day hoped to build a home.[29]

At the conclusion of the 1938–1939 academic year, Jeannette went, like a homing pigeon, to New York City for another summer of study at

Columbia University. Her rooms at 628 West 114ᵗʰ Street were conveniently located near the university and Miriam Tompkins' apartment. Jeannette enjoyed attending the New York World's Fair with friends before heading to Ludington for her annual visit to the lake. Seemingly unfazed by the recent demise of her relationship with Tish, Jeannette now cultivated her as a friend, evidently quite successfully. When Tish and Ruth went abroad during the summer of 1939, the letters they sent detailing their impressions of Europe on the eve of war made such an impression on Jeannette and her parents that Winslow even sent one to the *Ludington Daily News* for publication.[30]

Love Strikes Again

During her third year at Drexel, Jeannette, now forty-four, "really *fell* again," this time for a young woman in the half-time, three-year class for employed librarians that met on Wednesday evenings and Saturday mornings. As she had in the past, Jeannette wanted to find a cross between a pleasant and companionable friend and an ardent lover. She believed that sex was a necessary condiment to life, and was not shy about saying so, and she was an intellectual snob who seldom found anyone attractive if they were not intelligent. The young woman who caught her attention this time reminded her of the literary character Mademoiselle de Maupin—an elegant, tall, handsome, and sexy butch. In a movie, she would have been a fencer or a dashing cowboy, the one who won the girl. Jeannette's reaction was "characteristically instantaneous." As Barbara Grier, who came to know Jeannette well in the 1950s, recalled, she "definitely suffered from 'I took one look at you, that's all I had to do, and then my heart stood still.'" This tendency explains why in some of Jeannette's fiction her heroines could look at pictures on the wall and become faint with desire. Unfortunately for Jeannette, the student worked and lived in Wilmington, Delaware, a good half-hour away by train. Due to the lack of a car, the student's conscientious Roman Catholicism, and the fact that she lived under the close supervision of a widowed mother, "that passion joined a few earlier, in the Dept. of Utter Futility." Her efforts to court the woman included giving her a rather mannish silver and zircon ring but, as Jeannette lamented, "*She* let me know fairly soon she was already 'taken' by a Wilmington grade-school teacher."[31]

A student who fainted while working on a reference problem in the library helped Jeannette out of the gloom of disappointment one day in early 1940. A solicitous Dean Law asked if she would take the woman, Adelia Butcher Lund, home to recover. By this time, Jeannette had moved to an elegant old residence in Upper Darby township, approximately five miles away by streetcar. After traveling there by taxi at the school's expense (a fact that gave her great pleasure), Jeannette revived Dee (as she preferred to be called) with hot tea laced with bourbon. At that, Dee began to unload her problems. Her husband, Frederick H. Lund, was a professor of psychology at Temple University and had deserted her for one of his graduate students after sixteen years of marriage. Overwhelmed and despondent, she was living in a modernistic house on the far edge of Elkins Park with her college-age niece and did not know where to turn. Jeannette, on the other hand, immediately saw an opportunity and a solution: she needed someone to sublet her place during the summer and Dee needed to move out of her house.[32]

With Dee and her niece installed in the apartment, Jeannette headed for New York City to begin her summer school teaching at Columbia University. Her parents took great pride in her appointment to teach Bibliographic Method and Reading Interests and Habits of Adults, but if they had known how little she earned there they would have realized that the job was simply an excuse to spend the summer in the city. Lodging at Twenty-ninth Street, near Madison Avenue, she spent every spare hour in the New York Public Library, where she continued to detect examples of lesbian characters in works of literature.[33]

During the summer as they exchanged letters, Jeannette learned about Dee's background and realized that they shared several things in common—growing up in the Midwest in a household of women, a love of education, and experience traveling in Europe. A year older than Jeannette, Dee had taught school and met Lund, who she married in 1924, while studying at the University of Nebraska. Both did graduate work at Columbia University and enjoyed traveling to Europe.[34] The more she learned about Dee, the more convinced Jeannette became that they were compatible enough to live together. When Jeannette returned to Drexel at summer's end, they found a place large enough for Dee, her niece, and Jeannette to live comfortably. Once again Jeannette let convenience rather than love dictate her choice of partners.

Jeannette and Dee's life together offered a number of benefits, including larger living quarters and a hired helper to do some cooking and housecleaning. After only a short time, however, she realized that the relationship had no future. Dee had, Jeannette explained, "a *real* mother-fixation—I guess her husband had some grounds for his desertion—and all the emotion she needed was to sleep in someone's arms & feel 'mothered.'" For a woman like Jeannette, who enjoyed the physical expression of love, it was difficult to compromise. Always the pragmatist, she negotiated "some sort of half-way relationship" that never was wholly satisfactory to either woman, but it lasted until the niece married. After the summer of 1942, when Dee's divorce became final and she moved away from their West Chester Pike apartment, Jeannette downsized to a tidy little efficiency in the same building, where she remained for the duration of her time in Philadelphia. Despite the dissolution of their living arrangement, Dee and Jeannette appear to have remained cordial friends, with Dee helping Jeannette settle into her newer apartment and even traveling with her to Florida over the holidays.[35]

During her time with Dee, Jeannette lost a significant figure in her life when her father unexpectedly died on April 19, 1942. Winslow Foster had a history of heart trouble, but in characteristic fashion spent the day before his death working in the yard and writing in his diary. Only seventy-three years old, he had lived a full yet unfulfilling life, constantly searching for something just beyond the horizon, a trait that Jeannette shared with him. She had admired her father and for years had striven to earn his approval by doing well professionally. Once the man who had followed her studies and career with great interest was interred in a family plot at South Haven, Michigan, she no longer felt compelled to return to Michigan for regular visits.[36]

After her mother's death a year later, on September 3, 1943, Jeannette redefined her relationship with her two sisters. Anna, the dutiful daughter who had assumed responsibility for her mother during her final illness, had become a wife and mother living in a rural Illinois community. In letters to Jeannette she assumed an almost parental tone, expressing interest yet concern that her sister, somewhat like their father, could not find a satisfying position. She also chided her for working too hard and not taking good care of herself. In the years to come, Anna's relationship with Jeannette would be constrained. Her children grew up knowing that Jeannette, the aunt who sent them gifts, had some bad habits that they should not emulate. She drank too much, they were told, and was not careful with her money, but they never saw enough of her to judge for themselves. "I don't remember her being up here [at Hamlin Lake]," her niece Alison Cope Puffer recalled, "more than once or twice, visiting in a dress, in a working outfit." In contrast, Jeannette's youngest sister Helen grew closer to her in later life. Maturity diminished the eight-year age difference and the two women, who for a time both lived on the East Coast, enjoyed going to museums and concerts together. Linked by a shared interest in art and their childlessness, the two occasionally squabbled but seemed able to resolve most of their differences.[37]

The War Years

The wartime years proved quite challenging for the Drexel Institute Library School as Dean Law attempted to reposition the school so it would remain economically viable. As students left for active duty and Drexel's financial condition faltered, controversy erupted when President

George Rea attempted to sell art and manuscript collections in order to generate some much-needed income. In the fall of 1942, Jeannette had her family convinced that conditions at Drexel were so bad that she might lose her job.[38] Yet as one of the two library school faculty with doctorates, Jeannette seemed to enjoy the opportunities for leadership and service created by wartime exigencies. At faculty meetings she proposed creative plans for increasing library school enrollment by including the possibility of offering joint degrees with Temple University and the University of Pennsylvania, and she wholeheartedly supported the inauguration of a program in special librarianship. Eager to do her part for the war effort, she prepared reading lists intended to increase students' knowledge of current events, helped collect books for the Victory Book Campaign, and assembled and addressed the Drexel Service Men's Newsletter. She joined in discussions about defense preparations and efforts the school could make to rehabilitate war veterans. She also wrote scripts for a radio program that aired on Sunday afternoons beginning October 18, 1942. Jeannette may have gained ideas for the program from former Shorter College student and now friend Lillian Lee, who pioneered local educational broadcasting in Atlanta a few years earlier.[39]

Jeannette also remained active in the American Library Association, whose meetings she attended annually, and the American Association for Library Schools. In 1944 she began research for an AALS report concerning curricular requirements for library school degrees. Using her Graduate Library School training, she surveyed thirty-four library schools and prepared a systematic analysis of the results. The report, published in January 1946, weighed the merits of the MLS versus the BLS degrees. It appeared impossible to resolve the issues, Jeannette argued, as long as the same curricular content was offered at the undergraduate level in some schools and at the graduate level in others. As someone trained at Chicago, she had high expectations for her students, but many who were pursuing the equivalent of a second bachelor's degree did not feel compelled to do graduate work and some voiced complaints about the heavy workload required in her classes. After she left Drexel, however, the library school joined a national trend, replacing the BLS with the MLS, a graduate degree.[40]

The Hidden Agenda

During her years at Drexel, Jeannette continued her research on sex variance in literature and even began writing a draft of the manuscript. After the 1941 publication of George W. Henry's *Sex Variants*, she refined her definition of sex variance to include "women who are conscious of passion for their own sex, with or without overt expression."[41] Adopting a chronological approach, she wrote the book to include literature published through approximately 1910, let it rest, then revised everything she had written and extended it beyond 1910. Aware of the stigma attached to her research topic, she excelled in compartmentalizing her life, shoring up her professional reputation with committee service and professional publications while privately pursuing her life's passion. It was no small undertaking. By the time Jeannette completed research for the book in 1954, she had personally examined more than three hundred literary works, another three hundred scientific and psychiatric works dealing with homosexuality, and an additional two hundred titles for biographical and historical background.[42] Only a few of her closest friends and trusted colleagues knew the focus of her research. Those like Jennie Gregory were understanding and supportive, while others, like Clara Louise Thompson, questioned the wisdom of undertaking such a risky venture.[43]

By late 1938 Jeannette hinted at her interest in homophile literature in a letter to the editor of *Library Journal*. At a time when anyone who expressed interest in sexual, let alone lesbian or gay, topics was considered weird or questionable, this was a bold move. In an earlier issue, Randolph Adams had accused librarians of being the enemies of books.

Countering his statement that they did not do enough to preserve them, she declared that "there are two essential ways of looking at books, or perhaps at any product of human effort: the collector's and the scientist's. . . . To the latter any evidence of human experience, rare or common, is of value chiefly . . . as an aid in using knowledge of man's past and present for a better shaping of his future." As someone who had turned to printed works in order to understand her sexual orientation, Jeannette reiterated her belief in the power of reading: "The future lot of man may be ameliorated only by as accurate knowledge of past and present as is vouchsafed the current human intellect." Revealing a familiarity with sexological literature, she noted "the emotional satisfaction" she had experienced when examining the original manuscript from "certain chapters" by Havelock Ellis.[44] Knowledgeable readers would have realized that she was referring to his work on homosexuality.

For someone who obsessively searched for printed examples of gays and lesbians everywhere she went, whether she was visiting her family in Ludington, friends in Atlanta, or colleagues in Chicago, Philadelphia proved to be an ideal location to advance her research. Drexel's library, as she quickly discovered, had not collected such "questionable" literature, but when she searched the city's union library catalog she found that a number of other institutions in the area held relatively good collections. The University of Pennsylvania Library, for example, had a "pretty liberal" collecting policy, as did the libraries at Haverford College, Swarthmore, and Bryn Mawr, all easily reachable by interurban. The latter, she determined, was one of the few libraries with the work of lesbian writer Renée Vivien available for public consultation. As Jeannette read Vivien and the work of other French authors she may have given silent thanks to Helen Apfel, the Rockford College French professor who had prepared her so well for this task.[45]

Despite the richness of the area's publicly accessible libraries, none of them owned a copy of Catulle Mendès' Méphistophéla (1890). Noted for its detailed exploration of a lesbian's life spanning over five hundred pages,

Jeannette believed it had escaped the censors of the day because the main character is portrayed as morally depraved. Upon searching the Library of Congress Union Catalog, Jeannette found only four copies of the precious book listed in the nation's libraries, one of them in Philadelphia's Rittenhouse Club. She determined to have a look. Located at 1811 Walnut Street, this exclusive men's club had welcomed such prominent members as the author Henry James and University of Pennsylvania presidents, but never a woman. Arriving one Saturday morning, Jeannette formally requested admission to the Library, and was denied access even though she promised not to meet or talk with any of the members. Afterward, when complaining to a male assistant librarian at the University of Pennsylvania, she discovered that he was a member. Supportive of her work, he volunteered to borrow the book if she promised to read it in his office. Jeannette, who claimed she could read French at an amazing sixty pages per hour, spent the next three Saturday mornings seated at a secretary's desk in his outer office while she read the work. After finishing, she concluded that it "wasn't worth it, but it had its points."[46]

Jeannette's search for variant fiction also took her to Yale University to examine a rare copy of Mary Wollstonecraft's *Mary: A Fiction* (1788), which she believed to be the first novel on female variance written by a woman. Ever efficient, she combined research and professional responsibility by escorting her Drexel students on a field trip to Columbia University and several other area highlights, and then announced that they were adults and did not need a chaperone to find their way back to Philadelphia. Boarding a northbound train, she arrived in New Haven that evening and was at the University Library's entrance early the following morning, ready to spend the day reading. Familiar with Wollstonecraft's *A Vindication of the Rights of Women*, Jeannette believed that her biographers had focused on it while glossing over her fervent twelve-year attachment to Fanny Blood. In her opinion, the novel, which was based on the author's life, idealized "an innocent variant relationship as the highest form of emotional experience."[47]

Moving On

Between 1937 and 1948, Jeannette established herself professionally, making the Drexel Institute Library School her home institution while also teaching summer school at Columbia University and Emory University. Productive professionally, she served on ALA and AALS committees and published at least seven book reviews in *Library Quarterly* and in *College & Research Libraries*, all relating to her expertise in reading interests and reference work. Thriving in the urban environment among like-minded friends, she felt valued by the university because of her doctorate.

While she thrived professionally, Jeannette continued to be plagued by a vague feeling of unrest. Personally, she had not found a soulmate, someone with whom she could share her life. More mature and jaded than she had been in the 1920s, she still harbored a love of the romantic, which she sublimated into vivid imaginative prose based on people and episodes from her daily life. As with the poetry she had written earlier in the century, her short fiction was tied more to her desires than to her need for creative expression. Lacking suitable publication outlets, she tucked her stories away, optimistically waiting for a time in the future when they might be published. As much as she liked Philadelphia and its ready access to New York City, she continued to yearn for the South, persistently applying for summer teaching positions at Emory University until she finally succeeded in 1945.[48]

Wartime exigencies—caused in part because Drexel's predominantly male enrollment declined precipitously as students and faculty enlisted in the service—caused Jeannette a great deal of anxiety and led her to take a dismal view of the future there. These anxieties filled her letters home as she weighed the merits and liabilities of positions at other institutions. Conditions had improved by 1946, however, when the University of Southern California approached her about becoming director of their library school. Applying primarily because another job offer would be a bargaining chip when it came time to renegotiate her Drexel salary, she had little genuine interest in the position and no desire to uproot herself for a move to California.[49]

Drexel stabilized financially after World War II ended and Jeannette easily could have spent the remainder of her career there, but in 1947 Dean Marie Hamilton Law announced that she would be retiring the following spring. Jeannette knew her successor, Harriet Dorothea MacPherson, as the woman she first had been attracted to in 1938 when they both had taught summer school at Columbia University. "I realized," she reflected later in life, "that I could not work daily with her and keep my passionate fondness for her concealed." Fortunately, her need to move on coincided with an invitation from nationally prominent sex researcher Alfred Kinsey to become the first professionally trained librarian of the Institute for Sex Research in Bloomington, Indiana.[50]

❧ Six ❧

The Sex Researcher
and the Librarian

*I want to tell you again how much I appreciated your contribution to
our studies last week. . . . It was unusually satisfying to be able to discuss these things with someone intelligent enough to comprehend the
basic problems involved.*

ALFRED C. KINSEY TO JEANNETTE H. FOSTER, 25 JULY 1941[1]

In the fall of 1940, Indiana University professor Alfred C. Kinsey was
forced to make a choice: either give up his sex research or stop teaching the highly popular marriage course he had offered since 1938. Deciding to devote himself exclusively to sex research, he took Philadelphia by
storm that December when he delivered several lectures, including "Criteria for a Hormonal Explanation of the Homosexual," which attacked
the prevailing idea that homosexuality was caused by hormonal imbal-
ance. A year later, Jennie Gregory, an editorial assistant at the Harvard
Medical School's *Journal of Clinical Endocrinology*, wrote Jeannette for advice about two articles that had been submitted for publication. The first
was a statistical piece by Dr. Kinsey, the second "by an anti-statistical
man." Reading them both immediately, she replied without hesitation:
"Kinsey gets it."[2] When Jeannette reviewed his article in 1941, Kinsey's
name was not yet well known, yet by the end of the decade virtually

everyone would have heard of his controversial and pioneering accomplishments in the field of sex research.

Eager to make his acquaintance, Jeannette wrote to Kinsey on May 8, 1941, to express her interest in and support of his work. In the early 1940s, Kinsey's name was not a household word; his big fame would come later, after publication of *Sexual Behavior in the Human Male*. Conveying her "keen interest in the nature, cause and social effects of the phenomenon [of homosexuality] and practical possibilities in dealing with it," she shared openly about herself and her research for a comprehensive bibliography on the subject. Her perspective, she explained, was that of a layman with first- and secondhand experience, who had spent many years in college dormitories. Establishing herself as a serious scholar, Jeannette mentioned her faculty position at the Drexel Institute of Technology, her study of statistics at the University of Chicago, and her doctorate. Boasting that she had read "most of the easily available material in English on homosexuality" and had come to appreciate the value of case studies after the publication of Katharine Bement Davis's *Factors in the Sex Life of Twenty-two Hundred Women* (1929), Jeannette offered her case as one of the thousands he needed to collect. "I believe," she concluded, that "I lack any conventional reluctance to report frankly and completely." Moreover, she thought it would be possible to connect him with some of her college-educated girlfriends who "would contribute similar information."[3] This letter marked the beginning of a collegial, albeit sometimes testy, relationship between Jeannette and Kinsey, an association lasting until his untimely death in 1956. During a span of approximately fifteen years, Jeannette shifted from being an admiring fan to a discontented employee, but she never ceased to believe wholeheartedly in the value of his research.

With the exception of Clara Kinsey and those who gave their sex histories, women are virtually absent from accounts of Kinsey and his work. Biographies by James H. Jones and Jonathan Gathorne-Hardy, novels like T. C. Boyle's *The Inner Circle*, and commercial films and documentaries portray Kinsey working with a male research team. The reality, however, is that female library staff, research assistants, statisticians, and translators contributed significantly to Kinsey's pathbreaking work. Without the assistance of Foster and Jean Brown in the library, Cornelia V. Christenson as a research assistant, Dorothy Collins as a statistician, Alice W. Field as a legal expert, Hedwig Leser and Hazel Toliver as translators, and Eleanor Roehr and others in secretarial capacities, it would have taken longer to compile and publish *Sexual Behavior in the Human Male* (1948) and *Sexual Behavior in the Human Female* (1953).[4] Sharing work, social space, and a mission, Kinsey and his staff had a mutually beneficial relationship. In the case of Jeannette Howard Foster, for example, he gained firsthand knowledge about lesbianism among the educated middle class, and she had virtually unlimited access to one of the finest collections of material in the nation related to sexuality.

A Gold Mine of Information

From their first contact, Kinsey realized that Jeannette offered him an important opportunity to gain insight into lesbian behavior and identity among professional women. Replying to her initial letter, he expressed his heartfelt appreciation for her offer of assistance and emphasized how much he valued input from women like her. Explaining that he preferred to conduct in-person interviews rather than to gather data with a questionnaire, he volunteered to come to Philadelphia if she could help him get twenty-five to fifty histories from older women, especially female homosexuals. In a prompt response, Jeannette noted that her homosexual friends were "scattered all the way from Boston to Atlanta" and that she "could not hope to establish contact with any significant number of homosexual cases in this immediate neighborhood." If he was interested in older women talking about "just any type of sexual behavior," she continued, she could at best persuade a dozen subjects who were "scientifically free from reticence" to talk with him. Noting that she had contacts in New York City, she suggested that it might be possible to put him in touch with "a 'Village' group" in their early or middle thirties, "some of them associated with the old Howdy Club on Third Avenue," but, she cautiously added, she had only known them "secondhand" so she couldn't promise anything. In the 1937–1938 winter edition of *Going Places in New York City*, the Howdy Club, located at 47 West Third Street, was the only one of nineteen Greenwich Village places listed that catered to a gay crowd. Jeannette also proposed that she could connect with "a similar group in Boston" and she offered to "do a bit of scouting" when she attended the annual ALA conference in June.[5]

By 1941, Kinsey had amassed interviews from women and men in penal institutions, college students in his marriage classes, and others he met through his travels. Eager to tap Jeannette's knowledge as a lesbian, and to make contacts with her friends, Kinsey arranged to interview her while en route to her annual summer vacation at Hamlin Lake. Traveling by train, she arrived in Indianapolis on Wednesday, July 16, 1941, in time to have supper with Kinsey before he took her sex history at the Lincoln Hotel. Questioning her for three hours, nearly double the length of a typical session, he later apologized: "I am afraid that I wore you out," but it was "unusually satisfying to be able to discuss these things with someone intelligent enough to comprehend the basic problems involved." Kinsey, whose knowledge of male homosexuality had grown exponentially since 1939 when he evidently satisfied "his longing for a homosexual physical outlet," knew much less about female homosexuality. Jeannette was, as Kinsey coworker Paul Gebhard later recalled, "a gold mine of information."[6]

Boarding a bus, Jeannette left Indianapolis for Ludington on Saturday, where she spent a week of vacation reflecting on her interview with Kinsey. Thrilled to have met someone who rejected the disease model of homosexuality, she felt as if she had discovered a like-minded colleague, someone who shared her desire to alleviate people's mental anguish by giving them accurate and scientific knowledge about their sexuality. Assuring him that it had been a "real pleasure . . . to contribute my bit to the study," Jeannette emphasized that she had "enjoyed every minute of talk. If my energy flagged a bit at the end it may be laid to the previous night on a coach plus the shift from eastern to central time."[7]

Kinsey relied on key people like Jeannette to make connections that would lead to additional interviews. A week after interviewing Jeannette, he wrote once again to express his appreciation for her candor and to offer hope that she would aid him in making "further connections." The study would be much richer and more accurate, he stressed, with inclusion of "the type of history that your friends would represent." A dedicated correspondent, Jeannette had remained in touch with many of the lesbians she had known since her undergraduate days at Rockford College. Eager to support his research, Jeannette promised to contact "half a dozen good friends" in Georgia who were "more or less indigenous and connected with others." As soon as she had some free time, she assured him, she would "sell the idea of letting you visit there and interview them."[8]

After spending a week at the University of Chicago, where she attended a GLS library institute, Jeannette returned to Hamlin Lake for the remainder of her vacation. Mailing a half dozen or more letters to friends, she found their responses "more disappointing than surprising. . . . It seems very difficult to be convincing by mail." Perhaps, she informed Kinsey, "people find it easier to demur on paper than to one's face." As Kinsey's research would reveal, less than one-fifth of women with homosexual experience viewed their behavior as acceptable for themselves, and just under one-fourth considered it acceptable for other females. At best, she informed him, she had secured several "extremely grudging consents promising no further leads"—three in Atlanta and two in Rome, Georgia. The group, she continued, included women ranging in age from their mid-twenties to fifty-seven, with two of them married. Lesbians who taught at women's colleges feared losing their jobs while other friends, living in the South, would have found it shockingly dangerous to talk with Kinsey about their sexuality whether they were homosexual or heterosexual.

"I am extremely sorry," Jeannette apologized, "that the five others I expected to hear from favorably have not come across." Kinsey, confident that he could secure more interviews after "I once get on the ground" did not dismiss the possibility of going to Georgia, but indicated that he would focus on other trips first. In the interim, he encouraged her to help him make contacts in New York.[9]

When Kinsey wrote Jeannette on Christmas Eve 1942, he again expressed hope that she would be able to help him arrange interviews during his upcoming visit to New York City. From Florida, where she basked in the intermittent sunshine, came a mildly disappointing reply: "The only person whose name I feel free to give you without re-establishing contact with her beforehand *re* willingness to contribute," she explained, "is Miss Jennie Gregory. I think she can make a lot of contacts for you, many more than I could." Jennie did not disappoint, and both she and her companion, a nurse named Margaret Knowlton, shared their sex histories with him. Acknowledging their contribution in a complimentary follow-up letter, Kinsey wrote: "It was particularly good of you to come from Jersey and spend all the time that you did in contributing histories." Data "from individuals of your social level," he explained, were highly valued and he hoped they could help him make additional contacts in the future.[10]

Jeannette spent July and August 1943 in New York City doing biographical research and was eagerly anticipating Kinsey's arrival in the city in early September to attend a primate conference, meet with representatives of the Rockefeller Foundation, and collect more interviews. She hoped to recruit a few of her friends—"key people" who could lead to other interviews—to speak with him but the death of her mother on September 3 meant that she had to leave the city abruptly before finalizing the arrangements.[11] She finally connected with Kinsey in the spring of 1944 when he and Wardell Pomeroy, who had joined the Institute for Sex Research (ISR) staff in 1943, came East on an interviewing trip and stopped in Philadelphia. It would be an ideal opportunity, he suggested in advance, to interview some of Jeannette's friends in the area.

On March 7, when Kinsey invited Jeannette to attend his lecture at the Wistar Institute, she made several key contacts for him at Drexel. She gave a second sex history, this time to Pomeroy, because he needed practice with an experienced lesbian subject. Later that year, when reflecting on the visit, Kinsey acknowledged Jeannette's contribution to his research: "[W]e have gotten a splendid lot of histories out of her Drexel Institute." A gracious hostess, she also held a dinner party in Kinsey's honor, inviting Adelia (Dee) Lund and a few other friends. Kinsey was socially comfortable with lesbians, in fact with everyone except religious fundamentalists and psychoanalysts.[12] Exhausted from a day of interviewing, however, he was not his usual gregarious self when visiting Jeannette's apartment, and later apologized by sending Jeannette a copy of his book, *Edible Wild Plants*. It would, he suggested, "give you one more avenue of acquaintance with me."[13]

During the next few years, Kinsey sustained intermittent contact with Jeannette and Jennie Gregory in the hope that they could help him locate lesbians and others willing to be interviewed. Since Jeannette had never favored the bar scene, her contacts came primarily from the ranks of professionals. Jennie did connect him with a few of her friends and co-workers, but regrettably informed him that she had lost track of the contacts she once had in the Village. Kinsey would undoubtedly find more, she suggested, by "snooping around" than he would with her help "because the situation there has always been extremely fluid."[14]

From Philadelphia, Jeannette proudly kept Kinsey informed about her progress with the bibliography she was compiling of literature dealing with lesbianism. With the death of her parents, Jeannette felt freed to give serious consideration to publishing her book. Confident that the book's scholarly nature would enable her to pull it off without losing her job, she contacted several publishers while visiting New York in October 1946. In short order she learned that commercial publishers did not relish the prospect of adding a manuscript to their list "on so touchy a subject written by an 'amateur' without proper medical or psychiatric degrees."[15] In an attempt to establish the legitimacy of her work she stressed her previous scientific training and promised that her findings would be grounded in an overview of scientific writing on homosexuality. When those arguments failed, she mentioned her connection with Dr. Kinsey, but to no avail.

The Institute for Sex Research's First Librarian

Kinsey and the ISR staff worked furiously during the summer of 1947 to complete the manuscript of *Sexual Behavior in the Human Male* by a September 15 deadline and to proactively shape publicity surrounding its release. Excitement mounted in the month prior to the book's January 5 release as readers across the nation devoured articles about Kinsey and his study in such popular magazines as *Look*, *Harper's Magazine*, and *Science Illustrated*.[16] Final details relating to the book's copyediting and publicity consumed the institute's staff throughout the fall as they and university personnel braced themselves for the release of Kinsey's study nationwide.

In the midst of this chaos, Kinsey somehow found time to focus on matters closer at hand. Between 1941, when he had received his first grant of $1,600 from the National Research Council, and 1946, when the Rockefeller Foundation awarded the Institute for Sex Research a three-year $120,000 grant, Kinsey had transformed a shoestring operation into a fully staffed research institute. Using an estimated $10,000 of his own money, he built a collection of books, periodicals, and artworks to support his research. By 1946, it was growing at such a rate that it had become "impossible for him to keep up with it" because "large collections and even whole libraries were being given to the project" by donors who wished to remain anonymous. Campus administrators urged him to sell it to Indiana University but he refused, arguing that "there were many items in it ... that would cause consternation" if they appeared in the university library. On April 10, 1947, two days after incorporating the Institute for Sex Research (ISR), he gave the institute title to the histories, research materials, and his library collection. Out of necessity, Kinsey pressed interviewer Paul Gebhard into service as a part-time library worker and forced him to follow his boss's idiosyncratic practices, which included organizing books by his own pneumonic scheme rather than an approved library classification system. As psychiatrists and researchers around the country became aware of the library's potential as a resource, the pressure to appoint a professionally trained librarian mounted.[17]

Kinsey considered several factors as he pondered the appointment of a librarian to his staff. With interviewers, he sought men in their thirties or early forties who were happily married, and better yet, parents, because it gave them a patina of respectability. At the same time, however, he "did not want coworkers with orthodox sexual values." Taking an applicant's sex history revealed if he or she was sex shy, and gave Kinsey a sense of the person's ability to maintain strict confidentiality. It also was important to him that potential employees have excellent interpersonal skills, a genuine interest in sex research, and share Kinsey's openness about sexuality. Homosexual experience, at least in men, was considered a plus, but it was imperative that the potential employee give the appearance of respectability to the campus and community.[18] In addition to tact and discretion, lack of squeamishness about sex, and trustworthiness, candidates needed to possess educational credentials that would enhance the ISR's reputation. Finally, he or she must be compatible with Kinsey's existing team of researchers. Using these criteria, he had hired an inner circle of interviewers—Clyde Martin, Wardell Pomeroy, and Paul Gebhard—and others in support roles. As he pondered the appointment of a librarian in late 1947, Kinsey hoped that he could recruit someone whose credentials would strengthen the ISR's chances of successful grant applications.

Jeannette qualified in all of Kinsey's categories: as one of the first women in the nation to earn a PhD in library science, she had a solid grounding in the sciences as well as the arts; she seemed to be a discreet lesbian; she came from a cultured family and appeared highly respectable;

and she had a genuine enthusiasm for the study of sexuality, as evidenced in her efforts to compile a bibliography of lesbians in literature. The only negative, as far as he could determine, was the fact that she had undergone psychoanalysis in her early twenties. Kinsey had a very low opinion of psychoanalysis and was sharply critical of Freud because his model for "normal" development made heterosexuality the goal.[19]

In an initial letter describing the position to Jeannette, Kinsey explained that he sought a doctorally prepared librarian with tact and sensitivity. "Two-thirds of the books in our library," he stressed, "cannot legally be circulated, and there would be public disapproval if they knew of the material we have accumulated." The collection numbered approximately three thousand volumes and Kinsey doubted there was another "sex library in the country which surpasses it" unless it existed within the Library of Congress. "In addition to the scientific books," he explained, the ISR "has a unique collection of rare, and in many cases, original art materials, a fine selection of erotic fiction, a great many very old books . . . a most interesting collection of art materials, particularly in Japanese and Chinese art." Jeannette, who had studied at the Art Institute of Chicago during her youth, assured him that she felt comfortable with that medium, too.[20]

The possibility of a new position came at a welcome time for Jeannette, now in her eleventh year at Drexel. For several years she had felt restless, hoping to return to the South or at least to find a position more suited to her credentials and one that paid more. She had mined most of the libraries in the northeastern United States for sex variant literature, and knew that she would need to look elsewhere if she wished to find more. Leaving library education and taking a position with Alfred Kinsey, however, would in all likelihood mean that some doors would be closed to her in the future because of the controversy surrounding his research. Prior to 1948, she had compartmentalized her life, for the most part keeping her research on sex variant literature separate from her career. Now the two would merge. A risk taker, Jeannette welcomed the change because her undergraduate grounding in science, her agnosticism, and her progressive social views had prepared her well. On a personal level, she felt very comfortable with sex, but this job would be the first time that she could openly discuss her research and her sexual identity with colleagues.

Despite her deep interest in becoming a part of Kinsey's team, Jeannette wanted to avoid appearing too eager. When he wrote inviting her to join his staff, she responded that it might be possible "if practical details can be worked out to our mutual satisfaction." She had, after all, recently been promoted to a full professorship at Drexel, paying $4,000 for a nine-month appointment. As soon as she sent this reply, however, Jeannette had "second and third thoughts" and regretted her hesitation. As someone who read prepublication announcements of his forthcoming work in publishers' trade journals, she probably felt exceedingly flattered that he had thought of her as a potential member of his team. The job was, she explained in a subsequent letter to Kinsey, "exactly the work I want to do, that I am almost sorry to have given salary so prominent a place in my recent letter."[21] With that, Kinsey invited her to campus for an interview.

Nestled in the hills of southern Indiana, the campus of eleven thousand students was surrounded by poor farmland and seemed an unlikely site for what soon would become an internationally recognized center for sex research.[22] When Jeannette arrived on January 9, 1948, just three days after the release of *Sexual Behavior in the Human Male*, the campus and community were abuzz with excitement. Throughout the nation newspapers, tabloids, and magazines publicized the time bomb that Kinsey had set off with his work. Jeannette loved the exhilaration and excitement that punctuated her interview, which consisted of intense conversations with Kinsey, tours of the institute and campus, conversations with staff members, and a meeting with university librarian Robert Miller, who coincidentally was one of her classmates at the University of Chicago's Graduate Library School. Kinsey occasionally consulted Miller about library-related questions and wanted his input before making "any final decision about adding her to the staff."[23] By the time she left campus, Jeannette knew that she wanted to be part of this important and nationally recognized research project.

Kinsey wrote to offer Jeannette the position on January 17, the day before sales of *Sexual Behavior in the Human Male* reached forty thousand and went into another printing. In the midst of this postpublication flurry, hiring a librarian might have seemed like a mundane activity, yet Kinsey was determined to move forward with his research and believed that he needed Foster's services: "We think your command of our library problem is exactly the sort of thing we need." Of course, he explained, she would need to learn about the institute's way of doing certain things, but he was confident in her ability. Encouraging her to respond favorably to his offer, he invited her to become a member of "our research staff" at a generous salary of $4,650. Additionally, he proposed that School of Education dean Wendell W. Wright also would recommend her appointment as an associate professor of library science. Kinsey closed by reminding her that the position was "a great opportunity to push the research along by getting further command of these books." Jeannette knew it was a good offer, but she may not have known how well it compared to salaries received by other members of the ISR staff. Paul Gebhard, for instance, had joined the institute just two years earlier at a salary of $4,400 per year.[24]

Replying to Kinsey's offer on January 21, Jeannette began with effusive praise for *Sexual Behavior in the Human Male*, which she had just finished reading. Unable to contain her enthusiasm for the volume, especially the section on the definition of the homosexual, she noted that this was "ground I have beaten over inch by inch, and what you have written says beautifully all that I struggled to get into articulate form last summer. . . . Now I have confirmation from Authority that in my minute area I have been thinking with thoroughness, and that is heartening." As her letter continued, however, it became evident that she had some reservations about accepting the position. They did not stem from any concern about Kinsey's sexual advocacy or the nature of his findings, but rather from a practical streak in her personality. As much as she wanted to work with Kinsey and access to his vast and virtually untapped collection, she expressed concern about leaving a tenured position at Drexel for something less secure. Moreover, she also stood to lose a portion of her retirement annuity if she left Drexel before June 1950. Fortunately, Jeannette had grown to trust Drexel University president James R. Creese enough to confide in him about her research on sex variance and her need to access Kinsey's collections. Working to resolve the problem, Creese developed a plan that involved having a sympathetic physician prepare a letter stating that the demands of the Drexel position had taken too great a toll on her health and that she must find a less-strenuous position. The plan succeeded, and after a month of negotiation between Drexel administration and trustees, Jeannette went on a leave-of-absence from Drexel, accepted Kinsey's position with "utmost enthusiasm," and promised to report to work on August 1.[25]

Because of postwar housing shortages, Jeannette immediately began searching for accommodations, but her request raised eyebrows in campus offices. When completing the housing application form, she requested a three-or four-room apartment for herself and her forty-two-year-old "female housemate (permanent) and co-owner of property elsewhere." At a time when housing priorities stipulated that larger units went to married faculty with children, followed by married faculty without children, it was unprecedented for a single woman to make such a request. Jeannette attracted more attention to herself when she contacted the personnel office to inquire about the possibility of employment for her companion Elizabeth Smithers.[26] The two women may have met through mutual friends, since a number of women from Baltimore had enrolled in the part-time course for working librarians at Drexel.

Shortly after Jeannette's requests arrived on campus, university employees began gossiping about Kinsey's latest hire. This was still a time, Paul Gebhard recalled, when faculty were "supposed to be models for the students." Kinsey needed all of his employees to be above reproach in order to preserve the reputation of the project; therefore, he demanded an explanation. Shocked to learn of the "gossip emanating from the personnel office," Jeannette explained that she had been careful "not to imply any 'ardent interest in seeing that she [Smithers] was taken care of.'" "For the record," Jeannette declared defensively, "Miss Smithers is not among the people involved in the case history you have." Elaborating further, she noted that she had shared apartments with three different women since 1936 "without giving rise to the faintest speculation about personal relations." There should be nothing "intrinsically suspect about two unattached working women establishing a joint household for economy. . . . I have been counting heavily," she continued, "on the comfort of known companionship in adjusting to the new environment, and I shall be deeply disappointed if really baseless gossip destroys that possibility."[27]

Unfortunately, Jeannette had underestimated the campus climate. University president Herman B Wells supported Kinsey's research, but Indiana University's location in conservative southern Indiana meant that it had no openly gay or lesbian faculty members. Kinsey did not want his latest hire to become the first because the appointment of an "out" homosexual not only would draw unwanted attention to the institute but also would raise the specter of bias in research results. Kinsey, who traveled to the East Coast on business, met with Jeannette on June 2 and explained the situation to her in detail. He did not rescind his offer to hire her, but instead encouraged her to reconsider her request. The incident, she admitted to him, served "as a sharp lesson in the strenuous precautions a worker on the project must take to appear above suspicion," but she stood willing to make the sacrifice. Ultimately, Jeannette's desire to work with the institute's sex variant literature triumphed over her feelings for Smithers. Writing to the University housing office two weeks after meeting with Kinsey, she withdrew her initial application and instead applied for a one-room unit. When she moved into her temporary quarters at the Indiana University Union Club in August, Smithers remained behind in Chesapeake, Maryland.[28]

The Institute for Sex Research

When Jeannette reported for work at the Institute for Sex Research in late August 1948, she felt privileged to be in the eye of the storm as people throughout the nation discussed "The Kinsey Report" (as the press dubbed it). As Kinsey biographer James H. Jones has written, the publication of *Sexual Behavior of the Human Male* "precipitated the most intense and high-level dialogue on human sexuality in the nation's history." People everywhere were talking about the book, taking sides on the validity of his findings and methods. Because of the significance of his work and the sheer force of his charismatic personality, Kinsey succeeded in fending off inevitable attacks and preserving monetary support for his research from the National Research Counsel, the Rockefeller Foundation, and Indiana University. Jeannette's adoration of her employer and his recent accomplishment spilled over into the many letters she sent friends and relatives. Many years later her niece Alison, who was eighteen at the time, recalled the sense of pride she felt in having an aunt associated with the great Dr. Kinsey.[29]

At the institute, Jeannette's quarters initially consisted of a large room behind Kinsey's office in Biology Hall. Outfitted with tables, shelves, books, and cases of gall wasps, it provided Kinsey with ready access to his library and the librarian. In order for the staff to socialize with her, Gebhard recalled, they had to pass through Kinsey's office, something "one did not do lightly." Consequently, she was "sealed off for the workday" from most of her coworkers. She essentially was "a non-person" (because of her office's location) until the institute moved to larger quarters in Wylie Hall the spring of 1949. Jeannette, however, did not mind. Taking her work seriously, she enjoyed being left alone to follow her own course—as much as Kinsey would allow—and she was on a mission to discover if she had overlooked any examples of sex variance in literature. On occasion, however, she enjoyed talking one-on-one with Paul Gebhard, for instance, when he came to the library. According to translator Henry Remak, who began working for the ISR

PHOTO 17.　Institute for Sex Research Staff, circa 1950. First row, seated left to right: William Dellenback, Clyde Martin, Paul Gebhard, Wardell Pomeroy, unknown; second row, seated on step, left to right, Jeannette Howard Foster, Hazel Toliver, Hedwig Leser, Jean Brown, Dorothy Collins; standing, far left: Alfred C. Kinsey. The remainder are unidentified. (Courtesy, the Kinsey Institute for Research in Sex, Gender, and Reproduction)

in the early 1950s, the library was a place where one went for conversations of substance.[30]

It did not take long for Jeannette to realize that her new employer ran a tightly controlled operation. He had great difficulty delegating work, and could not refrain from checking on the smallest details. If someone packed material for shipment, he would unpack it to see if it had been packed correctly. At weekly meetings he solicited staff views, but only his prevailed. He knew precisely when employees arrived and left work, and had no hesitation when it came to probing into their lives outside of work. Staff members may have chaffed at Kinsey's controlling ways, yet they put up with them because they were convinced of the work's importance. Many of them good-naturedly followed him on hot summer days when he led a noontime procession to a nearby drugstore for ice cream. Jeannette, however, seldom joined them because she found it "somewhat foolish" to be traipsing along behind him like children with their father. In addition to such excursions, Kinsey enjoyed taking his staff for a Christmas lunch on campus in the Tudor Room. Statistician Dorothy Collins recalled that he viewed himself "in the role of Lord Bountiful," ordering for everyone. He also enjoyed delivering "hampers full of gifts" to his employees on Christmas Eve.[31]

Jeannette was not fazed by the imported pornography that seemed to arrive by the truckload or by the enormous number of anonymous erotic manuscripts sent by donors for Kinsey's library. Since they could not be sorted by author, Jeannette had to organize them by subject matter, an activity that she came to regard as boring but necessary. Anonymous authors didn't waste time, and after perusing the first page or two she knew if they were heterosexual, homosexual, sadistic, or focused on a particular fetish. Constant exposure to printed material, not conversations among staff, desensitized her to sexual slang and terminology. Indeed, Kinsey staff members learned to use a series of abbreviations so they could discuss their work in front of anyone. These included C for coitus, CX for extramarital coitus, H for homosexual, and GO for genital-oral contact.[32]

According to Kinsey staff members Gebhard and Collins, Jeannette quickly learned that "Kinsey had his own weird method of running a library" and in her professional opinion, the result "was haphazard." To an outsider, the process may have seemed inconsequential, but for Jeannette, Kinsey's method would become her breaking point. It was more a matter of will than it was of technique. After buying or receiving books as gifts, Kinsey would thumb through them in a seemingly casual manner, tossing them into one pile or another. Using a self-made pneumonic taxonomic system of approximately twenty-five categories, he expected books on medicine to be classified under M, prostitution under PR, modern fiction under MF, erotic books under

ER, and so forth. Prior to Jeannette's arrival, Kinsey instructed Gebhard to "put a piece of buckram adhesive tape on the back of the spine
down near the bottom" where he then wrote in white ink the category,
a line, and the first three letters of the author's name. Eager to impose
professional order on the collections, Jeannette fought "to persuade
Kinsey to use either the LC [Library of Congress] system or the DDC
[Dewey Decimal Classification] system," but "he would not budge." He
knew how his system worked, and did not want to have to memorize
other categories.[33]

Jeannette also came to know Kinsey as a compulsive collector who
acquired books in a haphazard way. After the publication of the male
volume, the library grew exponentially as he added a wide array of
erotic and pornographic materials, ranging from books to magazines to
artworks. An extremely busy man, Kinsey did not have time to select
books in a systematic manner and instead relied on friends and book
dealers to recommend titles. With royalties from *Sexual Behavior in the
Human Male* surpassing all expectations, he loosened up "quite a bit"
when it came to purchasing materials for the library and unfortunately
some people took advantage of him. Jeannette knew that he could not
read French. Yet when someone said, "Oh, Dr. Kinsey, I've got this list
of erotic French novels put out in the 1700s or 1800s," he would say,
"Okay, I'll buy them." Jeannette disapproved of his practice—not the
content of the books—and did not hesitate to let him know. When the
material arrived at the ISR, she would ask him, "Why did you buy this?"
His efforts to cover up his softness "ticked her off." When he traveled,
Jeannette complained, "Kinsey was reckless about refusing to carry a list
of 'library has' with him, and so acquired a number of DUPS." Ultimately, however, this worked to her advantage because he agreed to sell
her some of the duplicates she desired, including her prized copy of a
work by Louis Perceau. Jeannette was disappointed to learn that Kinsey
did not think there was much point to acquiring fiction; however, she
was able to work through his New York dealers who specialized in works
on sexuality to obtain some difficult to locate items for her personal li-

brary.[34] While at the ISR, she learned that she had not missed anything important in the sexual field.

In early 1949, Indiana University rebuilt the entire basement floor of Wylie Hall, with Kinsey supervising the details of soundproofing, fireproofing, security, and climate control. Upon moving into the new quarters in March, each staff member had a private office, and Jeannette reigned over the eight-thousand-volume library, which occupied a separate kingdom. Seated in a corner alcove, she was surrounded by works of bibliography, biography, psychology, and religion while her assistant's desk stood at the other end of the library, opposite the books on sadomasochism. One entire room contained books about art and artists, while a long hallway contained books on marriage and sex education, modern fiction, physical education, and more. Kinsey took great pride in his library stacks, opening them to invited guests only, but some ISR staff viewed the library as a bunker because wire mesh covered opaque windows and blinds shielded the books from direct light.[35] Jeannette, however, felt more professional in her new surroundings. When Jeannette joined the ISR team, it consisted of Kinsey, the three male members of his inner circle, and several women, among them library assistant Jean Brown and German translator Hedwig Leser. After dropping a bomb on the world and changing the way Americans thought and spoke about sexuality, Kinsey had the funding to more than double the size of his staff. When appointing new female employees, Kinsey sought intelligent women, but he also regarded hiring as a political activity. The appointments of Cornelia Christianson, wife of a senior economics professor, and Dorothy Collins, wife of the dean of faculties, for example, helped cement the relationship between the ISR and the university.[36]

While he could not govern what happened outside the workplace, Kinsey discouraged employees from becoming too friendly with one another. Women in the office, statistician Dorothy Collins recalled, were "not close enough [for their] relations to be good or bad." Generally, she elaborated, staff members did not know what each other did. Initially,

Jeannette felt closest to Paul Gebhard, who had oriented her to the library and with whom she shared a dry wit, observations about women, and frustrations caused by some of Kinsey's decisions. In contrast, she had little respect for Wardell Pomeroy. A psychologist eighteen years her junior, he possessed only an MA to her PhD. Good manners dictated that she treat him respectfully in the workplace, but she was disgusted with him on several counts. First, the scientist in her disapproved of his approach to the work, and his boast that if he was not accurate, he was at least fast. Working in intense bursts, he took frequent breaks for drinks or smokes. Pomeroy also had a "prodigious sexual appetite" for men and women, and as Paul Gebhard noted, his "main goal in life appeared to be sexual conquest." Jeannette was not a prude, and she knew that Kinsey believed that people would lead freer sexual lives if they were not restricted by religious or societal teachings, but she resented Pomeroy's advances for several reasons. She had little patience with most men, whom she considered to be rude and crude. While she liked the frankness with which Kinsey and his team of interviewers discussed sexuality, she disliked Pomeroy's vanity and refused to be coerced.[37]

According to Dorothy Collins, Kinsey was optimistic and cheerful, and tried to visit each staff member at least once a week. Polite and an attentive listener, he made them feel important and appreciated during these sessions. Other ISR staff found Kinsey to be an authoritarian, domineering, and exacting employer with an unsurpassed work ethic. Driven, he was usually the first to arrive at work and the last to leave, often returning in the evening to work past midnight. In exchange for the good salaries he paid them, Kinsey expected his staff to be at his beck and call and he had no qualms about limiting their personal interactions and even the time they took for lunch and restroom breaks. If American business was run the way college faculty handled their jobs, he informed them, "the nation would be bankrupt inside two years." Given the businesslike atmosphere that prevailed at the ISR, Jeannette and the others had little time for personal chitchat and, in her case, opportunity to discuss progress on her book.[38]

Life in Bloomington, Indiana

When Jeannette arrived in Bloomington, alone, she moved into the Indiana Memorial Union, but she soon found more permanent lodging in a nearby rooming house one block west of campus at 416 East Fourth Street, which she transformed into a homey environment with a few pieces of family furniture. Kinsey's librarian lived a relatively closeted life in Bloomington, but "wasn't at all bashful about being gay" when she was around understanding and sexually enlightened people like the institute staff. With her ISR coworkers, for example, she "would make remarks quite freely that would indicate her own orientation." Because she eventually let everyone know, Paul Gebhard reflected, "it made a very comfortable relationship." At times she even joined him in making "comments on the attractiveness of females who happened to be around. . . . She wasn't at all bashful about that," he recalled, although she did occasionally chide him, saying, "You're just interested in a pretty face; you're not interested in personality."[39]

In addition to working assiduously for Kinsey and on her own research and writing, Jeannette remained in contact with friends around the country through regular newsy letters. An enlightened few, like Jennie Gregory, expressed interest in her work with Kinsey and encouraged her research on sex variant women, but most preferred to distance themselves from both topics and to instead focus on shared professional interests and books they had read. Jeannette remained active in the American Library Association and in June 1949 traveled to New York City to deliver the results of her research on the minimum requirements for library schools.[40] Conferences like this, held in large cities, also offered a welcome change from the relatively sheltered environment of southern Indiana. Filling every waking hour, she visited her favorite haunts, reconnected with old friends, and perused bookstores for lesbian literature.

In 1950, Jeannette fell in love once again when Kinsey hired Hazel Toliver as a translator of Latin and Greek. A native of Arkansas, the attractive younger woman had been born in Fayetteville in 1909. An intelligent and industrious scholar, she graduated from high school at sixteen and enrolled at the University of Arkansas, where she earned a bachelor's degree in 1929. Hazel taught high school students for several years in her native state before returning to the University of Arkansas for a master's degree, which she earned in 1933. Returning to the high school classroom, she saved money and in 1942 moved with her mother to Iowa City to begin doctoral study in the classics. She completed her dissertation, "The Theater as a Force in Roman Society," in 1945, the same year she joined the faculty of Indiana University. After years of hard work to achieve her goal, she envisioned spending the rest of her life in scholarly pursuits.[41]

For five years Hazel had struggled to carve out a career for herself in a male-dominated field, but by 1950 it had become clear that she never would advance from instructor to a regular faculty position, at least not at Indiana University. When Kinsey offered her a position, she decided to make the change even though it meant translating Latin texts to provide him with evidence of the sexual crimes Catholic confessors elicited from their penitents. After joining the ISR staff, she confirmed his suspicion that earlier translators had omitted controversial passages in order to appease church censors. "The only way to really get the truth," she assured him, was "to get [the] original sources." After she promised to provide uncensored translations, Kinsey purchased an entire series of approximately one hundred classical books in Greek and Latin for her use.[42]

Hazel and Jeannette "became fast friends" soon after she joined the ISR staff. Thin, of medium-height, with a dark complexion, she wore her brown hair pulled into a bun at the nape of her neck. From the beginning Jeannette admired Hazel's wit, intellectual curiosity, and passion for scholarship. As they became friends, she learned that Hazel lived with her mother in a nearby apartment and had been her mother's primary source of support since her twenty-first birthday. Cantankerous and caustic, Myrtle Toliver claimed to be a widow for appearance's sake, but in reality her husband had left the family before Hazel's tenth birthday.[43] Jeannette found it easy to converse with Hazel about the classics (since two of her previous loves had been specialists in that field), books, and music. Taking lunches together and sharing long walks in the evenings, the two women grew close. "I got the impression," Gebhard explained, "that it was a sexual relationship," but "they were completely closeted, which I think they wanted, and Kinsey wanted." As Jeannette soon realized, however, Hazel was "much less highly sexed" than she was.[44] Over the course of the next three decades with Hazel, however, Jeannette would find the peace and contentment that had eluded her for so many years.

Discontent and Disillusionment

Jeannette believed wholeheartedly in the value of Kinsey's research, but several aspects of her work at the ISR fueled her growing dislike of the man. Persuasive and flattering, he had led her to believe that he respected and valued her scientific background and knowledge of sexual variance. Once she became his employee, however, she realized that he was a micromanager as well as a workaholic. He boasted of Jeannette's doctoral training to visitors but, in her opinion, made her handle his library as if she "had never had one hour of either training or experience." He refused to give her free reign in organizing the library according to a commonly accepted system like Library of Congress classification. Enlisting Gebhard on her side, she attempted "to get Kinsey to loosen up a bit [about using a standard cataloging system]" but never succeeded.[45]

Kinsey's benevolent dictatorship became another source of vexation for the fiercely independent librarian who found it difficult to submit to his controlling ways. He sought the best-educated people he could find for ISR positions, but refused to let them work autonomously. Accustomed to setting her own schedule as a faculty member, Jeannette chafed at Kinsey's dictatorial demands. "We . . . had no coffee break, we

didn't have a full hour for lunch, and whenever he called us in for special work, we showed up for it." "He snapped the whip," she continued,
and if visitors unexpectedly came at night, "he wanted his librarian
there to show off his library" and to serve refreshments. It was not uncommon for Jeannette to be working in her office "and all of a sudden
the door would fly open and here would be Kinsey with people peering
over his shoulder as he announced: "This is Jeannette Foster, our librarian, who is the first woman to get a PhD in library science." His statement, of course, was incorrect because she was not the first female to
graduate from the Graduate Library School with a doctorate. In short
order, she began to feel like an animal in the zoo. Jeannette had taken
the position expecting to be treated as a professional colleague because
of her PhD, but "the sense of hierarchy was always there." She was not
alone in this sentiment. Pomeroy, reflecting on his years with Kinsey,
compared himself and Gebhard to "workhorses, harnessed to the project
under Kinsey's direction."[46]

As a poet, writer, and scholar, Jeannette fumed when Kinsey limited
her interaction with institute guests, especially those she knew. When
her friend the writer Glenway Wescott arrived to read and evaluate
"some of the library's collection of erotica," Jeannette complained that
Kinsey "was damned set on keeping me among the hired help!" He had
his reasons. In this case, he had recently begun a sexual affair with the
visiting author and did not fully trust him to maintain silence about it.
One day, however, Wescott got into the library without Kinsey's
knowledge and had a "rare old time" with Jeannette discussing mutual
friends like Janet Flanner. On that occasion, she asked him if had ever
considered the possibility of a sexual relationship between Vita
Sackville-West and Virginia Woolf, all part of the world-famous
Bloomsbury group, with its crew of gay male and lesbian writers.
"Goodness, no!" he exclaimed, while promising to ask Harold Nichol-
son and let her know.[47]

Jeannette, who, according to her friend Barbara Grier, disliked most
males (except for gentle and sweet gay men), became outraged when

Kinsey and Wardell Pomeroy made sexual overtures to her. On the Kinsey heterosexual–homosexual scale, Gebhard explained, "0 was totally heterosexual, 6 was totally homosexual and a 3 was both equally, with 1 and 2 and 4 and 5 intermediate at either end." Kinsey, he continued, had evolved from a 1 in his twenties to a 4 by 1946, whereas Jeannette was a 6 and had no interest in the opposite sex.[48] Believing that homosexuality was genetically determined (even though it might be stifled by environmental influences), she felt that Kinsey had treated her "with typical male conceit," thinking "that a sympathetic 'laying on of hands' would cure *that* [her homosexuality]." Kinsey, Gebhard reflected, was "not in dire need for heterosexual expression" at the time Jeannette worked for him, but "there might have been a sexual element in his dealing with her. I can imagine him thinking it would be nice to have another willing female around, but not enough to warrant a big attempt at seduction." Kinsey also may have viewed the attempted seduction as a means of gaining insight into yet another dimension of lesbianism, but once rebuffed he resumed a cordial working relationship with Jeannette. Later, however, she would point to this incident as one of several steps on the path to her disillusionment with the sex researcher.[49]

By 1951, Jeannette had grown restive. She wanted more than anything to publish her book, but believed that Kinsey would never approve because people would associate her work with the institute. Her work there, while interesting, had grown tedious because of Kinsey's refusal to let her exercise professional autonomy. Meanwhile, the quiet and studious Hazel had never stopped yearning for a faculty position and had grown to hate her work at the ISR "like hell." Feeding on each other's discontent, they decided that it was time to leave Bloomington, hopefully together. Meeting Hazel, Jeannette recalled years later, was "the one good thing that came out of the whole four years." That fall, both women began applying for dozens of positions and grants that would enable them to pursue the research and writing they so dearly loved. Jeannette yearned to live once again in the South, but reality dictated that she and Hazel must apply wherever vacancies existed.

After the University of Kansas City (known by locals as KCU, and today as the University of Missouri–Kansas City) offered Hazel a position, Jeannette immediately submitted her name for consideration, too, and was rewarded with an appointment as reference librarian, to begin the following fall.[50] Eager to escape Kinsey's influence, the two women immediately began making plans for their move and the opportunity it provided for them to share a home for the first time.

When Jeannette submitted her resignation, she cited Kinsey's unwillingness to let her use either Library of Congress or Dewey Decimal Classification schemes to organize his library as the reason for her departure. "I can't be a librarian," she explained, because "you don't want a librarian. . . . You can get by with some sort of assistant." This is exactly what he would do after Jeannette's departure, and he would never again appoint a professional librarian.[51] Privately, Jeannette told friends that there were other reasons to exchange this position for a relatively lackluster one paying just two-fifths of her ISR salary. She had gone to Bloomington thinking that she would be an integral part of a team working at the forefront of sex education, but had found herself solely in a support role, and a clerical one at that. A self-assured woman who did not like to be bossed, she also wanted "to get away from him, because he was a 'come hither' boy, he had *charm*, gosh he was a magnetic man, I don't mean that I ever fell for him, but he had personality, the kind that could really get its claws in you. . . . He snapped the whip. I'm telling you, he was a dual personality, if ever there was one."[52] Jeannette thought too highly of herself and her scholarship to remain in such a hierarchical and controlling environment. She could not work for him, yet she respected his work and his efforts to dispel myths about human sexual behavior.

From 1952 until his death four years later, they sustained cordial communication, often initiated by Jeannette. It became her turn to flatter him, giving praise upon the publication of *Sexual Behavior in the Human Female* in 1954. "I expected," she confided, "to quarrel with parts [of the homosexual chapter], as you probably know, but I failed to find a sentence that did not convince me." She also sent him books for the Institute's library, called his attention to newspaper articles about his work, and expressed concern about its toll on his health. "Whatever personal tensions developed in the course of my job there," she wrote Gebhard and Pomeroy after learning of Kinsey's death, "I always believed wholeheartedly in Dr. Kinsey and his work. . . . I have always been sorry I could not make myself over sufficiently to give him more constructive service than I seemed able to do."[53]

When Jeannette first contacted Alfred Kinsey in 1941, she did so admiringly, eager to cultivate a relationship with the eminent sex researcher. Over the next seven years she took great pride in assisting him as he sought interview subjects. While she was not his primary source of lesbian interviews, she nonetheless became a vital conduit to the middle-class educated lesbian population. When Kinsey offered her the position of librarian in 1948, she was flattered to accept his position, offering as it did an opportunity for daily contact with his extensive library and more money than she had ever earned in her life. In an ensuing power struggle, Jeannette realized that she had to sacrifice her lover and live a closeted life if she wished to work for the sex researcher. Kinsey accepted Jeannette's homosexuality, but he clearly did not want it to jeopardize the ISR's standing at Indiana University, nor did he want her book on literary sex variance to be regarded as a sanctioned product of the Institute.

For three decades prior to joining the institute staff, Jeannette's sexual identity had shaped her relationships with others, governed the books she read, dictated her choice of research topics, and determined her career moves. Disillusioned and profoundly disappointed when Kinsey did not live up to her expectations of him, she knew she had to leave the ISR if she ever wished to publish her book. Her initial exhilaration at being part of this pioneering research team yielded to frustration as she attempted to apply her knowledge as a professionally trained librarian. On the other hand, she had gained access to additional sex variant literature and completed research for her pioneering bibliographic study. Like *Sexual Behavior in the Human Female*, which appeared the year after she left the institute, it would shatter myths and misunderstandings about female homosexuality and touch the lives of countless lesbians coming of age in the 1950s and beyond.

Seven

Sex Variant Women in Literature

If variance is to be always with us, calm acceptance of that fact may become as prevalent as the recognition of human evolution has come to be.

— JEANNETTE HOWARD FOSTER,
SEX VARIANT WOMEN IN LITERATURE[1]

In the 1950s homosexuals were condemned by the psychiatric and medical professions as pathological, by religious groups as immoral and sinful, and by the law as criminal. Women and men who had questions about their sexual identity had to brave asking librarians for access to psychological or medical texts about homosexuality in which they found themselves described as deviants. Kinsey's research findings heightened awareness and understanding of homosexuality at the same time that McCarthy and his minions branded homosexuals as a national danger and then attempted to ferret them, along with communists, out of federal positions and the military. Publishers faced censorship if their books contained obvious gay or lesbian content. Called to testify before a House committee that was investigating the proliferation of lurid paperbacks dealing with homosexuality, Ralph Daigh, of Fawcett Publications, defended the publication of Tereska Torres's *Women's Barracks*, the first-ever lesbian pulp novel. That particular book, he explained, sold more than 1.5 million copies because it contributed to the literature of human experience. The public, he pointedly reminded the committee, had become even more curious about such topics than ever before because of such hearings.[2] It was in this climate that Jeannette Foster, who was as obsessed with her research as Kinsey was with his, decided to publish *Sex Variant Women in Literature*.

Other gays and lesbians may have felt isolated and alienated in the 1950s, but Jeannette's high self-esteem and confidence in herself and her work fueled the conviction that a highly regarded press would want to publish the book and that its appearance would generate critical acclaim. From childhood she had been raised to regard her family as socially superior, and over time she had become highly opinionated and somewhat of an intellectual snob. So convinced was Jeannette of the superiority of her scholarship and the merit of her work that she could not imagine anyone finding fault with it, even if they objected to the subject matter. Librarianship also had provided her with an excellent platform from which to work, and in her more than twenty years in the profession, it had proven to be a welcoming field for gays and lesbians.

When it came to publishing a book about sex variance in the wake of the McCarthy era, Jeannette stood stubborn and fearless, guffawing at the idea that such an act could result in censorship or the loss of her job even though more people were losing their positions due to allegations of homosexuality than to accusations of left-wing sympathies. As someone in her early sixties, she had the comfort of being near retirement. Perhaps Jeannette also realized that people in the military or in federal- and state-government positions were far more vulnerable than was a librarian with a grandmotherly appearance. In retrospect, she was correct, and the Federal Bureau of Investigation never even opened a file on her. Jeannette did become furious and frustrated when she encountered obstacles or homophobia, but she refused to act afraid. She was like someone walking in an unsafe neighborhood—assuming that her book belonged in print and moving positively and directly to ensure that it happened.

Before the Stonewall Rebellion in 1969, few publishers risked bringing out works about homosexuality unless they were works of medicine, psychiatry, or pulp fiction in which the lesbian characters had an unhappy outcome. Even though the publication of *Women's Barracks* in 1950 ushered in the golden age of lesbian pulp fiction, writes Katherine V. Forrest, the moral imperative of the era dictated that "for unrepentant lesbian characters who did not convert to heterosexuality, madness, suicide, homicide awaited, or, at best, 'noble' self-sacrifice."[3] As Jeannette knew from her earlier experience, gays and lesbians found minimal satisfaction when they turned to printed works for evidence of their identity. Seeking to remedy this void, she boldly and proudly self-published *Sex Variant Women in Literature* under her own name in 1956. The first book to systematically analyze lesbian authors and themes, it struck a chord with countless readers because it affirmed that lesbians had been part of the human experience since the beginning of recorded literature. As she had anticipated, it offered an important counteractive to some of the religious taboos and psychiatric beliefs used to condemn homosexuality in mid-twentieth-century America.

Life after Kinsey

After leaving the Institute for Sex Research in the summer of 1952, Jeannette moved to Kansas City, Missouri, with Hazel Toliver. Purchasing their first home together, a small duplex within walking distance of the campus, they set up housekeeping with Hazel's mother. It was a very ordinary two-story under-over duplex with a steep and narrow staircase that led from the main floor to a loftlike second floor. At first glance, the second level appeared to be all books because of floor to ceiling bookshelves on three sides. A cozy space, it included a tiny kitchen, sitting space, and small bedroom. Hazel shared the downstairs unit—two bedrooms, a kitchen, tiny dining area, and bath—with her mother while Jeannette lived upstairs.[4] After years of living in college dormitories and boardinghouses, the two women were thrilled to have a home of their own.

Jeannette's relationship with Hazel defied definition and was unlike any she previously had experienced. Their strong emotional bond and intellectual compatibility made them excellent partners for one another, yet their physical relationship never fulfilled Jeannette's expectations. Hazel, who struggled with her sexual identity, had for the most part succeeded in repressing her physical desires. She was, Jeannette later recalled, never fully comfortable in her body or with her sexuality.[5] Jeannette, on the other hand, had grown up with a healthier sense of self and a scientifically grounded understanding of her sexual urges. She felt comfortable expressing herself verbally and physically. After experiencing unrequited love and a series of casual relationships, Jeannette overlooked Hazel's relative disinterest in sex because of the cherished companionship and stability she had found with her. As her actions during the course of the 1950s and 1960s would demonstrate, she cared very deeply for Hazel and wanted her to be happy.

Jeannette and Hazel began their respective positions at the University of Kansas City (hereafter KCU) in September 1952. Hazel was thrilled to have a full-time position as an assistant professor of classics and history, but feared that association with the controversial Kinsey research project might tarnish her reputation. Keenly aware of the gradual decline in classics programs, she responded to a question about her previous employment somewhat dismissively, noting that she had been a translator on a nameless Indiana University research project.[6] Jeannette, who felt less vulnerable than Hazel, took great pride in her affiliation with the noted sex researcher. Beginning her position as reference and interlibrary loan librarian with characteristic gusto, she in short order became "the great cajoler, coercer, and arbiter" in the travails of KCU graduate students. She also found time to join the University of Kansas City Book Club and to participate in area library meetings. In 1954 she became a regular contributor to an in-house publication known as the *Library Memo*.[7]

Kenneth J. LaBudde served as director of the KCU library and was an active scholar specializing in American studies. Jeannette and LaBudde, whom she believed to be a closeted gay man, were not close but developed a good working relationship during her eight years on the library staff. Both midwesterners, they had lived in Minnesota, although at different times. LaBudde had a genuine respect for Jeannette's research even though she enjoyed needling him whenever an opportunity arose.[8] Her appointment as reference librarian, however, posed a problem for him because in 1952 the professional staff of the library did not have faculty status. When Jeannette signed her initial appointment letter she had been given the rank of instructor in library science because the previous librarian had held that rank, and faculty status in recognition of her previous experience and academic preparation. While this rank was significantly lower than the full professor status she had held at Drexel, it nonetheless placed her on equal footing with teaching faculty. When the university administration sent her a contract for the 1953–1954 academic year, Jeannette discovered that it dropped all references to her position as an instructor and eliminated any reference to faculty status. Upon inquiring, LaBudde learned that KCU president Clarence Decker had struck out this clause without either of their knowledge and declared that "there was no such thing as faculty status for the professional librarians other than the director or the law librarian."[9] Taking a stand in support of her reappointment on the original terms, LaBudde encouraged the administration to grant Dr. Foster full faculty status, but without success.

During their first year at KCU, Hazel and Jeannette soon settled into a routine, but Hazel became restless because she had to teach in two departments when all she wanted to do was to specialize in her beloved classics. Devoting her spare time to reading and research, she made a concerted effort to remain professionally active. In addition to publishing various aspects of her research on the social influence of theater on Roman society, she attended conferences and delivered papers.

She also yearned to study abroad, and in the summer of 1954, Jeannette helped make this dream a reality. Leaving her mother in Jeannette's capable care, Hazel spent two and one-half glorious months traveling in England, Switzerland, Greece, and Italy. In addition to taking a cruise on the Aegean Sea, she stopped in Turkey and visited the ancient ruins of Troy as well as ruins of the Roman and Greek theaters that had for so long been the object of her research. When she returned to Kansas City, Missouri, her discontent with the KCU position increased because she had seen the world. As she explained to Alfred Kinsey in 1954, "I teach some courses outside my own field, and they have required a great deal of reading and preparation, leaving me comparatively little free time." Her goal, she explained, was to "one day be teaching entirely" in her field.[10]

Hazel's search for a more fulfilling position yielded results in the fall of 1955 when Northeast Missouri State Teachers' College, in Kirksville, offered her an appointment as associate professor of Latin. Jeannette, only five years away from retirement, concluded that it was not practical for her to make another move, so they struck a compromise. Hazel accepted the position and Jeannette remained behind in Kansas City to care for Hazel's mother, temperamental to begin with, but increasingly suffering from dementia. Jeannette's willingness to care for Myrtle Toliver was truly an act of love, Barbara Grier recalled, because it was like "caring for a rattlesnake." For the next two years Hazel commuted the nearly two-hundred-mile distance to Kansas City for monthly visits and when their schedules permitted the two women traveled together to professional conferences and spent summer vacations together.[11] Unfortunately, the Kirksville position also proved to be a disappointment, and in the fall of 1957 Hazel accepted a position as an associate professor of classics at Lindenwood College. The private women's school, located in St. Charles, Missouri, was nearly 230 miles from Kansas City, but Hazel promised that she would continue to make regular visits.

Researching and Writing the Opus

For at least two decades, Jeannette's search for literary works with sex variant content consumed her evenings, weekends, and vacations. Not only did
it require courage to undertake such a bold and controversial research topic
without suffering from profound self-consciousness, but also, it was an extremely ambitious project for the era. No one had previously attempted to
identify the writers from any period whose works contained any lesbian
content or characters. If published, their work was basically unknown, if
unpublished it was almost completely forgotten. Given the homophobia so
prevalent for centuries, earlier lesbian writers had concealed their work by
using coded language or by relying on gender neutral language to describe
relationships between women. Some of the writers obliterated their works,
while other works suffered in the hands of translators, editors, and publishers who sought to remove lesbian allusions from print.[12]

In true scholarly fashion, Jeannette had systematically combed
through each issue of *Publishers' Weekly* and *Cumulative Book Index*
looking for likely soon-to-be released titles. She also had consulted the
union catalogs from the Library of Congress, the Philadelphia Bibliographic Center, and the U.S. Surgeon General's Library to establish
which libraries owned the medical, psychiatric, and literary texts she
suspected of having homosexual content. Once she determined that an
author had written a book with a lesbian theme, she scoured all of the
works written by that author, searching for additional content. In her
thoroughness, she also examined subsequent editions or translations of
books, sometimes discovering that lesbian themes had been expurgated
in the later publications.[13]

Using her credentials as a librarian, her vast professional and personal
network, and her social skills to advantage, she tracked down elusive titles in libraries across the nation. At a time when anyone who seemed interested in anything sexual, let alone lesbian or gay, could be considered
a pervert, she disarmed librarians with her appearance, which resembled

a prim maiden aunt or grandmother. Until she knew whether or not a librarian was supportive, she proceeded cautiously. A well-bred woman, she could be tight-lipped when it was the smart thing to do, and carefree once she learned that it did not matter. After years of working in libraries, she knew that interlibrary loan personnel looked personally at all requests, and she did not want to jeopardize her access to that invaluable service. On numerous occasions, she made the acquaintance of supportive librarians who gave her access to little-known or hard-to-locate titles such as Catulle Mendès's *Méphistophéla*.

Liberal-minded professional colleagues and friends also helped Jeannette by negotiating interlibrary loans, adding "chance-encountered titles" to her list, and providing encouragement even when they had "no basic interest in the subject."[14] A few longtime friends like Jennie Gregory knew of her project, but she kept it separate and private when corresponding with many others, especially those who were fearful about being linked to homosexuality. Obsessed with her project, Jeannette willingly made the book her highest priority, sacrificing opportunities to develop close friendships. Ultimately, Hazel, who she met after a first draft of the book had been written, proved to be her most steadfast supporter. Hazel proofed everything that Jeannette wrote and offered her critique. As a scholar in her own right, she had great respect for Jeannette's research, appreciated the frustration she felt when trying to find a publisher for the book, and took great joy in seeing the final product. Jeannette deeply appreciated Hazel's input, but circumspectly did not mention her name, or indeed that of anyone else, in the book's acknowledgments section.

In her lifetime, Jeannette lived, worked, and studied in seventeen states, and spent extended periods in several of the nation's largest cities and publishing centers, where she scoured the shelves of bookstores and libraries in search of works containing references to lesbians or homosexuality. Several of her career moves were calculated to gain access to collections containing elusive works on sex variance. Indeed, Karla Jay once humorously proclaimed in a biographical essay about Jeannette,

"Her dedication was so great that had the only sexual library been the Pope's . . . she would have become a nun to gain access to it (or perhaps disguised herself as a monk since it is doubtful whether nuns are admitted to this collection)!"[15]

When she began her project, Jeannette planned to include only works that she had examined firsthand, but this proved to be impossible due to cataloging obscurities, inaccessible or lost material, and closed collections. Her quest took her to many college and university libraries, with the most fruitful collections being housed at Chicago, Emory, Indiana, Pennsylvania, Princeton, Yale, Bryn Mawr, and Swarthmore. Not surprisingly, she rated the public libraries of Chicago, Philadelphia, and New York City highly, and whenever she was in Washington, D.C., she frequented the Library of Congress. She found the libraries of Emory University Hospital, the New York Academy of Medicine, and the Philadelphia College of Physicians conducive to her search for medical texts. By 1948, when she joined the staff of the Institute for Sex Research, she claimed to have seen, by her own calculations, 96 percent of all titles that would be included in her book. The years Jeannette spent at the ISR, she explained, were especially valuable because they assured her that she "had overlooked no major area of writing on sex variance."[16]

Writing in the evening, on weekends, and during summers, Jeannette completed at least three hundred typewritten pages, which she would have shared with Hazel, by 1951. Initially she had envisioned an annotated bibliography, but she had so much insight into the authors and their books that it became a narrative work. Needing a block of time in which she could finish the manuscript and polish the narrative, she searched for grant funding and in October 1951 decided to apply for one of the prestigious fellowships awarded each year by the Guggenheim foundation to productive scholars and people with exceptional creative ability. If Jeannette had scanned a list of recipients, she would have observed that the awards tended to go to distinguished physicists, chemists, historians, sculptors, and novelists, most of them male.[17] Undaunted by the odds, she asked Drexel Institute President James R. Creese for a letter of reference, assuring him that "the survey neither pleads a cause nor pretends to many original conclusions." As if to prove her point, she noted that she had read several hundred scientific and psychological books and articles on sex variance in preparation for writing her book which, she stressed, was to be a dispassionate, scholarly, and historical overview. In his letter to Henry Allen Moe of the John Simon Guggenheim Foundation, Creese endorsed Jeannette's "keen judgment" and scholarly habits, noting that she was "a person of high standing in the library profession whose knowledge of library aids and techniques and whose judgment of books may be trusted." Creese was more cautious when discussing the subject of her research, noting that he had no means of appraising its value, only the fact that she would do it "honestly, with understanding, and in the spirit of careful scholarship."[18] Neither Creese nor Jeannette were surprised when her application proved unsuccessful in a year that saw awards going to such individuals as the political philosopher Hannah Arendt, poet Adrienne Rich, and historian Kenneth Stampp. Nevertheless, the very act of applying for the fellowship confirms Jeannette's determination to establish gay and lesbian research as a valid field of humanities scholarship. Unlike Edward Sagarin, who under the pseudonym Donald Webster Cory had published *The Homosexual in America: A Subjective Approach* (1951), she had taken the first step in boldly linking her name to the nascent field of gay and lesbian research.

Without the fellowship, it took Jeannette another three years to complete and revise the manuscript. In the spring of 1954 as she began putting the finishing touches on *Sex Variant Women in Literature* (which she referred to as her opus), she reflected on the path that had brought her to this point. Her search for the fiction, drama, and poetry that would fill its pages had begun when at the age of thirteen she had discovered Constance DuBois's "Lass of the Silver Sword." From that time forward, she had been on the lookout for more examples of same-sex love in literature, but initially this response had been instinctual rather than intentional: she simply sought confirmation that she was not alone in her love of women. As she had discovered, she was one of many lesbians, but she was virtually alone as a lesbian scholar.

In March 1954, the death of her beloved friend and mentor Miriam Tompkins gave Jeannette an added incentive to see her work in print. Only sixty-one years old, Miriam had opened many doors for her protégée by encouraging her to pursue a doctorate and influencing her interest in adult education and the study of readership.[19] As a library-school professor, she had instructed Jeannette in the compilation of annotated bibliographies, the format Jeannette initially used to organize her research for the book. Miriam also served as a sounding board and provided much-needed encouragement during the many years Jeannette spent compiling her findings. Eager to commemorate Tompkins' life, she chaired the committee of Emory University alumni that established a memorial in Tompkins' honor. Pausing to reflect on her friend's relatively short life, fifty-nine-year-old Jeannette felt an increased urgency to get her opus into the hands of readers who were searching for validation and support of their sexuality in print. Time was of the essence.

When it came time to select a title for the book, Jeannette "worked awfully hard" to find one that would begin with the word *sex* because she had learned from searching of bibliographies "that a title beginning with Sex couldn't be ignored." After mulling over prospective terminology for the book's title, she rejected the term *lesbian* (which she defined as a female who was sexually active with members of her own sex) because she wanted to include women whose emotional relations with other women "have all the intensity of physical passion." She also eliminated the term *homosexual* from consideration because she believed it was "most often applied to men," and the term *gay* as being too politically and emotionally charged. Settling on *Sex Variant Women in Literature* as the title for her book, she reasoned that the term *sex variant* was "not as yet rigidly defined nor charged with controversial overtones" as the terms she had discarded.[20] In his 1941 work, *Sex Variants: A Study of Homosexual Patterns*, psychiatrist George W. Henry had defined the sex variant as someone having emotional experience with others of his or her own sex. Based on personal experience and her reading, Jeannette concurred that passionate emotion played a more dominant role in women's lives than in men's. As a librarian, she was aware that the Library of Congress would assign a subject heading of sex deviate to such a work, but Jeannette hoped her use of the word "variant" would help in destigmatizing women who chose to live as bisexuals, cross dressers, and lesbians (women who had explicitly erotic relations with other women).[21]

Searching for a Publisher

Before she left Philadelphia in 1948, Jeannette had consulted three commercial presses in New York about the prospects for publishing her opus. George P. Brockway, of W. W. Norton & Company, proved to be the most sympathetic but warned her that "it might be hard to get it taken seriously" because her doctorate was in neither psychology nor psychiatry. When she finally completed the manuscript in June 1954, Jeannette sent him the introduction, conclusion, and an outline of the text, asking if he was interested in seeing the entire manuscript. A lot had happened in the intervening years: Kinsey's publications, the Beats, the homoeroticism in the work of Tennessee Williams and Gore Vidal, the increased visibility of lesbian pulps by writers like Valerie Taylor and Ann Bannon, and the formation of lesbian and gay organizations like the Daughters of Bilitis and Mattachine. Despite being in the midst of the Cold War era, it seemed that there had never been a better time to publish a book like Jeannette's, yet Brockway "answered most kindly that he was not [interested]" because such a book "did not promise to be profitable enough for a good commercial risk." Jeannette's rich vocabulary, complex sentence structure, assumption of the reader's prior knowledge, refusal to provide translations of French and German terms, and verbose style, compounded by her academic approach to the subject, resulted in dense prose. Readers who expected to be entertained found otherwise when they read such passages as:

> In the extravagance of the plot and the description of the hero, which oc-
> cupies a good quarter of the tale, one might suspect satire upon the Byro-
> nism which was sweeping Europe, except for the romantic seriousness of
> the whole. Another long interpolated essay is an arraignment, mordant in
> brilliance, of the cruelty, stupidity, and license of Parisian life, in which one
> detects echoes from Rousseau: in such an 'unnatural' milieu excesses of evil
> are only to be expected.[22]

Such prose, Brockway suggested, was "exactly the sort of thing that university presses were designed to put out" and she would be wise to place it with "the best of them."[23]

Wasting no time, Jeannette mailed a prospectus for the book to several (she claims the number was six or seven) university presses, among them the University of Chicago Press, who rejected it, claiming—as she anticipated—that "it was in a field they had never entered and didn't anticipate entering." Jeannette chose other presses based on works they had published. She approached Columbia University Press because its King's Crown imprint had published Dorothy Yost Deegan's *Stereotype of the Single Woman in American Novels* (1951). Their response, however, was that "it was an expansion of a dissertation written there, and was rather outside any field they intended to push." She briefly considered Oxford University Press because it had recently issued a second edition of Mario Praz's *The Romantic Agony* (1951), which discussed erotic aspects of Romanticism, but decided against it because "all their authors seem internationally known." With the exception of the University of Florida Press, any other presses that she sent a prospectus to remain unidentified, but the results were all the same: her work was deemed well written but not suitable for their lists.[24]

Jeannette next contacted Rutgers University Press, because it had published Roy Basler's *Sex, Symbolism and Psychology in Literature* in

1952, and acting director Alan E. James "rose to the bait." According to her account of this episode, written in 1957 when her memory was still fresh, she submitted her complete manuscript to Rutgers in July 1954. If this is accurate, that means that she had received minimal consideration and indeed prompt rejections from the other presses, and that she most likely submitted prospectuses for the book to them simultaneously. According to Jeannette, Rutgers sent the manuscript out for review by literary and psychiatric experts, and by February 1955 had received favorable opinions from Rutgers professor of psychology Morgan Upton and Basler, an expert on U.S. history and literature who also had a good grasp of French and German. "I thought we were all set," she explained.[25]

Unfortunately, James stepped down from his post in December 1954, and his replacement, William Sloane, was less inclined to publish the book. On March 8, 1955, at his first meeting with the University Press Council, *Sex Variant Women in Literature* was rejected. In Jeannette's opinion, Sloane and the Council viewed Basler's volume as an aberration on their list, "and his and mine weren't a line *they* anticipated developing."[26] When weeks passed and Rutgers had not returned her manuscript, Jeannette traveled by train to New Brunswick, only to discover that an assistant, a woman who lived on the outskirts of the Village, had found it of immense interest and was circulating it among her friends.[27] At that point, Jeannette knew she would have a market for the book if she could only find a publisher.

Subsidy Publishing

Discouraged, yet determined to see her work in print, Jeannette turned to subsidy publishing, or what is today known as the vanity press. She knew that such presses had questionable reputations, in part because they were flooded with material from "perverts [her phrasing] who hoped at last to get their stuff [pornography] published," but could be valid outlets for works of limited appeal. Perhaps she ran across David

K. Dempsey's article in the July 1955 *Harper's Magazine*. Entitled "How to Get Published, More or Less," it advised authors to think twice before turning to a subsidy publisher. Jeannette evidently decided there was no other choice. Even though the quality of subsidy books had improved thanks to the efforts of Edward Uhlan, founder of Exposition Press in 1936, she chose not to send her book there because he was Jewish and she narrow-mindedly believed that he would automatically reject it because there was "nobody as biblically opposed to homosexuality as the Jews, and the Orthodox Jews."[28]

After reviewing the output of several other subsidy presses, Jeannette decided to try Pageant Press. According to Judith Serebnick, who worked as a clerk-typist for Pageant in 1953, the press had published one homosexual novel that year and it was selling so well that runners repeatedly had to deliver more copies to bookstores. Jeannette claimed that she considered Pageant because "I liked the physical style of a few things I'd seen from there." The editor received her manuscript enthusiastically, she recalled, "And no wonder! Sure they'd publish, it was an impressive volume and blah-blah-blah," but she would need to pay $6,200, considerably more than a year's salary. "Sez I," Foster later said, "Not today, thanks."[29]

Next, Jeannette turned to Vantage Press, with offices at 120 West Thirty-first Street in New York City. Jeannette's research in *Publishers' Weekly* revealed that in 1954 it stood seventh among the largest American publishers, following such firms as Doubleday, Macmillan, and Harper. It had grown steadily in the past three years, eclipsing both Exposition Press and Pageant Press in annual output. By her reasoning, Vantage could therefore afford less profit on each item. Upon inquiry, she learned that their charges would be $4,450, approximately two-thirds of Pageant's fee.[30] So determined was she to publish the book that she decided to withdraw the sum from her meager savings account. After reviewing a lengthy contract with the minutest care and questioning several points, she felt satisfied with the editor's answers and signed a contract in February 1956. In retrospect, she would regret her choice.

Jeannette's first headache with Vantage occurred shortly after signing the contract when representatives of the press asked her "for an enormous list of persons and libraries" that she thought would be good sales prospects. Alarmed that Vantage might try to exploit her connection with Dr. Kinsey and the ISR for advertising purposes, she pestered the publisher until someone gave her an agreement in writing that Vantage would not exploit her connections. Jeannette's primary worry when it came to Kinsey was that he would not like an obviously lesbian title linked to the Institute. Seeking additional reassurance that Kinsey would not sue her or obstruct publication, Jeannette next turned to his legal counsel, Harriet Pilpel. The two women had met when Pilpel, legal counsel for the Planned Parenthood Federation of America and a senior partner in the law firm of Greenbaum, Wolff and Ernest, had visited the Institute for Sex Research on business.[31] Drawing conclusions similar to those she had made about Uhlan, Jeannette avoided any references to sex variance, homosexuality, or lesbianism when she wrote on January 30, 1956. "When Dr. Kinsey hired me," she explained, "I had been for twenty years accumulating examples in fiction, drama and poetry of certain phases of feminine sex experience." Dr. Kinsey, she continued, knew of her intention to publish and "warned me that if anyone used a connection with the Institute to advertise my work, author and publisher would be prosecuted." Jeannette wanted it known that she had gathered most of the material for her book prior to joining the ISR. As if to prove her integrity, she explained that she had omitted "a number of items—especially in the 'galant' field [French amorous literature]—of which I had never heard before I came to the Institute," from the manuscript. The few titles she had read at the ISR, she rationalized, were books she could have consulted at other libraries or obtained through interlibrary loan, had she taken the time.[32]

Pilpel did not hesitate to forward Jeannette's letter to Kinsey, even though Jeannette had expressly requested that it be kept confidential. After reviewing the matter with his inner circle, he concluded that Dr.

Foster was "unnecessarily disturbed over possibility of difficulty. We went a good deal further than she seems to have grasped," he explained, "in assuring her that we had respect for her scholarship and that we thought a book of the sort she was writing would be of value . . . provided it was made clear that it was not a product of the Institute staff's thinking." The one thing Kinsey wanted Jeannette to clarify in her acknowledgments was that any bona fide scholar would have had access to the materials she consulted. She never had, he stressed, "access to any material that was confidential nor to material connected with the histories of persons who were subjects in our study." In conclusion, Kinsey reiterated that his main concern all along was to keep the publisher from exploiting Dr. Foster's connection to the Institute for sensational purposes. If that could not be done, he concluded, he would "simply have to let the press understand that this book is no more a product of the Institute's research than a number of other things where scholars from other places have come in and utilized our library."[33]

Jeannette had another reason for being nervous about Kinsey's response to the forthcoming publication of her book: George W. Henry, a man for whom he had great disdain, had written the preface. Believing that the book would do better "when it comes to college sales and all that" if she had a specialist validate its contents, Jeannette had considered asking one of her female friends—"one a psychoanalyst [Phyllis Greenacre], one a psychiatrist, and the third a specialist in women's cases [probably her physician and friend Dr. Ella Roberts], but two are unmarried and the third divorced, and I wasn't willing to ask them to lend their names to exactly this sort of volume." Greenacre pooh-poohed Jeannette's choice of Dr. Henry, dismissing him as "an old fuddy duddy, pretty much an old woman in pants." Jeannette understood the basis for her friend Phyllis's criticism, but at the same time appreciated several things about Henry's work. "I've never thought quite so poorly [of Henry] as you-all do," she wrote Paul Gebhard, "though I know he's no intellectual giant." To the world at large, she explained, "he *is* one of the living 'specialists' on homosexuality."[34]

In order to understand Henry's reputation, it is helpful to begin with the 1934 publication of sex researcher Robert L. Dickinson and Lura Beam's *The Single Woman: A Medical Study in Sex Education* (1934). This work included a candid and nonjudgmental analysis of homosexuality and attracted the attention of a lesbian activist named Jan Gay. Born Helen Reitman, the daughter of anarchist and birth-control advocate Ben Reitman had begun conducting interviews with lesbians after she visited Magnus Hirschfeld's Institute for Sexual Science in the 1920s and learned how to conduct sexuality surveys. Unable to publish the findings from her three hundred interviews because she lacked the necessary medical and scientific training to make her work credible, she joined forces with sex researcher Thomas Painter, and then with Dickinson, who organized the Committee for the Study of Sex Variants in 1935 to supervise and fund their research.[35]

George W. Henry was one of the nineteen medical and scientific specialists whom Dickinson, in consultation with Gay, recruited for service on the committee. With Gay's assistance in locating subjects, Henry conducted additional interviews with men as well as women and took measurements of genitals in an attempt to demystify homosexuality. Unfortunately, argues the historian Henry W. Minton, Dr. Henry took over her research and "[t]he emancipatory potential of her project as well as her original contribution was thus subverted into a psychiatric treatise on homosexuality." His results reinforced stereotypes of male homosexuals as innately effeminate, artistic, or narcissistic, and suggested that at least one lesbian turned to same-sex love because she was ugly. While he considered homosexuals and lesbians to be "socially maladjusted individuals," he nonetheless viewed them as "the unfortunate targets" of prejudice.[36]

Despite Henry's somewhat contested reputation, Jeannette felt deeply grateful to him for writing a preface to the volume and believed his name would lend an added measure of credibility to the book. On a personal level, she found him to be "an old lamb," who willingly read "the whole 400-odd pages in fuzzy carbon, corrected a point or two . . .

and warned me of one or two passages which might get me sued for libel by deceased authors' surviving relatives." Still, the one comfort she took in Dr. Kinsey's death in 1956 was "that he never saw the volume carrying that preface. It would have seemed to him, I'm afraid, rather like a nose-thumbing gesture."[37]

Jeannette's next publication headache occurred when Vantage sent her galley proofs at an inconvenient time and she found them riddled with errors. The manuscript, she complained, "had evidently been vetted by a number of different readers, one at least of whom was scarcely literate, and had butchered my 'deathless prose' to the point where I wouldn't have the result appear over my name." As someone who had spent years teaching English grammar, and who routinely made penciled corrections in the margins of library books, Jeannette could not rest until she had restored the text to its original prose. When she returned the corrected proofs to Vantage, the staff tallied the cost and informed her that she owed an additional $2,000. If she did not have it on hand, they offered to take it out of her royalties. "It will take quite a few sales to reimburse me for what the thing cost," she noted a month after its publication, "and frankly I'm too much of a realist to expect profit."[38]

According to their agreement, Vantage was obligated to publish her book within 240 days of her signing the contract. As 1956 came to a close without evidence of the book's appearance, Jeannette's frustration reached a boiling point. Vantage insisted that the book had been produced, but she had not yet seen one of the anticipated thirty-five hundred copies. Determined to have the book in hand before year's end, a budget-conscious Jeannette worked with an attorney associated with the KCU law school and they "wrung out one copy, and the news that the volume had been held up by one of Vantage's lawyers, who felt that a number of passages might be considered libelous." Throughout December 1956 and January 1957, Jeannette devoured "tomes on the Law of the Press" and wrote "bitchy letters to dear Mr. Alan Pater [at the press]." Suffering from a variety of stress-related ailments including "ulcers, gall

stones, hemorrhoids, insomnia, skin allergy, and leprosy of the disposi-
tion," she finally breathed a sigh of relief when in February 1957 Vantage
Press finally released *Sex Variant Women in Literature: A Historical and
Quantitative Survey* for sale.[39]

In *Sex Variant Women in Literature*, Jeannette undertook the Herculean task of summarizing approximately twenty-six hundred years
(from 600 BCE to the early 1950s) of literary portrayals of female sex
variants, whom she defined as lesbians, bisexuals, and transsexuals. Geographically, her study included examples from English, American,
French, German, Italian, Russian, Spanish, and Portuguese literature,
with the emphasis on works in English, French, and German, the languages she read fluently. Practicality forced her to limit her research to
areas where she personally had sufficient knowledge. Hazel provided assistance with ancient literature, especially Greek and Latin, but without
help from someone knowledgeable in Arabic or oriental languages, Jeannette had to impose limits on the book's scope. Years later, subsequent
generations of scholars would begin to fill this void.[40]

More than a listing of titles with lesbian themes and images, her narrative included plot summaries, critical analysis, and relevant historical
data for each text and biographical information for each of the authors—
both famous and lesser known. Filling her accounts full of passion and
adventure, she told stories of female authors like the Brontë sisters, Margaret Fuller, Emily Dickinson, and Katherine Mansfield, and explored
lesbian themes in the work of such male writers as Henry James, Emile
Zola, and Honore de Balzac. She also included such outright lesbian
novels of the twentieth century as Josephine Tey's *To Love and Be Wise*
(1950) and Patricia Highsmith's *The Price of Salt*, written under the
name Claire Morgan. In all, she evaluated an amazing 324 titles, and her
book became the first work of nonfiction to counter the age-long prejudice against sexual variance.

Despite its appearance in the wake of the McCarthy era, Jeannette
claimed that she never experienced censure for its subject matter. Careful readers of her text, however, can see that even though she did not ap-

pear to be concerned about the impact of increased government scrutiny, Jeannette took precautionary efforts to justify variance by grounding her work in the literature of science and psychology, a practice that others continued into the 1970s. Following the publisher's advice, she distanced herself from the subject matter and established her scholarly objectivity by concocting an introduction—partly based on her undergraduate experiences, but largely fictional—explaining how she came to write on the theme of sex variance. "The germ from which this book has grown," she explained, occurred nearly forty years earlier "when a student council voted . . . to dismiss two girls from a college dormitory unless they altered their habits." Portraying herself as a naïve junior council member who did not understand the significance of their infraction, she told of going to the library, where she learned about homosexuality by reading the work of Havelock Ellis. She concluded by hoping that her efforts to shed light on the subject would help others avert "minor tragedy." Years later, when questioned about the veracity of this story, she explained that she had not been on the student council, but had heard about it from a friend. "I'm not sure," she recalled, "that either of us really knew what was involved."[41]

Excluding legal fees, postage, and the unknown cost of her years of research, Jeannette had spent approximately $4,500 of her life savings to get her book into print. Vantage sold nearly eleven hundred copies and then recouped the $2,000 cost of author's corrections (which Jeannette had refused to pay) by selling unbound pages to British publisher Frederick Muller, Ltd., in 1958. Muller brought out a British edition later that year.[42] Ultimately, the only money she received from the 1956 publication of her work was the $240 a secondhand book dealer paid for the twenty-four hundred unsold copies remaining from the original print run. As a money maker, the book was not a success; however, one measure of success is the presence of Jeannette Foster's volume in libraries more than fifty years after its publication: in 2007 the 1956 edition remained available in thirty-five states and three countries outside of the United States, while the 1958 edition is held by libraries in twenty-three states and six other nations, among them the Netherlands, Spain, and South Africa.[43]

Publicity and Reception

A proud author, Jeannette sent a copy of *Sex Variant Women in Literature* to Paul Gebhard and Wardell Pomeroy at the Institute for Sex Research, to be added to the collection, while others undoubtedly went to her longtime friends, Jennie Gregory, Lenore Ward, and Clara Louise Thompson. "I've had phone calls from Georgia and the east coast," she reported, "and at least a dozen students, having got wind of it, are waiting to plunk their $5 at the U. bookstore when the book is in stock."[44] She also sent copies to her sisters, who had mixed reactions. According to Jeannette: "My *own* sister [Helen] & her husband, well established in Ft. Myers, Fla., *probably* wouldn't give a whoop, but I couldn't swear even to that! My sister [Anna] . . . wouldn't have my 1956 opus in her house! But she had kids." By 1957, however, Anna's children would have been adults. According to Jeannette's nephew, Winslow Cope, his mother may have felt unprepared to discuss the book if someone saw it in her home and asked about it, yet later in her life she did keep it on the bookshelves along with everything else, indicating that she was more supportive than Jeannette realized.[45] In 1957, however, Jeannette expected far more praise and recognition for her book than she received. There was no book party or signing, and if it were not for her efforts to alert friends about its publication, they would not have known that it at last was in print.

As a librarian, Jeannette knew how important it was for a book to be reviewed. Even a bad review would be better than no review, because it alerted readers to a book's existence. Eagerly awaiting reviews in national review sources, she was bitterly disappointed and blamed Vantage for failing to promote it: the 1956 edition of *Sex Variant Women in Literature* was never reviewed in the *New York Times* or in other national book review sources. Vantage did run a display add for "Latest Vantage Titles" in the *New York Times* on April 7, 1957, touting the book as "A scholarly study of the sex deviate as she appears in literature from Sappho's day to now."[46] Lacking confidence that Vantage would send review copies to the list of periodicals she had provided, Jeannette took matters into her own hands. Writing to Del Martin and Phyllis Lyon at *The Ladder* (which would not achieve a circulation of seven hundred until the end of the decade), she enclosed a review copy of her book and the Vantage Press broadside. Eager to help his friend publicize her book, Paul Gebhard also wrote to *The Ladder* from the Institute for Sex Research to draw readers' attention "to a book which has recently appeared and which should be of especial interest to you."[47]

Fortunately, the book fared better locally. A favorable mention appeared in the *Kansas City Star*'s book page on March 2, correctly acknowledging the book as "the first of its kind." Praising her narrative as objective and based on more than twenty years of research, the reviewer (who undoubtedly was an academic) also found her prose "brisk and compelling." Even when writing about Renée Vivien, one of the more openly lesbian authors she studied, for example, Jeannette's narrative was anything but brisk. She noted, for instance, that Vivien's "poetry has been pronounced most perfect in form of any French verse written in the first quarter of the century, and this quality is the more remarkable in that her native language was not French but English."[48]

In March 1957, the University of Kansas City "University News" carried a headline proclaiming KCU [Kansas City University] LIBRARIAN AN AUTHOR and another review appeared in the *KCU Campus Newsletter*. Noting the long years Dr. Foster had spent doing research for the book "during those evening, Saturday and vacation hours that scholars alone can find," reviewer Kenneth LaBudde (who may have written the review at Jeannette's prodding) downplayed the book's sex variant content and instead framed it as a study in the "psychology of reading (and writing, for that matter)" and emphasized that it grew out of her "dissertation on classifying fiction by the characteristics of its readers."[49]

The book was not without its critics. Lesbian pulp novel and fantasy writer Marion Zimmer Bradley did not hesitate to dismiss vanity-press books as next to worthless. Writing in *The Ladder*, she declared that "Miss Foster would have done better to keep her manuscript unpublished until it could find a commercial publisher." At a time, she continued, "when any inept scribbler, talentless and aspiring, can have his or her vapid babblings committed to print simply by paying the printer, those who seriously publish their own serious works must of necessity be tarred with the same brush." Bradley, herself a collector and bibliographer of lesbian literature, criticized several aspects of the book. In addition to lacking psychological analysis, she continued, there were some "glaring" omissions. She accused Jeannette of including some unconvincing material, pointing specifically to Jeannette's proofs of Emily Brontë's sex variance and that of the biblical Ruth. Despite these differences of opinion, Bradley recognized the significance of publishing a book about sex variance in the conservative 1950s. "As far as I know," she explained, "except for a few privately circulated leaflets in mimeograph, it is the first work of its kind, and an absolute necessity for those who are interested in the social aspects of Lesbianism." Novelists, she continued knowingly, "played a valuable social role because their works "portray the Lesbian *as she appears in society*, not in the limited portraiture of the psychologist's casebook" which, as lesbians of the 1950s knew, was negative.[50]

Perhaps Bradley had been correct in her critique, and Jeannette should have persisted until a commercial or university press agreed to undertake her project, but after more than two decades of research she knew it was time to disseminate her findings. Just two years earlier, in September 1955, eight women had met in San Francisco over drinks and dinner to found the nation's first lesbian organization, the Daughters of Bilitis (DOB). Emerging in the same climate of hostility and fear that shaped publishers' reactions to *Sex Variant Women in Literature*, the DOB sought to offer a counternarrative to the religious leaders, medical authorities, and political figures who condemned homosexuality and persecuted gay men and women. Like founding members Del Martin and Phyllis Lyon, Jeannette recognized how important it was for isolated lesbians and gay men to find validation for their lives in print. Sending for a membership application several months after her book appeared, she commended their work "toward social acceptance of the homophile" even as she noted that her half century of experience had left her "a bit pessimistic about seeing its [gay acceptance] success within my lifetime."[51] Yet things had begun to change, in part because of her pioneering effort to lift the veil of silence that surrounded lesbian life.

This Volume's First Fan

During the fall of 1956, a woman in her early twenties named Barbara Grier was working in the catalog department of the Kansas City, Kansas, Public Library. Intensely preoccupied with the detection of literature with lesbian characters and content, she had been collecting it for seven years and was quite proud of the fact that by 1956 she had accumulated nearly one hundred titles, a number of them appearing under the Fawcett, Pyramid, or Berkley imprints. Much like Jeannette, she had developed a system of routinely scouring library and book trade sources for newly published titles with possible lesbian content. It was in that manner that she discovered Fay Adams, *Appointment in Paris* (1952), Guy des Cars, *The Damned One* (1956), and Carol Hales, *Wind Woman* (1953). One day, while scanning *Cumulative Book Index,* she was taken by surprise when she read about a forthcoming publication, *Sex Variant Women in Literature.* When she called the local Cokesbury Bookstore to place an order for it, the clerk casually mentioned that the author worked at KCU. Wasting no time, Grier called the campus library on September 19, 1956, and asked to speak with Miss Foster. "*Dr.* Foster," corrected library director Kenneth LaBudde, was not available that day. Undeterred, she obtained Jeannette's phone number from directory information and placed the call, only to have it answered by a gruff voice belonging to Myrtle Toliver. When Jeannette came to the phone, she was delighted to discover that her caller was someone with a deep interest in lesbian literature.[52]

When Barbara Grier first met Jeannette in February 1957, her initial impression was of a prim and proper woman who used stationery with her name embossed on it and wore Nelly Don dresses, Ground Gripper shoes, and porkpie hats. Thirty-eight years and one day older than Barbara, she had the appearance of a grandmother, with warm eyes and a ready smile. Jeannette, however, soon dispelled Barbara's initial impression. One day when she was on her way to dinner with Barbara and her partner Helen L. Bennett, Jeannette tripped on the stairs of their apartment and said "fuck." Barbara was amazed, not by the profanity, but by the fact that she had never heard an adult female say "fuck" in public. As Jeannette later explained, she had not used such words prior to her work at the Institute for Sex Research, but regular exposure while there had desensitized her to them.[53]

Euphoric to discover someone else who shared her passion for the detection of lesbian literature, Jeannette gave Barbara a copy of *Sex Variant Women* at that first meeting inscribed "For this volume's first fan." "I think," Grier explained, "it is safe to say that her most serious attachment was to the one book."[54] Her true love, it had given her satisfaction as no lover ever could. She had stopped working on it only because she knew there were others, like herself, who would benefit from finding validation of their existence in print. If she had waited, the book most likely would not have found a publisher until the 1970s and the rise of the gay liberation movement, whose contours would have been different had her book not raised awareness of the lesbian's historical presence.

For the next few years the two women, equally obsessed with lesbian literature, spoke almost daily by phone, dined out occasionally, and spent Sunday afternoons together when Bennett visited her family. Jeannette was thrilled to have found someone who shared her obsession and genuinely appreciated her lifework. Until they met, she had regarded herself as unique, and it was not until later that women like Christine Pattee, Maida Tilchen, and others took up the cause. As Jeannette and Barbara grew close, they also shared many observations about life and tidbits from their personal histories. Jeannette also gave Grier copies of the novels, short fiction, and poetry she had written earlier in the century, still harboring the hope that one day they would be published. Barbara, who had come out to her mother at the age of twelve, enjoyed Jeannette's frankness and her obvious comfort with her sexual identity. "Jeannette," she explained, "did not suffer from any doubts about lesbianism. . . . She seemed never to have considered anything else, either."[55] In short order, Barbara became Jeannette's protégée, learning her techniques for identifying books with potential lesbian content. That knowledge would aid her in preparing the "Lesbiana" column she wrote for *The Ladder* (virtually the only lesbian book review in the world at that time) and the checklist of lesbian literature that she compiled with the lesbian author Marion Zimmer Bradley.

Jeannette's work also had a significant impact on others. In the fall of 1962, for instance, Lillian Faderman was a graduate student at the University of California, Los Angeles. One day while searching the shelves of the English Reading Room for another work—possibly, she recalls, an E. M. Forster novel—she happened upon *Sex Variant Women in Literature*. "I certainly wouldn't have known to look for Foster," reflected Faderman, who was at the time very closeted, "nor would I have dared to 'look up' such a book." Intrigued by the work, she "read it standing up in the stacks, returning many times to read a bit more." Whenever anyone happened to pass by, she recalled, "I made sure that the title was not visible. Those were scary times for gay people." As Faderman well knew, students could be kicked out of universities for being homosexual, and she "desperately wanted to be credentialed as a scholar, to get a PhD, to become a professor." In the years to come, she never forgot *Sex Variant Women in Literature*, and "Foster became a model . . . of how one could do serious scholarship about lesbian subject matter." Over the course of the next decade Faderman grew in the conviction that she could be braver. Beginning with lesbian articles, she moved on to write *Surpassing the Love of Men*, hoping that "someday my own work might be as crucial to other scholars as her work was to me."[56] In the 1960s and beyond, as Jeannette's monumental book became the basic sourcebook for homophile researchers and students of lesbian literature, it would bring her into contact with such lesbian and gay activists as Tee Corinne, Barbara Gittings, Karla Jay, Jonathan Ned Katz, and Marie Kuda. Through their friendship and intervention, her scholarly and creative work gained even greater visibility, even as her understanding of what it meant to be homosexual in the twentieth century continued to evolve.

⚘ Eight ⚘

Hail and Farewell

Why didn't I write her then? . . . Now I never can. . . . Always going to someday, when I found the time—and courage enough to say what had to be said. . . . Always seemed there was all the time in the world for it. A sort of treat, saved for the future.

—JEANNETTE HOWARD FOSTER
WRITING AS JAN ADDISON, 1957[1]

The quest to research and publish *Sex Variant Women in Literature* had driven Jeannette for several decades, but after it finally appeared in early 1957, it was time to reevaluate her goals and priorities. So much had changed in the world and in her life since she first came out to herself in the 1910s. During decades of living a compartmentalized life, she watched as gays and lesbians become increasingly visible in popular culture. She savored lesbian expression in the music of blues artists in the 1920s and 1930s, took delight in the proliferation of lesbian pulp novels in the 1950s, and welcomed the emergence of a gay and lesbian periodicals in the late 1940s and 1950s. In time, the isolation that she and many others of her generation had experienced began yielding to a growing sense of community. In turn, the dynamic networks that grew from such print-based organizations as the Mattachine Society and the Daughters of Bilitis gave rise to a campaign for recognition and rights. On a personal level, Jeannette had made the journey from unrequited love to a caring and committed relationship. As an author, she began seeing her fiction and poetry in print, and after decades as a successful career woman, Jeannette went indomitably ahead into a future that would bring her well-deserved recognition and many caring friends.

Time to Reassess

Jeannette's health and relationships had suffered during the long years she spent working on *Sex Variant Women in Literature*. Plagued by chronic insomnia and digestive problems, she found solace in sleeping tablets, laxatives, and liquor. In the years to come, a sedentary lifestyle, a constant struggle to keep her weight down, and creeping arthritis would limit her activities. Since the death of their parents, she had remained in regular correspondence with her sisters, but they were not especially close, primarily because Jeannette had remained closeted with them and they would never really know her as an individual.[2] On the other hand, she had grown to regard Hazel as her family, the person with whom she could be herself and for whom she would willingly make many sacrifices. After all, she had helped care for Hazel's mother, who, somewhat ironically, did not die until after Jeannette entered a nursing home. Yet theirs was a relationship that defied definition. "We were (and are)," she wrote in 1975, "wholly compatible intellectually, but . . . there has never been overt lesbianism between us."[3] It is possible that Jeannette chose to censor her description of their relations out of respect for Hazel's wishes; after all, she had chosen for them to retire near family members with whom she remained closeted.

Jeannette's choice of terminology as she reflected on a lifetime of lesbian relationships underscores both the changes that had occurred in her lifetime and the range of relationships on a lesbian continuum. All of her loves were lesbian, but some, especially those occurring early in the twentieth century, were grounded in emotional connection, while others, predominantly those during the 1930s and beyond, included physical "completeness." Even though Jeannette never found a lover who could return her feelings in kind, there is no doubt that she and Hazel loved each other, and each was an important part of the other's life. It was in 1960, shortly before Jeannette retired from KCU, that she came to the realization that she no longer had "the faintest hint of sexual hunger, need, or even interest." Beautiful women would still catch her eye, but aside from a knowing look or a witty remark, her experiences would be vicarious.[4] This was fortuitous because by that time Hazel had met and grown fond of another woman.

For most of her teaching career, Hazel had yearned for a more fulfilling position, one that would allow time for immersing herself in research. As a woman, however, she often found herself saddled with basic courses and service commitments while her male colleagues received grants and fellowships and pursued their research. Ever the pragmatist, Jeannette encouraged Hazel to follow her dream, even if it meant they had to live apart. After only three years of sharing a house in Kansas City, Hazel became an associate professor of Latin at Northeast Missouri State Teachers College, in Kirksville. Two years later, in 1957, she moved yet again, this time across the state to St. Charles, to become a professor of classics at the all female Lindenwood College. Instead of dislodging Hazel's mother, Myrtle, Jeannette and Hazel agreed that she would remain behind with Jeannette in Kansas City.

It was at Lindenwood that Hazel met Dorothy (Dot) Hall Ross in the fall of 1957. A strikingly beautiful brunette in face and form, she was a mere four years older than Hazel. Adopted, she had grown up on a farm and loved the out-of-doors. Athletic yet introverted, the young brunette had joined the faculty of Lindenwood College as an instructor in physical education in 1946.[5] Closeted to the point of repression, Dot struggled with her sexual identity. As difficult as it was for an isolated rural woman to identify as a lesbian during this time, it was even harder for someone like Dot, who would throughout her life work with female athletes in schools and at summer camps.[6] Everyone knew that high school and college administrations would fire a homosexual without hesitation for being morally suspect, and it appears that she internalized the homophobia of her era, working diligently to discourage homosexual impulses in the young women who were her charges.

PHOTO 18.   Jeannette made her home with Dorothy (Dot) Ross
(1905–1986) and Hazel Toliver (1909–1997) from 1960–1975.
(Courtesy of the Lindenwood University Library)

If Hazel had been uncomfortable with her sexuality, she would not
have accepted a position at the Institute for Sex Research, nor would
she have attached herself to Jeannette, who was hardly tactful or closeted. She found herself drawn to Dot, despite the physical education instructor's outward disapproval of same-sex relationships, and the two
soon became close friends. Recognizing that they were compatible and
complementary, they made plans to begin sharing an apartment in the
fall of 1958. Jeannette, who had enough previous experience to know,
recognized the mutual attraction that existed between Hazel and Dot.
Confiding in her friend Barbara Grier, she told of seeing them sneak a
kiss in the garage when they thought no one was watching.[7]

Jeannette grew to accept the situation because she knew that Hazel
did not take good care of herself, something Dot did rather well. A doer
rather than a thinker, Dot was a talented cook, and enjoyed being admired for her skill at such things as carpentry, plumbing, and gardening.
Hazel, on the other hand, was more reclusive, loved to bury her head in
a book, and prepared food out of necessity. Because of their love for
Hazel, Dot and Jeannette tolerated one another but occasionally made

PHOTO 19.   The four-plex at 130 Gamble Street, St. Charles, Missouri, where Jeannette lived with Hazel and Myrtle Toliver, Dot Ross, and Elizabeth Dawson from 1960–1974. Jeannette's unit was on the upper right and she used to open the window so her cat Dilly could sun himself on the porch roof. (Photo by the author)

barbed remarks to one another. To visitors in their home, however, the three women appeared to enjoy each other's company, constantly teasing one another and sharing a sardonic sense of humor.[8]

As Jeannette's retirement from the University of Kansas City drew near, the three women began making plans for a shared future. Hazel envisioned them collectively purchasing a spacious residence where they all could live (including her mother), but when Lindenwood College offered a suitable property for sale, she fretted nervously about the possible repercussions if administrators discovered Jeannette's self-imposed notoriety as a lesbian.[9] To ward off any risk, only Dot and Hazel's names appeared on the title when they bought a two-story brick fourplex, located just one block from campus at 130 Gamble Street. Officially, Hazel and her mother would occupy one unit, Dot a second, Jeannette a third, and a renter the fourth. Selling the Kansas City duplex, Jeannette became a silent partner in the new investment, placed her hundreds of books in storage, and moved with Myrtle Toliver and their cats into 4346 Harrison Street for the remainder of her time there in Kansas City. By the summer of 1960, when Jeannette said farewell to KCU and moved to St. Charles, Dot had become an integral part of Hazel and Jeannette's family.[10]

Early Days of Retirement

St. Charles had been founded by French Canadians in 1769, served as the first state capitol in 1820, and had been a site on the Oregon Trail. Its setting along the Missouri River continued to exude a nineteenth-century atmosphere in many portions of the town. The sedate and historic community appealed to work-weary Jeannette, who eagerly anticipated retirement as a time she could "begin savoring life as it hourly passes." She had grown weary, she explained to Margaret Anderson, of the "diabolic age of rush, 'status seekers,' automotive engine exhaust and noise by land or by air, and no time for charm!"[11]

Jeannette, who still had a high level of energy, had acquired her father's love of history and decided to volunteer at the St. Charles County Historical Society. It served many school groups and the teacher in Jeannette enjoyed giving them tours and history lessons. When she was not at the museum, watching Myrtle, or doing household chores for herself, Dot, and Hazel, she filled her time with correspondence and reading. In a typical week, she borrowed and read an average of twenty books per week from the public library. The mail carrier also wore a path to her door as he delivered a constant stream of mail-order books, periodicals, and letters from correspondents around the globe.

After the publication of *Sex Variant Women in Literature*, Jeannette had begun re-reading the stories and poems she had written over the course of her lifetime, pondering the possibility of preparing them for publication. With the exception of "Lucky Star," which appeared in *Harper's Magazine* in 1927, they had remained unpublished because of the lack of suitable outlets for works with obvious lesbian content. In early 1957 when Jeannette learned about *The Ladder*'s experience, she realized the good news: at last there might be a venue for publishing some of her earlier works. In the coming decade and a half, she would at last see some of her short fiction, poetry, and novellas published on its pages.

The Ladder had been preceded in 1947 by *Vice Versa*, the first gay and lesbian periodical in the nation, but in all likelihood Jeannette never saw that hand-typed Los Angeles-based publication, created and distributed by Edythe Eyde under the pseudonym Lisa Ben. Its short-lived existence, however, signified that change was in the wind. In the 1950s, the McCarthy Era categorization of homosexuals as emotionally unstable and morally corrupt prompted a stalwart crew of gays and lesbians who boldly began to counter negative depictions of themselves in the media by establishing several gay and lesbian periodicals. The impact of these publications, which included *ONE* (Los Angeles, 1953), *The Mattachine Review* (Los Angeles, 1955), and *The Ladder* (San Francisco, 1956), was decreased gay and lesbian isolation, and even more importantly, a heightened positive visibility of this demonized minority.[12] While the first two appealed to a primarily male readership, *The Ladder* became the first regularly published lesbian periodical to have a national audience. Its title, inspired by Radclyffe Hall's 1928 novel, *The Well of Loneliness*, encouraged readers to use this publication as a ladder to escape their lonely existence. Beginning with its first twelve-page mimeographed issue in October 1956, founding editor Phyllis Lyon (under the pseudonym Ann Ferguson) sought to combat negative images of lesbians in society. Like Lisa Ben's *Vice Versa*, *The Ladder* contained short fiction, poetry, and lists of books, films, plays, and songs with gay and lesbian themes.[13]

The Ladder, which eventually had a subscription base of nearly four thousand (plus a far larger readership of people who read copies borrowed from friends), served as a forum in which women could raise consciousness by discussing such critical topics as lesbian identity and homosexual rights. Perhaps more importantly, it created a sense of

community among geographically dispersed and socially isolated readers. Most, of course, wrote using pseudonyms, primarily because they
feared losing their jobs or being ostracized by their families if it were
known that they were homosexual. After a few issues appeared, editor
Phyllis Lyon boldly decided to exchange her pseudonym for her real
name, but few others followed suit.[14]

In the early days, *The Ladder* staff sometimes had difficulty filling its
pages, and therefore welcomed contributions of prose and poetry from
readers. After sending money for a subscription in June 1957, Jeannette
immediately submitted one of her stories and finally found herself in
the right place at the right time.[15] Over the next eleven years, *The Ladder* would publish seven of her stories, one of them a novella appearing
as a four-part serial. Most contributors used pseudonyms because they
wanted to protect their identities, but Jeannette seemingly did so because she wanted people to associate the name Jeannette Howard Foster with her scholarly work. She used the name Hilary Farr for longer,
more literary pieces and drew upon her grandfathers' names when she
chose Abigail Sanford for her poetry and Jan Addison for her short fiction. At times, however, she felt a bit apologetic that she had saddled
her paternal grandfather, the man she loved as much as her father, with
such flippant fiction.

Jeannette's earlier life had provided a wide array of experiences and
locales as settings for her short fiction. Situating stories in such familiar
urban locations as New York and Chicago, her characters were drawn
from her life and those of her friends. Several pieces address the inter-
related themes of regret for missed opportunities and the importance of
seizing the moment. Appearing in September 1957 under the pseudonym Jan Addison, "Hail and Farewell" featured a librarian named
Agnes Dawes who, while reading a professional journal, discovers the
obituary of Lynn Currier, an American author who had written a queer
novel entitled *Quicksands*. Agnes recalls reading the book in a single afternoon and asking herself why she never wrote Currier to convey her
heartfelt appreciation for the courage to say what had to be said. The

story's message struck a chord with a *Ladder* reader from San Leandro, California, who, like Jeannette, hungered to know of authors who shared her love for other women. Describing the story as "haunting," she explained that it reminded her "of a time when I . . . knew the loss of an unknown, unseen friend."[16]

Unlike the main character in "Hail and Farewell," Jeannette often wrote to authors whose work she admired. As a result, her correspondents included such women as the the poet Elsa Gidlow and Hazel E. Barnes, the philosopher who introduced French existentialism to Americans through her translation of Sartre's *Being and Nothingness*. Reflecting on her brief association with Foster, Barnes recalled: "She wrote to tell me she had liked something I had written, and I wrote to thank her." While their correspondence was superficial, Barnes remembered "one very lovely thing that she did. I must have mentioned that I was leaving for Europe on a particular ship. When I got on board, I found she had sent me an orchid!"[17]

Encouraged by the appearance of "Hail and Farewell," Jeannette next submitted a story entitled "Life Class," printed under the pseudonym Jan Addison. This time, the story explored the importance of acting upon one's instinct, something that Jeannette wished she could have done more of throughout her life. Based on a time in her youth when she took classes at the Art Institute of Chicago, it also drew inspiration from Jeannette's tense relationship with her mother. The main character, Vanessa, won a scholarship to study art despite her older step-sister Mag's objections to her being exposed to loose-living art students. At the institute, Van (as she is called) develops a crush on the nude model, Garda. Awestruck in her presence, she is unable to paint and explains to her instructor that this is the first time she has ever seen a naked body. Braced by a small glass of alcohol he gives her, Van is consumed with a desire to preserve Garda's beauty on canvas and begins to draw. At the end of the course, Garda and Van meet on the street, feel an instant attraction, and Garda invites Van to leave home and move in with her, which, the reader is led to conclude, she does.[18]

In a story ahead of its time entitled "A Man's World," Jeannette offers a positive portrayal of lesbian love and parenting. In contrast with depictions of lesbians in the pulp fiction of the 1950s, her characters are like the lesbians she knew in real life—talented, intelligent, and emotionally well-balanced. Painter Jerry Ashburn is hired to paint two women, Paige and Wylie, at their rural Virginia estate. They love each other and want to have a baby, so they arrange for Paige to seduce the painter and become pregnant. Time passes, and one day many years later Jerry meets his daughter, whom Paige and Wylie have raised. Presenting lesbian love in an ideal light, his daughter declares: "I never knew anything could be so—beautiful."[19] While the story was progressive concerning lesbian themes, it showed its age when it came to racial sensitivity. Set in the South, it included African-American servants speaking in dialect, which *Ladder* editor Helen Sandoz, writing under the pseudonym Ben Cat, found offensive. "Had I been asked about the story," she explained, "I think I would have objected to several passages of dialect that appear." Hoping that none of the readers were offended, she promised that it would never happen again.[20]

In her fiction, as in her life, Jeannette also explored the sexual dimension of lesbian life, acknowledging that flesh-and-blood women had physical desires. Sometimes she based stories on aspects of her earlier experiences. In "Narrow Escape," which appeared in the February 1963 issue of *The Ladder*, the main character Mel has just seen *Mädchen in Uniform* (a 1931 German film with lesbian content) for the fifth time.[21] As she boards a bus to go home, she spots a "pencil-slim" girl with shingled hair who meets and then quarrels with an older woman. Mel follows the girl, whose name is Jimmy James, when she exits the bus and inquires suggestively: "Anybody collapse if you're not home tonight?" Jimmy turns to Mel, much like Jennie Gregory had done with Jeannette in 1931, and says: "We both know we're in love with somebody else." Mel concurs, adding "and neither of us likes promiscuity. In theory." The story comes to a jolting halt when Mel is snapped back to realty, only to find herself daydreaming on the bus. In real life Jeannette, like the character Mel, too often had played it safe by dreaming rather than jumping straight into reality.

Jeannette's unpublished works, more risqué than her standard fare, show another side of the romantic librarian, one intrigued by behaviors in which she could never indulge. Almost voyeuristic, they position the narrator as a cautious observer of a bolder lesbian lifestyle based on Jennie Gregory's days in the Village. Set in the early 1940s, "The Funniest Thing" is told by a married woman named Suzy who is taking night classes at New York University while her husband serves overseas in the army.[22] In the class she meets a stunning heiress named Kay Gaither (modeled on Gregory), with a penchant for life on the wild side. The two spend the night together and after a few drinks and kisses, Suzy falls asleep. The next morning she wonders if her memories of "the biggest bang I ever experienced" were real or a dream. When Kay, who lives in the Village, takes Suzy to visit her wealthy step-grandmother (modeled on Jennie Gregory's aunt), Suzy suspects that she is being used as protective cover since she is much milder than most of Kay's other friends. Meanwhile, Kay falls for a poet of purple prose named Malvina, who concocts a blackmail scheme that involves slipping Kay a Mickey Finn and seducing her in a sadistic scene—involving nakedness, green metal snakes, an emerald-hilted silver dagger, and a Middle Eastern belly dance—that is filmed by a "pansy" running a hidden camera. Coming to her rescue, Suzy persuades Kay to tell her grandmother, who saves the day and the family reputation by paying off Malvina with an expensive gift.

In her second unpublished Abby Sanford story, the reserved narrator (who, like Jeannette, is not part of the bar scene) stands in stark contrast to more promiscuous examples of lesbian behavior. "Why I'm a Cautious Soul" features a female bookstore employee in Chicago who is asked to welcome a couple of women to the city. Freda and Charlie stop by her apartment for a drink and directions to area gay bars, then invite her to accompany them. When she declines, they stay at her place and become increasingly drunk. Both start "directing their steam" at the narrator. First one, then the other, pursue her, with Freda making "a brilliant campaign of it" until the narrator admits that "if I hadn't a partner—I might even have fallen, for she carried a higher charge than anyone I'd met since the old Village days."[23]

Jeannette's best work, the novella "Temple of Athéne," appeared in the late 1960s under the pseudonym Hilary Farr and explores the complexity of unrequited love.[24] The story begins when Theodora K. Hart (named for Jeannette's University of Chicago dance instructor Theodora Burnham) takes a faculty position at the all-female Radnor College. While on the train she encounters and instantly becomes infatuated with an attractive woman who, she later learns, is Radnor College president Anna Lenox Van Tuyl (based on Jeannette's beloved Clara Louise Thompson). Through flashbacks, Theodora recalls her first love (modeled on Edna Grace Thompson), the kisses they shared in the moonlight, her Victorian scruples, and "hellish hygiene." Certain passages of the story are informed by Jeannette's study of science and homosexuality, especially a passage in which another colleague on the faculty declares that "Our sort" needs to understand "our own endocrine reactions." Like Clara Louise and Jeannette, Van Tuyl and Theodora are separated by a ten-year difference in age. Despite the attraction that exists between them, Van Tuyl represses her homosexual urges and tells the younger woman that she must do the same or leave the college. Unable to comply, Theodora leaves Radnor College much like Jeannette had left Thompson and Shorter College— with a new touchstone for measuring her feelings.

Spurred on by her success in publishing stories, Jeannette also submitted some of her unpublished poetry to The Ladder. Five appeared in late 1958 under the pseudonym Abigail Sanford. Entitled "Horizons," "To One Departing," "Healing," "Sonnet Out of Serenity," and "Vignette from a Campus Window," all but one of them originally had been written in the 1920s as she coped with her unrequited love for Thompson. In the 1950s, she also translated several of Renée Vivien's poems— "Mournful Bacchante," "Prolong the Night," and "Sonnet"—as well as some original poems and stories by the French novelist, essayist, and critic Marcel Proust, some of which appeared in *The Ladder* in 1959. As a gift for her friend Barbara Grier, Jeannette decided to undertake a translation of Renée Vivien's *Une Femme M'Apparut* (*A Woman Appeared to Me*). Taking careful measures to avoid her supervisor's notice because she would have loved catching Jeannette "doing private business on library time," she borrowed the French text from the Library of Congress and "worked hard to make the trans[lation] literally correct without sounding stiff & stilted." Jeannette was pleased many years later when Naiad Press published her effort and a reader wrote to express appreciation for her "high quality" translation.[25]

Politicization

Jeannette did not regard herself as political, but as the conformist 1950s yielded to the more radical 1960s, she found herself being drawn into the politics of lesbian publishing. Her decision to publish *Sex Variant Women in Literature* under her own name rather than a pseudonym had been a bold step, yet in doing this Jeannette was not making a political statement. She was proud of her scholarship and wanted recognition for it.[26] As younger women read her book and began writing to her about its impact on them, however, Jeannette realized the degree to which her research was contributing to lesbian consciousness raising and the creation of a sense of community needed before a lesbian rights movement could flourish. It had not been her original intention, yet she took pleasure in seeing her work's wider relevance.

Jeannette had, of necessity, joined professional associations during her career but never viewed herself as a joiner. Since *The Ladder* was the official organ of the Daughters of Bilitis, however, she had taken out a membership in order to receive the publication. By the time she joined, Jeannette had spent many years observing and experiencing the homosexual's struggle for acceptance in American society and she understood the necessity for that recognition. Too many of the women she had known over the years feared condemnation by family and friends, loss of jobs, and even loss of property, simply because of who they were. "I think you are engaged in a commendable effort toward social accep-tance of the homophile," she wrote in 1957.[27] Jeannette's attitude to-ward homophile activism made a dramatic change between 1960 and 1970, and while she never would become a front-line activist, her book would jettison her into the center of the homophile and then the gay liberation and feminist movements.

While Jeannette was a loyal contributor to *The Ladder*, she never fully embraced the DOB as a group or gay rights as a cause. In a letter to Margaret Anderson in 1960, she made snobbish references to the DOB, *The Ladder*, the men at Mattachine, and other groups crusading for the social recognition of the homosexual. Although members of the DOB claimed to be assimilationists, she branded them as separationists and refused to attend their conventions or to moderate their panels, ex-plaining: "I don't want to opt myself out of the human race." In her eyes, she had lived openly and for the most part people had not rejected her because of her sexual orientation.[28] Four years later, her tone had begun to change. Proudly noting that she had been a member of DOB and subscriber to *The Ladder* "almost from their birth," she attended the 1964 national DOB convention, held in New York City at the Barbizon-Plaza on Central Park South. While there she met DOB leaders Del Martin and Phyllis Lyon, spoke with Marijane Meaker about her pulp fiction, and briefly reconnected with former Kinsey coworker Wardell Pomeroy, who spoke before the group. At a social gathering, a male Columbia University library school alumn surprised her with a kiss. As she listened to presentations by members of the clergy, psycholo-gists, psychoanalysts, and others, she contrasted her journey with that of the friends with whom she stayed. One of them was a former lover (probably Lenore Ward), yet lived such a closeted lifestyle that Jean-nette could not bring herself to tell her the nature of the meetings she attended.[29]

While Jeannette preferred to wield the pen rather than a placard, her submissions to *The Ladder* in the 1960s reflect a gradual change in outlook. In 1960, she became embroiled in a controversy involving the portrayal of lesbians in *The Ladder* and pulp fiction. While her response may have been prompted by personal feelings, the exchange placed her in the midst of a larger discourse about the politics of lesbian publishing. When lesbian pulps first appeared in the early 1950s, Marijane Meaker (who wrote under the pseudonym Vin Packer) knew that she must portray lesbian characters as morally bankrupt and unhappy. Lesbian readers, eager to find any representation of themselves in print, bought the books in large numbers but felt troubled by the negative images of themselves in print. As the times changed and publishers began to relax, Meaker began a new series of books under the name Ann Aldrich, publishing *We Walk Alone* (1955) and *We, Too, Must Love* (1958). In a critique of these works, which appeared in April 1958, Daughters of Bilitis (DOB) president Del Martin criticized Meaker for continuing to perpetuate negative stereotypes of lesbians and sought to enlighten her by giving the author a year's subscription to *The Ladder*.[30] After reading every issue for the year 1958 from cover to cover, Meaker remained unconvinced; in fact, she decided that it was time to question the DOB's agenda and methods.

In "The Ladder, Rung by Rung," an essay that appeared in her next book, *Carol in a Thousand Cities* (1960), Aldrich challenged the claim that the DOB was dedicated to promoting the integration of the homosexual into society. As proof, she analyzed the fiction appearing in *The Ladder* for 1958 and announced that it fell into four categories: "Job Be Damned," "Lesbians as Near-Transvestites," "Our Love Is Better Than Your Square Love," and "Whistling in the Dark about Years to Come." Striking back at those who criticized her negative depictions of lesbian life, Aldrich described *The Ladder's* own portrayals as "pretty grim. You can't get to work on time; your innards give out from too much alcohol when you're about forty-eight; you're fated for carpentry and argyle socks, and in your middle age you're not supposed to try to dance. If this Ladder is an approach to Lesbos," she concluded, "it seems hardly worth the climb."[31]

After reading *Carol in a Thousand Cities* in June 1960, Jeannette felt
enraged by Aldrich's condescending tone. "I spent more time than I
should yesterday," she confided in a letter to Barbara Grier, "kicking one
of Miss A's teeth in." In a withering critique that appeared in the August issue of *The Ladder*, along with one written by Grier, Jeannette dismissed Aldrich as an inferior writer, someone with "superlative early
training in Writing to Sell" who had "diarrhea of the pen." Grier, perhaps unknowingly, honed in on one reason for Jeannette's impassioned
defense of *The Ladder* and DOB: Aldrich had slashed "to ribbons every
story without exception that appeared in THE LADDER during the
year 1958," including Jeannette's "Life Class." Placing it in the "Job Be
Damned" category, with a strain of "Our Love Is Better than Yours,"
Aldrich had mocked the dialogue, which included such words as "gasp-
ing" and "shaking." Aldrich's first category was accurate, since the main
character Vanessa did decide to call in sick the next morning so she
could be with her new lover. Overall, Jeannette's story fared no better or
worse than the others under review, but the comments angered her. Sar-
castically noting that "the pore li'l [sic] amateur short-shorts for THE
LADDER seem pretty rough-hewn" to Aldrich, she suggested that the
pulp novelist was not really sure of her identity and therefore had no
right to criticize *The Ladder*'s content, which was for lesbians.[32]

Jeannette should have stopped there, but she unfortunately continued with a haughty reference to her literary knowledge and her ability
to deduce authorship by analyzing "style, background, names, allusions,
etc." Based on that expertise, she speculated that Ann Aldrich and
Ann Bannon (author of *I am a Woman*, *Women in the Shadows*, and
Journey to a Woman) were one and the same person. In the October
issue, however, several readers, including Bannon, wrote to correct her
error and to chastise Jeannette for a "disgusting bit of name-calling,
mud-slinging propaganda." While Bannon offered a tongue-in-cheek
apology for her "slick and dysenteric" writing, another reader demanded to know how such comments helped "gain respectability and
acceptance for your magazine and ultimately for the Lesbian?"[33] The

incident served as a baptism by fire into the contested terrain of modern lesbian literature.

The *Carol in a Thousand Cities* debate evidently did not knock Jeannette off of the pedestal on which readers of *Sex Variant Women in Literature* had placed her. Women who had read and drawn inspiration from the book continued writing to let her know how it had touched their lives. One, a lesbian novelist, poet, and social activist named Velma Tate, wrote Jeannette to express her appreciation for her monumental work. Nearly twenty years younger, Tate had divorced her husband in 1953 and moved to Chicago. Her first novel, *Hired Girl*, appeared that year, followed by her first lesbian novel, *Whisper Their Love* (1957), under the pen name Valerie Taylor. Ultimately, she would write hundreds of poems and numerous pulp fiction classics including *The Girls in 3-B*, *Stranger on Lesbos*, and *A World Without Men*. Striking up correspondence with one another, the two women would become lifelong friends, bound together by their love of lesbian literature and writing.

Others who contacted Jeannette included the English author Mary Challans (1905–1983), who under the pseudonym Mary Renault would write fourteen novels, the first five containing the suggestion of lesbianism, and the latter works set in ancient Greece and dealing with male homosexuality. Jeannette's familiarity with Greece, acquired from Clara Louise Thompson and Hazel Toliver, and the breadth of her reading provided ample topics for correspondence with Renault, but in time they also shared anecdotes from their personal lives and travels.[34]

Many of Jeannette's correspondents will remain a mystery because in 1974, in anticipation of moving into a nursing home, she burned letters she had received over the years to protect her correspondents' identities. Jeannette had briefer exchanges with a number of other authors and poets, ranging from Anna Elisabet Weirauch to Jody Shotwell.[35] As she dispensed advice and shared life experiences with her correspondents, Jeannette began making connections between her lesbian past and the homophile movement's quest for identity and recognition. After so many years grounded in an individual ethos, she had begun to see herself as part of the homophile movement, which was defined by difference yet strengthened by mutual interdependence.

May Sarton at Lindenwood

While reading the early works of May Sarton, Jeannette had become enamored with the poet and author, and for some time had suspected her of being a lesbian. She may have encountered her briefly in 1962 when Sarton visited the Lindenwood campus, but three years later the two women had an opportunity to become friends when Sarton spent the fall semester as a poet-in-residence. Moving into a unit of the four-plex temporarily vacated by English professor Elizabeth Dawson, she lived across the hall from Jeannette, and the two women had many opportunities to talk about their shared appreciation for literature, poetry, and New England culture.[36] Sarton, who was recovering from an infatuation with Wellesley College president Margaret Clapp, had had her contract terminated after making a nuisance of herself with persistent telephone calls, love poems, and letters. Herself a veteran of many crushes and unrequited loves, Jeannette had little sympathy for Sarton's self-pity, but did devour the love poems she shared with her.[37]

Already the author of eight novels, seven volumes of poetry, and numerous short stories, Sarton felt freed after the death of her parents to reveal, albeit tacitly and judiciously, her homosexuality to readers. In *Mrs. Stevens Hears the Mermaids Singing*, published in the fall of 1965, she presented a female homosexual character (Hilary Stevens) in a positive light. A significant step toward the emergence of modern lesbian identity in mainstream literature, Sarton's literary coming out represented a calculated risk in the pre-Stonewall era: publishers could reject her work, employers could dismiss her, and readers could refuse to buy her books.[38]

Jeannette admired *Mrs. Stevens* and identified with the main character, who—like herself—had sublimated "her passionate attractions in poetry."[39] The more she came to know more about Sarton's personality, however, the more Jeannette grew disillusioned with her. At times when

Jeannette, Hazel, Dot, and Sarton shared meals and animated dinner conversation in Jeannette's kitchen, Sarton lost her temper and one time even took her shoe off and pounded it on the table to emphasize a point. Indeed, wrote Jeannette, "her *complete* self-centeredness came to the surface more and more." After Sarton left Lindenwood, she continued to send Jeannette copies of her published books, which Jeannette dutifully read. In the early years, she sent Sarton long critiques by return mail, but within a few years she had become thoroughly frustrated with Sarton's responses because she was "completely unable to foresee how she would react to *anything* I wrote to her." Ultimately, their correspondence died an inevitable death, as Jeannette put it, "of malnutrition at both ends!"[40]

Life in St. Charles

Life at 130 Gamble Street settled into a predictable and comfortable routine, with the occupants forming a congenial and cohesive household. Soon after Myrtle moved into the back room of Hazel's downstairs unit, it became evident that they could not live together harmoniously, so Hazel and Dot remodeled and enlarged Dot's unit, converting two sunporches into bedrooms. With Myrtle in the smaller unit, Hazel and Dot moved in together, leaving the upstairs to Jeannette and a tenant. Jeannette's unit had a window overlooking the sunroom roof, which she opened so her cat Dilly could sunbathe. Down-to-earth and practical, Jeannette contributed to the household by making plans and seeing that things were accomplished. In addition to volunteering at the local historical society, she did basic housekeeping tasks and shopping. She enjoyed the occasional cocktail parties they hosted, and her love of reading remained unabated. In addition to lesbian fiction, she began re-reading such classics as Dickens and Kipling, as well as novels with New England themes or characters. Dot, a compulsive workhorse and a tidiness fanatic, did manual labor, ran errands, and fixed things that needed attention. Hazel, who was occasionally withdrawn, generally kept Jeannette and Dot entertained with her lofty and at times comic conversations.[41]

Both Dot and Jeannette helped care for Myrtle, who lived with them the entire time they were in St. Charles, because they wanted to alleviate some of the lifelong burden Hazel had known. A cantankerous woman at best, she had been dependent on Hazel since 1929, but with age and dementia her personality and behavior grew even more difficult to manage. Hazel's relationship with her mother had always been tense, but no nonsense Jeannette handled Myrtle firmly and well. There was never any question of hiring someone; they simply made her care a part of their routine.

During those years Hazel and Jeannette continued to make occasional trips together, sometimes accompanied by Dot. In the summer of 1964, they visited Chicago, where they dined with Valerie Taylor at the Tip Top Tap cocktail lounge in the Allerton Hotel. Years later Taylor recalled how the head of the Chicago chapter of the Daughters of Bilitis, a branch that had only a handful of people, decided to host a dinner in Jeannette's honor even though she and her partner were in the midst of a move. When Jeannette walked into the chaotic environment and saw a mattress leaning against the wall in the hall of the new apartment she looked at the mattress and said with her characteristic wry wit, "Oh, I see we're going to have an orgy." With that, the ice was broken, and everyone enjoyed a noisy evening of good food and conversation.[42] In addition to visiting Chicago and New York City in 1964, Jeannette made several mid-winter trips to Florida as she had done for so many years previously.

In the mid-1960s, Jeannette's health began to show signs of deterioration and she began consulting with a physical therapist and osteopath on a regular basis. For years she had suffered from mild emphysema, which she blamed on childhood exposure to coal smoke. An insomniac for many years, Jeannette depended on sleeping tablets, and an obsession with bowel regularity caused her to take a daily laxative. Injuries took longer to heal, and an infected thumb that troubled her before Thanksgiving, 1970, persisted well into the next year, making it difficult for her to type. Modifying her routine somewhat, she continued to volunteer at the local historical society but did hire a weekly cleaning woman.[43]

Dot's retirement from Lindenwood in the spring of 1970 coincided with Jeannette's failing health and she began to assume more responsibility for household chores, including the care of Myrtle Toliver, now eighty-seven. As the three women began to anticipate Hazel's retirement in the spring of 1974, they weighed their options. Jeannette had a niece and nephew living in Illinois, but was not close to either, and Dot had no immediate family. Hazel, on the other hand, had many relatives living in Pocahontas, Arkansas, a community of approximately five thousand residents, and one of her aunts had been well cared for at the Randolph County Nursing Home. Operating on the assumption that it would be good for Hazel, the youngest of the trio, to be near family members, Jeannette and Dot agreed that Pocahontas, Arkansas, a sleepy southern village where the Ozarks met the Delta, should be their final destination. Purchasing several wooded acres on a promontory overlooking Baltz Lake, Hazel, Dot, and Jeannette made plans to have a home constructed by the time Hazel retired from Lindenwood in 1974.

Jeannette would never be able to fully enjoy the house on Baltz Lake. In the fall and winter of 1973, the arthritis in her right hip worsened to the point that she could no longer shop for groceries, liquor, and medicine or do household chores. By Christmas she had suffered a couple of falls in her quarters and could no longer walk safely downstairs to visit Hazel and Dot. Entering the hospital for a complete medical examination, she had a myelogram, which involved the removal of some spinal fluid and its replacement with a dye. It not only indicated a fractured vertebra and a crushed intervertebral disc, necessitating a spinal operation, but also, as Jeannette came to believe, the myelogram permanently affected her memory as well as the strength in her right hand. Aware that her privacy would soon become a thing of the past, and that she did not want certain items "kicking around among my stuff," Jeannette prepared for the operation by sending her entire collection of *The Ladder* to Barbara Grier and by destroying some of her personal papers.[44]

On January 7, 1974, Jeannette had lumbar spinal surgery, which unfortunately left her with debilitating nerve damage affecting the sphincter muscle that controlled the urethra.[45] Bedfast, she never again walked without the aid of a walker or a steel brace worn on the right leg, up to the knee, with shoes like those of a heavy laborer. Upon her discharge from the hospital on February 1, she entered a private recuperative home in St. Charles, which she found quite distasteful. As someone used to reading lesbian books and corresponding with a host of gays and lesbians around the country, Jeannette had difficulty adjusting to the lack of privacy. At the home, which Jeannette referred to as a "G. D. Jackson St. dump," she had difficulty sleeping because her "supposed caretaker" came home at all hours of the night. Transferring to another place, located five miles away, she was not permitted to use the phone but learned to sneak into the front room when the attendant was busy in the basement laundry.[46]

May Sarton, with impeccable timing, sent Jeannette a copy of her 1973 novel, *As We Are Now*, beginning with the epigraph, "As you are now, so once was I; Prepare for death and follow me." She knew from reviews that the novel eerily paralleled her experience during the first half of 1974 and vowed that she would never read it. "I . . . felt that meeting it personally," she explained, "was all I could take without having M.S.'s nakedly penetrating version to face also!" In chilling detail, the novel tells the story of Caro Spencer, who after surgery is deposited in a substandard nursing home in rural New England. An overburdened staff treat the intelligent woman, who is used to better circumstances, in a demeaning way, cruelly stripping away her autonomy and dignity. In an act of resistance, she commits her observations to a carefully hidden journal before ending the terror of her confinement by destroying the home and herself in a fire. Jeannette believed that *As We Are Now* was based on the psychiatrist and author Dr. Marynia Farnham's experience in a nursing home.[47]

With Jeannette incapacitated by her surgery and Hazel finishing the school year, Dot assumed responsibility for packing Jeannette's papers, books, and other personal effects in preparation for the move. Jeannette never again returned to the fourplex at 130 Gamble Street. On August 1, an ambulance transported her to Pocahontas, Arkansas, her seventeenth state of residence. Their new home stood on a miniature promontory overlooking the water in three directions. Perhaps the setting reminded Jeannette of the Fosters' summer cottage at Hamlin Lake. The road to their home was blacktopped, as was their drive, but there was not another house in sight. When the fourplex sold the following October, they bought additional land on either side to ensure their privacy.

The three women devoted many hours to making the house into a home. Dot shouldered a great deal of the responsibility for unpacking, Hazel attended to business matters and organized their household goods, and Jeannette, working from a seated position because of her infirmity, alphabetized their books, which Hazel in turn placed on the shelves that covered every available inch of wall space in the study. Although Jeannette had disposed of many of her periodicals and some personal papers before the move to Arkansas, she still owned two thousand or more books, which she now combined with Hazel's hundreds and dozens of others they had acquired from Lindenwood colleagues. They had so many that when a local man helped unload their Bekins moving van, he declared, "My God, those women have more books than the Public Library!"[48]

From the beginning of their residence in Pocahontas, Hazel's relatives invited the three women to family dinners, took them on occasional outings to Jonesboro, and included them in holiday festivities. Jeannette thought family members descended on the lake house out of curiosity at the prospect of three old maids making their home together. In addition to each other, the three women loved pets. Hazel had a soft spot for any cat she encountered, Jeannette had feline companions for most of her life, and Dot had grown up on a farm. Six cats accompanied them on the move from St. Charles, including Jeannette's Dilly, Dickey (also known as Sir Richard Steele), a neurotic pale gold asthmatic male named Biscuit, and Fluff, a full-blooded Persian given to them by their St. Charles veterinarian. In time they also acquired several dogs.[49]

Jeannette was delighted to rejoin her companions, but she knew it was temporary. Never a thin woman, her weight increased after the surgery to approximately one hundred and seventy pounds, making it difficult for Hazel and Dot to provide the physical care she needed. She had placed her name on the waiting list at the Randolph County Nursing Home well before she left St. Charles, and it was just a matter of time before they had a vacancy for her. The first notification arrived on December 23, 1974, but she begged off, citing holiday celebrations. When a second vacancy occurred the following March, she knew she had to accept or move to the bottom of the list. In a typed note to her closest friends, Jeannette announced on March 29 that she would have a new address as of April 1. She was not yet helpless, but was conscious of "deteriorating abilities daily" and knew that once she did need help neither Hazel nor Dot possessed adequate strength. "I *hate* to go," she told Barbara Grier. "I love it here, the view, the quiet, the 7 cats, *and* my cherished old pals." She could return for visits, but it would not be the same. Ever the realist, she concluded: "There is no choice, so I mustn't waste strength rebelling. . . . There are worse fates!"[50]

❦❦❦ *Nine* ❦❦❦

Gaiety Must Be Gaining Respectability!

To understand her mind, examine Sex Variant Women.
To get some idea of the scope of her education and interests, look into the Vivien.
And to read her heart, read some of her poems.

—VALERIE TAYLOR, 1978[1]

In 1968, Chicagoan Marie J. Kuda spotted a copy of *Sex Variant Women in Literature* in the author Valerie Taylor's apartment when she attended a newsletter meeting for Mattachine Midwest, one of Chicago's first successful gay rights organizations. "I was stunned!" she recalled. Kuda, who had an undergraduate degree in English literature, had spent countless hours searching the library stacks for evidence of her identity "beyond the 'sinful' labels of my church and the 'sick' stigma of medical writers" and was so taken with Jeannette's book that she sat cross-legged on the floor devouring it page by page.[2] Gay historian Jonathan Ned Katz also was unaware of Jeannette's earlier work, and in the early 1970s he decided to write a book that would prevent subsequent generations from thinking that "they were the first gay people on earth." In the process of his research for his groundbreaking *Gay American History* (1976), he discovered *Sex Variant Women in Literature*. In 1998, when reflecting on his initial encounter with Jeannette's book, Katz recalled a "kind of mystical aura around it (and her)." As someone who also sought to recover the gay and lesbian past, he found it "utterly unearthly, completely amazing, that someone was able to gather so much information so many years earlier, when it was so much harder, when there was so little interest, so little emotional support for such work, and so great an active dislike of such research."[3]

With the Stonewall Rebellion of 1969 serving as a catalyst, members of the New Left countercultural movement known as gay liberation began calling for social change even as activists looked for proof of their existence in a closeted past. Fueled and inspired by the civil rights movement, the women's movement, and the black power movement, advocates of gay and lesbian liberation militantly sought an end to their persecution. In this pre-Internet era, they also recognized the power of the printed word to mobilize and empower, and their rediscovery of Foster's *Sex Variant Women* and her lesbian poems (written earlier in the century) jettisoned her to the status of lesbian foremother. Ironically, her upper-middle-class childhood and academic training meant that she was at times shocked by the protests, violence, and disorder shaking the nation. On the other hand, she took great pleasure in the heightened gay and lesbian visibility occurring in the wake of Stonewall, for instance, when publications like *Time* magazine and the *New York Times* published such feature stories as "The Homosexual: Newly Visible, Newly Understood" and "What It Means to be a Lesbian." The academic in her also would have been pleased to see the first issue of the *Journal of Homosexuality* in the fall of 1974.[4]

Recognition

In mid-1974, Chicagoans Valerie Taylor, Marie Kuda, and Susan Edwards brainstormed the first Lesbian Writers Conference, to be held in Chicago, the city where Margaret Anderson and her lover Jane Heap had first published the *Little Review*. The following September, women writers arrived for the three-day event, which convened in a Unitarian Universalist church, viewing exhibits, attending workshops, and reading from their own work. Participants received a twenty-eight-page annotated bibliography entitled *Woman Loving Women* that had been prepared by Kuda and Taylor because they wanted women to know of their history. In her keynote address, Taylor highlighted Jeannette's contributions to the study of lesbian literature, noting that pioneers "don't always live to see their experiments accepted—when they do it's a great thing." Upon receiving a printed copy of Taylor's address, Jeannette acknowledged: "I'm much flattered to know that Marie Kuda dedicated the Conference to me—*I am just not that significant*, though it does me good to be known outside the circle of my immediate personal friends."[5]

A few months earlier, Jeannette had received a different form of recognition from the American Library Association. The ALA Task Force on Gay Liberation, established by Israel Fishman in 1970, strived "to encourage the creation, publication, and dissemination of more and better materials on Gay people and the Gay movement, and to raise the issues of discrimination against Gays within the library profession."[6] Recognizing the important role books had played in the lives of countless gays and lesbians, it created a Gay Book Award in 1971. Initially, according to Task Force chair Barbara Gittings, members informally discussed books until they reached a consensus concerning the winner. The first award went to Alma Routsong in 1971, who under the pen name Isabel Miller had written *A Place for Us* (later published under the title *Patience and Sarah*). Three years later, on July 9, 1974, Miller presented the third Gay Book Award to Jeannette Foster for *Sex Variant Women in Literature*. Unable to receive the award in person because of her declining health, she sent a message expressing her "delight and overwhelmed gratitude at being chosen," noting with pleasure that the "long-respected ALA is willing to admit the existence—and even honor it—of Gaiety!"[7]

Recognition of *Sex Variant Women in Literature* by lesbians and librarians generated interest in making the long-out-of-print book accessible. In July 1974 Gittings optimistically announced in an ALA press release that

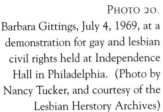

PHOTO 20.
Barbara Gittings, July 4, 1969, at a
demonstration for gay and lesbian
civil rights held at Independence
Hall in Philadelphia. (Photo by
Nancy Tucker, and courtesy of the
Lesbian Herstory Archives)

Sex Variant Women in Literature would "soon be commercially republished" because of the demand for its use in college courses on gay literature.[8] Following on the heels of the ALA Gay Book Award, Valerie Taylor published a tribute to Jeannette in the October 1974 *Chicago Gay Crusader*, underscoring the significance of *Sex Variant Women in Literature* as "a germinal work, a basic sourcebook not only for homophile researchers but for lovers of literature, students of social trends, and the growing forces of fighters for human liberation." In the early 1970s, she reminded readers, librarians who sought to build collections of gay literature used it as their primary selection aid. Encouraging younger readers to purchase the book when it was republished, she praised it as being "compactly written, well-documented, soundly judgmental, and a joy to read."[9] Almost overnight, *Sex Variant Women* became the cornerstone to gay literary history.

It was in this context that Jeannette, the woman who had been forced to self-publish twenty years earlier, found herself being courted by several people who wished to reprint her classic study. Valerie Taylor wrote urging Jeannette to let the Lavender Press of Chicago reissue *Sex Variant*

Women in Literature while W. Dorr Legg, a founder of *ONE*, the first openly marketed gay and lesbian periodical in the nation, expressed interest in including it in a multivolume set to be published by Garland Press. Arno Press managing editor Leslie Parr inquired about including Jeannette's book in a similar venture, a series to be edited by Jonathan Ned Katz, but by the time she inquired, Jeannette had decided to let another press undertake the project. The 69-volume Arno reprint project, *Homosexuality: Lesbians and Gay Men in Society, History and Literature* (1975), included such classic texts as *Sexual Inversion* by Havelock Ellis and a complete run of *The Ladder*. After surveying the scene, Jeannette observed: "There seems to be a perfect *rash* of amateur publishing groups rushing to put out gay writing of all sorts."[10]

The Two Barbaras

Two individuals who wanted to see Jeannette's book republished at times appeared to be competing with one another for the privilege of shepherding it into print. Barbara Gittings, as Jeannette noted, was "talking (vaguely but optimistically) about getting my Opus reissued by W. W. Norton [who ironically had rejected the book in 1956] or Penna. [sic] State Press . . . and B. Grier is pleading the excellence of Diana Press in Baltimore." While she had known Grier since the late 1950s, she had only met Gittings through correspondence that year. The two Barbaras, she knew, were "mortal enemies" because of the falling out they had while working on *The Ladder*. In Jeannette's opinion, the problem was that "they both *have* to *run things*." In later years, Gittings attributed their differences to the fact that she had been made editor of *The Ladder* in 1963 instead of Grier, while Grier attributed their conflict to differences in movement philosophy and priorities.[11]

At first glance, Gittings seemed well placed to help Jeannette get the book republished. Born in 1932, the energetic young woman come out to herself during freshman year at Northwestern University dropped out, and moved to Philadelphia when she was just eighteen. During the next eight years Gitting's search for information about her sexual identity led her to Edward Sagarin, who under the name Donald Webster Cory had published *The Homosexual in America*. Sagarin told her about the Mattachine Society in Los Angeles. Traveling to California in 1956, she visited the editorial offices of *ONE*, attended her first Daughters of Bilitis meeting, and became acquainted with DOB founders Phyllis Lyon and Del Martin. With their encouragement, she founded a chapter of the Daughters of Bilitis in New York City two years later. Her tireless commitment to the cause led to her appointment as editor of *The Ladder* in 1963, a position she held for three years.[12]

Jeannette observed several significant changes in *The Ladder* during Gittings's editorship, among them a move away from an emphasis on assimilation, public image, and reliance on heterosexual experts to validate the homosexual's existence to the practice of having homosexuals speak for themselves. Gittings added the word *lesbian* to the masthead in March 1964 (*The Ladder: A Lesbian Review*) and replaced line drawings on the covers with photographs of lesbians who appeared happy and wholesome. Attempting to increase *The Ladder's* appeal to gay males because she wanted to build bridges with men, she published an increasing number of articles by men as well as scientific studies pertaining to male homosexuals. Jeannette, like Del Martin, had a problem with the male attitude toward women generally, and disliked the direction *The Ladder* was taking under Gittings's leadership.[13]

In Jeannette's opinion, Gittings also was a bit of a dilettante, attempting to juggle editorial responsibilities with picketing at the White House, the Pentagon, the Civil Service Commission, and the State Department. Pulled in many directions, Gittings struggled to keep the publication on schedule, which became a significant problem since DOB leaders relied on *The Ladder* to publicize upcoming meetings. Removing Gittings from the editorship in the summer of 1966, Del Martin and Phyllis Lyon served as acting editors until Helen Sandoz (a former DOB president) could assume the responsibility in November 1966. Sandy, as her friends called her, had been associated with *The Ladder* for many years and had used her skill as a graphic designer to create a number of memorable cov-ers. During her term as editor, which spanned from late 1966 through August 1968, Barbara Grier served as poetry and fiction editor.[14]

The year 1968 was an especially volatile time throughout the nation, with the assassinations of Bobby Kennedy and Martin Luther King Jr., student antiwar protests, and riots at the Democratic National Conven-tion. It also was a time of discord and change for the DOB. At its August 1968 meeting, Rita Laporte became president and brought a radical fem-inist perspective to that office. In contrast with earlier DOB leadership, she argued that lesbians should fight for the liberation of their sisters rather than dilute their force by aligning with gay men. The "real gap within humanity," she argued, "is that between men and women, not that between homosexual and heterosexual."[15]

That fall, Barbara Grier, who had been involved with *The Ladder* for more than a decade, writing a review column entitled "Lesbiana" and serving as fiction and poetry editor since 1966, succeeded Helen Sandoz as editor of *The Ladder*. Dropping the subtitle "A Lesbian Review," Grier stressed that *The Ladder* "has long needed to take a more active look at the current world." With her strong literary background, Grier also raised *The Ladder's* literary quality by securing contributions from such prominent and talented writers as Jane Rule, Isabel Miller, Rita Mae Brown, Dolores Klaich, Lee Lynch, Valerie Taylor, Helen Rose Hull, He-lene Rosenthal, and Judy Grahn. During the next four years, Grier worked diligently to expand *The Ladder* in size, circulation, and distribu-tion, but dissension arose among some DOB leaders, who objected to the publication's increasingly feminist political stance. Begun as a forum where lesbians could express themselves with pride, it initially had em-phasized public image and acceptance. After a short alliance with male homosexual goals, the new generation of lesbians demanded that atten-tion be given to such weighty issues as the dual oppressions based on gender and sexual orientation.[16]

Grier and LaPorte worked well together. As their impatience with the DOB grew, they developed a plan to liberate *The Ladder* from an

organization that they regarded as out-of-date and torn apart by disen-
sion. In the summer of 1970, LaPorte, with Grier's enthusiastic approval, took the addressograph plates containing *The Ladder's* mailing
list, along with other files, to her home in Sparks, Nevada. The two jus-
tified the act, arguing that they were saving the magazine from extinc-
tion, while DOB leaders pointedly referred to it as "the theft." Without its
mailing list, the primary means of reaching membership, DOB's national
board dissolved. *The Ladder* continued under Grier's ambitious editorship
for another two years, but ceased with its August-September 1972 issue
due to lack of financial backing. As Lillian Faderman observes, larger
forces helped dictate this publication's fate. With the proliferation of lesbian publishing houses such as Daughters, Inc., and Naiad Press, as well
as lesbian periodicals such as *The Furies, Lesbian Connection,* and *Lesbian
Tide;* feminist publications that included lesbians, such as *off our backs;*
and feminist lesbian/gay periodicals such as *Gay Community News* and
Come Out!, women had a wide array of outlets for validating their identities, displaying pride, and venting anger.[17] For sixteen years, *The Ladder*
had alleviated the isolation of thousands of lesbians, provided readers
with quality fiction, served as a vehicle for communication, and became
a powerful consciousness raising tool. A new generation of lesbians built
on this foundation to create new vehicles for print, action, music, and
community-based gay liberation movement.[18]

The Diana Press Edition

Jeannette would have enjoyed seeing a mainstream publisher reissue her
book and at first allowed herself to be flattered by Gittings's optimistic
promises. Writing to Grier about Gittings's plans, she asked if her friend
would consider updating the volume from 1954 to the present for a fifty-
fifty split in the profit. With her practical experience in publishing, Grier
knew that the exponential increase in works having gay and lesbian content would have made an expanded volume completely unwieldy and far
too costly to publish in a commercially driven market. Discouraging the

idea of updating the book "to the length of the Britannica," she stressed to Jeannette that her book should remain unaltered. Fearing that Jeannette might hastily sign or write something granting Gittings the right to act on her behalf, Grier urged her to appoint a literary executor, preferably her long-time companion Hazel Toliver.[19]

Despite an improved climate for the publishing of feminist works, it is unlikely that Gittings could have brokered an agreement with Penn State University Press or W. W. Norton, but that question became a moot point when Jeannette lost faith in her ability to deliver. As flattered as she initially was by Gittings's attempts to place the book with a major press, Jeannette ultimately dismissed her as an eternal optimist, someone who promised more than she could deliver. Unfortunately, Gittings made several errors in her interactions with the author of *Sex Variant Women*. First, she delayed in mailing her the Gay Book Award prize, explaining that she wanted to show it to her friends first. As the weeks turned to months, an impatient Jeannette fumed: "I'd say by now the whole gay population of Phila. must have done so." Second, Gittings assumed that Jeannette would want someone to act as her de facto agent with publishers. After Jeannette's frustrating experiences with Rutgers University Press and Vantage Press in the 1950s, however, she had become very fearful of losing control of the book and any royalties it might yet earn. A well-intentioned Gittings contacted Vantage Press about the right to photoprint *Sex Variant Women in Literature*, but Jeannette interpreted this move as an attempt to gain rights to the book. In a letter to Vantage, Jeannette demanded to know: "Have I, as author, not some claim to any profits which might accrue from a new edition?"[20]

As Jeannette pondered the possibility of being republished, Dot Ross and Hazel Toliver unpacked more of her personal library and in the process discovered a copy of Bettie Wysor's *The Lesbian Myth: Conversations and Insights* (1974). The author had asked Jeannette for permission to quote from *Sex Variant Women in Literature* in her forthcoming book, but that request had arrived when she was ill, and while in a mental fog she had given Wysor her unconditional consent. After perusing the complimentary copy,

Jeannette was appalled: Wysor, she claimed, not only had misspelled names of authors and titles but also had included quotes verbatim without acknowledgment. "I think she made a pretty sorry mess—inconsistently handled—of what I *tried* to treat fairly."[21] The errors perturbed Jeannette, but another thought troubled her even more. With Wysor's work, published by Random House no less, why would anyone consider purchasing her dated book from 1956? When Jeannette questioned Gittings, she replied that Wysor's was "heavy going" and that the market for gay and lesbian books was large enough for both books, as well as for the recently published *Woman Plus Woman: Attitudes toward Lesbianism* by Dolores Klaich. A magnificent work, it offered a historical overview of lesbianism with emphasis on the damage done by the religious and medical communities, and had a completely different scope from Jeannette's book. Digesting this information, Jeannette informed Grier that she thought it would be fun to give Wysor a run for her money by taking the book to a paperback concern.[22]

Eager "to have her book in circulation before the present wave of enthusiasm has cooled down," Jeannette gave Grier permission to initiate contact with the women of Diana Press, who were preparing to publish several anthologies of material excerpted from the now-defunct *Ladder*. Begun in 1972, the Baltimore-based Diana Press was founded by a group of women who wanted to develop skill in printing. At least two—Coletta Reid and Nancy Myron—had been part of the Furies Collective. Begun in Washington, D.C., in 1971, the collective created a newspaper entitled *The Furies* to give voice to the cause of lesbian separatism. Calling sexism the root of all other oppressions, they denounced capitalism, racism, and imperialism. Lesbianism, they argued, was a political choice that women must make if they were to end male supremacy. Other members of the collective included Rita Mae Brown, Charlotte Bunch, Helaine Harris, and Joan Biren. After disbanding, members went on to establish Olivia Records, *Quest: a Feminist Quarterly*, and Women in Distribution, Inc.

Operating on principles similar to that of the Furies, the women of Diana Press believed that feminist businesses offered a solution to women's economic dependence on men and that "there were women's words that could not be spoken or heard because all publishing companies were owned by men." Starting with practically zero capitalization, Reid, her partner Casey Czarnik, and others worked to make the press self-supporting, but to do so required some compromises in their worldview. They faced the conundrum of trying to operate a business in the face of an anti-business attitude. Czarnik lost some supporters when she signed a lease-buy option on a platemaker because they did not approve capital-equipment expenses.[23] Operating with a small team of women, Diana Press began as an instant print shop, accumulating skills and equipment before undertaking its first book project, Rita Mae Brown's *Songs to a Handsome Woman*, in 1973. Keeping the two businesses separate, they did quick printing to cover expenses and small salaries, and they attempted to operate the publishing business as a self-supporting endeavor. Working with secondhand equipment, they published three books and a calendar in 1973, then another three books, a calendar, and a date book in 1974. Based on this track record, and on her positive interactions with them, Barbara Grier had every confidence that the women of Diana would do a professional job with Jeannette's book. Explaining to Coletta Reid that Jeannette was elderly and unwell, she asked to be kept informed about negotiations so she could provide assistance if needed. Jeannette, she explained further, lived in a "good and loving household," but her companions were "relatively indifferent to her work in terms of her writing, and fairly blasé about the book, not understanding interest in it."[24]

By late January 1975, Reid and two other women at Diana had read *Sex Variant Women*, pronounced it "wonderful!" and decided that it should be reissued. Technically, they felt it would be a relatively simple task since all of it except the afterward by Grier was already typeset. Reid optimistically projected that they could begin printing the following April despite the fact that the press had been contending with a host of trials, including equipment that kept breaking down and a fire the previous December that had consumed the third floor and roof of their building. "It seems like the goddesses have had it in for us," Reid exclaimed. "Maybe our strength is being tested?!"[25] It would be tested further still.

When Reid sent samples of Diana Press work to Jeannette, along with a letter conveying interest in the project, she also must have raised the possibility of borrowing money. On a generous impulse Jeannette replied that while she already had loaned money to Hazel and Dot for an "income tax emergency," she might be able to loan Diana $5,000 after April 1. In the meantime, she sent them a check for $20 to cover the postage on the sample materials they had sent her. After this exchange she observed in a letter to Grier that "All these 'queer' new non-commercial presses must be operating on a *broken* shoe-string." Diana's financial limitations, however, did not deter Jeannette, who liked the idea of a women's press, especially one catering to lesbian readers, reissuing her book. "What I *hope*," she replied to Reid in early February, "is that the project may be profitable enough to pay you hardworking women on the Press staff for your efforts." The prospect of seeing her book in print again brightened Jeannette's outlook during the final days before her move to the Randolph County Home on April 1, 1975. In an exuberant note to Grier, she proclaimed: "I HAVE SIGNED THE CONTRACT WITH Diana Press!" After all these years, she reflected, "it does brick me up no end to think of the dear ol' Opus really seeing the light of day, & not just being any longer a Bad Smell in a Dark Corner!"[26]

Once Grier had prepared the afterward and bibliography of notable lesbian literature published from 1955 to 1974, she sent it to Jeannette for review, stressing that any profit generated by the book categorically belonged to Jeannette and underscored that it was "an honor and a privilege to be able to do anything for you."[27] Jeannette, aware that feminist presses had many obstacles to overcome, among them the lack of adequate funding, was not surprised when her book had not appeared by September 1975. "It sounds," she wrote Coletta Reid, "as though you'd be accomplishing a near-miracle if the thing *were* ready before Christmas." Finally, the following April, *Sex Variant Women in Literature* began appearing in bookstores, but Jeannette did not receive her author's copies for another month. "The BOOK arrived this morning," she exclaimed in a letter to the women at Diana Press, "and it's an absolutely PERFECT job! I am simply *swelled* with pride, and I congratulate every one who had anything to do with its production!" The 420-page paperbound book featured an attractive cover designed by Casey Czarnik, Coletta Reid's lover and a partner in Diana Press, on a Strathmore textured pink paper. Inspired by Renée Vivien, the cover was printed in yellow, purple, and red to emphasize Vivien's symbolism carried into daily life: "violets for the first love, lotus and tiger lilies for the second, iris for the third." Jeannette loved the "concealed sexual suggestion of the cymbidium and the warmth of the colors."[28]

In her review of the book for the *Lesbian Tide*, Joy Fisher encouraged lesbian feminists to buy *Sex Variant Women in Literature* because it would give them "a tangible token of lesbian courage." Her only major criticism was of the book's binding, which was glued rather than stitched and, as Jeannette herself noted, fell apart almost as soon as someone opened it.[29] Wanting to print a small run of the book in a library binding, Reid asked Jeannette for a $1,000 publication subsidy. Upon conferring with Dot and Hazel, who controlled her checkbook, Jeannette reported the sad reality of her own financial condition. "I AM TO NO END SORRY not to be enclosing a check for the $1000, but simply ain't got," she concluded. Perhaps, she added hopefully, Diana could take the money from her royalties to produce a hardcover edition. That was not to be. As Reid explained that fall, she doubted if there would be any profit for either of them until well into the second printing. "The book," she reported with regret, "is not selling as well as we had hoped—due to the price." Eight dollars was a bit high at a time when paperback originals sold for twenty-five to thirty-five cents and hardcover books from three to five dollars.[30]

From her Pocahontas, Arkansas, nursing home, Jeannette remained unaware of the challenges wracking Diana Press that would ultimately contribute to its downfall. In early 1976, the women of Diana Press joined (essentially by selling their business to) the Feminist Economic Network (FEN), an association of women's businesses premised on sharing skills and resources. The plan was for them to remain a separate entity as far as operations, while using their assets as a basis to support more women's businesses. In April 1976, FEN members made the controversial purchase of a building for women's businesses in Detroit, Michigan, but within six months the organization had dissolved, and Diana Press was sold back to the original owners. Through their interactions with other feminist businesses, however, Reid and Czarnik had grown close to members of the Oakland (California) Feminist Women's Health Center and learned that the city's Women's Press Collective was on the verge of closing. After considering the overcrowded condition of their Baltimore quarters and the cheaper cost of real estate in Oakland, they decided to move. Before the nine women and their equipment could reach Oakland, however, lesbian feminist Martha Shelley published a paper entitled "What is FEN?" in which she accused FEN members of underhanded dealings. The fact that FEN had been a capitalist venture struck a nerve with lesbians and feminists who believed that capitalism had to be smashed in order to end oppression and sexism. Arriving in the Bay Area amidst rumors and speculation, the Diana Press women felt unfairly hassled as they struggled to establish themselves and rebuild trust among the women's community. The move was a financial disaster, and even worse, tensions escalated internally.[31]

Ambitiously committing to publish eleven books in the fall of 1977, Reid and Czarnik ordered paper and supplies on credit and geared up for production. When Reid wrote to Jeannette in early October 1977 to report on sales figures for *Sex Variant Women* (by then in its second printing), she indicated that they had finally succeeded in "getting things operational" enough to publish *She Who* by the poet Judy Grahn. Jeannette's book, she predicted, would begin making a profit halfway through the sale of the second printing. On October 25, 1977, only a few days after Reid sent that upbeat letter, vandals destroyed much of Diana's equipment, back list, and current work. Czarnik, who understandably was feeling very paranoid at the time, felt that it had been a political attack, but she was not sure of its origin. Diana Press had been involved with the Gay Freedom Parade in San Francisco a short time before, distributing flyers and postcards, so the source could have been right-wing retaliation. On the other hand, she thought that it could have been internal. The Diana Press group had grown larger because of its involvement with the Feminist Women's Health Clinic, and there might have been other discontent. Disheartened by the attack, some of the women left the Press, and those who remained began to disagree about the direction they should take the press in the future. Overburdened with trying to survive, Coletta Reid all but ceased communication with authors.[32]

Feeling a moral obligation because she had encouraged Jeannette to let Diana Press publish her work, Grier consulted with attorney and business partner Anyda Marchant that fall and then advised Hazel to request a royalty statement, to be sent by certified mail. She did not like to think that the women at Diana, many of them from working class backgrounds, would take advantage of Jeannette because she was "elderly, unable to protest, upper middle class white, and therefore, fair game." If Reid failed to respond this time, she advised, the next step would be to have an attorney send a scare letter. By early December 1977, when Hazel still had heard nothing, she turned the matter over to a local attorney, who recommended suing if Reid maintained her silence. While Reid did write Jeannette in February 1978, indicating that the book had hit the break-even point and that Jeannette had $1,383.72 due her in royalties, she reiterated that "our financial situation is extremely precarious" and she did not enclose a check with the letter. A month later, several of what Hazel referred to as the "cheated authors"—Elsa Gidlow, Zsuzsanna Budapest, Ruth Geller, and Rita Mae Brown—were consulting with James R. Taggart, a San Francisco-based attorney, about a joint suit.[33] In a drawn-out investigation on Jeannette's behalf, Taggart learned that the press had sold 2,270 copies. After negotiation that extended until May 1979, he drew up an agreement stipulating that Diana Press would return the negatives of the book to Jeannette, that she was released from the publishing agreement with Diana Press, that Diana Press would pay her the $1,383.72 due her as of December 31, 1978, and would thereafter provide sales summaries and payments at six-month intervals, and that Jeannette would release them from any breaches in the written contract.[34]

By 1978, Jeannette's mind had begun to fail, and she fortunately did not comprehend the problems Hazel Toliver was having in attempting to claim the royalties due her. In an attempt to explain her actions, Coletta Reid admitted to errors in judgment, but stressed that she had not deliberately withheld royalties from Foster or other authors. *Sex Variant Women in Literature*, she elaborated, was a reference work and could not be expected to immediately recoup the cost of production.[35] Even worse than being accused of taking advantage of an aging lesbian confined to a nursing home was the rumor that Reid and her associates sabotaged the press themselves. "I may have exhibited bad judgment," she explained to Grier in February 1979, in making an ill-timed move to the west coast, in trying to expand without adequate resources, and for "not realizing that after the vandalism we should have completely cut back and not attempted any more publishing." In December 1979, the press did send Jeannette her final payment, part of which was used to cover legal fees, and the remainder went to pay nursing home expenses. In the end, this lesbian feminist press also was a victim of the times, and in 1980 Coletta Reid and Casey Czarnik, who was by then a silent partner, signed papers for Chapter 11 bankruptcy.[36] Despite its painful death, Diana Press had provided an important service by making *Sex Variant Women in Literature* available to yet another generation of women.

Womanpress and Two Women

In 1976, Jeannette would have not one, but three, works published by women's presses, the first by Diana Press, the second by Womanpress, and the third by Naiad Press. As a lesbian booklover, Jeannette took pleasure in seeing women's presses established, and she had a deep appreciation for the many obstacles—financial and other—that they faced. From her room in the Randolph County Nursing Home she attempted to stay aware of newly published lesbian titles through correspondence with friends and publication announcements in some of the periodicals she read. Jeannette was so addicted to books that she continued to order them through the mail or from friends despite her limited income and the fact she had nowhere to store such titles in her nursing home room.

Capitalizing on the improved climate for small press books and women's writing, Marie Kuda had founded Womanpress as a sole proprietorship after the initial five hundred copies of *Women Loving Women* were exhausted. Operating from the workshop of friends who had a hobby press in their coach house, she published a second edition of *Women Loving Women* and the text of Lesbian Writers Conference keynote speeches. In early 1976, Kuda had an opportunity to read Jeannette's poems and was blown away, not so much by the quality of the poetry but by its lesbian content, written many years before the publication of Radclyffe Hall's *The Well of Loneliness*. In a letter conveying her appreciation to Jeannette, she wrote, "I am so glad you preserved the poems. Beyond their beauty and form, is the history of an era lost to many of our younger women; a pre-pollution time vibrant with color and smells, heartache, rejection, anticipation and love." Eager to rescue them from oblivion, she began exploring the possibility of publishing a volume featuring the poetry written by Jeannette Foster and Valerie Taylor. Explaining to Jeannette that her press was "a nascent venture with minimal resources," Kuda promised that she would be compensated with boundless enthusiasm and confidence.[37]

Kuda's first challenge was to select those poems which should be included in the anthology from the nearly sixty that survived. Reading through them, she chose the ones that resonated with her for one reason or another. "I particularly like: Illusion, White Night, New England Portrait, the amusing Foreward." After selecting twenty-nine of Jeannette's and twenty-seven of Taylor's for the volume, Kuda and Jeannette continued to correspond about the poems throughout the spring of 1976. In response to Kuda's questioning, Jeannette explained that she had never expected to see her poetry published outside of her college paper or *The*

Ladder. She had written it, she explained, simply to capture her mood on paper, and that had been satisfaction enough. Kuda, on the other hand, found great satisfaction in the creation of the physical book. While she did not hand set all the type for the poetry, she confessed to doing much of it, putting "all the love and care it is so worthy of" into the project. "I want the day to come," she continued, "when your poems and those of women like you can be read by proud women to a mixed audience 'and not a dry eye in the house.'"[38] Jeannette was pleased that changes in her lifetime had at long last resulted in an outlet for her poems, but if she ever thought that her work, especially *Sex Variant Women in Literature*, had played a role in bringing this day about, she kept it to herself.

The following August, Kuda took the galley proofs for *Two Women* with her to the first National Women in Print Conference, which brought approximately 150 women booksellers, printers, publishers, illustrators, distributors, and newspaper and magazine women together at a Camp Fire Girls camp outside Omaha, Nebraska. While there, photographer Tee Corinne first heard about two writers—Valerie Taylor and Jeannette Foster. She had never read any of their writing, so when Kuda shared the proofs of the poetry anthology with her, she curled up in her lover's Volkswagon van "and read, feeling as if each page was a gift, a message from the past which resonated deeply in my present." She knew then that she must go to Arkansas to photograph Jeannette. In the meantime, she ordered copies that she gave her friends, telling them "We have a life in poetry—a record, songs."[39]

In September 1976, Jeannette enthusiastically examined the package containing her ten author's copies of *Two Women: the Poetry of Jeannette Foster and Valerie Taylor*, bound in goldenrod yellow paper. Her poems filled the first half of the volume and spanned the years 1914–1934, while Taylor's were written between 1940 and 1975. It filled Jeannette with pride to see her work published alongside that of her friend and someone for whom she had great respect as a poet. "I was amazed at how decent my verse 'sounds' in print!" she exclaimed with pleasure to Kuda. "You can't imagine how much good you've done an old woman by printing them." Upon close inspection, she found one typographical error in her "Sapphics to One Called Helen" and in characteristic fashion corrected all of her copies by hand. "But don't *you* worry about it, for God's sake!" she informed Kuda. "Most readers won't know how Sapphics ought to scan anyhow!"[40]

As someone who had spent years trying to get her work published in a male-dominated publishing world, Jeannette was thrilled that she had lived long enough to see the rise of women's presses. A pragmatist, she realized that the battle was not yet won because such presses typically struggled financially. Praising Kuda for the work she was doing on behalf of the women's cause, Jeannette declared that she would "die willingly" the day that Womanpress, Diana Press, and others like it became self-supporting. That day would remain an elusive goal because of conflicting beliefs among the editors of women's presses. When the Lesbian Writers Conference III convened in Chicago in September 1976, Kuda requested permission to sell the Diana Press volume at a discounted rate to conference attendees, but financially strapped Diana Press publisher Coletta Reid would not consent. "It is not fair to women's bookstores," she explained in a letter to Grier. Female authors and publishers deserved just compensation for their work and should not have to sacrifice. Forced to sell the book to conference attendees at full price, Kuda compromised by giving a free copy of *Two Women: the Poetry of Jeannette Foster and Valerie Taylor* to everyone who purchased *Sex Variant Women*.[41]

To celebrate the publication of *Two Women*, some of Kuda's friends and several women from the Lesbian Writers Conference held a party on September 23, 1976. After a reading from the book, one of the women put a roll of paper down and invited everyone to write a note to Jeannette. In addition to Kuda, those signing the scroll included Paula Adams, a member of the board of directors of Mattachine Midwest; singer and songwriter Ginni Clemmens; and Sandra Szelag, a Unitarian Universalist minister and co-chair of the Unitarian Universalist Gay Caucus in the 1970s. "Thanks to women like you," wrote playwright and actress Jan Bina, "it's easier for me to work as an artist." Activist Torrie

Osborn effusively praised *Sex Variant Women* as the "most important book *ever* written for lesbians," noting that she was basing her thesis research on Foster's publication. After reading both *Sex Variant Women in Literature* and *Two Women*, poet Penelope Pope wrote that she felt "AFFIRMED. That what I do and what I write is part of a living continuum. That I am part of a viable tradition." Jane Melnick, a writer for *In These Times*, described Jeannette as "one of the true heroines of the lesbian movement" and expressed an ardent wish that she could "feel the pride in your accomplishments you deserve."[42]

When read from cover to cover, Foster and Taylor's poetry spanned seven decades of lesbian life and illustrated the shift from romantic to a more physical form of love. It dawned upon Jeannette that women of Valerie's generation had lived a less constrained life. In an effusive letter to her coauthor, she exclaimed that she loved the sensuality expressed in Valerie's poems, containing references to a lover's body and to making love. Any lesbian who picked up the volume, she anticipated, "would know in a *minute* that practically all my experience 'never happened'— outside my overheated imagination." Actually, upon reflection, she realized that Kuda had edited out the two or three poems "registering success" in love.[43]

Jeannette agonized over who should receive her author's copies of *Two Women*. The trouble, she explained to Valerie Taylor in late October, was "that most of my gay friends were either ignorant of that side of me, *or* were *adoreds* [sic] enough older to be all extinct by now. It's very frustrating to realize the penalty for having worshipped *older* women!" A listmaker, she asked Kuda to send the volume with invoices to two former "old students of mine, who are at present affluent enough to pay the bill!" She also sent Kuda a list of libraries where she had worked. Inspired by the news that several prestigious schools, among them Yale, Brown, and the University of Southern California, had purchased the book, she concluded that "Gaiety *must* be gaining respectability!" and sent Kuda an even more "daring" list of people to receive fliers about the book. These included

PHOTO 21.
Pen friends for the final two
decades of Jeannette's life,
Valerie Taylor led the effort to
organize the Sisterhood Fund.
(Photo by Tee Corinne, and
courtesy of the Lesbian
Herstory Archives)

friends, colleagues, and correspondents living in ten states, including the philosopher Hazel Barnes, Barbara Gittings, and Dolores Klaich.[44]

While a number of women were thrilled to see their heroine's poetry published, the poet Elsa Gidlow gave the anthology a mixed review. The book was, she began, "a generous service to women and Lesbians in making it possible for this intimate writing of two Lesbians to be read," but she found some of the poems embarrassing. Writing from a late-twentieth century viewpoint, she criticized many of Jeannette's contributions as "sentimental and not well crafted: she was too content with clichés of the period." Among the best, she noted, were "A Song Unuttered," "Sapphics," and "Aftermath" (which "has genuine feeling, directly expressed, without sentimentality"). "The Wave" also was a "poignant, direct, a well-made poem that moves one," but could have been improved. She found the last three lines of "Leap Year Night" defeatist and questioned how Jeannette, who could not have been more than 40 when she wrote it, would have given up at such an early age. Concluding her letter on a charitable note, she conceded that "Lesbian readers less exacting than I will buy and cherish this book for emotions that so many will share."[45]

Home Is the Hunter

Jeannette fully expected that her third work to appear in print in 1976 would be a novel, *Home Is the Hunter*. Inspired by events from the late-1930s and written in the 1950s, the wordy yet suspenseful story told of Camilla Mallory, a concert pianist, who while recovering from a nervous breakdown returns to the inherited home of her deceased and much beloved cousin. While there she becomes infatuated with Marcy, her cousin's daughter, who is being mistreated by her con-artist father. Aware of Camilla's lesbianism, which she has kept carefully closeted, the father attempts to blackmail her. The story, which drew upon personal experiences and geographic details from Jeannette's years in New York, Philadelphia, Ohio, and Chicago, concludes with Camilla rescuing the younger girl and hints that they will have a glorious future together.[46]

When presses began asking Jeannette if she had any unpublished work, she retrieved the manuscript from storage and reread its nearly eighty thousand words, concluding that it was "Old Hat, too long for its plot to carry the reading interest," and there was "a sort of 'tone' about the style that's not up to the minute."[47] She was correct about that, but Valerie Taylor, who typed the manuscript for Jeannette in the 1960s, appreciated the fact that her protagonists were "fully developed women, not bed-hoppers or stereotype lesbians." They live, she elaborated, "real lives predicated on the idea that lesbianism is a normal and joyous way of life, that tenderness and human responsibility can accompany passion." Publishers and readers were not ready for that message in the 1950s and 1960s, as Taylor discovered when she asked her agent to attempt placing it in the "straight fiction market." Likewise, when Jeannette tested it on the "boys at One," she remembered, "Hal Call SCORNED it—same as I feel about some Male H stuff!"[48] By the early 1970s, however, Taylor believed publishers would be more receptive.

In 1975 Taylor began encouraging her friend to submit her unpublished fiction for publication, believing that it would be an ego boost as well as a source of extra money. It was, she claimed, "as good as anything that has been published" and she classified one of Jeannette's novels (she was referring to *Home Is the Hunter*) "in the same category with *The Price of Salt* and Bannon's best." Convinced, Jeannette briefly considered sending her novel to Diana Press, but changed her mind after their disastrous fire and move.[49] Then, as Kuda was preparing the contract for *Two Women* in early January 1976, Jeannette summoned the courage to ask if Womanpress ever published fiction. Her inquiry, she qualified, should be immediately disregarded "if it's impertinent." Kuda, whose admiration for Jeannette had grown as she worked on the poetry anthology, replied that she would "love to do your novel" but that it would be a year or two before it would be "within the realm of financial possibility." Offering the possibility of an eighteen-month option with first refusal rights, Kuda (who had received assurance of the novel's merit from Valerie Taylor) vowed that she would publish the work "if I have to set each page of type myself—it is only a question of time."[50]

Previously, Jeannette had published all of her fiction under pseudonyms, and she had originally written *Home Is the Hunter* using the pseudonym Hilary Farr. Times, however, had changed, and she admired the way so many younger women uninhibitedly exercised their freedom. Pondering the question of which name to use for the book, she boldly declared: "I no longer have any reluctance to use my own name . . . Oh, go on & use 'Jeannette Foster' if you think it has sales value! I'll be buried soon enough 'to make no matter.'" She also doubted that the book would be sweeping the reading public, and that the chances of anyone in rural and remote Pocahontas stumbling across it were minuscule. In July she signed and ecstatically returned a contract to Kuda. "All I hope now," she exclaimed, "is that I'll still be alive to enjoy my 'bicentennial'—3 books issued by 3 different houses."[51] Unfortunately, *Home Is the Hunter* never appeared under the Womanpress imprint because it was too long and Kuda's press lacked adequate resources. Several other small presses, among them Metis, A & M Press, and a third group in Arizona, also declined to publish the wordy tome.[52] Even though *Home Is the Hunter* remains unpublished to this day, Jeannette did live to see a third work printed in 1976, by Naiad Press.

Naiad Press

Naiad Press was founded on January 1, 1973, by Barbara Grier, her partner Donna McBride, attorney Anyda Marchant, and her partner Muriel Crawford, when Marchant asked Grier for assistance in getting her novel published. Written under the pseudonym Sarah Aldridge, *The Latecomer* appeared in 1974 and was promoted by sending an announcement of its publication to the entire mailing list from *The Ladder*. During the next thirty-one years, Naiad would go on to publish such best-selling works as Jane Rule's *Desert of the Heart*, Sheila Ortiz Taylor's *Faultline*, and mysteries by Katherine V. Forrest. Operating the press from their rural Bates City, Missouri, home Grier and McBride worked in Kansas City during the day and spent countless hours brush cutting, planting, gardening, baking bread, and canning fruits and vegetables. "We are working toward a time when we can virtually live year round on the produce from the land," Barbara explained.[53] By 1976 Grier and McBride also had published five additional titles under the Naiad Press imprint, two of them written by Marchant as Aldridge. In the summer of 1976, they discussed publishing Jeannette's novel, but had reservations because of the cost involved in publishing a book of this length. Instead, Naiad decided to publish Jeannette's translation of Renée Vivien's *Une Femme M'Apparut* (*A Woman Appeared to Me*), which Jeannette had done years earlier as a birthday gift for Barbara. Writing to Jeannette with their plans, Grier and McBride promised that it would be "a little book, finely produced . . . with a photo cover and a good scholarly introduction by Gayle Rubin."[54]

On a personal level, Jeannette found Vivien fascinating and during the course of her lifetime had done "one *heap* of research" on her and even con-

PHOTO 22.
Jeannette's protégée and friend,
Barbara Grier, circa 1976
(Photo by Donna McBride, and
courtesy of Barbara Grier and
Donna McBride)

templated writing a novel about her. Vivien had begun life as Pauline Mary
Tarn and had adopted the name Renée Vivien early in her writing career.
With her lover Natalie Barney she wrote poetry inspired by the ancient
Greek poet Sappho, and during her short lifetime (she died at age thirty-
two) Vivien wrote an amazing thirteen books of poetry, two novellas, and
three volumes of short fiction and prose poetry that addressed themes of
lesbian love, death, and lust. Although Jeannette never felt fully satisfied
with the translation, it had been done with her characteristic thoroughness
and, as others have noted, captured Vivien's "unique style and feeling."[55] In
her introduction, Gayle Rubin underscored the significance of this publication by reminding readers how the "same silence which makes the practice of lesbian history so arduous also obscures the work of those who
succeeded in illuminating a lesbian past." Like Foster's *Sex Variant Women
in Literature*, which had been out of print for two decades, Vivien's career
had languished in obscurity until Jeannette's translation enabled lesbians of
the 1970s to connect with one of their literary foremothers.[56]

Beginning in the mid-1970s, Jeannette Foster's name and work experienced a renaissance, in large part due to the emergence of feminist and lesbian presses. After struggling unsuccessfully for most of her life to get a few items in print, she took great delight in the three works she had published in 1976. Convinced that male-dominated mainstream presses discriminated against feminist and lesbian works, she sent a note of appreciation to Anyda Marchant: "Think of all us Victims of Male Chauvinism you are saving from oblivion!"[57] Personal growth and the development of community, she knew from personal experience, depended on the printed word, and she was thrilled to witness and be a part of the feminist and lesbian publishing boom of the 1970s. It would appear, she noted, that general public tolerance of lesbianism was on the increase, but thinking back to the "move of comparative tolerance in the 1890s," Jeannette fully expected a backlash. "The 'GOOD,'" she noted, "are sure to become conscious of trends, and get on their snow-white steeds for a 'decency' crusade pretty soon—damn their pious hides!"[58] From her nursing home room in rural Arkansas, Jeannette saw glimmers of a future that would include the rise of the moral majority, but she could not anticipate the impact of economic changes on the publishing world. By the early 1980s small independents like Diana Press and Womanpress would fade away and the rise of media conglomerates would soon follow.

Had it not been for the flourishing women's and lesbian press movement of the early 1970s, Jeannette easily could have sunk into obscurity. The rediscovery of *Sex Variant Women in Literature* by post-Stonewall gays and lesbians, however, meant that at last Jeannette would receive the recognition she deserved for her pioneering work. Through correspondence with this younger generation of lesbians, Jeannette developed a deeper appreciation for the path she had traveled from romantic friendship to gay pride, and the many bridges she had crossed along the way.

⚶ Ten ⚶

Exit Laughing

Sometimes I'm reduced to envying that monk in Siberia
Whose life it grew dreariah and dreariah—
Till he burst from his cell
With the hell of a yell
And eloped with the Mother Superiah!
— JEANNETTE HOWARD FOSTER, 1977[1]

In June 1977 Tee Corinne and her partner Honey Lee Cottrell made the pilgrimage to the Randolph County Nursing Home in Pocahontas, Arkansas, to photograph Jeannette Foster. The receptionist, unaware of Jeannette's area of expertise, informed the two women that "Miss Foster" was expecting them, and that she could not understand why so many people came from great distances to see her. Entering the room bearing long-stemmed red Richmond roses, they found Jeannette standing at the foot of her bed looking "neat and matronly in a print dress, her short curly silver hair well combed. After sending the nurse to find a vase, Jeannette turned to them with a sparkle in her eyes and said, "Great legs." Even at 81, she still had an eye for women. Joined a few minutes later by Barbara Grier and Donna McBride, the five women left the home to dine in a local restaurant. All of them, except Jeannette, were wearing slacks and had short hair. According to Tee, the word lesbian was said "loudly enough and frequently enough that we caused quite a stir." After lunch

PHOTO 23.
Seated from left to right, Tee
Corinne, Barbara Grier. Standing
from left to right, Donna J.
McBride and Honey Lee Cottrell.
Taken in Kansas City, June 1977,
before driving to Pocahontas for a
visit with Jeannette. (Photo by
Honey Lee Cottrell, and courtesy of
Barbara Grier and Donna McBride)

they adjourned to the Baltz Lake home where Hazel and Dot lived. It was there that Honey and Tee took photographs. In one of them Jeannette was looking at the lesbian comic book, *Dynamite Damsels*, by Roberta Gregory, laughing as she read it. It was a pleasant day.[2]

The following year Tee stopped to visit Jeannette again. It was September, and she was traveling with a new lover, one who lacked interest in lesbian history and visiting old ladies in nursing homes. Tee went to Jeannette's room alone. Although she had called ahead, Jeannette was still in bed, and it was obvious that her health had declined significantly during the intervening year. Uninhibited, she pulled a portable toilet on wheels out from under the bed and used it while talking to Tee about the problems of having arthritis. "Despite the casualness and nonchalance of her behavior," Tee recalled, "I sensed that she was aware of the intimacy and outrageousness of peeing in front of me and took delight in the activity." It was a hot and humid Arkansas day, and Tee had dressed in a tank top, cut off jeans, and sandals. She chose to sit on the wooden arm of a chair, stretching a little from her cross-

Photo 24.
Lesbian photographer Tee
Corinne shot this image of
Jeannette during a 1977 visit to
Pocahontas, Arkansas. (Photo
by Tee Corinne, and courtesy
of the Special Collections and
University Archives,
University of Oregon Libraries)

country drive. Jeannette sat in front of her, looking at Tee's left foot and then the right, left knee and then the other, up her legs to her hips, hands, arms, breasts, and finally her face. "Oh, yes," she said and smiled, leaving Tee tingling all over. In 1985, when Tee designed the cover for the Naiad Press edition of *Sex Variant Women in Literature*, she thought of that day. "I wanted the cover to have a sultry question-ing seductiveness," she remembered, "as rich with possibilities as the way her eyes had caressed me."[3]

Jeannette could not evade the effects of aging, but as Valerie Taylor observed, she met them "with grace and humor, making necessary concessions, without fuss, and holding fast to important things." With the approach of her eighty-second birthday, she jokingly expressed concern about being sentenced to another decade of existence. "Can you think of any sadder end than dying of boredom?" Lest anyone think she was depressed, she hastened to add that she was "not all that bored yet!"[4] As long as her arthritic hands allowed her to write and she could see, Jeannette lived vicariously through letters from friends and by reading and rereading her beloved books. The interest shown in her life and work, especially in 1976, temporarily revived her failing mind and she freely responded to questions posed by the young gays and lesbians who contacted her. Those accounts are invaluable today for the light they shed on lesbian life during the first half of the twentieth century.

Back into the Closet

Mentally alert but an invalid by virtue of her spinal problem, Jeannette pragmatically chose to enter a nursing home because she knew the demands of her care would become too much of a physical burden for Dot and Hazel, seventy and seventy-four, respectively. Jeannette consciously attempted to closet herself when she moved to the home primarily because she wanted to protect her friends. In a community the size of Pocahontas, Jeannette explained to friends living elsewhere, "it would be absolute suicide to have it known one was gay." Indeed, Arkansas was not a receptive environment for gays and lesbians, and in March 1977, the state legislature recriminalized same-sex acts between consenting adults. Personally, she explained, she did not "give 'one whoop & hurrah in Hades'" when it came to herself, but she hated for her companions "to get tarred with the same brush." She would live out her life as an "Eternal Imposter," if it would safeguard their reputations.[5] This was easier said than done. As she looked around the nursing home, Jeannette was convinced that she had spotted several women among the nurses who could be lesbians. "There's one, a *gorgeous* butch, who's as mean as hell," she reported to Karla Jay, "& I'm told—by another nurse—that her sister once worked here, had 'favorites' among the patients, & got fired—so this one isn't making the same mistake." If she could spot them, she reasoned, it was logical to assume that they could identify her as a lesbian. She became all the more convinced after one of the young attendants lent her a magazine with a female baseball umpire on the front cover.[6]

As a cosmopolitan woman, one of Jeannette's biggest adjustments was to life in a semiprivate room with women from different educational, regional, sexual, and socioeconomic backgrounds. She strived to be courteous and sociable to them and their family members, doing little favors whenever possible and sharing treats mailed to her by friends like Valerie Taylor. She found her first roommate, a dirt farmer's wife named Clara Hurn, friendly, sane, and acutely pious yet congenial even though she never finished grade school and had only lived one winter away from Randolph County. She was, Jeannette explained, her "first acquaintance with virtual illiteracy." Few residents of the home, she stressed, comprehended the significance of a PhD, let alone the fact that she possessed one.

An agnostic since the late 1910s, Jeannette refused to attend religious services held in the home. Seeking to mollify a concerned Mrs. Hurn, she explained that she was a Unitarian, but then had to define it. Upon hearing the explanation, Mrs. Hurn became certain that she "wasn't 'saved' and expressed daily regret." Other well-intentioned residents of the home spent, or as Jeannette said, "wasted," time trying to "save" her. "GOD," she wrote a year and a half after entering the home, "how I loathe the Bible Belt, smack in the middle of which I seem to have landed. I *tell* you, when I entered Ark. I fell off the edge of civilization!"[7]

Twice each week, Hazel and Dot gave Jeannette much-needed relief from the nursing home when they brought her to the lake house for day visits. There, she spent long afternoons cataloging their collective library, eating delicious home-cooked food that Dot prepared, enjoying convivial conversation, playing with the cats, and drinking sherry. Dot and Hazel had created a special space in the library for a few volumes from her "hidden collection"—albeit on a lower shelf obscured by a piece of furniture so Hazel's young high-school age niece would not accidentally find them. She was bright enough, they speculated, to know "all about gaiety," and would "spread the news like mad if she suspected Dot & Hazel."[8] Even that space, Jeannette worried, was not especially private.

Still, that was where she kept the psychological and medical texts about homosexuality she had used to prepare her life's work and her treasured works of lesbian literature spanning from Sappho to the latest novel by her friend Valerie Taylor. At the end of each visit, she selected a volume or two to take back to the home with her for the coming week's reading.

For a woman whose identity had shifted during the course of her lifetime from variant to lesbian, and who for decades had lived unabashedly as a woman-loving woman, returning to the closet proved to be a difficult assignment. In national publicity surrounding the American Library Association's Gay Book Award in 1974 she had freely admitted to having deep emotional attachments to a number of women, including six with whom she had "physical expression." The publication of *Sex Variant Women in Literature*, *Two Women*, and the Renée Vivien translation in 1976 brought further attention to her as a lesbian writer. After the 1976 printing of *Sex Variant Women*, the local librarian called one day after work to bring Jeannette a sack full of review sheets in which she found the Diana Press edition of her book featured as a starred review in *Booklist* describing her book as a study of "women who are conscious of passion for their own sex." Other residents of the community may have read Karla Jay's profile of her in *MS Magazine*, entitled "Lesbianism from the Bible On," but it is doubtful if many discovered that Jonathan Katz had dedicated his *Gay American History* (1976) to her and Mattachine Society founder Henry Hay.[9]

Jeannette's lesbianism was so central to her identity that it remained intact despite the ravages of old age and the reality of life in a nursing home. Try as she might, she could not quell her lifelong habit of admiring women. After Karla Jay came to interview her in June 1975, Jeannette wrote to say that she found herself "thinking both during your visit & afterwards that it was lucky for our peace of mind that I have passed so far beyond twenty-eight myself or I should undoubtedly make a nuisance of myself pursuing you." All passion had been spent, she elaborated, but she nonetheless found it gratifying "to recognize 'the potential affinity.'"[10] As a young lesbian searching for her history, Karla enjoyed

Jeannette's tart wit, positive outlook on life, ongoing interest in activities of the Gay Academic Union, and willingness to share openly about her lesbian past.

Likewise, Jeannette had many reasons for liking Karla, among them her passion for life and her comfort with her sexuality. In her frank letters to the older woman, Karla shared openly about her work, writing, and relationships—sexual and otherwise. In the process, she became a lifeline connecting Jeannette to news of the gay world, and she also became a source of vicarious pleasure. Karla, who had been born in Brooklyn in 1947, had her social consciousness awakened in the late 1960s when she witnessed the student uprisings on the Columbia University campus. Politicized, she threw herself into the Redstockings, a radical feminist and Marxist group that included such members as Alix Kates Shulman and Rita Mae Brown, and into the Gay Liberation Front. Committed to promoting lesbian visibility, she edited (with Allen Young) *Out of the Closets: Voices of Gay Liberation* (1972) and *After You're Out: Personal Experiences of Gay Men and Lesbian Women* (1975).[11]

Despite the more than fifty years difference in their ages, a special bond formed between the aging foremother and the lesbian activist as they exchanged lengthy letters in the ensuing months. The serialized biographies they shared with one another prompted Jeannette to reflect on the differences that existed between them, largely because of the eras in which they had come of age. Karla's story, she noted, had convinced her that "no matter how emancipated we imagine ourselves, mentally, we are rooted to the bone in the mores of our generation." Jeannette admired and envied "the freedom you've enjoyed in having experience with both men and girls," but simply could not imagine emulating it.[12] From the safety of her nursing home room, however, she could express the fervent wish that she had been in New York to take part in Lesbian Pride Week. "The semi-nude dance in the street near Columbia," she exclaimed, "I'd have loved to see! How times have changed since I taught a sedate summer term there in 1940!"[13]

As Karla's activities consumed more and more of her time, and Jeannette's mind began to fade, their correspondence slowed to a trickle. Yet,
when there was a fire in Karla's apartment in early 1977, the generous-
hearted Jeannette sent her a check to help her "keep body & soul together."
In one of her last letters to Karla, Jeannette wondered if she would ever see
"the east" again and yearned for "the wildest chance" that Karla would
make another trip through Arkansas to alleviate some of the boredom and
dreariness that had dampened her optimistic outlook. Yet even in this letter of woe Jeannette rallied to comment on a head nurse who would tempt
her if only "I were young, slim, spry, and the way I *wish* I'd been at 19!" At
eighty-two, she was not yet ready to change her ways.[14]

After the MS article, gays and lesbians around the nation had reason
to assume that Jeannette was living openly as a lesbian. Writing to their
heroine, the woman they had come to know as their lesbian foremother,
well-meaning admirers unwittingly sent lesbian periodicals, newspapers,
and newsletters to her at the nursing home. After Karla Jay sent a copy
of *After You're Out*, Jeannette wrote to acknowledge the book, which she
had kept hidden in her room. "Now brace yourself for a shock," she explained, "but I am *not* out of the closet yet," at least not in the nursing
home. In all likelihood, she was not fooling anyone because Jeannette
typically stored her overflowing correspondence and reading material in
an unlocked drawer and she continued her lifelong habit of ordering lesbian books through the mail or from friends. In her eagerness to see new
books when they arrived at the home, she sometimes asked attendants to
help open the packages. Keeping an open mind to the end, Jeannette
may have preferred old-fashioned romance to the newer literature, but
her intellectual curiously demanded that she stay abreast of current
trends. Therefore, people walking down the hall could see her eagerly
turning the pages of Robin Jordan's *Speak Out, My Heart* and Jane Rule's
Lesbian Images.[15]

Despite her physical limitations, Jeannette remained a voracious
reader and an avid correspondent. After devouring an issue of the
Chicago Gay Crusader sent to her by Valerie Taylor, she let her know that

the "*male ads* in the Crusader were not to my taste, and I know the bars & grills they touted wouldn't be either!"[16] Even though her friendship with May Sarton had soured, Jeannette made a point of acquiring her recently published books as well as any biographies written about her. When Jeannette offered to pay Barbara Grier and Donna McBride for the Naiad Press books they sent, Barbara declared: "You MAY NOT buy any NAIAD PRESS books. You are an honorary NAIAD PRESS person for ever. . . . I love you, adore you, and you are not to send me any money for anything. You are and always have been the most generous person on earth . . . but it is time to NOT be. You are more than entitled to receive anything I might humbly publish . . . you have enriched my life in more ways than I can ever repay."[17]

Jeannette, who enjoyed reading anything that Valerie Taylor wrote, impatiently begged her to send carbons of new manuscripts because she could not wait for the published works. After devouring Taylor's draft of *Prism*, a novel exploring lesbian love and sex after sixty, Jeannette expressed concern that it would be difficult to find a publisher who would "dare bring out in public print your exquisitely realistic '69' scene. . . . It exceeded in graphic vividness anything I have hitherto met in print." She clearly was not too prudish to discuss the subject with her friends, noting that she knew a "pair who regularly celebrated their ecstasy in just that fashion."[18]

Taylor, Marie Kuda, and others also sent Jeannette newly published volumes of lesbian poetry. Reading them, she explained, had made her keenly aware of her work's old-fashionedness. Many of the poems in Claudia Scott's "Portrait," she noted, were "intellectually beyond me," although she loved the sound of them as much as she did a concerto by Jewish composer Arnold Schoenberg, which she heard on television one evening. She pronounced Penelope Pope's *The Enclosed Garden* charming even though she felt too old-fashioned to fully comprehend the verse. The younger generation, she realized, had begun to use idioms of thought that were not native to her eighty-two-year-old reading habits, yet they succeeded in conveying "wonderfully well the emotional moods out of which the—to me—unexpected words grow; and after all," she reflected, "what else is poetry for?"[19]

Correspondence, Her Lifeline

When Jeannette moved to the relative isolation of Pocahontas, or Pokey, as she loved to call it, the mail carrier became her lifeline to the outside world. Her twice-weekly visits with Hazel and Dot, while pleasant, were not enough for a woman with Jeannette's need to communicate. Channeling conversation into correspondence with distant friends, the act of letter writing preserved her sense of belonging to a community, provided an outlet for venting frustration, and helped her transcend the boring and monotonous routine of her nursing home existence. It is impossible to reconstruct Jeannette's address book, but it would have included her sisters Anna (until her death in April 1975) and Helen, who continued the family habit of sending regular newsy letters. Throughout her life, Jeannette had made a concerted effort to remain in contact with many of her former loves. Clara Louise Thompson and Miriam Tompkins had passed away by the time she entered the home, but she corresponded with Grace Taylor, Jennie Gregory, and Lenore Ward, as well as with former Shorter and Drexel students, authors whose books she had admired, and a host of new acquaintances who initiated contact after reading *Sex Variant Women in Literature*.[20] Jeannette struck up a pen friendship with Anyda Marchant, who wrote *Latecomer* under the pseudonym Sarah Aldridge, because she enjoyed Marchant's portrayal of "our" world. For the most part, Jeannette's correspondents, who included former students and colleagues, were lesbian or knew that she was.[21]

Pocahontas was the smallest community in which Jeannette had ever lived, and at first she fretted that the post office was not adequately prepared to handle her correspondence with friends in such remote places as South Africa and Greece. She also worried that local postal officials would discover that she was mailing and receiving literature with lesbian content. On occasions when Jeannette wanted to mail homosexual books from her library to friends elsewhere, she had to rely on Dot to wrap materials in a way that "the P. O. here didn't refuse them." In 1976 when Valerie Taylor sent Jeannette the manuscript of her novel *Prism*, it arrived torn lengthwise, prompting Jeannette to fret that the "P.O. authorities could have gained not only the fact that it was fiction, but even, I fear, what sort of fiction—tho none of the *erotic* passages were legible." Her concern was not unfounded, having lived through an era when people had lost their jobs for receiving material deemed obscene because of its homosexual content in the mail. It also stemmed, in part, from her years at the Institute for Sex Research, where she had observed Kinsey's legal battles over alleged violations of the Comstock Act, which outlawed the sending of obscene material through the mail.[22]

Correspondence with younger gays and lesbians gave Jeannette opportunities to reflect on the changes that had occurred for gays and lesbians since her childhood. She found some of the younger generation's ideas amusing. It was silly, she thought, to refer to history as herstory, and she referred to lesbians who went on unemployment rather than working for men as "idiots." Raised to be a "proper" lady, she was "most definitely turned off" by "very butchy boys—also *very* butchy gals" who wore leather jackets and rode motorcycles. While she enjoyed the way young lesbians like Karla Jay spoke so frankly about their sexuality, she noted that her generation "had grown up concealing our gayness as if it were syphilis!" It was a hard habit for many to break. When Karla Jay prepared to write the *MS Magazine* article, Jeannette stressed that she did not want to out herself or the women she had loved in her lifetime. "I can't tell you why," she explained, but "I would feel as if I had been permanently stripped naked." It was, she noted, "just the way we were brought up."[23] Shaped by her era, Jeannette always had been careful to protect the identities of her closeted lovers and had spent much of her life operating under the principle of "don't ask, don't tell." Even though a younger generation of lesbians viewed Jeannette as courageous for publishing *Sex Variant Women in Literature* under her own name, she had done so out of pride for her scholarship, not to make a statement about her sexuality.

Uninhibited

Jeannette's interest in sexuality remained unabated despite her age and residence in a nursing home. In February 1977, while devouring *Lavender Herring: Lesbian Essays from the Ladder* (Diana Press, 1976), she paused long enough to exclaim that she was "having the time of my life" reading "so much FIRST CLASS PROSE!" It was so good, Jeannette confided, that she had enclosed the volume in a leather envelope to conceal its title because "the gals wouldn't let me bring it back here with me as long as the word *Lesbian* was visible." In her eagerness to see the next volume, which she understood to be about "how *women* can give each other most pleasure," she wrote Barbara Grier to see if she would let her read it in a rough draft. "Somehow I don't think it will teach me much— but you never know!" Reading *Lavender Herring*, *Sinister Wisdom* (a lesbian periodical founded in 1976), and other publications prompted her to recall her earlier life and loves. "I really have enjoyed living and loving, when and how I have done it!" she informed Grier.[24]

Inspired by Karla Jay's openness, Jeannette began to share intimate details from her life history with her and subsequently with Jonathan Katz. Most of the women who were near Jeannette's age had lived carefully closeted lives out of fear that they would lose their jobs, homes, family, and friends. She seldom reminisced about the past with them, but when writing to younger gays and lesbians, she felt free to include explicit details about earlier relationships. Writing matter-of-factly, she discussed such topics as tribadism (mutual masturbation), casual sexual encounters, and serial monogamy. Imagine Hazel's horror if she happened upon such topics in Jeannette's unfinished letters, lying on a table in her room at the nursing home or spilling out of a handbag. Prompted by such incidents, Hazel spent many hours thinking about the need for privacy in nursing homes.[25]

In September 1977, Jeannette completed four pages out of fifteen pages of a detailed Sexuality Survey administered by Karla Jay and Allen Young. After responding to questions dealing with sex, emotions and love, specific sexual acts, and other sexual preferences, she grew weary of answering and wrote a concluding note: "I think I've said enough to be quite clear on my attitude! And I've lived with it 82 years!" Emotional involvement, she explained, was critical to her relationships and she preferred her partner to be feminine. Her willingness to answer questions about such topics as cunnilingus, dildos, and bondage stands as a testimony to her remarkably open mind.[26]

That fall, the historian Jonathan Katz also wrote Jeannette with the news that he would like to include her story in a sequel to *Gay American History.* Eager to help, she sent him a detailed response of approximately fifteen hundred words in which she discussed her experiences with crushes, physical intimacy, and Alfred Kinsey. Katz, sensing that he had tapped a wealth of information, replied with delight, and requested permission to come to Pocahontas for an interview with her. When his follow-up letter went unanswered he wrote again on December first, explaining that he was simply trying to clarify what he could and could not say about her in the book. "Do you not want me to include any direct references to your own Lesbianism? Or are you simply worried about references referring to other women?" It would, he assured her, be easy to disguise them if that was the case.[27] Unfortunately, Jeannette never responded.

Hazel Intervenes

Jeannette had begun noticing lapses in her short-term memory in early 1976, when she was eighty. Unable to remember when she received or read books sent to her by friends, she exclaimed: "I really am beginning to worry about the holes in my mind!"[28] She would ask Hazel to order books, only to have her "cry out 'Why, you've had that for weeks, & looked it through out here 2 or 3 times!'"[29] Part of the problem was that her books and files of correspondence were stored at the lake house where she could not easily use them to refresh her memory.

Meanwhile, as Jeannette's responses to Katz and Jay indicate, her long-term memory may have been too excellent for comfort. Hazel and Dot would have had valid reasons to worry about the impact of Jeannette's lesbianism on their lives. As two unmarried women living together, they faced a difficult time in a rural southern community. On several occasions someone had vandalized their mailbox and Hazel anticipated that worse would occur if people suspected them of being lesbians. "This is a very small town," she explained to Barbara Grier, "full of (from my point of view) kind-hearted but definitely narrow-minded people. Since we hope we are permanently settled here, we do not want tongues wagging about us or neighbors being afraid to associate with us. I'm sure you understand the problem." Hazel was so concerned about her reputation that she overcame her social phobia and with Dot accepted a cousin's invitation to join the Church of Christ.[30] The fact that neither woman had attended church for years and Hazel's goal for retirement had been to remain uninvolved suggests that this decision was a measure intended to deflect gossip.

Driven by concern for her reputation in the community, Hazel overlooked how central and vital Jeannette's lesbianism was to her identity and how crucial contacts with the outside world were for her day-to-day happiness. Informing Jeannette that some of her mail was getting lost, she convinced her that it would be best to have all of it sent to the Baltz Lake address, especially since she was managing her business and financial affairs. In December 1977 Hazel began informing correspondents that Jeannette no longer possessed the concentration necessary to respond to their letters. Even though she sent a critique of Penelope Pope's poetry to Valerie Taylor that month, she refused to write Christmas cards, something she had done dutifully for years. "We do not know why she cannot make herself write," wrote Hazel to Valerie Taylor, "unless it is because of her short attention span." That was just one reason for her sudden change of habit. "Just NOTHING," she complained, "happens in these Rest Homes—so what is there to write about?"[31] As a result, however, people who had been accustomed to receiving her long and detailed letters ceased writing as frequently.

Once Jeannette's mail was transferred to the lake address, it became easier for Hazel to control gay and lesbian access to her. Responding to Katz on Jeannette's behalf, she explained that he had not offended Jeannette while informing him that "she does not wish to be identified as a Lesbian. She lives in a very small conservative town and in a nursing home where the other residents would be shocked at any mention of homosexuality. . . . She has made every effort since moving here to keep that aspect of her life hidden. . . . There have already been a few [open references to her lesbianism], about which, I think, she is sorry." If he chose to send further correspondence to Jeannette, Hazel advised, he should conceal the fact that she had told him about her "failing mental and physical condition." After a few more overtures in an attempt to convince Hazel of Jeannette's historical significance, Katz respected Toliver's request: neither Jeannette nor *Sex Variant Women in Literature* are mentioned in his *Gay/Lesbian Almanac* (1983). On the other hand, Hazel encouraged Jeannette to write a short biographical essay for Valerie Taylor, who planned to speak about Jeannette's life and work at an upcoming Lesbian Writers Conference. The finished piece is a testimony to her still-sharp long-term memory but at the same time suggests that Hazel probably discouraged her customary frankness: while it contained remarkably accurate details about her childhood, education, and career, it was noticeably devoid of information about her life as a lesbian.[32]

By the end of 1977, Jeannette's mental and physical condition deteriorated to the point that the nursing home upgraded her status from self-care to intermediate care, meaning that she now required some regular assistance. Friends who did not see her for many months or even years at a time were struck by the effects of age on the once-brilliant mind. It was hard, Barbara Grier explained, to see her long-time friend "come apart at the mental seams." Despite the obvious love and care

Jeannette received, it did not compensate "for the general sadness of the whole thing."[33]

In early February 1978, Hazel wrote a form letter "To the friends of Jeannette Foster" to inform them of the change. "Jeannette still loves you and is pleased when she gets a letter from you," but in addition to being confined to bed much of the time and walking "with constant fear of falling," she had begun suffering from confusion. "She frequently calls us," Hazel elaborated, "and does not know where she is, imagining that she is in Philadelphia or in some other place where she once lived. Yet when we talk with her she is quite intelligent, and she has not forgotten us or any of her old friends."[34]

Once she could no longer look forward to daily mail delivery or express herself freely, some of the purpose and zeal went out of Jeannette's life. Without avenues for freely discussing that about which she had encyclopedic knowledge and opportunities to share her life experiences with others, she floundered. Growing depressed, she became withdrawn and told her sister Helen that she prayed every night that she "would not wake up the next morning."[35] With cataracts impairing her vision, the woman who once devoured whole books in an afternoon now found it difficult to read more than four or five pages of a large-print book at a time. She eagerly anticipated cataract surgery in the summer of 1979 and was quite disappointed when the surgeon decided against performing the operation, reportedly because of her age. In Valerie Taylor's opinion, Jeannette was precipitated into senility by the cataracts that rendered her unable to read.[36] Occasional letters and gifts from friends brightened her days, but much of the time she felt cut off from the world that had given her life and purpose.

The Sisterhood Fund

Throughout her working life Jeannette had planned for retirement by investing in four pension plans, but as a single working woman who spent much of her life in the female-intensive profession of librarianship, her earning power had been modest. When she entered the Randolph County Home as a self-care resident in 1975, her pension income was sufficient to cover monthly fees and prescriptions, but as the cost of care and medicine increased, it became evident that her savings would prove to be inadequate. The retirement annuity she had established in 1922, for instance, paid only $17.75 per month in 1976. Once she needed intermediate care, her monthly fees exceeded her income and Hazel and Dot had to make up the difference.[37] Hazel knew that it was only a matter of time before Jeannette became a full-care patient.

Even though she wanted to protect Jeannette's identity as a lesbian, Hazel believed that one way to generate income was by pushing Diana Press to pay the royalties due Jeannette from the 1976 publication of *Sex Variant Women in Literature*. She explained in a letter: "I understand that it *has* been forced to pay some authors lately." Working with the local attorney who had prepared their taxes and San Francisco attorney James R. Taggart throughout 1979, she learned that Jeannette was due $1,383 for the 2,270 copies of the book that had sold. In December 1979, when Jeannette finally received her royalty payment, a portion went to the attorney and the remainder covered her nursing home expenses until the following February. Describing his relationship with Diana Press as "extremely difficult and abrasive," Taggart said that he was "sorry that Jeannette had ever become involved with it."[38] He failed to comprehend that the book's publication had made a contribution to lesbian history that far surpassed any monetary gain. With negatives for the book in her possession, Hazel hoped to find another company willing to republish the book and pay Jeannette royalties, but had no success.

Eager to relieve some of Jeannette's financial difficulties, Valerie Taylor concocted a plan to solicit donations from gays and lesbians who had been touched by her life or her book. Combining forces with photographer Tee Corinne and author Lee Lynch, Taylor established the Sisterhood Fund in early 1980. Due largely to Taylor's efforts, articles about Jeannette's plight appeared in numerous gay and lesbian periodicals throughout the nation. Despite her desire for anonymity, Hazel resigned herself to the fact that her name, as Jeannette's power of attorney, would appear in appeals for donations. In the coming months, the San Francisco Lesbian and Gay History Project circulated a plea from Taylor on Jeannette's behalf, suggesting that if thirty women would each send five dollars a month, the woman who had contributed so significantly to their education would be able to "exist and die in decency." Naiad Press enclosed notices about the Sisterhood Fund with book orders and spread the word through personal correspondence, and feminist bookstores posted notices on bulletin boards. Seattle's *Out and About* ran an article entitled "Jeannette Foster, She Needs Our Help," while the *Gay Chicago Magazine* wrongly stated that "Janet" Foster was being "forced out of her nursing home and being dumped into the streets" because her money had run out. "If we don't recognize our own heroes," the author urged, "who will?" Jeannette would have found the suggestion that gay bars host benefit nights in her honor rather amusing since she had never enjoyed the bar scene. A benefit dance held in Cincinnati in 1980 "raised consciousness about older women and about Jeannette." One of the organizers, author and activist Victoria Ramstetter, had recently seen Judy Chicago's *The Dinner Party* (a feminist artwork representing famous women from the mythological past to the mid-1970s), which brought home to her "how much information is lost about lesbians and other women, and how important research like Jeannette's is."[39]

Taylor had hoped for a good response but found herself "moved and, yes, a little astonished by the quick response of women all over the country." By April 1980, she informed donor Joan E. Biren, they had received enough pledges "to keep her going, unless too many people forget or lose their jobs." For Taylor, Jeannette's need was emblematic of a larger problem. At sixty-six, she knew that she would join aging lesbians like Jeannette, who she viewed as "discriminated against doubly in the job market . . . because most of us don't have families to help us."[40] Surviving correspondence indicates that approximately one hundred twenty-two people donated money to the Sisterhood Fund during the last eighteen month's of Jeannette's life, some on a one-time basis, others monthly.

Hazel meticulously recorded donations, ranging from $5 to $150, on index cards from donors who included Mattachine Society founder Henry Hay, Chicago playwright Lucina Kathmann, Marijane Meaker, with whom Jeannette had feuded in *The Ladder*, feminist writer and academic Gayle Rubin, staff members from the Institute for Sex Research, and activists Torrie Osborn, Emily Rosenberg, Ron Sable, and Arlie Scott. The women of Casa Nuestra, the Arizona lesbian community where Taylor had moved in 1979, sent $125, noting appreciatively that they owed her "sustenance in these last difficult years" because of all she had done for them. Many other donors enclosed notes of appreciation for Jeannette's contribution to lesbian history, which Hazel read aloud in the hopes that they would lift her spirits. "She seems to enjoy them and is grateful for both the messages and the money."[41]

While some individuals made one-time donations, many others sent regular checks. In October 1980, Hazel noted that a Deborah A. Thomas had been sending fifty dollars each month since May. Another regular donor, Henry David Payne III, wrote from Lubbock, Texas, to see if he could visit Foster on his way to Illinois. Betty Bruther represents one of many who responded to the call for help. As a young woman, she first encountered *Sex Variant Women in Literature* when one of her friends purloined it from the Indianapolis Public Library. After it circulated among a small group of friends, the book ended up in Bruther's personal library, where it remained until she quietly returned it to the library years later. Upon learning about the Sisterhood Fund from a Naiad Press notice, she wanted to help support the aging author of this treasured book and began donating small sums of cash whenever possible. She recalled feeling "that as a relatively young woman I could afford to donate money to help an elder who had studied lesbian literature and had done groundbreaking work in a time when the subject was neglected or portrayed in a negative light."[42]

In April 1981, a few months before Jeannette's death, Hazel noted with surprise that donations continued to arrive "in surprising amounts." As many donors realized, the time had come to contemplate

the need for "congenial retirement homes for women."[43] Social programs geared toward heterosexuals were based on the assumption that
a woman would benefit from her husband's retirement. Aging lesbians,
however, faced a dilemma. Those who had been estranged from their
families because of their sexual identities were reluctant to turn to
them for financial assistance. In Jeannette's case, her closeted existence with her family meant that she was not close enough to her surviving niece and nephew to call upon them for assistance. Fortunately,
her gay and lesbian family stepped forward to surround her with their
love and support.

Decline

During her final years, Jeannette had ample reason to become depressed.
Cut off from correspondence that had been her lifeline, she resigned herself to a monotonous existence. For a woman of her intellectual capacity
and former energy level, the years from 1978 until her death in 1981
proved "dull and anything but congenial." She continued to visit "the
gals" at the lake, but less frequently. "I think she likes to be here," Hazel
explained, "but often she doesn't want to get out of bed and get going in
the morning. She does everything so slowly now that it takes ages to get
her started." Hazel had already begun to mourn the loss of her companion. "I miss the conversations we used to have," she elaborated. "There
are so many things she doesn't remember, and too she just doesn't seem
to be interested in talking about anything except the cats or what she
sees when she looks out into the yard."[44]

Jeannette spent Christmas and New Year's Eve 1979 at the lake house
even though it had become such a problem to transport her and she no
longer had control of her bladder or bowels. It was a sad time for Hazel
because she could not tell that the holiday meant anything to her former
companion, even though she seemed to enjoy looking at cards from old
friends. Seeking someone to blame for Jeannette's deteriorating condition, Hazel criticized her attending physician for having the attitude

"that everyone at the home is just waiting to die and so there's no need to worry about anyone there."[45] In the midst of managing Jeannette's finances and care, Hazel had another concern. In early 1980 Dot suffered a recurrence of breast cancer. Dot, however, took the matter in style, awaking from her mastectomy and astounding other patients "by walking around the halls and talking with everyone."[46] She got along so well that the doctor let her come home several days early. While Hazel had no life-threatening illnesses, the stress of caring for her friends and her on-going battles with sciatica left her drained of energy.

Hazel believed that Jeannette's spirits would lift if more of her work appeared in print, which seemingly contradicted her wish for Jeannette to remain closeted. Quite likely, she assumed that few if any residents of the rural Arkansas community would ever hear of its publication by small lesbian or feminist presses. She knew that Marie Kuda had the first option to publish Jeannette's *Home Is the Hunter*, but lacked the financial wherewithal. After conferring with her attorney in October 1980, Hazel decided to seek out another publisher, even if it meant risking a lawsuit, because its publication "would make her feel so good." Perhaps Hazel told Jeannette of her efforts to get the book into print, because in late 1980 she briefly snapped out of her depression after months of sitting in her room having nothing to do with anyone. It amazed and pleased Hazel and the nursing home staff when she started "going around the home and talking to people." Hazel, who urged Taylor to find a publisher to print some more of Jeannette's poems, was profoundly disappointed when Mosaic Press rejected them in 1981. She had hoped that Jeannette would live to see something more of hers in print because "she needs a lift."[47] But it was not to be.

Jeannette's final four months of life were spent in and out of the hospital. On April 3, 1981, her physician's younger replacement ordered Jeannette to enter the hospital because her stomach had grown so large that he suspected a tumor. A series of tests and the doctor's questioning revealed that her nightly reliance on laxatives since the 1950s had rendered her bowels incapable of elimination. As long as tubes remained inserted to drain her abdomen, "her middle would shrink until it looked almost normal," but as soon as they were removed her abdomen, hands, and feet would swell. Practically blind from cataracts, on a liquid diet due to her bowels, and suffering from hardening of the arteries, she returned to the home. She no longer knew Hazel consistently and sometimes referred to her as Helen (her sister's name), but seemed to recognize Dot because of her height. Attempting to console herself, Hazel reflected that she had seen this happen before, with her mother, grandmother, and aunts. "It always seems a pitiful condition; yet it has occurred to me that perhaps the condition leaves the person who has it less unhappy than it does his or her friends."[48]

On May 26, Jeannette appeared to have a heart attack, but when she was admitted to the hospital, physicians concluded that her symptoms stemmed from hardening of the arteries and her ongoing bowel problem. In and out of the hospital during the next few days, she fluctuated between playing possum "when she doesn't want to be bothered" and then talking with Hazel and Dot in an animated fashion. "She seemed almost her old self," Hazel reflected, except she no longer asked questions about anything. "I get a lonely feeling after I've seen her," Hazel confided to Valerie Taylor, "because I realize that the Jeannette I knew is gone." In those final days and hours she began to mourn the loss of her love, her intellectual partner, and the woman who had selflessly cared for Myrtle Toliver so Hazel could pursue research and a career. She had been through the death of a loved one before, "but that doesn't keep it from hurting when it happens again to some one I've known so long and so well."[49]

Spending her final days asleep and unaware of her surroundings, Jeannette Howard Foster passed away on July 26, 1981, three months shy of her eighty-sixth birthday. She had approached death as she had everything else in her life, headlong and with optimism tinged with realism. As her friend Valerie Taylor reflected, "No one was ever less like the dusty erudite professor of tradition. Witty and warm, a connoisseur of good food and drink, enchanted by a poem or a sunset or the antics of a pet cat," she had "spent almost 80 years developing as a person—the dedicated worker and the zestful companion in balance." Beloved by her friends, an enigma to her family, she had touched the lives of many through letters, poems, stories, and especially through the culmination of her life's work, *Sex Variant Woman in Literature*.[50]

One day after her move to Pocahontas, Hazel and Dot had driven Jeannette to the Chesser Cemetery, located six miles southwest of town. On a hill overlooking a farm field, it was shaded by tall oak trees and conveyed an atmosphere of peace and tranquility. Looking it over with a critical eye, she decided that it would be her final resting place. Immediately after her death, Hazel had arranged for a brief graveside service "such as Jeannette would have approved," but since it rained on July 28, the day of her funeral, approximately twenty-four people gathered instead in a small room at the funeral home to pay their respects. Jeannette's sister Helen, eighty-two, could not make the journey from her home in Fort Myers, Florida, and Jeannette's lesbian friends were not informed about the service until after it was over. After a short talk about Jeannette's life and accomplishments, one of Hazel's young male cousins led the group in an unknown song that Hazel felt was "suitable for the occasion and for Jeannette." After the short service Jeannette was interred in a plot that already contained Hazel's mother Myrtle, who had died in October 1975, and would one day receive Hazel and Dot's remains. Hazel was pleasantly surprised by "how people knew her [Jeannette] and remembered her from the time when she had all her mental faculties and so had made a strong impression on them."[51]

The day after the funeral Hazel and Dot filed a petition for probate of Jeannette's will and the appointment of a personal representative in the Probate Court of Randolph County. Bequeathing all of her worldly goods equally to Hazel and Dot, she left few material possessions—clothing, a small amount of jewelry, approximately two thousand books, file boxes of letters received, an eighteen-year-old cat named Dilly, and unpublished novels, short stories, and poems. After paying Jeannette's outstanding final expenses, the residue of the Sisterhood Fund was used to fix up Jeannette's grave and purchase her "small and simple but solid tombstone."

PHOTO 25.   Jeannette is buried in the Chesser Cemetery, Randolph County, Arkansas. Her tombstone was purchased with money from the Sisterhood Fund. (Photo by the author)

Hazel returned checks that arrived after her death along with a note of appreciation and Valerie Taylor mailed a mass letter to those who had so generously donated money for Jeannette's care during her final years of life, urging those who wished to contribute further to establish a lasting memorial to establish a gay retirement home in their communities. "Nothing," they concluded, "would have given Jeannette more pleasure, and nothing could do her more honor."[52]

   In the months following her death, women across the nation honored her memory in a variety of ways. In August the five-year-old Michigan Womyn's Music Festival, which would grow into one of the largest celebrations of lesbian culture in the nation, was dedicated to her memory. Barbara Grier began making plans to reissue *Sex Variant Women in Literature* and also contacted Hazel with a plan to transfer Jeannette's books to a library that maintained a special collection of books relating to women. The idea appealed to her until lesbian book collector Christine Pattee sent Hazel a catalog of lesbian literature and expressed interest in purchasing items from Jeannette's collection. Recognizing their potential value, Hazel decided that she should avoid acting too hastily, and informed Valerie Taylor that she had decided to keep them for awhile. Ultimately, Pattee purchased one box of pulp paperback fiction for three hundred dollars.

PHOTO 26.
Jeannette Howard Foster was the author of *Sex Variant Women in Literature* (from left to right, Vantage Press, 1956; Diana Press, 1976; Naiad Press, 1985). She translated Renée Vivien, *A Woman Appeared to Me* (Naiad Press, 1976), and her poetry appeared in *Two Women: the poetry of Jeannette Foster and Valerie Taylor* (Womanpress, 1976). (Photo by Carol McCafferty)

Examining them upon their arrival, she noted that Jeannette, in typical fashion, had written the real name of pseudonymous authors such as Marion Zimmer Bradley on the title pages. The fate of the remaining books is unknown, but in 1981 Hazel indicated that she wanted them to go to someone who "would appreciate the fact they had been Jeannette's.[53]

After Jeannette's death, Hazel and Dot continued to live in the house at Baltz Lake. Jeannette's beloved cat, Dilly, died in January 1983 at the age of twenty. Dot, who had become Hazel's bulwark, at times drove herself to exhaustion taking care of Hazel, who suffered from hypothyroidism. In addition to looking after everything in the yard, Dot poured herself into gardening. "I suppose it's all natural for a hyperthyroid and a Physical Education major," Hazel observed. On April 27, 1986, Dorothy Ross passed away at the Randolph County Medical Center at the age of eighty. She was interred at the Chesser Cemetery in the same plot where Jeannette lay. Hazel Toliver, who survived Dot by eleven years and four months, passed away on August 29, 1997, and is buried alongside Jeannette, Dot, Myrtle Toliver, and several other relatives.[54]

When mourning the passing of her friend and lover, Hazel reflected: "The loss of a real friend is the loss of a part of one's life because there's no one left to share the memories of that period with." Companions for thirty-one years, Hazel had attended family functions with Jeannette and Jeannette met Hazel's other relatives after the move to Pocahontas. Their intellectual compatibility was *par excellence*, and for years Hazel grieved "the loss of someone with whom I could discuss ideas that we had a common interest in." She also regretted that a person of Jeannette's brilliance had not received greater recognition during her lifetime. "I am sure," as Hazel wrote somewhat bitterly, "that she always felt that she was rather a failure since only her original book and her poetry were published out of all that she wrote and the first was brought out by two dead-beat outfits." After seeing some of the tributes written after Jeannette's death, she fervently wished that Jeannette "could have known how the women felt about her."[55]

Epilogue

As gays and lesbians throughout the nation paid tribute to Jeannette Foster, they remembered the courage, intellectual brilliance, and determination that enabled her to research, write, and publish *Sex Variant Women in Literature*. Barbara Grier, who was "this book's first fan," sent it to author Lee Lynch in the late 1960s or early 1970s. In her early twenties, Lynch was doing research into lesbian literature and was stunned to find an entire book dedicated to the subject. "It was powerfully validating," she recalled. "What a gift Jeannette gave us all . . . the bedrock of lesbian and gay studies today." Lynch, who never met Jeannette Foster, was so inspired by her that she modeled a fictional character named Augusta Brennan on her in the novels *Old Dyke Tales* and *Rafferty Street*.[1] Jeannette's book made a difference in the lives of countless women from many walks of life. Susan Wiseheart, one of the founding members of Arcadia (a lesbians' land collective), discovered the book in the early 1970s when she was first coming out. "What I didn't have," she explained, "was any knowledge of the community of lesbians." Reading *Sex Variant Women in Literature* "gave me an enormous sense of being part of a long-lasting always present group that spanned centuries." This discovery filled her with "joy at finally realizing who I was and a strong sense of bonding with women as a group," and helped counter some of the negative messages with which lesbians have had to contend. Others, like Robin Cohen, a Colorado woman who learned of Foster's work in 1980, took inspiration from her example and began collecting lesbian literature. Honoring Jeannette as the "foremother who first delivered to us our stories," Cohen developed an educational slide show about lesbian literature.[2] Inspired by Jeannette, she and many others began exploring their history.

As growing numbers of women and men went to libraries in search of gay-related books, they often started with *Sex Variant Women in Literature*. As an undergraduate at the University of Chicago in 1959, Bill Kelley wanted to see what he could find on homosexuality. At that time he did not know the word *gay*, having been raised in a rural part of the mid-South. He learned it after discovering Donald Webster Cory's *The Homosexual in America*, which was housed in the library's Rare Book Room, most likely to protect it from theft. After that he consulted Jeannette's bibliography, which he found useful "as a guide to finding gay-related material in general." After obtaining a stack pass, he discovered that gay materials listed in the catalog often were missing from the shelves "no doubt because people would indeed rather steal them than check them out by signing their names."[3]

After Christine Pattee discovered and read "every word" in *Sex Variant Women in Literature*, she systematically hunted down every title where Jeannette had something positive to say about the characters or the writing. Her interest in lesbian literature led her to collect lesbian literature and to establish Independent Woman Books because of her desire to share her "love of lesbian literature with women around the country, and none of this would be possible if Jeannette had not shared her monumental work with us."[4]

A number of individuals consider themselves to be Jeannette's literary and intellectual heirs. Jonathan N. Katz recalled that he "loved the idea that she could see and know that her early work had meant so much to those of us who came later." Likewise, in *Surpassing the Love of Men* (1981), Lillian Faderman acknowledged her debt to Barbara Grier and

Jeannette Foster, noting that their "pioneering bibliographic works were indispensable to my own work." It was her "fondest wish," she continued, "that I may be as helpful to future scholars as they were to me." In the dedication of *Lesbian Histories and Cultures*, editor Bonnie Zimmerman acknowledged several people, including Jeannette, for their "pioneering work in creating and promoting lesbian scholarship."[5] Maida Tilchen followed in Jeannette's footsteps literally and figuratively. While working as a secretary in Indiana University's Goodbody Hall, she received permission to use the Institute for Sex Research library during her lunch hours. It was there that she held a rare copy of Foster's legendary 1956 book in her hands (it was before the Diana Press edition appeared). "It just didn't seem possible to me—she was so heroically unreal to me, how could she have been in a place I was?" Building on Foster's shoulders, Tilchen's research at the institute's library and her "endless collecting" of lesbian pulps resulted in many articles on pulp fiction and lesbian literature. For many years, starting in 1975, she and a friend held a monthly lesbian and gay literary circle in Bloomington, Indiana. Noting that several members of the group went on to publish their own novels, Tilchen wrote, "I'd like to think that the spirit of Jeannette Foster inspired us."[6]

Jeannette's legacy also survives in the work of her protégés. She was a woman-loving woman, yet she also chose to nurture and support gay men. In 1959 she loaned Joseph (Joe) P. Gregg money so he could do graduate work at her alma mater, the University of Chicago's Graduate Library School. Attending there from 1959 to 1961, he graduated in 1964 after completing his MA.[7] While working at Northeastern Illinois University as an acquisitions librarian, he read that a gay and lesbian library would open in Chicago and thought that becoming involved would be "continuing something that Dr. Foster began with her book in the 1950s." Taking the position meant coming out for Gregg, a closeted man, but like Foster, he decided to put his professional expertise to work for his people. In 1981 Gregg became codirector of Chicago's Gerber–Hart Library, dedicated to the collection of gay and lesbian books, magazines, newspapers, newsletters, and other materials.

Using a $7,500 grant from the Chicago Resource Center, Gregg and his codirector Ruth Ketchum purchased books that they designated as the Jeannette Foster Collection of Lesbiana.[8] Chicagoan Marie J. Kuda also worked to ensure that Foster's name and legacy lived on long after her death. In 2000, two years after Foster was inducted into the Chicago Gay and Lesbian Hall of Fame, Kuda joined with local activist Arlene Halko to establish the Jeannette Howard Foster Memorial Sewing Circle and Book Club.[9]

Another protégée, Barbara Grier, is known for her work as a bibliographer, editor, reviewer, collector, and publisher. Building on the knowledge and techniques for decoding lesbianism in literature that Jeannette shared with her in the 1950s, Grier extended Jeannette's work in several subsequent bibliographies. Writing under the pseudonym Gene Damon, she and Lee Stuart published *The Lesbian in Literature* in 1967—a bibliography that listed about three thousand English-language books published before 1966 that concerned lesbianism or had lesbian characters. In addition to compiling two subsequent editions of the publication in 1975 and 1981, she cofounded Naiad Press, which eventually became the nation's leading publisher of lesbian literature. For a number of years, Grier had hoped to reprint *Sex Variant Women in Literature*, but given the length of the book and the associated costs of publishing, Naiad was not stable enough during its first decade of existence to tackle the project. In 1985, however, Ann Stokes sought a publisher for *A Studio of One's Own*, an account of her efforts to build a refuge for lesbian artists on a beautiful mountainside in New England. She wanted the book to be published in a more expensive format than Naiad customarily did, and Grier wanted someone to subsidize the cost of publishing Jeannette's book. After telling Stokes about Jeannette's book and the need to get it into print as quickly as possible, the two women struck a deal: Naiad would publish *A Studio of One's Own* according to her requirements if she would pay the cost of publishing *Sex Variant Women in Literature*.[10]

Having previously obtained permission from Hazel years earlier, Grier disassembled two clean and perfect copies of the 1956 Vantage edition in order to photo-offset the book, a much cheaper process than retypesetting. This time Jeannette's book received more widespread publicity than either of the earlier editions, with reviews appearing in a variety of gay and lesbian publications. Reviewers recognized that it was a Herculean accomplishment for the mid-1950s and praised Foster for her open-mindedness in documenting lesbian resistance in the form of literature, but the text had begun to show its age. By the time author Katherine V. Forrest found the book in the 1980s, for example, it had become "more of a historical document," yet she was deeply impressed and "admired it as the piece of extraordinary scholarship it most surely is."[11]

When Jesse Monteagudo reviewed *Sex Variant Women in Literature* in the context of 1980s scholarship, he noted the omission of variant works in Oriental languages as well as titles in Spanish, Italian, Swedish, Russian, or Yiddish, and criticized her failure to translate French and German excerpts into English. Another reviewer, writing in the *New York Native*, criticized the omission of writing by women of color and noted that Jeannette had been "constantly glancing nervously over her shoulder at science and psychology."[12] Without question, the McCarthy era had subtly influenced Foster's presentation of her research, but it had not silenced her. As the *New York Native* reviewer's criticisms testify significant social and cultural progress had occurred between her book's first appearance in 1956 and its reissuance three decades later. Superceded by the revolution in lesbian studies that it had engendered, *Sex Variant Women in Literature* nonetheless represented a critical step on the road to gay liberation, a touchstone for what Jeannette Howard Foster had believed was possible.

NOTES

INTRODUCTION

1. Paul Gebhard verified the authenticity of this anecdote in an e-mail to the author, 13 October 2007.

2. John D'Emilio, *Sexual Politics, Sexual Communities: The Making of a Homosexual Minority in the United States, 1940–1970*, 2d ed. (Chicago: University of Chicago Press, 1983), 21.

3. JHF to M. Kuda, 1 April 1976, Marie Kuda Archives (hereafter MKA), Oak Park, Illinois.

CHAPTER 1

1. "Valentines," *Two Women: The Poetry of Jeannette Foster and Valerie Taylor* (Chicago: Womanpress, 1976), 8, (hereafter *TW*), also reprinted in *Two Women Revisited: The Poetry of Jeannette Foster and Valerie Taylor* (Austin, Tex.: Banned Books, 1991), 12 (hereafter *TWR*).

2. Jeannette Howard Foster (hereafter JHF) to Karla Jay, 2 May 1975, Karla Jay Papers (hereafter KJP), Box 3, Manuscripts and Archives Division, New York Public Library.

3. JHF to Valerie Taylor, 12 September 1976, *Valerie Taylor Working Papers #1: Letters from Jeannette Howard Foster, Hazel M. Toliver, Dot Ross to Valerie Taylor* (hereafter *VTWP #1*) (Wolf Creek, Ore.: Tee A. Corinne), 1997; Winslow Howard Foster, *Ancestry of Winslow Howard Foster and That of His Wife Anna Mabel (Burr) Foster* (Ludington, Mich., 1941).

4. "Ada Lydia Howard (1829–1907)," *Dictionary of American Biography* Base Set. American Council of Learned Societies, 1928–1936. Reproduced in *Biography Resource Center* (Farmington Hills, Mich.: Thomson Gale, 2007). http://galenet.galegroup.com/servlet/BioRC. For more on Mt. Holyoke's founding, see Lillian Faderman, *To Believe in Women: What Lesbians Have Done for America: A History* (Boston: Houghton Mifflin Company, 1999), 178.

5. Winslow Howard Foster, *Ancestry of Winslow Howard Foster*. For more on the Salem witchcraft trials, see Paul Boyer and Stephen Nissenbaum, *Salem Possessed* (Cambridge, Mass.: Harvard University Press, 1976); Carol Karlsen, *The Devil in the Shape of a Woman* (New York: W. W. Norton, 1987); Mary Beth Norton, *In the Devil's Snare* (New York: Vintage, 2003). The film based on Sarah Cloyces's story is *Three Sovereigns for Sarah* (PBS, 1985).

6. Maris A. Vinovskis and Richard M. Bernard, "Beyond Catherine Beecher: Female Education in the Antebellum Period," *SIGNS: Journal of Women in Culture and Society* 3 (1978): 857, 868. In Massachusetts the percentage of females engaged in the teaching profession increased from 56.3 percent in 1834 to 77.8 percent in 1860.

7. Susan Morton Houghton (1838–1924) married Addison Houghton Foster (1838–1906). For information on the families, see "Houghton," in Charles H. Chandler, *The History of New Ipswich, New Hampshire, 1735–1914* (Fitchburg, Mass.: Sentinel Print, 1914), 477–79; "Susan M. Foster [obituary]," *Chicago Daily Tribune*, 16 March 1924, 10. There is no known connection between this line of the family and the Houghton Library at Harvard College.

8. *Ancestry of Winslow Howard Foster*, 68–70. According to a Foster family photograph album, ca. 1869–1936, FFP, the house stood at 97 Hoyne Avenue.

9. *Woman's Medical School, Northwestern University (Woman's Medical College of Chicago): The Institution and Its Founders: Class Histories, 1870–1896* (Chicago: H. G. Cutler, 1896), 41–2, 44, 147, 158; "Mary Harris Thompson," in Rima Lunin Schultz and Adele Hast, eds., *Women Building Chicago, 1790–1990: A Biographical Dictionary* (Bloomington, Ind.: Indiana University Press, 2001), 8; Eve Fine, "Medical Education," *The Electronic Encyclopedia of Chicago* (Chicago Historical Society) http://www.encyclopedia .chicagohistory.org/pages/805.html (accessed 5 February 2007).

10. JHF to Valerie Taylor, 7 November 1974, VTWP #1; *Ancestry of Winslow Howard Foster*, 67–9. For more on Addison Howard Foster, see A. T. Andreas, *History of Chicago* (Chicago: A. T. Andreas, 1884–1886), II: 533.

11. Sanford Burr (1838–1901). Burr's company served from June to October 1862 in Virginia. See "John Scales, "Dartmouth Cavalry Company B, Seventh Squadron Rhode Island Volunteer Cavalry," http://history.rays-place.com/nh-cw/dartmouth.htm (accessed 17 January 2007); *Ancestry of Winslow Howard Foster*, 68–9.

12. Eliza Jane Osgood (1835–1899). For details on the family, see *Ancestry of Winslow Howard Foster*, 68–9. According to Jeannette Foster's nephew, the family did not discuss any reasons for these congenital problems.

13. *Ancestry of Winslow Howard Foster*, 69. For more on Burr's contributions to Winnetka, see Lora Townsend Dickinson, *The Winnetka Story* (Winnetka, Ill.: Winnetka Historical Society, 1956), 86; Caroline Thomas Harnsberger, *Winnetka: The Biography of a Village* (Evanston, Ill.: The Schori Press, 1977), 211. South Haven is a port city located along the shore of Lake Michigan.

14. Foster family photograph album, ca. 1869–1936, 10–3, FFP.

15. "Classical Music" and "Choral Music," *The Electronic Encyclopedia of Chicago* (Chicago: Chicago Historical Society, 2005) (accessed 22 July 2007).

16. Foster family photograph album, ca. 1869–1936, 13, FFP; Carrie Burr Prouty diary (1891), 3 November 1891, FFP. Carrie Burr did not move to Michigan with her family, because she had married Carlton Prouty on 25 March 1886.

17. *Ancestry of Winslow Howard Foster*, 69.

18. *Ibid*. Foster family photos, FFP.

19. Winslow Foster, 1900 manuscript population census, Cicero, Cook County, Illinois, 1900; JHF to Valerie Taylor, 12 September 1976, *VTWP #1*. For more on turn-of-the-century Oak Park, see Carlos Baker, *Ernest Hemingway: A Life Story* (New York: Charles Scribner's Sons, 1969), 7; Michael Reynolds, *The Young Hemingway* (New York: Basil Blackwell, 1986), 1, 4, 5, 9. Hemingway's father, Clarence (1871–1928) was a physician in Oak Park, and undoubtedly would have known Addison Howard Foster. The streets of Oak Park were renumbered in 1908, and it is unclear whether the Fosters lived at 216 or 316 North Harvey in 1894.

20. *Ancestry of Winslow Howard Foster*, 69. Sanford Burr died in the home on 20 July 1901.

21. JHF to Karla Jay, 2 May 1975, Jay Papers.

22. JHF to Jonathan N. Katz, postmarked 2 November 1977, Jonathan N. Katz Papers (hereafter JNKP), box 3, New York Public Library.

23. JHF to J. N. Katz, 2 November 1977, JNKP; JHF to Karla Jay, 12 April 1975, KJP; JHF to Valerie Taylor, 7 November 1974, *VTWP #1*.

24. *Ancestry of Winslow Howard Foster*, 69; JHF to Karla Jay, 2 May 1975, KJP. May 1 was known as "moving day" because so many families moved to new apartments or flats. See "Moving Days," *The Electronic Encyclopedia of Chicago*, (Chicago Historical Society, 2005) http://www.encyclopedia.chicagohistory.org/pages/852.html.

25. Edmund W. Kearney, *Chicago State College 1869–1969: A Centennial Retrospective* (Chicago: Chicago State College Centennial Commission, 1969), 9.

26. JHF to Karla Jay, 2 May 1975, KJP. For more about the Parker School, see "Critic Department," *Organization and Course of Instruction, Chicago Normal School*, September, 1902, 2–3; "Arthur Zilversmit, "Progressive Education," *The Electronic Encyclopedia of Chicago* (Chicago Historical Society, 2005).

27. JHF to J. N. Katz, 18 October 1977, JNKP; Ellen Skerrett, "Beverly," *The Electronic Encyclopedia of Chicago* (Chicago Historical Society, 2005) http://www.encyclopedia.chicagohistory.org/pages/134.html (accessed 13 January 2007); Winslow Howard Foster, manuscript population census, 7th Ward, Chicago, Cook County, Illinois, 1910. At the turn of the century, Beverly was known as Beverly Hills.

28. JHF to J. N. Katz, 18 October 1977, JNKP; JHF to Karla Jay, 2 May 1975, KJP.

29. Carrie Burr Prouty diary, 1902–1913, FFP.

30. JHF to Valerie Taylor, 26 September 1976, *VTWP #1*.

31. Carrie Burr Prouty diary, 1902–1913, FFP.

32. Foster family photograph album, ca. 1869–1936, 113–114, FFP.

33. JHF to Karla Jay, 2 May 1975, KJP.

34. For more insight into perceptions of sexual inversion during the late nineteenth century, see George Chauncey Jr., "From Sexual Inversion to Homosexuality: Medicine

and the Changing Conceptualization of Female Deviance," *Salmagundi* 58–59 (Fall 1982–Winter 1983): 114–46.

35. JHF autobiography enclosed in Hazel Toliver to Valerie Taylor, 21 July 1978, *VTWP #1*.

36. JHF to Karla Jay, 12 April 1975, KJP; JHF to J. N. Katz, 27 September 1977, JNKP; JHF to Valerie Taylor, 26 September 1976, *VTWP #1*. For more on attitudes about masturbation in the early-twentieth century, see Alan Hunt, "The Great Masturbation Panic and the Discourses of Moral Regulation in Nineteenth- and Early-Twentieth-Century Britain," *Journal of the History of Sexuality* 8 (1998): 576.

37. JHF to Karla Jay, 2 May 1975, KJP; JHF to Valerie Taylor, 26 September 1976, *VTWP #1*.

38. See part III, chapter 1 in Lillian Faderman, *Surpassing the Love of Men: Romantic Friendship & Love Between Women from the Renaissance to the Present* (New York: Perennial, 1998), especially p. 311.

39. Foster discusses her reading in JHF to Karla Jay, 27 September 1977, KJP; Josephine Dodge Daskam, "A Case of Interference," *Smith College Stories* (New York: Scribners, 1900), 37–64; Mary Constance Dubois, "The Lass of the Silver Sword," *St. Nicholas: An Illustrated Magazine for Young Folks* (December 1908–October 1909), and published as a novel under the same title (New York: Century Publishing Co., 1911). For a discussion of "Lass of the Silver Sword," see Lillian Faderman, "Lesbian Magazine Fiction in the Early Twentieth Century," *Journal of Popular Culture* 11 (1978): 800–17.

40. JHF to Karla Jay, 17 July 1975, KJP.

41. JHF oral history, 5 June 1975, KJP.

42. JHF to J. N. Katz, 27 September 1977, JNKP; JHF to Karla Jay, 2 May 1975 and 17 July 1975, KJP. For information about Calumet High School, see JHF autobiography, in Toliver to Taylor, 21 July 1978, *VTWP #1*.

43. Martha Vicinis, "Distance and Desire, English Boarding School Friendships," *SIGNS* 7 (Summer 1984): 601.

44. JHF to Karla Jay, 2 May 1975, KJP; Carrie Burr Prouty diary (1902–1913), 11 May 1909–11 August 1909, FFP.

45. Carrie Burr Prouty diary (1902–1913), 26 November 1909, 29 November 1909, 3 September 1910, 8 October 1910, FFP.

46. Winslow Howard Foster, manuscript population census, Murphy Precinct, Grants Pass, Josephine County, Oregon, 1910. "Foster, 41" is listed as owner of a fruit farm living with a farm laborer named Earnest Reece. Deeds for purchase and sale of property are on file in the Josephine County, Oregon, courthouse, dated 16 March 1910, 4 March 1911, 24 April 1912, 13 February 1920, 3 July 1936. Foster bought the land with two partners, purchased additional land in 1920, and sold out during the Depression.

47. Carrie Burr Prouty diary (1902–1913), 22–23 February 1910, 15 March 1910, 22–25 March 1910, 12–13 April 1910, FFP.

48. Carrie Burr Prouty diary (1902–1913), 26 May 1910, 9–11 August 1910, 10 September 1910, 15 September 1910, FFP.

49. JHF to Karla Jay, 2 May 1975, KJP.

50. Carrie Burr Prouty diary (1902–1913), 26 October 1911, 19 March 1912, 26 April 1912, 18 July 1912, FFP.

51. According to family lore, they registered Jeannette at Wellesley when she was a child. See JHF to Karla Jay, 2 May 1975, KJP.

52. The tuition scholarship was worth approximately $120. For more, see "Assistance to Students at the University of Chicago," *Bulletin of Information* 12 (12 May 1912): 3. The reference to the physician is from JHF to J. N. Katz, 18 October 1977, JNKP.

53. Carrie Burr Prouty diary (1902–13), 19 July 1912, 27–31 July 1912, 16 August 1912, 1 September 1912; 2 September 1912, FFP; Winslow Cope e-mail message to the author, 19 January 2007.

CHAPTER 2

1. "A Song Unuttered," *TW*, 108, also reprinted in *TWR*, 18. Foster's poems were typed by Valerie Taylor and are housed in the Valerie Taylor Papers, series #7627, box 1, Rare and Manuscript Collections, Carl A. Kroch Library, Cornell University, Ithaca, New York. Taylor returned the original notebooks to Foster.

2. Margaret Anderson (1886–1973) founded *The Little Review* in 1914. She was a lesbian, feminist, editor, and author, widely known as a leading light in the modernist movement. See "Anderson, Margaret Carolyn," *Women Building Chicago, 1790–1990: A Biographical Dictionary* (Bloomington: Indiana University Press, 2001), 38–9. In addition to publishing works of poetry and short fiction, Anderson and her partner Jane Heap published short fiction, the political writings of anarchist Emma Goldman and articles on feminism and psychoanalysis.

3. For more on Flanner, see Brenda Wineapple, *Genet: A Biography of Janet Flanner* (Lincoln: University of Nebraska Press, 1989).

4. JHF to Karla Jay, 2 May 1975, KJP; JHF to J. N. Katz, 18 October 1977, JNKP.

5. "Alone," in *TWR*, 14. For a discussion of the crisis of religious faith on early twentieth century college campuses, see Barbara Miller Solomon, *In the Company of Educated Women: A History of Women and Higher Education in America* (New Haven, Conn.: Yale University Press, 1985), 90–2.

6. See Solomon, *In the Company of Educated Women*, 95–100.

7. See "Breckinridge, Sophonisba Preston," p. 114–6, "Talbot, Marion," p. 865–8, in *Women Building Chicago*; "Miss Gertrude Dudley [obituary]," *Chicago Daily Tribune*, 22 June 1945, 18. Dudley, born in November 1869, lived in Kelly Hall with Talbot in 1900. See "Gertrude Dudley," manuscript population census, 34th Ward, Chicago, Cook County, Illinois, 1900.

8. Lillian Faderman, *Odd Girls and Twilight Lovers: A History of Lesbian Life in Twentieth-Century America* (New York: Penguin, 1991), 61; *Wolf Girls at Vassar: Gay & Lesbian Experiences, 1930–1990*, compiled and edited by Anne MacKay (New York: Ten Percent Publishing, 1992), iv.

9. JHF to Karla Jay, May 2, 1975, KJP.

10. Lillian Faderman, *To Believe in Women*, 140–1.

11. *Circular of the Departments of Mathematics, Astronomy and Astrophysics, Physics, Chemistry, 1912* (University of Chicago, 1912), 5. Beecher Hall is located on a quadrangle at 5830 University Avenue. JHF to Valerie Taylor, included with Hazel Toliver to Taylor, 21 July 1978, *VTWP #1*; JHF to Karla Jay, 2 May 1975, KJP; Carrie Burr Prouty diary (1902–1913), 3 November 1912, FFP.

12. Beecher House, *Cap and Gown*, 1913 (University of Chicago, 1913), 265; Beecher House, *The Cap and Gown*, 1914 (University of Chicago, 1914), 275.

13. JHF to Margaret C. Anderson, 8 June 1960, Margaret Anderson-Elizabeth Clark Collection, Beinecke Library, Yale University.

14. Jeannette Howard Foster Transcript, University of Chicago registrar's office; *Cap and Gown*, 1913, 1914; JHF to Valerie Taylor, 28 January 1975, MKA; "Janet Flanner, Reporter in Paris for the *New Yorker*, Dies at 86," *New York Times*, 8 November 1978, B-10.

15. Janis Londraville and Richard Londraville, *The Most Beautiful Man in the World Paul Swan, from Wilde to Warhol* (Lincoln: University of Nebraska Press, 2006); Carrie Burr Prouty diary (1902–1913), 2 November 1912, FFP; "Chosen Queen of Carnival," *Chicago Daily Tribune*, 21 May 1913, 17. Hinman had been a teacher at the Francis Parker School before establishing a dancing school.

16. JHF to Karla Jay, 2 May 1975, KJP; Mary Pryor, Rockford College archivist, to the author, 13 March 2006; David Pavelich, University of Chicago archivist, e-mail to the author, 13 March 2006. Burnham is listed as "Assistant in Physical Culture," *University of Chicago Circular of Information: Departments of Arts, Literature, and Science, 1912*, p. 64, and again in 1913, p. 66.

17. JHF to J. N. Katz, 2 November 1977, JNKP; JHF to Valerie Taylor, 28 January 1975, MKA. Winifred Pearce is listed as a dance instructor in "Chosen Queen of Carnival," *Chicago Daily Tribune*, 21 May 1913, 17.

18. "Prouty Quickly Weds Again," *Chicago Daily Tribune*, 2 November 1912, 3; Carrie Burr Prouty diary (1902–1913), 25–28 December 1912, FFP. For examples of Jeannette's contributions and family conditions, see November 1912, 27 December 1912, 28 December 1912, 3 January 1913, 18 January 1913, 23 January 1913, 4, 11 February 1913, FFP.

19. Jeannette Howard Foster transcript, University of Chicago registrar's office.

20. Carrie Burr Prouty diary (1902–1913), 23 November 1912, FFP; "Divorced, Weds in 3 Days," *Chicago Daily Tribune*, 7 March 1913; Glenda Riley, *Divorce: An American Tradition* (New York: Oxford University Press, 1991), 128–9.

21. For example of Jeannette's activities, see Carrie Burr Prouty diary (1902–1913), 15 November 1912, 22 November 1912, 24 March 1913, 26–27 March 1913, 12 April 1913, FFP; for Prouty's impressions of Sadler's lecture, see 10 November 1912; William S. Sadler, *The Physiology of Faith and Fear, or, The Mind in Health and Disease* (Chicago: A. C. McClurg, 1912).

22. Foster sold some of the Oregon land to his partner on 24 April 1912, according to deeds filed in the Josephine County, Oregon, courthouse. For insight into the Foster

family's summer activities at Hilltop Cottage, see Carrie Burr Prouty diary (1902–1913), 12, 21, 23–26 June, 2–5, 12–14, 17–20, 24 July, 7 August 1913, FFP.

23. Carrie Burr Prouty diary (1902–1913), 17, 24–25, 30 July 1913; 15–16, 19, 21–22 August 1913; 3, 8 September 1913, FFP; *Official Publications of the University of Chicago, 1912*, p. 8.

24. Carrie Burr Prouty diary (1902–1913), 8 November 1913, 11 December 1913, FFP. By 1920, Burnham was living with her widowed father, eighty-three, and bachelor brother Charles in Waltham, Massachusetts, while working as a private secretary to an Episcopal priest, the Reverend Julius Sauber, whom she later married.

25. JHF to Karla Jay, 2 May 1975, KJP. Foster refers to her beloved as E.G.T. to protect her identity, but provided enough details that it is possible to determine her identity using a combination of student registers and Anna B. Foster college diary (hereafter ABF college diary), transcribed by Winslow H. Cope, FFP. The *Annual Register of the University of Chicago, 1913–1914* shows both Foster and Taylor resided in Beecher Hall during the autumn, winter, and spring quarters. It housed eighteen undergraduate and twenty-four graduate students.

26. Grace Taylor to Carl Taylor, postmarked 16 April 1945, Carl Taylor Papers, Rare and Manuscript Collections, Cornell University; Grace Taylor, manuscript population census, Adel, Dallas County, Iowa, 1910, boarding in the household of Chauncy Forrester.

27. JHF to Karla Jay, 2 May 1975, KJP.

28. JHF to Valerie Taylor, 26 September 1976, *VTWP #1*.

29. The reference to kissing is from JHF to Karla Jay, 2 May 1975, KJP. Grace's older brother, Alva Wilmot Taylor, a pastor in the Disciples of Christ church, would later gain fame as a social gospel prophet and labor arbitrator while her younger brother Carl, known for his work as a rural sociologist, was appointed to several New Deal agencies in the 1930s. See *Alva Wilmot Taylor: A Register of His Papers in the Disciples of Christ Historical Society* (Nashville, Tenn.: Disciples of Christ Historical Society, 1964); "Carl Cleveland Taylor," *American National Biography* (New York: Oxford University Press, 1999): v. 21, 355–6. Edna Grace Taylor became a teacher in Council Bluffs, Iowa, see "Teachers Assigned in Bluffs Schools," *Council Bluffs Nonpareil*, 22 August 1953, 21. The reference to her companion Dora is in E. G. Taylor to Carl Taylor, postmarked 16 April 1945, Carl Taylor Papers.

30. "White Night," *TW*, 1; *TWR*, 4.

31. The brother was probably Alva Wilmot Taylor, author of *The Social Work of Christian Missions* (Cincinnati: The Foreign Missionary Society, 1911), and she went to teach at the Nanjing Higher Normal Institute, called the Liangjiang Normal College until 1915. The quotes are from JHF to Karla Jay, 2 May 1975, KJP.

32. JHF to Karla Jay, 2 May 1975, KJP; "Dr. Irving D. Steinhardt, 1914," in Jonathan Ned Katz, *Gay/Lesbian Almanac: A New Documentary* (New York: Harper & Row, 1983), 358–9. For additional insight into early-twentieth-century medical attitudes toward homosexuality, see Jonathan N. Katz, *Gay American History* (New York: Thomas Y. Crowell Company, 1976), chapter 2 ("Treatment, 1884–1974"); Jennifer Terry, *An American Obsession* (University of Chicago Press, 1999).

33. JHF to J. N. Katz, 21 July 1978, JNKP; JHF to Valerie Taylor, enclosed in Hazel To-liver to Taylor, 21 July 1978, *VTWP #1*.

34. Carrie Burr Prouty was an activist and believed in service to her community. She served as president of the Winnetka Public Library Board, 1906–1945, and president of the Winnetka Historical Society, 1937–1938, 1939–1942. She also wrote *Stories Jesus Heard and Stories Jesus Told* (W. A. Wilde Co., 1929).

35. JHF to Del Martin and Phyllis Lyon, 25 February 1973, Lyon-Martin Collection, Box 23, Folder 15, GLBT Historical Society, San Francisco; William S. and Lena K. Sadler, *The Mother and Her Child* (Chicago: A. C. McClurg & Co., 1916).

36. William S. and Lena K. Sadler, *Living a Sane Sex Life* (Chicago: American Pub-lishers Corporation, 1938), 97. JHF spoke of her psychoanalysis in a letter to Alfred C. Kinsey, 8 May 1941, Foster–Kinsey Correspondence, Kinsey Institute for Research in Sex, Gender, and Reproduction (hereafter Kinsey Institute).

37. *Sixty Eighth Official Bulletin of Rockford College, 1917–1918* (Rockford, Illinois: The College, 1917), 18–9.

38. JHF transcript, University of Chicago registrar's office, contains a notation of her transfer to Rockford College, 31 August 1915; JHF to Karla Jay, 2 May 1975, KJP.

39. Solomon, *In the Company of Educated Women*, 89, 99–100. For additional insight into homosocial behavior on women's college campuses, see Elaine Kendall, *Peculiar In-stitutions: An Informal History of the Seven Sister Colleges* (New York, Putnam's, 1975); Helen Lefkowitz Horowitz, *Alma Mater: Design and Experience in the Women's Colleges from Their Nineteenth-Century Beginnings to the 1930s.* 2d ed. (Amherst: University of Massachusetts Press, 1993).

40. C. Hal Nelson, ed., *Rockford College: A Retrospective Look* (Rockford, Ill.: Rockford College, 1980), 92.

41. Jeannette Howard Foster transcript, Rockford College registrar's office; *The Ances-try of Winslow Howard Foster*, 70.

42. Jeannette Howard Foster, "Parcel Post vs. Romance," *The Taper* 7 (Midwinter 1916–1917): 19–21.

43. "Reassurance," *TW*, 3; also *TWR*, 6.

44. "Ashes" and "Désirée," in *TW*, 4–5; *TWR*, 7–8.

45. Lillian Faderman, *Odd Girls and Twilight Lovers*, 13, 20, 87.

46. JHF oral history, KJP; Havelock Ellis, *Studies in the Psychology of Sex* Volume 2, *Sexual Inversion* (Philadelphia: F. A. Davis, 1901). It was reissued in 1913 under the title *Sexual Inversion*. Edith Lees Ellis, a lesbian and wife of Havelock Ellis, lectured on "Sex and Eugenics" in Chicago on 4 February 1915. See Katz, *Gay/Lesbian Al-manac*, 160.

47. JHF oral history, KJP.

48. "Resolve," *TW*, 6; *TWR*, 9.

49. "Reassurance," *TW*, 3; *TWR*, 6.

50. JHF Oral History; JHF to Karla Jay, April 12, 1975, KJP. For more on Anna Howard Shaw, see Faderman, *To Believe in Women*, 40–60.

51. Faderman, *To Believe in Women*, 185.

52. Clara Louise Thompson, Appointment Bureau registration blank, 4 April 1923, Thompson Biographical Folder, University of Pennsylvania Archives, Philadelphia.

53. "Conversations with Alice Paul," oral interview conducted by Amelia R. Fry, 1972–1973, Bancroft Library, University of California, Berkeley; "College Women Will Work for Suffrage," *Sheboygan (Wisconsin) Press*, 10 March 1915, 5.

54. CLT, "A Shadow," *The Taper* 1 (Spring 1915), "Courage," *The Taper* 1 (Autumn 1915), "Defeat," *The Taper* 1 (Commencement Number 1916).

55. "Désirée," *TW*, 5, and *TWR*, 8.

56. JHF to J. N. Katz, 2 November 1977; for insight into lesbianism and the National Woman's Party, see Lillian Faderman, *To Believe in Women*, 93-94; for references to spending time in Thompson's quarters, see ABF college diary, 20 September 1917, 2 December 1917, 6 March 1918, FFP; "Flash," *TWR*, 11.

57. "Chains," *TWR*, 13.

58. "Platonics," *TWR*, 15. In her oral history, JHF attributes the anthology to an editor named Smitkind.

59. JHF oral history, KJP; JHF to J. N. Katz, 18 October 1977, JNKP.

60. *Rockford College Cupola* (yearbook), *1918* (Rockford, IL: The College, 1918), see p. 19 for JHF's senior picture and list of activities; ABF college diary, entries for her freshman year, 1917–1918; Foster family photograph collection, FFP.

61. C. Hal Nelson, ed. *Rockford College: A Retrospective Look* 94 (State Street is in Rockford, Illinois); ABF college diary, 10, 22 March 1918, FFP.

62. "Chicagoans Graduated," *Chicago Daily Tribune* 13 June 1918, 14. ABF college diary, June 9–13, 1918, FFP.

63. ABF college diary, 14 June 1918, FFP.

64. ABF college diary, 27, 29 June 1918, FFP.

65. ABF college diary, 17, 27 June 1918; 24, 31 July 1918; 5, 14, 27 August 1918, FFP.

66. ABF college diary, 24, 26–7, 31 July and 24 August 1918, FFP.

67. "June graduates, Morgan Park High," *Suburbanite Economist*, 22 June 1917, 5; "Phi Beta Kappa," *The Barnard Bulletin* 26 (9 June 1922): 1. Bleecker would transfer to Barnard College as a junior, graduating Phi Beta Kappa in 1922.

68. ABF college diary, 10 September 1918, FFP.

69. Based on author's visit to Shelbyville, Kentucky, and the Wakefield Scearce Galleries, 7 August 2006.

70. Reverend John Tevis's remarks serve as an introduction to his wife's 489 page autobiography, Julia Ann Hieronymus Tevis, *Sixty Years in a School-room: An Autobiography of Mrs. Julia A. Tevis* (Cincinnati: Western Methodist Book Concern, 1878); Telephone interview with Rosella Davis, Shelbyville, Kentucky, 4 August 2006.

71. ABF college diary, 8 and 25 October 1918, FFP.

72. ABF college diary, 22 November, 9–12 December 1918, FFP.

73. ABF college diary, 2 January 1919, 1 October 1917, FFP. If the accusations were true, Goodwin might today be considered a pedophile rather than a homosexual.

74. "Rockford College Inaugural, *Chicago Daily Tribune*, 19 October 1902, 6; "Julia H. Gulliver, Educator, Is Dead," *Chicago Daily Tribune*, 28 July 1940, 30.

75. ABF college diary, 16 February 1919, FFP; Julia Gulliver to Edith Bramhall, 30 April 1919, Gulliver correspondence, Rockford College Archives; Information about James Gardner Goodwin is from Linda Hurteau, Alumni Association, Wesleyan University, Middletown, Connecticut, to Mary Pryor, 28 November 2005.

76. ABF college diary, 16–18, 20 February 1919, FFP; "Veteran Woman Educator Quits Rockford Post, Man to Head Seminary for the First Time in 72 Years," *Chicago Daily Tribune*, 14 March 1919, 11.

77. For more on this change in climate, see Lillian Faderman, *Surpassing the Love of Women*, 308–9. Gulliver to William Arthur Maddox, March 8, 1919, quoted in C. Hal Nelson, editor, *Rockford College: A Retrospective Look*, 95.

78. For more on the dismissal of faculty, see *Rockford College: A Retrospective Look*, 87–96.

79. ABF college diary, 7, 9, 11 May 1919, 21 June 1919, 18 August 1919; 28 December 1919, FFP.

80. Lillian Faderman, *Odd Girls and Twilight Lovers*, 13, 20, 87, 93.

81. Nancy F. Cott, *The Grounding of Modern Feminism* (New Haven, Conn.: Yale University Press, 1987), 158–60. For examples of women visible in the arts, see Deborah Gorham, *Vera Brittain: A Feminist Life* (Toronto: University of Toronto Press, 2000) and the work of Gale Wilhelm, author of *We Too Are Drifting* (1935).

82. For a discussion of what the dismissed faculty did after leaving Rockford, see "Faculty of 1918–1919," *Rockford College Taper* 9 (November 1919).

83. San Francisco passenger lists records, Ancestry.com library edition. By 1920, Taylor was teaching public school. See Grace Taylor, 1920 federal census, Harlan, Harlan Township, Shelby County, Iowa.

84. *TW*, 9; *TWR*, 16.

85. ABF college diary, 29 December 1918, FFP.

86. ABF college diary, 5–6 April 1919, FFP; JHF to Valerie Taylor, enclosed in Hazel Toliver to Valerie Taylor, 21 July 1978, *VTWP #1*.

87. Lieutellas Taylor, 1920 manuscript population census, Harlan, Harlan Township, Shelby County, Iowa; Grace Taylor in the John C. Lutz household, 1930 manuscript population census, Council Bluffs, Pottawattamie County, Iowa; "Teachers Assigned in Bluffs Schools," *Council Bluffs Nonparallel*, 22 August 1953, 21. According to Grace Taylor to Carl Tayler, 16 April 1945, Carl Taylor Papers, Cornell University Libraries, Grace made her home with a woman named Dora. The Social Security Death Index lists Taylor's death at age 94 in Pinellas, Florida, on 24 April 1978.

88. "Barter (A Triolet and an Unsent Valentine)," 1922, *TWR*, 21.

89. ABF college diary, 27 June 1919, FFP.

90. For a description of Janesville, see John V. Stevens, *Medical History of Janesville, Wisconsin, 1833–1933* (Janesville, Wis.: J. V. Stevens, 1933).

91. J. E. Lane, 4th Ward, Janesville, Rock County, Wisconsin, 1920 manuscript population census. Foster, Hairgrove, and Venable lived in the household of J. E. and Anna

Lane, on South Jackson Street. "Faculty," *Phoenix Yearbook*, 1921, 10, 14; "Meeting of Loani Band," *Janesville Daily Gazette*, 9 June 1920, 3.

92. "High School to Have Nine New Teachers," 2 September 1919, 3; "High School Notes," 7 February 1920, 5; "Youthful Orators Enter Beloit Meet," 23 April 1920, 5; "High School Picnic at Blackhawk," all from the *Janesville Daily Gazette*, Janesville, Wisconsin; "Her Thrilling Moment," *Phoenix Yearbook* 9 (Janesville, Wis.: Janesville High School, 1921), 129.

93. For examples of Jeannette's visits to campus, see ABF college diary, , 10–11 October 1919, 1–2 November 1919, FFP.

94. For a description of the Christmas holidays, see ABF college diary, 17–31 December 1919, FFP.

95. ABF college diary, 21–22 February 1920, 3 April 1920, 9–10 April 1920, 1–2, 14–15, 29–31, May 1920, 13 June 1920, FFP.

96. JHF to Valerie Taylor, enclosed with Hazel Toliver to Valerie Taylor, 21 July 1978, *VTWP #1*.

97. ABF college diary, 18, 20 June 1920, 20–27 July 1920, 4–29 August 1920, 2 September 1920, FFP.

Chapter 3

1. *TW*, 25; also in *TWR*, 41.

2. Anderson to JHF, 28 May 1960, in Anderson, *Forbidden Fires* (Tallahassee, Fla.: Naiad Press), 155–6.

3. Anderson, *Forbidden* Fires, 42–3, 80.

4. JHF to Anderson, 8 June 1960, Margaret Anderson-Elizabeth Clark Collection, Beinecke Library, Yale University Anderson, *Forbidden Fires*, 159–60.

5. According to family lore, the family discouraged Anna's interest in becoming a nurse because the profession lacked status. *The Ancestry of Winslow Howard Foster*, 70; ABF diary (1921–4), 3 January 1921, FFP.

6. For further discussion of literary treatments of lesbianism in the 1920s, see Lillian Faderman, *Odd Girls and Twilight Lovers*, chapter 3, "Lesbian Chic: Experimentation and Repression in the 1920s," pp. 62–92; Faderman, "Lesbian Magazine Fiction in the Early Twentieth Century, " *Journal of Popular Culture* 11.4 (1978): 800–17.

7. ABF diary (1921–1924), FFP.

8. Jeannette Howard Foster transcript, University of Chicago registrar's office.

9. *Official Publications of the University of Chicago, The Colleges and Graduate Schools* 21 (April 1921), 209.

10. Elsa Gidlow to M. Kuda, 23 October 1976, MKA. In both *TW*, 11 and *TWR*, 19, the poem "Sapphics to One Called Helen" has an error in the first line, which should end in Athéne rather than Athens. See JHF to M. Kuda, 10 October 1976, MKA.

11. H.D.'s *Sea Garden* (Boston: Houghton Mifflin, 1916) featured feminine images of Greek mythological figures. For more on H.D., see Hilda Doolittle "H.D." *Feminist Writers* (St. James Press, 1996), and for Lowell's treatment of lesbianism, see Faderman,

"Warding off the Watch and Ward Society: Amy Lowell's Treatment of the Lesbian Theme," *Gay Books Bulletin* I (Summer 1979): 23–7.

12. ABF college diary, 28 June 1921, FFP. Winslow Foster sawed the cottage in two, moved half of it twelve feet away, and constructed a living room in the newly created space; for examples of activities with the family see ABF college diary, 16–18 September 1921, FFP; ABF diary (1921–1924), 16 and 23 October 1921, FFP.

13. JHF transcript, University of Chicago registrar's office.

14. Biographical information on Fuller is from "(Sarah) Margaret Fuller," *Feminist Writers* (St. James Press, 1996) Reproduced in *Biography Resource Center*. Farmington Hills, Mich.: Thomson Gale. 2007, http://galenet.galegroup.com/servlet/BioRC. For a more recent treatment of Fuller and lesbianism, see Mary E. Wood, "'With Ready Eye': Margaret Fuller and Lesbianism in Nineteenth-Century American Literature," *American Literature* 65 (March 1993): 1–18.

15. Jeannette Howard Foster, "Literary Allusions in the Works of Margaret Fuller," MA thesis, University of Chicago, September 1922, p. 1

16. JHF, "Literary Allusions," 7, 24–5, 35. She did address the question of variance in Fuller's life in Jeannette Howard Foster, *Sex Variant Women in Literature* (New York: Vantage Press, 1956), 138–9.

17. ABF diary (1921–1924), 10 and 22 June 1922; 25 July 1922; JHF transcript, University of Chicago registrar's office.

18. Solomon, *In the Company of Educated Women*, 174.

19. "Additions to Faculty," *The Hamline Oracle*, 13 October 1922; faculty numbers are from the *Annual Catalog, 1922–23* (Hamline University, January 1922). The number of women excludes the nurse and librarian, but includes the dean of women, two other instructors in English, one instructor in Romance languages, and one instructor in physical education. "Faculty," *1924 Hamline Liner* (St. Paul, Minn.: Hamline University, 1924), 27.

20. "English Club Plans Program," *The Hamline Oracle*, 1 December 1922, 1.

21. *Directory of Hamline University, 1923–24*, Hamline University Archives, St. Paul, Minnesota; *Annual Catalog, 1923–24* (Hamline University, January 1923), 55; Jeanette [sic] H. Foster, "Reminiscence," *The Hamline Review* (November 1923), 11.

22. Charles Shirley, manuscript population census, Orleans, Orange County, Indiana, 1900; Mary Shirley biographical file, Smith College Archives, Northampton, Massachusetts. Shirley taught at Hamline from 1922–1924, then became an assistant instructor at the University of Minnesota, where she received her MA in 1925 and PhD in 1927; JHF to Karla Jay, 27 May 1975, KJP.

23. Anna discusses her time in Urbana in ABF diary (1921–1924), FFP, beginning in September 1922. After completing his course of study, Winslow Foster became Chief Structural Engineer with Porkins, Follows & Hamilton, Chicago Architects, and remained with them until 1930, when his position ended because of the Depression. His work included designing the structural steel and reinforced concrete for such projects as Evanston Township High School (Illinois), Teachers' College (Ann Arbor, Michigan), and Manitowoc High School (Wisconsin).

24. ABF diary (1921–1924), 15 January 1924, FFP.

25. JHF to Valerie Taylor in Hazel Toliver to Valerie Taylor, 21 July 1978, *VTWP #1*.

26. In 1929 the Italian dictator Benito Mussolini presented Rome's sister city with a reproduction of an original Etruscan sculpture, the Capitoline Wolf with Romulus and Remus. For information on Rome, see George Magruder Battey, *A History of Rome and Floyd County, State of Georgia, United States of America, 1540–1922* (Atlanta, Ga.: Webb and Vary Co., 1922); for a picture of Shorter College in the 1920s, see Robert G. Gardner, *On the Hill: The Story of Shorter College* (Rome, Ga.: Shorter College, 1972), 217–68.

27. This description is based on a poem by Lenore Harvey, "From Shorter Hill," *The Chimes* 22 (October 1930): 41–2.

28. Gardner, *On the Hill*, 220; JHF oral history, KJP. For insight into campus activities, such as mock weddings and proms, see *The Argo*, 1924–1930.

29. Gardner, *On the Hill*, 223; Board of Trustees minutes, 8 June 1926, Shorter College Archives; *Periscope* 6 (24 January 1925), JHF transcript, University of Chicago Registrar's Office. In the summer of 1926, Jeannette took two courses in Old English, which she passed with high distinction, a course in recent aesthetic theory, and she audited a survey of English literature and a course in literary realism.

30. See Board of Trustees Minutes, 8 June 1926, Shorter College Archives; Florence Fleming, *Higher Education for Southern Women: For Church-Related Women's Colleges in Georgia, Agnes Scott, Shorter, Spelman, and Wesleyan, 1900–1920*. PhD dissertation, Georgia State University, 1985, p.113; Gardner, *On the Hill*, 220, 223, 235.

31. Hilary Farr (pseudonym for JHF), "Temple of Athene," *The Ladder* (December 1967), 20–8; (January 1968), 4–9, 32–40, (February/March 1968), 7–9, 20–37, (April 1968), 22–7; the quote is from (December 1967), 28.

32. The reference to drawing strangers across a room is from JHF to Margaret Anderson, 8 June 1960, Margaret Anderson-Elizabeth Clark Collection, Beinecke Library, Yale University; "Aftermath," *TW*, 13; *TWR*, 25.

33. "To One Called Helen," "Lady Elusive," "Survival," *The Chimes*, December 1924, 17; Faderman, *To Believe in Women*, 248.

34. Faderman, *Surpassing the Love of Men*, 326. Davis earned her PhD from the University of Chicago in 1900; JHF to Margaret Anderson, 8 June 1960, reprinted in Anderson, *Forbidden Fires*, 160.

35. JHF to Anderson, 8 June 1960; "A Lovely Lapse," in *TW*, 14, and *TWR*, 26.

36. Farr, "Temple of Athene." Foster's earlier life often served as inspiration for the stories she penned, which in turn shed light on her earlier emotional experiences.

37. In "Temple of Athene," Theodora reflects on her first kisses, shared with a woman (probably drawn from Jeannette's earlier love, Grace Taylor); the reference to completeness is from JHF to J. N. Katz, 27 September 1977, Katz Papers, NYPL; the reference to abstention is from Farr, "Temple of Athene," *The Ladder* (April 1968), 26.

38. "Anniversary," *TW*, 18; *TWR*, 29.

39. "The Final Mutiny," *TW*, 23; *TWR*, 37.

40. "Bluff," *TW*, 22; *TWR*, 33.

41. "Untitled Sonnet" (1925), *TW*, 21; *TWR*, 32.

42. "Foreword," *TW*, 16; *TWR*, 28.

43. JHF to Anyda Marchant, 25 August 1974, MKA. In JHF to Karla Jay, 21 June 1975, KJP, she discusses the student of her first "experience."

44. Lenore Ward, "In Defense of Cats," *The Chimes* (June 1924), 34; "Senior Statistics," *Periscope* 7 (3 June 1927). Less social than many of her classmates, Lenore's extracurricular activities revolved primarily around her academic interests: Polymnian and Chi Delta Phi (both clubs for English majors), and the Classical Club. "Dear Hands," *Two Women Revisited*, 34.

45. "Camarata Has Enjoyable Meeting," *Periscope* 7 (3 April 1926); "Phi Kappa Alpha," *Periscope* 7 (3 December 1926); Miss Foster Entertains Chi Delta Phi at Dinner," *Periscope* 7/8 (May 21, 1927), 1.

46. "Personals," *The Chimes* (May 1922), 65. Clara Louise Thompson toured Europe in 1922 with Ada Belle Patrick (Shorter class of 1922).

47. Announcements for comparable trips given in other years include "News of Faculty Members," *The Periscope* (August 1926): 18; "Dr. Ware Announces Plans for European Party This Summer," *The Periscope* 8 (February 1928). The trip is described in detail in the Elizabeth Beverly Scrapbook, "My European Trip," Shorter College Archives.

48. Jeannette returned to the United States on the Veendam, leaving Southampton 10 August 1927 and arriving in New York on 20 August 1927. See "New York Passenger Lists, 1820–1957," Ancestry.com.

49. According to Jeannette, her first "experience" occurred when she was thirty-four or thirty-five, which would be either 1930 or 1931; "Morning After" (1925–1930), *TWR*, 36.

50. "Sonnet Out of Serenity," *TWR*, 40.

51. Jeannette Howard Foster, "Lucky Star," *Harpers* 155 (October 1927): 624–35.

52. Lynn D. Gordon, *Gender and Higher Education in the Progressive Era*, (New Haven: Yale University Press, 1990), 198. Somewhat mysteriously, she also had acquired an adopted daughter named Grace, an eighteen-year-old high school senior, described in "University of Pennsylvania Placement Service," 30 January 1928, Clara Louise Thompson Biographical File, University of Pennsylvania Archives. Further information about Thompson is available in "Shorter Teacher Dies Sunday After Extended Illness," *Rome, Georgia, News-Tribune*, 3. She resided at 1011 Oakland Avenue.

53. Fleming, *Higher Education for Southern Women*, 530. Cousins did not complete his doctorate until 1968. Foster described her disgust at the inequitable salaries in JHF to J. N. Katz, 18 October 1977, JNKP.

54. Oak Park Land Co. to Jeannette H. Foster, Deed Book 133, p. 475, 20 October 1928, Floyd County Court House, Rome, Georgia; Oak Park Land Company to Clara Louise Thompson, Deed Book 133, p. 476, 23 October 1928.

55. Jeannette H. Foster to Clara Louise Thompson, Deed Book 138, p. 320, 31 May 1929, Floyd County Court House, Rome, Georgia.

56. When Foster published *Two Women* in 1976, she requested that notices of the book be sent to both women.

57. Unemployed, Winslow Howard Foster spent his time doing research on the family at Chicago's Newberry Library. *The Ancestry of Winslow Howard Foster*, 70. Foster described her surgery and financial situation in JHF to Clara E. Howard, 28 January 1931 and 14 April 1931, Library School Dean's Correspondence, Emory University, Atlanta, Georgia.

58. "Song," *TW*, 28; *TWR*, 43.

59. Martha Vicinus, *Intimate Friends: Women Who Loved Women, 1778–1928* (Chicago: University of Chicago Press, 2004), 187.

CHAPTER 4

1. "The Wave," *TW*, 31; *TWR*, 47.

2. Fewer than half of the students who entered Hollins during the 1930s graduated. See Erin Brisby, "College Women of the 1930s," *The Filson Club History Quarterly* 64 (1 January 1990): 48. Information about Hollins College enrollment was compiled by Beth Harris, archivist, Wyndham Robertson Library, Hollins University.

3. JHF to Valerie Taylor, in Hazel Toliver to Taylor, 21 July 1978, *VTWP #1*; information about the service scholarship is found in JHF, Application to Library School, Foster Library School Alumni File (hereafter LSAF), Emory University Archives (hereafter EUA).

4. JHF to Atlanta Library School, 20 January 1931; JHF to Clara E. Howard, 28 January 1931; JHF to Clara E. Howard, 13 February 1931; JHF to Clara E. Howard, 21 March 1931, LSAF, EUA. Foster also considered applying to her father's alma mater, the University of Illinois, but that program required two years of study. Lenore Ward was working as a stenographer for the Retail Credit Company in Atlanta in 1931.

5. Thomas H. English, *Emory University, 1915–1965: A Semicentennial History* (Atlanta: Emory University, 1966), 35–36. Although affiliated with Emory in 1925, the first library school classes were not held on campus until 1930. The Julius Rosenwald Fund was established in 1917 to aid schools, colleges and universities, and charities, with an emphasis on aid to African Americans. Increased standards meant requiring applicants for admission to possess a bachelor's degree. Concern about age is evident in this statement in *The Emory University Catalogue* (Atlanta: Emory University, February 1931), 203: "Persons over thirty-five are advised not to make application unless they have been engaged in library work." Foster questioned Howard about the age requirement in JHF to Clara E. Howard, 28 January 1931, LSAF, EUA.

6. JHF to Clara E. Howard, 28 January 1931; LSAF, EUA. Tuition at Emory was fifty dollars per quarter, plus the cost of supplies. Howard to JHF, 23 March 1931, LSAF, EUA.

7. JHF Library School Application for Admission, 12 February 1931, LSAF, EUA; Ruby U. Hightower and Clara L. Thompson to Emory University Library School, 15 February 1931; Paul Cousins to Emory University Library School, 16 February 1931, LSAF, EUA.

8. JHF to Louise King, 25 February 1931; King to JHF, 3 March 1931; JHF to King, 11 March 1931; King to JHF, 13 March 1931, LSAF, EUA.

9. JHF to Louise King, 13 July 1931. According to the *Atlanta City Directory*, 1932, JHF took a room at 1182 Clifton Road, NE, and Lenore lived at 1035 Amsterdam Avenue.

10. Joanne E. Passet, "Men in a Feminized Profession: The Male Librarian, 1887–1921," *Libraries & Culture* 28 (Fall 1993): 385–402. According to James V. Carmichael Jr. e-mail message to the author, 8 May 2007, most of the remaining women in the class led relatively ordinary lives.

11. Clara E. Howard to Phineas L. Windsor, 31 August 1932, LSAF, EUA.

12. "Tompkins, Miriam D(owning)," *Who's Who in Library Service* (New York: H. W. Wilson, Co., 1933), 413.

13. "The Wave," *TW*, 31; *TWR*, 47.

14. "Sketch for a Portrait," *TWR*, 50.

15. "Leap Year Night," *TW*, 30; *TWR*, 48–49.

16. "Gary O. Rolstad, "Adult Education," *World Encyclopedia of Library and Information Services*, 3d ed. (Chicago: American Library Association, 1993), 36.

17. "Report on the work of Jeannette Foster in Cataloging," May 1932, LSAF, EUA.

18. Prior to the 1950s, graduates of library schools received a second bachelor's degree, the bachelor of library science, rather than a master's degree. Jeannette was part of an American Association of Library Schools committee in the 1940s that made recommendations concerning the replacement of the BLS with a master of library science degree.

19. "ALA Personnel Division, Jeannette Howard Foster," form completed by Clara E. Howard, 8 April 1932; Clara E. Howard to Phineas L. Windsor, 31 August 1932, LSAF, EUA.

20. Miriam D. Tompkins to Hazel Timmerman, 8 April 1932, LSAF, EUA.

21. JHF to Clara E. Howard, 6 August 1932, LSAF, EUA. McDiarmid would serve as president of the American Library Association in 1948 and 1949.

22. JHF to Clara E. Howard, 12 July 1932, LSAF, EUA. For more on the history of the Graduate Library School see John V. Richardson, *The Spirit of Inquiry: The Graduate Library School at Chicago, 1921–51* (Chicago: American Library Association, 1982).

23. JHF to Clara E. Howard, 6 August 1932 and 24 August 1932, LSAF, EUA. She registered with the Southern Teachers' Agency, the American Librarians' Agency, the Albert Teachers' Agency, and the Fisk Teachers' Agency, and the Fisher Teachers' Exchange.

24. *The Ancestry of Winslow Howard Foster*, 71; Clara E. Howard to Phineas E. Windsor, 31 August 1932, LSAF, EUA; Amelia Krieg, University of Illinois, to Clara E. Howard, 8 September 1932, LSAF, EUA.

25. JHF to Clara E. Howard, 13 September 1932, LSAF, EUA.

26. Arthur E. Morgan, "The Antioch Program," *The Journal of Higher Education* 1 (December 1930): 497–502; *Antioch College Catalog for 1932–33* (Yellow Springs, OH: Antioch College, 1932), 9, 15.

27. JHF to Clara E. Howard, 30 October 1932, LSAF, EUA. Lyle later became known for his text, *The Administration of the College Library*.

28. JHF to Karla Jay, 7 July 1975, KJP; Antioch College, "Weekly Faculty Notes," 13 January 1933, Antiochiana Collection, Antioch College, Yellow Springs, Ohio.

29. The meeting is described in Antioch College, "Weekly Faculty Notes," 14 October 1932; JHF to Karla Jay, 27 May 1975, KJP.

30. Gregory (1908–1978) was the niece of Edwin James Armstrong and was enumerated with her parents in "John F. and Rose Gregory," Federal Population Census, Elmira, Chemung County, New York, 1920 and 1930; "Death Notices," *Newark (NJ) Star Ledger*, 27 October 1978; JHF to Karla Jay, 27 May 1975, KJP; "Mrs. Jessie W. Armstrong," undated clipping from Antioch College Archives [1956].

31. JHF to Karla Jay, 27 May 1975, KJP. Gregory is enumerated with her parents, John and Rose Gregory, Elmira, Chemung County, New York, manuscript population census, 1910, also in 1920 and 1930; her death notice appeared in the Newark, N.J., *Star Ledger*, 27 October 1978.

32. JEF to Clara E. Howard, 30 October 1932 and 29 January 1933, LSAF, EUA. Evidently the college administration decided to lay off the science librarian during June, July, and August as a means of effecting a salary savings.

33. Clara E. Howard to JEF, 15 February 1933, LSAF, EUA.

34. JHF to Clara Howard, 28 February 1933, Howard to JHF, 3 March 1933, LSAF, EUA.

35. Clara E. Howard, Report on Applicant's Admission to the GLS [for Jeannette H. Foster], [February 1933], LSAF, EUA.

36. Faculty Meeting Minutes, 23 March 1933, Box 1, Graduate Library School Records, 1928–1979, University of Chicago Archives; Richardson, *The Spirit of Inquiry*, 111. GLS faculty included Louis Round Wilson, Pierce Butler, Leon Carnovsky, Douglas Waples, and William M. Randall.

37. JHF to Clara E. Howard, 2 April 1933 and 9 April 1933; Howard to JHF, 4 April 1935, LSAF, EUA.

38. JHF to Valerie Taylor, 21 July 1978, in Hazel Toliver to Taylor, 21 July 1978, VTWP #1.

39. JHF Transcript, University of Chicago registrar's office; the school's curriculum is described in *The Graduate Library School, Circular of Information* 33 (25 October 1932).

40. JHF to Karla Jay, 27 May 1975, KJP; Mary M. Shirley, "Academic and Professional History," Smith College Archives, Northampton, Massachusetts.

41. JHF to Clara E. Howard, 5 February 1934, LSAF, EUA; according to Richardson, *The Spirit of Inquiry*, 111, the Carnegie fellowships went to Ethel M. Fair and Mary E. James; *The Ancestry of Winslow Howard Foster*, 70.

42. JHF to Karla Jay, 27 May 1975; "Greenwich Village," *The Encyclopedia of New York City*, edited by Kenneth T. Jackson (New Haven: Yale University Press, 1995), 506–9.

43. JHF to Karla Jay, 27 May 1975, KJP. The woman in question, who Jeannette never named, subsequently married, had two sons, and still was exchanging Christmas cards with her in 1974.

44. *Graduate Library School Bulletin* (University of Chicago, 25 October 1932), 14. JHF to Karla Jay, 27 May 1975, KJP; JHF to Valerie Taylor, in Hazel Toliver to Valerie Taylor, 21 July 1978, *VTWP#1*.

45. Richardson, *The Spirit of Inquiry*, 125.

46. Beginning in 1927, the Julius Rosenwald Fund provided grants which helped establish school libraries for African Americans and rural whites living in the South. In many instances, these libraries served as de facto public libraries for their communities.

47. Foster's original thesis proposal is described in JHF to Clara E. Howard, 5 February 1934, LSAF, EUA; GLS Faculty Meeting Minutes, 7 August 1935, Graduate Library School Records, 1928–1979, Box 1, University of Chicago Archives; JHF transcript, University of Chicago registrar's office; Foster, "An Approach to Fiction Through the Characteristics of its Readers," *Library Quarterly* 6 (April 1936), 124–74, the quote is from page 168.

48. JHF to Karla Jay, 27 May 1975, KJP; Mary Shirley biographical file, Smith College Archives, Northampton, Massachusetts.

49. JHF to Karla Jay, 27 May 1975, KJP.

50. Ibid.; Winslow Howard Foster Diary (1936–38), 3 April 1936, 11 April 1936; 4 January 1937, FFP. JHF spent her vacation in Jacksonville, Florida.

51. JHF, "More Definite Terms to Describe Types of Reading; Abridged," *ALA Bulletin* 30 (August 1936): 682–4.

52. Flexner, who had spent the early years of her career as head of the circulation department at the Free Public Library of Louisville, Kentucky, embarked on the most productive period of her career when she became head of the NYPL Readers' Advisory Service office in 1929. For insight into Flexner's work, see "Only Half of Adults Can Read with Ease," *New York Times*, 9 August 1936.

53. JHF to Karla Jay, 17 November 1975, Karla Jay Papers, Box 3, NYPL.

54. JHF to Tommie Dora Barker, 5 March 1937; Barker to JHF, 8 March 1937, LSAF, EUA.

55. JHF to Karla Jay, 27 May 1975, KJP.

CHAPTER 5

1. Jeannette Howard Foster, "Another Philadelphia Story," unpublished manuscript in the Barbara Grier and Donna McBride Collection (hereafter GMC), San Francisco Public Library (hereafter SFPL).

2. Winslow Howard Foster diary (1936–1939), 9 June 1937, FFP.

3. The Committee grew out of the George–Deen Act (June 1936), which authorized increased Federal appropriations for vocational education.

4. Winslow Howard Foster diary (1936–1939), 9–20 June 1937, FFP; the NRC librarian, a Mr. McCarthy, was leaving for another appointment. The North Interior Building, now the General Services Administration Building, stood across from the Main Interior Building. Office locations were N-7131 for the ACE and N-6137 for the NRC. George D. Franchois to the author, e-mail, 11 May 2007.

5. Paul T. David to Floyd W. Reeves, 22 June 1937, Advisory Committee on Education Records, Franklin D. Roosevelt Library, Hyde Park, N.Y.

6. JHF to Mr. Merrill, "Staff needs of Library," 27 August 1937, Advisory Committee on Education Records, FDR Library; JHF to Karla Jay, 27 May 1975, KJP.

7. Ralph M. Goldman, "In Memoriam, Paul Theodore David," PS: Political Science and Politics (March 1995); JHF to Karla Jay, 27 May 1975, KJP.

8. JHF to Karla Jay, 27 May 1975, KJP

9. Jan Addison (pseudonym for JHF), "A Man's World," The Ladder (July 1968), 13–25 and (August 1968), 31–45.

10. JHF to Karla Jay, 27 May 1975, KJP. For general information about the campus, see Drexel Institute of Technology Bulletin 14/11 (November 1937).

11. JHF to Karla Jay, 27 May 1975, KJP. Law (1884-1981) lived on Tulpehocken Street in 1937. She later made her home with Margaret Gerry Cook, who graduated from the library school in 1926 and who served on the library school faculty from 1948–1952. See Cook to Katherine Ohler, 19 October 1981, Drexel University Archives and "A Visit with Marie Hamilton Law," GSLS Newsletter no. 8 (Winter 1976), n.p., Drexel University Archives (hereafter DUA).

12. The statue at Drexel Institute represents one of three versions carved by William Wetmore Story and was given to Drexel in 1892 by Sarah H. Peterson. For more on Story, see Jan M. Seidler, "A Critical Reappraisal of the Career of William Wetmore Story (1819–1895), PhD dissertation, Boston University, 1985.

13. Guy Garrison to Kevin Martin, 6 May 2005, shared with the author by Martin, discusses Kathryn Oller's impressions of Foster during the 1938–1939 academic year when she took several courses from her. For additional insight into Drexel's history, see Miriam N. Kotzin, A History of Drexel University: 1941–1963 (Philadelphia: Drexel University, 1983), and Edward McDonald and Edward M. Hinton, Drexel Institute of Technology, 1891–1941, (Philadelphia: Drexel Institute, 1942) For the library school's history, see Guy Garrison, A Century of Library Education at Drexel University: Vignettes of Growth and Change (Philadelphia: Drexel University College of Information Studies)1992.

14. Winslow Howard Foster diary (1936–1939), 4 and 23 September, 5, 11, and 27 October, 1, 10, and 24 November, 8 December 1937, FFP; Guy Garrison to Kevin Martin, 6 May 2005.

15. Library School Faculty Meeting Minutes, 5 November 1937, 7 January 1938, 21 January 1938, 25 February 1938, 19 May 1938, Drexel University Archives; "Bibliographic Leviathan," [University of Missouri-Kansas City] Library Memo 5 (November 1959), 3–4; Drexel Library School Association Newsletter, April 1941.

16. JHF to Karla Jay, KJP.

17. JHF to Karla Jay, 27 May 1975, KJP; "Henry A. Pool" and family, U.S. population census, Middleton, New Castle County, Delaware, 1930. Letitia, 27, attended the Drexel Institute Library School after earning her bachelor's degree from the University of Delaware, and joined the Drexel Institute library staff as a cataloger immediately after

graduating from library school. Tish is described in "Letitia Evans Pool," *The Blue & Gold, 1922 Yearbook* (Newark, Del.: University of Delaware), 72.

18. JHF to Anyda Marchant, 13 December 1976, MKA, JHF to Karla Jay, 17 January 1976, KJP; Winslow Howard Foster diary (1939–1941), 7, 12, and 21 December 1939, FFP; see Ann[a] Cope to Dear Folks, 5 January 1943, Foster Family Correspondence, FFP, for an example of Jeannette's letters being filled with stories of illness and overwork.

19. JHF to Karla Jay, 27 May 1975, KJP; Winslow H. Foster diary (1936–1938), 25 April 1938, FFP.

20. Grier to the author, 23 and 26 July 2007.

21. "Miriam D. Tompkins of Columbia Staff," *New York Times*, 4 March 1954. Miriam taught Reading Interests and Habits of Adults, and Public Library in Adult Education.

22. JHF to Alfred C. Kinsey, 21 October 1943 and 6 October 1944, Foster–Kinsey Correspondence, Kinsey Institute.

23. "Dr. Ella Roberts, 58, Cardiac Specialist," *New York Times* 25 October 1963, 31; Phyllis Greenacre (1894–1989) left the Payne Whitney clinic in the late 1940s and went into private practice in Manhattan.

24. JHF to J. N. Katz, 18 October 1977, JNKP; Garrison, *A Century of Library Education at Drexel University*, 9. Harriet MacPherson (1892–1967) earned a BA from Wellesley College in 1914, studied in the New York Public Library school, earning a certificate in 1917, and then earned an MA (1924) and a PhD (1929) from Columbia University.

25. Winslow H. Foster diary (1936–1938), 9 June 1937, 19–20, 23–24 August 1938, 6 September 1938, FFP.

26. Ruth is enumerated with her father, Carolus Harry, Manuscript Population Census for 1920, 22nd Ward, Philadelphia, Pennsylvania. The daughter of a Lutheran clergyman, Ruth Harry majored in English at Hood College, then earned a BS in Library Science from Drexel in 1938.

27. Library Science Faculty Meeting Minutes, 31 October 1938, 6 January 1939, DUA; Ann[a] Foster Cope to Dear Parents, 1 November 1938, Foster Family Letters, FFP; Winslow H. Foster diary (1936–1938), 23–26 December 1938, FFP.

28. Library Science Faculty Meeting Minutes, 2 December 1938, 20 January 1939, DUA.

29. Winslow Howard Foster diary (1939–1941), 23 February 1939, FFP; JHF to Karla Jay, 27 May 1975, KJP.

30. JHF to Dear Folks, March 1939 [two letters without the day noted], Foster Family Correspondence, FFP; Winslow H. Foster diary, 18 May 1939, FFP; according to *Rockford College Alumni News*, Winter 1946–1947, Foster still owned the Atlanta property. Lenore still lived at 1035 Amsterdam Ave.

31. Library School Faculty Minutes, 18 May 1939, DUA; JHF to Anyda Marchant, 21 October 1974, and JHF to Anyda Marchant, 16 May 1976, MKA. This correspondence refers to visiting the Pool family cottage at Rehoboth Beach in 1939 or 1940; "Describes Recent Atlantic Crossing on Neutral Vessel," *Ludington Daily News*, 21 September 1939. Letitia and Ruth spent several years together, but in 1942 Ruth accepted a wartime posi-

tion with the Coast Artillery School in Fort Monroe, Virginia, and left Letitia behind in Philadelphia.

32. Grier e-mail to the author, 15 May 2007; JHF to Karla Jay, 27 May 1975, KJP. Jeannette attributed this phrase to the *New Yorker*.

33. Jocelyn K. Wilk, Columbia University Archives, e-mail to the author, 22 June 2007; "Dr. Frederick Lund [obituary]," *New York Times*, 23 December 1965, 27.

34. JHF to Karla Jay, 2 March 1975, KJP; Foster Employment Record, Columbia University Archives. Twenty-four years later she would encounter one of the men she taught that summer in New York City when she attended a national meeting of the Daughters of Bilitis.

35. "Mary A. Butcher," manuscript population census, Wymore, Gage County, Nebraska, 1910, 1920; "Adelia Butcher Lund," *Who's Who in Library Service* (Chicago: American Library Association, 1943). The daughter of a drayman who died when she was only seven, Dee grew up in rural Wymore, Nebraska, the second of four sisters.

36. JHF to Karla Jay, 27 May 1975, KJP; JHF to Dear Everybody, 5 January 1943, Foster Family Correspondence, FFP.

37. "Ill Four Hours, W. H. Foster Dies," *Ludington Daily News*, 20 April 1942. After cremating his body, the family interred him in the Burr family lot at South Haven, Michigan.

38. Jeannette's mother died in Potomac, Illinois, where she lived with her daughter Anna. See "Former Resident of Ludington Dies," 8 September 1943, *Ludington Daily News*; Anna Foster Cope to family, 29 September 1942, 8 March 1943, Foster Family Letters, FFP; Alison Cope Puffer and Winslow H. Cope, oral interview with the author, 3 December 2005.

39. Miriam Kotzin, *A History of Drexel University, 1941-1963* (Philadelphia: Drexel University, 1983), 47; Ann[a] Foster Cope to family, 19 April 1943, Foster Family Letters, FFP.

40. Library School Faculty Meeting Minutes, 2 October 1942, 4 December 1942, DUA; "Miss Lillian Lee [obituary]," 15 March 1988, *Atlanta Journal-Constitution*, C-1.

41. Jeannette Howard Foster, "Library School Opinion on Degrees and Curriculum." (Philadelphia: Drexel University, 1946); Library School Faculty Meeting Minutes, 16 March 1945, DUA.

42. Foster, *Sex Variant Women in Literature* (New York: Vantage Press, 1956), 12.

43. For a complete listing of the works she consulted, see the bibliographies in Foster, *Sex Variant Women in Literature* (New York: Vantage Press, 1956).

44. During this period she published a number of book reviews, including JHF, "Review of *Replacement List of Fiction*," *Library Quarterly* 10 (January 1940), 124–5; JHF, "Review of *Subject Guide to Reference Books*," *College and Research Libraries* 4 (March 1943), 165-7; JHF "Review of *Exploration in Reading Patterns*," *Library Quarterly* 13 (July 1943), 270–1; JHF, "Review of *Reading Interests and Needs of Negro College Freshmen Regarding Social Science Materials*," *Library Quarterly* 13 (October 1943, 353-355; JHF, "Review of *Program of Instruction in Library Schools*," *Library Quarterly* 14 (July 1944), 252–3; JHF,

"Review of *Library in the Community*," *Library Quarterly* 15 (January 1945), 78–9; JHF, "Review of *On Judging Books*," *Library Quarterly* 18 (January 1948), 69–71.

45. Jeannette Howard Foster, "Open Letter to a Colleague," *Library Journal* (November 1938), 858–9.

46. See the concluding paragraph of "Describes Recent Atlantic Crossing on Neutral Vessel," *Ludington Daily News*, 21 September 1939, for a description of JHF's summer research at the Ludington Public Library; JHF, "Acknowledgements," *Sex Variant Women in Literature* (New York: Vantage Press, 1956), 7; Renée Vivien, born Pauline Mary Tarne in 1877, was a British-born woman educated in Paris. In 1898, when she reached her majority, she adopted the name Renée Vivien, under which she became best known for poetry celebrating lesbian erotic love.

47. JHF oral history, KJP.

48. JHF, *Sex Variant Women in Literature* (New York: Vantage Press, 1956), 55, 60.

49. JHF LSAF, EUA.

50. JHF manuscript entry for *Who's Who in Library Service*, LSAF, EUA; Ann[a] Foster to Dear Family, 29 September 1942, Foster Family Correspondence; JHF to Tommie Dora Barker, 22 October 1946 and 31 October 1946, LSAF, EUA.

51. JHF to J. N. Katz, 18 October 1977, JNKP.

CHAPTER 6

1. Alfred C. Kinsey (hereafter ACK) to JHF, 25 July 1941, Foster–Kinsey Correspondence, Kinsey Institute for Research in Sex, Gender, and Reproduction (hereafter Kinsey Institute), Bloomington, Indiana.

2. JHF to Karla Jay, 27 May 1975, KJP; JHF oral history, KJP; James H. Jones, *Alfred C. Kinsey: A Public/Private Life*, (New York: W. W. Norton and Co., 1997), 425. The article Foster read in manuscript form appeared as Alfred C. Kinsey, "Homosexuality: Criteria for a Hormonal Explanation of the Homosexual," *Journal of Clinical Endocrinology* 1 (May 1941): 424–8.

3. JHF to ACK, 8 May 1941, Foster–Kinsey Correspondence, Kinsey Institute; Katharine Bement Davis, *Factors in the Sex Life of Twenty-two Hundred Women* (New York: Harper & Brothers,1929).

4. Jones, *Alfred C. Kinsey*; Jonathan Gathorne-Hardy, *Kinsey: Sex The Measure of All Things: A Life of Alfred C. Kinsey* (Bloomington: Indiana University Press, 2000); T. Coraghessan Boyle, *The Inner Circle* (New York: Viking, 2004); *American Experience: Kinsey* (Alexandria, VA: PBS Home Video, 2005).

5. JHF to ACK, 22 May 1941, Foster–Kinsey Correspondence, Kinsey Institute; "The Howdy Club," *Going Places in New York City* (Brooklyn: The Brooklyn Daily Eagle, winter edition 1937–1938), 38.

6. ACK to JHF, 25 July 1941, Foster–Kinsey Correspondence, Kinsey Institute; JHF to Karla Jay, 27 May 1975, KJP; Paul Gebhard oral interview with the author, Bloomington, Indiana, 14 July 2005. For more on Kinsey's interviews, see Jonathan Gathorne-Hardy,

Kinsey: Sex the Measure of All Things, Chapter 7. Kinsey's experiences with homosexuality are discussed on p. 137.

7. Winslow H. Foster diary (1939–1941), 18 July–3 August 1941; Jones, *Alfred C. Kinsey*, 520, 624; JHF to ACK, 5 August 1941, Foster–Kinsey Correspondence, Kinsey Institute; Gebhard interview with the author, 14 July 2005.

8. Jones, *Alfred C. Kinsey*, 372, discusses follow-up notes; ACK to JHF, 25 July 1941; JHF to ACK 22 May 1941; JHF to ACK, 5 August 1941, Foster-Kinsey Correspondence, Kinsey Institute.

9. According to "Attitudes of Females Toward Homosexual Activities," *Sexual Behavior in the Human Female*, 501, nearly 17 percent of the 5,940 women interviewed for *Sexual Behavior in the Human Female* admitted to some homosexual experience. ACK to JHF, 1 October 1941, Foster–Kinsey Correspondence, Kinsey Institute. The identities of the women Jeannette contacted remain unconfirmed; Lenore Harvey, Lillian Smith, and Clara Louise Thompson would have been among those from Georgia that she invited to participate.

10. JHF to ACK, 31 December 1942; ACK to JHF, 26 January 1943, Foster–Kinsey Correspondence, Kinsey Institute; ACK to Jennie Gregory and Margaret Knowlton, 26 January 1943, Gregory–Kinsey Correspondence, Kinsey Institute.

11. JHF to ACK, 21 October 1943, Foster–Kinsey Correspondence, Kinsey Institute; Jones, *Alfred C. Kinsey*, pp. 438 and 443 discusses the conference and Rockefeller Foundation.

12. Gebhard e-mail to the author, 22 October 2007.

13. ACK to JHF, 2 March 1944, 24 May 1944, Foster–Kinsey Correspondence and Jennie Gregory to ACK, 19 January 1945, Gregory–Kinsey Correspondence, Kinsey Institute.

14. Gregory to ACK, 10 February 1945, Gregory–Kinsey Correspondence, Kinsey Institute.

15. JHF to ACK, 11 November 1946; ACK to JHF, 18 November 1946, Foster–Kinsey Correspondence, Kinsey Institute.

16. For examples of prepublication press coverage, see Harold B. Clemenko, "Toward a Saner Sex Life," *Look* (9 December 1947): 106–7; Albert Deutsch, "The Sex Habits of American Men," *Harper's Magazine* (December 1947): 493; "A Scientist Looks at America's Sexual Behavior," *Science Illustrated* (December 1947): 34; Fred Myers, "The Truth about Sex in America," *Reader's Scope* (December 1947): 154.

17. Jones, *Alfred C. Kinsey*, 458; Paul Gebhard discussed Kinsey's management of the library in his oral interview, 14 July 1005, Bloomington, Indiana; for insight into the mounting pressure to use the collections, see Wardell B. Pomeroy, *Dr. Kinsey and the Institute for Sex Research* (New York: Harper & Row, 1972), 229–30.

18. Jones, *Alfred C. Kinsey*, 476, 479-80.

19. Foster boasted of being psychoanalyzed in JHF to ACK, 8 May 1941, Foster–Kinsey Correspondence, Kinsey Institute. See Jones, *Alfred C. Kinsey*, 298–300 for Kinsey's attitudes on Freudian psychiatrists.

20. ACK to JHF, 25 November 1947 and 21 March 1948, Foster–Kinsey Correspondence, Kinsey Institute.

21. JHF to ACK, 1 December 1947, 3 December 1947, Foster–Kinsey Correspondence, Kinsey Institute.

22. Gilbert Bailey, "Picture of a Postwar Campus," *The New York Times Magazine*, 21 December 1947:14.

23. ACK to Robert Miller, 29 November 1947, Foster–Kinsey Correspondence, Kinsey Institute.

24. ACK to JHF, 17 January 1948, Foster–Kinsey Correspondence, Kinsey Institute; Foster personnel papers, Indiana University Archives; for Gebhard's salary, see Jones, *Alfred C. Kinsey*, 497.

25. JHF to ACK, 21 Jan. 1948, 27 February 1948, Foster–Kinsey Correspondence, Kinsey Institute. The sales of *Sexual Behavior in the Human Male* reached 40,000 by January 19, 1949, and the month after its publication, it had gone into a sixth printing. For sales statistics, see Gathorne-Hardy, *Kinsey*, 269. References to the retirement annuity are in JHF to James R. Creese, 11 October 1951, Creese Correspondence, DUA, and to the leave of absence in *Drexel Library School Alumni Association Newsletter* 7 (April 1948).

26. Indiana University Faculty Housing Application for Jeannette Howard Foster, 21 February 1948, Indiana University Archives; JHF to ACK, 6 May 1948, Foster–Kinsey Correspondence, Kinsey Institute. Born near Baltimore in 1906, Smithers was the daughter of a dentist and a high school teacher. She was enumerated with her father, Delmar Smithers, in federal manuscript population census, Chesapeake, Cecil County, Maryland, 1930. According to an oral interview with Dorothy Collins, 27 July 2005, first priority in housing assignments in the postwar years went to married faculty with children, then married without children, then single faculty, then married students with children.

27. JHF to ACK, 6 May 1948, Foster–Kinsey Correspondence, Kinsey Institute.

28. JHF to ACK, 6 May 1948 and ACK to JHF, 28 May 1948, Foster–Kinsey Correspondence, Kinsey Institute; Foster to Faculty Housing Committee, 14 June 1948, and J. A. Franklin to Foster, 13 July 1938, Housing Committee Records, Indiana University Archives; Elizabeth C. Smithers, Social Security Death Index Record. In Paul Gebhard oral interview, 14 July 2005, he notes that there were no openly gay or lesbian faculty members at Indiana University in the late 1940s, and only a few years earlier, under President William Lowe Bryan's administration, faculty members were asked to resign if they divorced.

29. Jones, *Alfred C. Kinsey: A Public/Private Life*, 574, 599. Alison Cope Puffer interview, 3 December 2005.

30. Gebhard to author, e-mail messages dated 13 October 2006, 25 October 2006; Gebhard interview with the author, 14 July 2005; description of meals at the Tudor Room is from Dorothy Collins oral interview, 27 July 2005; Henry Remak oral interview with the author, 23 February 2007, Bloomington, Indiana.

31. Gathorne-Hardy, *Sex the Measure of All Things*, 217–9; Gebhard to author, e-mail messages dated 13 October 2006, 25 October 2006.

32. Paul Gebhard e-mail to the author, 13 October 2007.

33. Gebhard oral interview, 14 July 2005; Dorothy Collins oral interview, 27 July 2005.

34. Gebhard oral interview, 14 July 2005; JHF to Karla Jay, 9 August 1975, KJP; JHF oral history, KJP.

35. Gebhard oral interview with the author, 14 July 2005. For a description of the library, see Gathorne-Hardy, *Kinsey*, 329–30.

36. See Gathorne-Hardy, 329–32 for information on the appointment of female staff. The title page of *Sexual Behavior in the Human Female* lists six women and seven men working for the project, excluding Foster and translator Hazel Toliver, who left the Kinsey Institute before the book appeared.

37. Dorothy Collins oral interview, 27 July 2005; Gebhard oral interview, 14 July 2005; JHF to J. N. Katz, 18 October 1977, JNKP; Gathorne-Hardy, *Sex, the Measure of All Things*, 247. For a description of Pomeroy, see Jones, 482, and "Pomeroy, Wardell B.," *Contemporary Authors Online*, Gale, 2007, Reproduced in *Biography Resource Center* (Farmington Hills, Mich.: Thomson Gale. 2007), http://galenet.galegroup.com/servlet/BioRC (accessed 27 July 2007).

38. Gathorne-Hardy, *Kinsey*, 331; JHF oral history, KJP; Gebhard e-mail to the author, 2 November 2007.

39. Gebhard oral interview, 14 July 2005.

40. *Rockford College Alumna* 25 (July 1949), 15; "Study Librarian Requirements," *New York Times*, 6 June 1949, 5.

41. Hazel Toliver Biographical File, Indiana University Archives, Bloomington, Indiana.

42. Gebhard oral interview, 14 July 2005; Toliver's research is discussed in Herman Briscoe to William Ainsworth Parker, American Council of Learned Societies, 5 June 1952, Dean of Faculties Correspondence, Indiana University Archives. For examples of the censorship she found in Benjamin Jowett's translation of Plato's *Symposium*, see C. A. Tripp, "Alfred C. Kinsey (1894–1956)," in Vern L. Bullough, ed., *Before Stonewall: Activists for Gay and Lesbian Rights in Historical Context* (New York: Harrington Park Press, 2002), 20–21.

43. Barbara Grier discussed Hazel's traits in e-mail message to the author, 24 March 2006; Hazel and Myrtle Toliver are enumerated in the federal manuscript population census with James A. Toliver, Fayetteville, Washington County, Arkansas, 1910; and separately in Fayetteville, Washington County, Arkansas, 1920 (where Myrtle is listed as a widow) and Sallisaw City, Sequoyah County, Oklahoma, 1930.

44. Gebhard oral interview, 14 July 2005; JHF oral history, KJP; JHF to Karla Jay, 27 May 1975, KJP.

45. J. H. Foster oral history; KJP; JHF to Karla Jay, 27 May 1975, KJP; Gebhard oral interview, 14 July 2005.

46. JHF oral history, 5 June 1975, KJP; Gebhard oral interview, 14 July 2005; Pomeroy, *Dr. Kinsey and the Institute for Sex Research*, 235-236; Grier e-mail to the author, 21 October 2006.

47. JHF oral history, KJP; JHF to Barbara Grier, December 1974, GMC, SFPL; Jonathan Gathorne-Hardy, *Kinsey*, 354. For a biography of Wescott, see Jerry Rosco, *Glenway Wescott Personally: A Biography* (University of Wisconsin Press, 2002).

48. Barbara Grier e-mail to the author, 21 October, 2006; Gathorne-Hardy, *Kinsey*, 83.

49. JHF to J. N. Katz, 18 October 1977; Gebhard e-mail to the author, 6 September 2005.

50. JHF to Karla Jay, 27 May 1975, KJP; J. H. Foster LSAF, EUA.

51. After Foster's departure, Kinsey appointed her assistant, Jean Brown, librarian, but she did not have a library degree.

52. Gebhard oral interview, 14 July 2005; JHF oral history, KJP.

53. JHF to ACK, 2 March 1954 and JHF to Gebhard and Pomeroy, 12 September 1956, Foster-Kinsey Correspondence, Kinsey Institute.

CHAPTER 7

1. JHF, *Sex Variant Women in Literature* (Tallahassee, Fla.: The Naiad Press, Inc, 1985), 354.

2. "Perverts Called Government Peril," *New York Times*, 19 April 1950, p. 25; "Publisher Defends Lurid Paper Books," *New York Times*, 2 December 1952, 33; "U.S. Ousted 425 on Morals," *New York Times*, 13 April 1953, 20.

3. Katherine V. Forrest, ed., *Lesbian Pulp Fiction: The Sexually Intrepid World of Lesbian Paperback Novels, 1950–1965* (New York: Cleis Press, 2005), x, xiv.

4. The house stood at 2004 E. Thirty-first Street. For a description, see Barbara Grier e-mail to the author, 30 March 2006.

5. JHF to Karla Jay, 27 May 1975, KJP; for a description of the relationship, see Grier e-mail to the author, 24 March 2006.

6. "Named to K.C.U. Posts," *Kansas City Star/Times*, 10 August 1952; "Add Sixteen to Faculty," *The University News*, 24 September 1952, 2; "Memorandum on Appointment to Staff," for Jeannette H. Foster and Hazel Toliver, 16 March 1953, President's Papers, Loc. #30894, File #45, University of Missouri–Kansas City University Archives (hereafter UMKC Archives). Hazel was to receive $4,100 and Jeannette $3,500 for the 1953–1954 academic year.

7. "Across Campus," *Information on Faculty-Staff*, 15 March 1954, p. 4. For information on the book club, see Untitled Clipping, *Kansas City Star/Times*, 8 November 1952; for information about serving as hostess for a reception see Untitled clipping, *Kansas City Star/Times*, 13 June 1956, UMKC Archives.

8. Kenneth LaBudde to President Earl J. McGrath, 10 September 1953, UMKC archives; "Kenneth J. LaBudde," *Directory of American Scholars*, 9th ed. Gale Group, 1999. Examples of his articles appear in *American Quarterly*, volumes 2, 10–12, 16–18, 20. Reproduced in *Biography Resource Center*. Farmington Hills, Mich.: Thomson Gale, 2007. http://galenet.galegroup.com/servlet/BioRC. Document Number: K1612511421. According to the Social Security Death Index, LaBudde died 25 March 2000.

9. Kenneth J. LaBudde to Earl J. McGrath [Decker's successor], 10 September 1953, President's Papers, Loc. #31192, file #33, UMKC Archives.

10. "Dr. Toliver Visits Sites of Ancient Cultures," *Information on Faculty/Staff* (12 October 1954), 1. For an example of Hazel's research, see Hazel Toliver, "Plautus and the State Gods of Rome," *CJ* 48 (1952): 49–57. Hazel Toliver to Alfred Kinsey, 19 April 1954, Toliver–Kinsey Correspondence, Kinsey Institute.

11. Barbara Grier e-mail to the author, 30 March 2006; JHF to Paul Gebhard, 11 April 1957, Kinsey–Foster Correspondence, Kinsey Institute; "Did You Know?" *This Week at Our University*, 13 May 1958, 3. They attended meetings of the Classical Association of the Middle West, the Foreign Language Conference, and the American Library Association.

12. See Karen M. Keener, "Out of the Archives and Into the Academy: Opportunities for Research and Publication in Lesbian Literature," *College English* 44 (March 1982): 301–13, for a fuller discussion of the obstacles to lesbian scholarship during Foster's lifetime.

13. The Library of Congress Union Catalog was published in 1946 and in 1948 was designated the National Union Catalog. See William J. Welsh, "Last of the Monumental Book Catalogs," *American Libraries* 12 (1981): 465. For more on Jeannette's research process, JHF to Karla Jay, 17 November 1975, KJP.

14. "Acknowledgements," JHF, *Sex Variant Women in Literature*, 7.

15. Karla Jay, "The X-Rated Bibliographer: A Spy in the House of Sex," in Karla Jay and Allen Young, eds., *Lavender Culture* (New York University Press, 1978): 259.

16. "Acknowledgements," *Sex Variant Women in Literature*; JHF oral history; KJP.

17. For a list of Guggenheim recipients in 1952, see John Simon Guggenheim Memorial Foundation, "Foundation Program Areas, 1952," http://www.gf.org/52fellow.html (accessed 18 June 2007).

18. JHF to James R. Creese, 11 October 1951; Creese to JHF, 22 October 1951, Henry Allen Moe to Creese, 23 November 1951, Creese to Moe, 27 November 1951, DUA.

19. Tompkins died on March 2 in her apartment at 400 West 119th Street, New York City. For her obituary, see "Miriam D. Tompkins of Columbia Staff," *New York Times*, 4 March 1954. According to Gary O. Rolstad, "Adult Education," *World Encyclopedia of Library and Information Services*, 3d ed. (Chicago: American Library Association, 1993), 36, "The teaching of Miriam Tompkins for 30 years, at Emory University and then at Columbia University, was probably a greater influence during the 1930s and 1940s than any other single educational factor in building the cadre of adult services specialists who gave leadership to the field."

20. JHF oral history, KJP.

21. JHF, *Sex Variant Women in Literature*, 11.

22. Foster, *Sex Variant Women in Literature*, 63.

23. JHF to Paul Gebhard, 3 March 1957, Foster–Kinsey Correspondence, Kinsey Institute.

24. Dorothy Yost Deegan, *Stereotype of the Single Woman in American Novels: A Social Study With Implications for the Education of Women* (New York: Octagon Books, 1975

[c. 1951]). Praz, an Italian-born critic of English literature, first published *The Romantic Agony* in 1933, a comprehensive survey of the erotic and morbid themes by European authors in the late eighteenth and nineteenth centuries.

25. JHF to Gebhard, 3 March 1957, Foster–Kinsey Correspondence, Kinsey Institute. Basler, a Lincoln scholar who had headed English departments at several colleges and universities in the southern U.S., joined the Library of Congress staff in 1952. The text of these readers' reports has not survived.

26. Agenda, Rutgers University Press Council Meeting, 8 March 1955, Rutgers University Press Papers, Rutgers University Archives; JHF to Gebhard, 3 March 1957, Foster–Kinsey Correspondence, Kinsey Institute. For some reason, when Jeannette retold this story in subsequent years, she always claimed that the receptive editor died and his successor did not want *Sex Variant Women* to be the first title appearing under his management. Press protocol dictated that the University Press Council had the final vote on whether or not a book appeared in print, so evidently a majority of the members did not want *Sex Variant Women in Literature* to be among the first titles appearing under Sloan's management.

27. When William Sloan joined the press, he arranged for Helen Ada Stewart, who lived at 28 West Eleventh Street with Rita Forenbach, to become an executive editor. See Helen Ada Stewart appointment papers, and William Sloane to Mason W. Gross, 27 December 1954, Rutgers University Press papers, Rutgers University Archives.

28. JHF oral history, KJP. For more on subsidy presses, see Edward Uhlan, *The Rogue of Publishers' Row: Confessions of a Publisher* (New York: Exposition Press, 1956).

29. Judith Serebnick, personal interview with the author, 10 June 2005, Bloomington, Indiana; JHF to Paul Gebhard, 3 March 1957, Foster–Kinsey Correspondence, Kinsey Institute.

30. "Publishers' Output in 1954, *Publishers' Weekly* 167 (22 January 1955), 346–9; "Publishers' 1954 Output of Titles Analyzed," *Publishers' Weekly* 167 (22 January 1955), 305–6; JHF to Margaret Anderson, 8 June 1960, reprinted in Anderson, *Forbidden Fires*,157; JHF to Gebhard, 3 March 1957, Foster–Kinsey Correspondence, Kinsey Institute.

31. Harriet Fleischel Pilpel was a member of the New York bar and senior partner at the law firm of Greenbaum, Wolff & Ernst, a firm that specialized in First Amendment Issues. Between 1937–1991, she participated in twenty-seven cases before the U.S. Supreme Court, and also had a monthly column in *Publishers' Weekly*.

32. JHF to Pilpel, 30 January 1956, Foster–Kinsey Correspondence, Kinsey Institute.

33. ACK to Harriet Pilpel, 13 February 1956, Foster–Kinsey Correspondence, Kinsey Institute.

34. JHF to Paul Gebhard, 3 March 1957, Kinsey Correspondence, Kinsey Institute. Henry served as director of the psychiatric clinic at New York Hospital from 1926–32 and attending psychiatrist from 1932–1954. He also was on the staff of Bloomingdale Hospital (New York Hospital–Westchester Division) in White Plains and on the faculty of Cornell University Medical College. Elizabeth M. Shepard, archivist, Cornell University, e-mail message to the author, 1 June 2007.

35. Robert Latou Dickinson and Lura Beam, *The Single Woman, A Medical Study in Sex Education* (Baltimore: The Williams and Wilkins Co., 1934); Helen Reitman (later known as Jan Gay), born in Chicago in 1902, died 1960.

36. Henry Minton, *Departing from Deviance* (Chicago: University of Chicago Press, 2001), 5, 33–57.

37. JHF to Gebhard, 3 March 1957, Foster–Kinsey Correspondence, Kinsey Institute.

38. Ibid.

39. Ibid.

40. Paul and Jane Bowles brought some Arabic-based literature to light, and Yukio Mishima's work led to increased interest in gay Asian literature.

41. JHF, "Foreword," *Sex Variant Women in Literature*, 3; JHF to Karla Jay, 12 April 1975, KJP.

42. Jeannette Howard Foster, *Sex Variant Women in Literature* (London: F. Muller, Ltd., 1958).

43. Library holding information is available from WorldCat library database by searching key words "sex+variant+women foster" at www.worldcat.org.

44. JHF to Paul Gebhard, 3 March 1957, Foster–Kinsey Correspondence, Kinsey Institute.

45. JHF to Marie Kuda, 6 March 1976, MKA; Winslow F. Cope e-mail to the author, 21 June 2007.

46. It was advertised along with such tantalizing titles as *Indian Animal Stories for Children* and *A History of Employer's Associations in the U.S.* "Latest Vantage Titles," *New York Times* (7 April 1957), 266.

47. Letters from JHF and Paul H. Gebhard, "Readers Respond," *The Ladder* 1 (May 1957), 20.

48. "Women Sex Deviates in Books," *KC Star/Times*, 2 March 1957; Foster, *Sex Variant Women in Literature*, 158.

49. Kenneth LaBudde, KCU Librarian an Author," *University News* (March 15, 1957), 4.

50. Marion Zimmer Bradley, "Variant Women in Literature," (review) *The Ladder* 1 (May 1957): 8–10. *The Ladder* circulation statistics are from Rodger Streitmatter, *Unspeakable: The Rise of the Gay and Lesbian Press in America* (Boston: Faber and Faber, 1995), 28.

51. JHF, Letter to the Editor, *The Ladder* 1 (June 1957): 25.

52. Barbara Grier to JHF, 19 September 1977, GMC, SFPL.

53. Grier to the author, e-mail message, 29 December 2006.

54. Grier to the author, e-mail message, 21 October 2006.

55. Grier to the author, e-mail message, 21 October 2006.

56. Faderman, e-mail to the author, 30 December 2006. For more on Faderman's work, see also "Lillian Faderman," *Contemporary Authors Online*, Gale, 2007. Reproduced in *Biography Resource Center* (Farmington Hills, Mich.: Thomson Gale, 2007). http://galenet.galegroup.com/servlet/BioRC. Document Number: H1000030301.

CHAPTER 8

1. Jan Addison [pseudonym for JHF], "Hail and Farewell," *The Ladder* 1 (September 1957):9.

2. According to Winslow F. Cope e-mail to the author, 25 June 2007, Jeannette often stayed with her sister Helen and brother-in-law Russell Fisher when she attended library meetings in Chicago, but one year, circa 1962 or 1963, they had a falling out, and she stayed with Winslow and his wife Alora. Later they learned that Helen had voiced displeasure with Jeannette's drinking, but since Helen and Russell both drank there must have been an additional cause, possibly Jeannette's lesbianism, at the center of the estrangement.

3. JHF to Karla Jay, 27 May 1975, KJP.

4. JHF to Valerie Taylor, 22 April 1976, *VTWP #1*.

5. 1928 Yearbook, Central Missouri State University (now Central Missouri University) (Warrensburg, Mo., 1928), 176. According to the Indiana University registrar's office, Bloomington, Indiana, Ross also did some graduate work at there in the summer of 1953.

6. Grier e-mail to the author, 24 March 2006.

7. Grier e-mail to the author, 11 June 2007.

8. Grier e-mail to the author, 11 June 2007; JHF to Karla Jay, 2 March 1975, KJP.

9. Grier e-mail to the author, 8 June 2007.

10. JHF to Karla Jay, 27 May 1975, KJP; JHF to Anyda Marchant, 21 October 1975, MKA; "Tea Honors Dr. Foster," *This Week at Our University*, 24 May 1960, 2. Jeannette retired on 29 July 1960. For insight into the relationship of the three women, see Barbara Grier, e-mail to the author, 12 June 2007.

11. JHF to Anderson, 8 June 1960, Margaret Anderson–Elizabeth Clark Collection, Beinecke Library, Yale University.

12. Roger Streitmatter, *Unspeakable: The Rise of the Gay and Lesbian Press in America* (Boston: Faber and Faber, 1995), 22.

13. Streitmatter, *Unspeakable*, 9, 26.

14. Marcia M. Gallo, *Different Daughters: A History of the Daughters of Bilitis and the Rise of the Lesbian Rights Movement* (New York: Carroll and Graff, 2006), Chapter 2, "Climbing the Ladder," 21–38.

15. JHF [letter to the editor], *The Ladder* 1 (June 1957): 25.

16. Jan Addison (pseudonym for JHF): "Hail and Farewell," *The Ladder* 1 (September 1957): 7–11; B.S., San Leandro, California [letter to the editor], *The Ladder* 2 (November 1957): 24.

17. Hazel E. Barnes to the author, 14 April 2006.

18. Jan Addison, "Life Class," *The Ladder* 2 (May 1958): 4–8.

19. Jan Addison, "Exit Laughing," *The Ladder* 5 (Nov. 1960): 10–3.

20. Ben Cat (pseudonym for Helen Sandoz), "Timely Topics," *The Ladder* 12 (July 1968): 27.

21. Jan Addison, "Narrow Escape," *The Ladder* (Feb. 1963): 7–10. In *Mädchen in Uniform*, fourteen-year-old Manuela von Meinhard is sent to boarding school where she develops a crush on Fraulein von Bernburg, a popular and compassionate teacher. When both are dismissed, Manuela plans to commit suicide but is saved by schoolgirls and the Fraulein castigates the headmistress.

22. Abby Sanford (pseudonym for JHF), "The Funniest Thing." In a folder labeled "Manuscripts by Others–Jeanette Howard Foster," GMC, SFPL.

23. Abby Sanford, "Why I'm a Cautious Soul." In a folder labeled "Manuscripts by Others–Jeanette Howard Foster," GMC, SFPL.

24. Hilary Farr (pseudonym for JHF), "Temple of Athene," *The Ladder* 12 (December 1967): 20–8; (Jan. 1968): 4–9, 32–40, (February–March 1968): 7–9, 20–37, 39–40 (April 1968): 22–7.

25. JHF to B. Grier, 5 June 1976, 11 October 1976, 30 December 1976, December 1976 [Christmas card], GMC, SFPL. Jeannette's poems under the name Abigail Sanford include, "Bluff," *The Ladder* (June 1961): 14; "Changling," *The Ladder* (July 1961): 14; "After Farewell," *The Ladder* (September 1962): 15; "Brief Victory," *The Ladder* (December 1963): 7; "Valentine: For One Called Helen," *The Ladder* (Feb. 1964): 8; "Aftermath," *The Ladder* (June 1964): 7 (written in 1924); "Survival," *The Ladder* (June 1964): 11 (originally written in 1923); "Crescendo," *The Ladder* (September 1965): 19; "Rain," *The Ladder* (November 1965): 12. Her translated poems, also published under Abigail Sanford, include "Poems of Renée Vivien translated for THE LADDER," *The Ladder* 4 (1959): 14–5; "In the Twilight by Marcel Proust," *The Ladder* 5 (December 1960): 4–8; (February 1961): 24; (March 1961): 4. Foster wrote about the translation of *Une Femme M'Apparut* in JHF to Barbara Grier, 30 December 1976, GMC, SFPL.

26. JHF, review, *Laughter of Aphrodite*, by Peter Green, *The Ladder* 10 (April 1965): 11–2; JHF, review, *Mrs. Stevens Hears the Mermaid Singing* by May Sarton, *The Ladder*, (April 1965): 11–3; JHF, "The Poet Within," *The Ladder*, (April 1966): 11–3; JHF, "The Lesbian in Literature: A Bibliography" (Review), *The Ladder* 11 (September 1967): 17-18; JHF, "Somerville and Ross, a Biography" (Review), *The Ladder* 11 (February–March 1969): 26–7; JHF, *An Impersonation of Angels*, by Frederick Brown (Review), *The Ladder* 13 (April–May 1969): 29–31; JHF, *The Sleep of Reason*, by C. P. Snow (Review), *The Ladder*, April–May 1969): 26–7; JHF, *Whipped Cream* by Geoffrey Moss, *The Ladder* (April–May 1971): 31–2.

27. B. Grier e-mail to the author, 23 May 2007, JHF, June 1957. JHF, [letter to the editor], *The Ladder* 1 (June 1957): 25.

28. JHF to Margaret Anderson, 8 June 1960, Margaret Anderson–Elizabeth Clark Collection, Beinecke Rare Book and Manuscript Library, Yale University Library.

29. JHF to Del Martin and Phyllis Lyon, 25 February 1973, Lyon-Martin Collection, box 23, folder 15, GLBT Historical Society, San Francisco; "Homosexual Women Hear Psychologists," *New York Times*, 21 June 1964, 54.

30. Del Martin, "Open Letter to Del Martin," *The Ladder* 2 (April 1958): 4–6. For more on this episode, see Gallo, *Different Daughters*, 66–9.

31. Ann Aldrich, *Carol in a Thousand* Cities (New York: Fawcett/Gold Medal, 1960), 237–47; the concluding quote is from 247.

32. JHF to Barbara Grier, 20 June 1960, GMC, SFPL; Gene Damon, "An Evening's Reading," *The Ladder* 4 (August 1960): 7; Jeannette H. Foster, "Ann of 10,000 Words Plus," *The Ladder* 4 (August 1960): 7–9.

33. Foster, "Ann of 10,000 Words Plus," *The Ladder* 4 (August 1960): 7–9; Ann Bannon, *The Ladder* 5 (October 1960): 24. M.S., California, *The Ladder* 5 (October 1960): 24.

34. Mary Renault to JHF, 7 July 1962, GMC, SFPL; JHF to Valerie Taylor, [Christmas 1975], *VTWP #1* refers to hearing from Renault at Christmas.

35. Hazel Toliver to J. N. Katz, 5 July 1978, JNKP.

36. JHF to May Sarton, 23 January [1971], May Sarton Papers, box 160, folder 3, New York Public Library; JHF to Sarton, [31 October 1966], May Sarton Papers, box 157, folder 5, NYPL; St. Charles (Missouri) City Directories, 1961–1970. For more on Sarton's term as poet-in-residence, see "May Sarton Challenges Lindenwood College," *Linden Bark* 14 February 1962, Lindenwood University Archives, St. Charles, Missouri.

37. JHF to Valerie Taylor, Labor Day, 1975, MKA. For more on Sarton's love for Clapp, see Margot Peters, *May Sarton: A Biography* (New York: Ballantine Books, 1998).

38. Ray Pierre Corsini, "Down Memory Lane with Hilary," *New York Times* (24 October 1965) p. BR53; "May Sarton," *Gay & Lesbian Biography* (St. James Press, 1997). Reproduced in *Biography Resource Center* (Farmington Hills, Mich.: Thomson Gale. 2007). http://galenet.galegroup.com/servlet/BioRC.

39. JHF, "*Mrs. Stevens Hears the Mermaid Singing*" (review), *The Ladder* 10 (April 1966): 11–3.

40. JHF to Valerie Taylor, Labor Day 1975, MKA; JHF to Valerie Taylor, 2 October 1976 and 11 November 1976, *VTWP #1*. Sarton continued to send Foster copies of her books until the late 1970s. In September 1976, for example, Sarton had sent *As We are Now* (Norton, 1973), and a few months later she sent the British edition of *A World of Light: Portraits and Celebrations* (1976).

41. JHF Oral History, KJP, and Barbara Grier e-mail to the author, 3 July 2007, discusses living arrangements in the St. Charles fourplex.

42. Tee Corinne and Caroline Overman, "Valerie Taylor Interview," *Common Lives, Lesbian Lives* #25 (Winter 1988): 61–72, the quote is from p. 67.

43. JHF to Elsa Gidlow, 6 February 1971, Elsa Gidlow Papers, GLBT Historical Society, San Francisco.

44. JHF to Valerie Taylor, 19 April 1976, *VTWP #1*. Jeannette also believed the spinal problem negatively affected her right-hand endurance, and thus her handwriting. See JHF to Karla Jay, 2 March 1975, KJP.

45. JHF oral history, KJP; JHF to Valerie Taylor, 19 April 1976, *VTWP #1*.

46. JHF to Barbara Grier, 4 October 1974 and 5 November 1974, GMC, SFPL; JHF to Karla Jay, 29 March 1975 and 12 April 1975, KJP.

47. JHF to Valerie Taylor, 15 September 1974, *VTWP #1*. For Farnham's obituary, see "Dr. Marynia Farnham, Author, 79," *New York Times*, 30 May 1979.

48. JHF to Karla Jay, 15 February 1975, KJP; JHF to Valerie Taylor, 26 March 1975, MKA.

49. JHF to Anyda Marchant, 7 October 1974, MKA. When Hazel died in 1997, she left $10,000 for the care of surviving animals, with the residue to go to the Randolph County Humane Society. See Hazel Toliver, "Last Will and Testament," 5 September 1997, Probate Court, Randolph County, Arkansas.

50. JHF to B. Grier, 7 August 1976, JHF to B. Grier, 29 March 1975. In folder labeled "Foster Correspondence," GMC, SFPL.

Chapter 9

1. Valerie Taylor, "Jeannette Foster, Forerunner," Valerie Taylor Papers, box 25, Cornell University, Ithaca, NY. Henry Gerber had founded the Society for Human Rights in Chicago in 1924.

2. Marie J. Kuda, "Jeannette Howard Foster (1895–1981) Literary Pioneer: A Personal Reflection," Outlines, 11 November 1998.

3. J. N. Katz to M. Kuda, 15 February 1998, MKA. Many others women and men also found the book and wrote to Jeannette about it. See JHF to B. Grier, 22 November 1976, Foster Correspondence, GMC, SFPL.

4. "The Homosexual: Newly Visible, Newly Understood," Time, 31 October 1969; Merle Miller, "What it Means to be a Lesbian," New York Times Magazine, 17 January 1971.

5. For a history of the Lesbian Writer's Conference, see Marie J. Kuda, "Women Loving, Women Writing," Outlines (30 September 1998): 18, and M. Kuda e-mail to the author, 4 July 2007. The publication they distributed was Marie J. Kuda, ed., Women Loving Women: A Select and Annotated Bibliography of Women Loving Women in Literature (Chicago: Lavender Press, 1974). Taylor's remarks at the conference were published as Valerie Taylor, For My Granddaughters (Chicago: Womanpress, 1975). The quote is from JHF to Valerie Taylor, 27 September 1975, VTWP #1.

6. ALA Social Responsibilities Round Table Task Force on Gay Liberation, Press Release, 9 July 1974. Sent to the author by Barbara Gittings.

7. Ibid. For more on the ALA Social Responsibilities Round Table Task Force on Gay Liberation, see Barbara Gittings, "Gays in Library Land: The Gay and Lesbian Task Force of the American Library Association: The First Sixteen Years," in James V. Carmichael Jr., ed., Daring to Find Our Names: The Search for Lesbigay Library History (Westport, Conn.: Greenwood Press, 1998), 81–93. Jeannette's award was a 16″ by 20″ photo of an Auguste Rodin drawing of two women entitled "The Embrace," and another of a Winslow Homer painting featuring two women dancing together on the seashore.

8. ALA Social Responsibilities Round Table Task Force on Gay Liberation, Press Release, 9 July 1974.

9. Valerie Taylor, "A Personal Appreciation, Homage to a Sister," Chicago Gay Crusader (October 1974): 3.

10. JHF to Barbara Grier, 20 January 1975; Grier to JHF, 21 March 1975; JHF to Grier, 19 October 1974, Foster Correspondence, GMC, SFPL.

11. JHF to *Valerie* Taylor, 7 November 1974, MKA; Gittings to Kuda, 2 July 2005, MKA.

12. "1958: Barbara Gittings," in Jonathan Katz, *Gay American History: Lesbians and Gay Men in the U.S.A.: A Documentary History* (New York: Thomas Y. Crowell Company, 1976), 420–33; Del Martin, "It's Time for a Change," *The Ladder* (January 1963): 5–6, 22–24.

13. Kay Tobin Lahusen, "Barbara Gittings," in *Before Stonewall: Activists for Gay and Lesbian Rights in Historical Context*, Vern L. Bullough, ed. (New York: Harrington Park Press, 2002), 243; Rodger Streitmatter, *Unspeakable*, 55.

14. B. Grier, email to the author, 7 June 2007. For more on Martin, Lyon, and Sandoz, see Phyllis Lyon, "Del Martin," *Before Stonewall*, 160–8; Del Martin, "Phyllis Lyon," 169–178; Stella Rush, "Helen Sandoz a.k.a. Helen Sanders a.k.a. Ben Cat," *Before Stonewall*, 145–7.

15. Rita Laporte to Barbara Gittings, 20 August 1968, personal papers of Frank Kameny, Washington, D.C., quoted in John D'Emilio, *Sexual Politics, Sexual Communities: the Making of a Homosexual Minority in the United States* (Chicago: University of Chicago Press, 1983), 229, fn 10; Rita Laporte, "An Open Letter to Mary Daly," *The Ladder* (October–November 1968): 25 and Laporte, "Of What Use NACHO?" *The Ladder* (August–September 1969): 18–9, quoted in D'Emilio, *Sexual Politics, Sexual Communities*, 229.

16. Gene Damon (pseudonym. for Barbara Grier), "Editorial," *The Ladder*, (September 1968): 2; Gallo, *Different Daughters*, 178.

17. Lillian Faderman, *Surpassing the Love of Men*, 380–1; Strietmatter, *Unspeakable*, 152; Gallo, *Different Daughters*, 160–1; Gene Damon, "Editorial," *The Ladder* 16 (August/September 1972): 3.

18. Gallo, *Different Daughters*, 183–4.

19. JHF to B. Grier, 23 September 1974, discusses the B. Gittings to JHF, 31 August 1974; B. Grier to JHF, 30 September 1974, Foster Correspondence, GMC, SFPL.

20. JHF to B. Grier, 4 October 1974; JHF to B. Grier, 5 November 1974, Foster Correspondence, GMC, SFPL. Jeannette did not realize that photo-offsetting was customary practice and having that guarantee would make the book easier to market.

21. JHF to B. Grier, 4 October 1974, Foster Correspondence, GMC, SFPL; Bettie Wysor, *The Lesbian Myth* (New York: Random House, 1974); Bettie Wysor to the author, 24 March 2007.

22. JHF to B. Grier, 4 October 1974, Foster Correspondence, GMC, SFPL; Dolores Klaich, *Woman + Woman: Attitudes Toward Lesbianism* (New York: Simon and Schuster, 1974).

23. JHF to B. Grier, 4 October 1974, Foster Correspondence, GMC, SFPL; Kathy Tomyris and Coletta Reid, "Diana Press: An Overview, 1972–1979," Diana Press File, June L. Mazer Lesbian Archives, Los Angeles; Katherine Czarnik, e-mail to the author, 19 July 2007, 5 November 2007. The four volumes Jeannette refers to are *Lesbiana: Book Reviews from The Ladder, 1966-1972* (Naiad, 1976); *The Lavender Herring: Lesbian Essays from the Ladder* (Diana Press, 1976); *Lesbian Lives: Biographies of Women from the Ladder* (Diana, 1976); and *The Lesbians Home Journal: Stories from the Ladder* (Diana, 1976). For historical context, see Alice Echols, "Cultural Feminism: Feminist Capitalism and the Anti-Pornography Movement," *Social Text*, No. 7 (Spring-Summer 1983): 43.

24. B. Grier to JHF, 30 September 1974, Foster Correspondence; B. Grier to Coletta Reid, 23 October 1974, Diana Press Correspondence, GMC, SFPL.

25. Coletta Reid to B. Grier, 25 January 1975, Diana Press Correspondence, GMC, SFPL. The fire was reportedly caused when someone in the third floor apartment fell asleep smoking.

26. The reference to sending money is from JHF to Ms. Czarnik, Myron & Reid, 31 January 1975, Diana Press File, June L. Mazer Archives, Los Angeles; to "Queer" presses is from JHF to B. Grier, 17 January 1975, Foster Correspondence, GMC, SFPL; to profit is from JHF to Miss Reid, 3 February 1975, Diana Press File, June L. Mazer Archives; to signing the contract is from JHF to B. Grier, 12 April 1975, Foster Correspondence, GMC, SFPL.

27. JHF to B. Grier, 1 May 1975, Foster Correspondence, GMC, SFPL.

28. JHF to Coletta Reid, 22 Sept. 1975 and JHF to Coletta Reid and Sister Publishers, 21 May 1976, Diana Press File, Mazer Archives. The information on the book design is from Katherine Czarnik to the author, 19 July 2007.

29. Joy Fisher, "Old Testament of Lesbian Courage," Lesbian Tide 6 (November/December 1976): 39; JHF to Valerie Taylor, 29 October 1976, VTWP #1.

30. JHF to V. Taylor, 22 November 1976, VTWP #1; JHF to Coletta Reid, 13 July 1976; C. Reid to JHF, Fall 1976, Diana Press File, June L. Mazer Lesbian Archives; C. Reid to B. Grier, n.d. [late summer 1976], Diana Press Correspondence, GMC, SFPL.

31. Katherine Czarnik, e-mail to the author, 31 July 2007. According to Czarnik, "nobody ever forgave us for that. Years later, some women quit our softball team in Oakland because we put FEN on our T-shirts." Czarnik, who came from the New Left, was a director on FEN's board For more on the subject, see Ginette Castro, American Feminism: A Contemporary History (1990), 253. For Martha Shelley's report against FEN, see Detroit Feminists Women's Health Center Collection, Walter P. Reuther Library of Labor & Urban Affairs, Wayne State University.

32. Coletta Reid to JHF, 17 October [1977]; "Diana Press: An Overview, 1972–1979," [p. 2], Diana Press File, June Mazer Archives; Czarnik e-mail to the author, 5 November 2007.

33. B. Grier to Coletta Reid, 24 June 1977, B. Grier to Hazel Toliver, 20 October 1977, Hazel Toliver to B. Grier, 12 December 1977 and 26 March 1978, Diana Press Correspondence, GMC, SFPL.

34. James R. Taggart to Coletta Reid, 2 February 1979, 23 February 1979, 12 April 1979, 17 April 1979; Attorney Barbara E. Price to BG, 15 March 1979, Price to Reid, 14 March 1979, Diana Press Correspondence, GMC, SFPL; Grier e-mail to the author 2 July 2007.

35. "Diana Press, an Overview, 1972–79," Diana Press File, June L. Mazer Lesbian Archives.

36. Coletta Reid to B. Grier, postmarked 14 February 1979, Diana Press Correspondence, GMC, SFPL; Hazel Toliver to Valerie Taylor, 11 January 1980, VTWP #1; "Diana Suspends Publishing, Apologizes," The Lesbian Tide 8 (May/June 1979), 14–5; Katherine Czarnik e-mail to the author, 19 July 2007.

37. M. Kuda to JHF, 17 March 1976, 12 Feb. 1976, MKA; Kuda e-mail to the author, 4 July 2007. The dates of active printing for Womanpress were circa 1975 through 1982. When Women in Distribution, Inc., which distributed the output of Womanpress, went bankrupt, Kuda lost her book stock and ceased.

38. M. Kuda to JHF, 12 February 1976; JHF to M. Kuda, 1 April 1976; M. Kuda to JHF, 17 March 1976, MKA.

39. Tee A. Corinne, "Introduction," *TWR*, v.

40. JHF to M. Kuda, 10 October 1976, MKA.

41. JHF to M. Kuda, 19 April 1976, MKA; C. Reid to B. Grier, n.d. [late summer 1976], Diana Press Correspondence, GMC, SFPL; Kuda e-mail to the author, 22 July 2005.

42. [*Two Women* Publication Party Scroll], 23 September 1976, MKA.

43. JHF to Valerie Taylor, 26 September 1976 and 11 October 1976, *VTWP #1*.

44. JHF to V. Taylor, 29 October 1976, *VTWP #1*; JHF to M. Kuda, 22 October 1976, MKA.

45. Elsa Gidlow to Marie Kuda, 23 October 1976, MKA; Kuda to author, 22 July 2005 Gidlow (1898–1986) was an Anglo-Canadian-American poet and philosopher whose writings were explicitly lesbian. See Elsa Gidlow, *Elsa, I Come With My Songs: The Autobiography of Elsa Gidlow* (San Francisco: Druid Heights Press, 1986).

46. JHF to M. Kuda, 1 April 1976, M. Kuda Archives. The manuscript of *Home Is the Hunter*, Manuscripts by Others-Foster, GMC. Foster givers a further history of the manuscript in JHF to BG, 29 November 1974, Foster Correspondence, GMC, SFPL.

47. JHF to M. Kuda, 6 March 1976 and 19 March 1976, MKA; JHF to Valerie Taylor, 6 March 1976, MKA. When Barbara Grier saw the manuscript in the late 1950s, it appeared to be on yellowed paper but in the mid-1970s Jeannette dates the writing of the story to the mid-1950s.

48. Valerie Taylor, "A Personal Appreciation, Homage to a Sister," *Chicago Gay Crusader* (October 1974), 3; JHF to Karla Jay, 30 September 1975, KJP. Hal Call was director of publications for the Mattachine Society in the mid-1950s.

49. Valerie Taylor to Barbara Grier, 26 May 1975, Taylor Correspondence, GMC, SFPL; JHF to Valerie Taylor, 11 October 1975, *VTWP #1*.

50. JHF to M. Kuda, 5 January 1976, and M. Kuda to JHF, 12 February 1976 and 17 March 1976, MKA.

51. JHF to M. Kuda, 1 April 1976 and 11 July 1976, MKA.

52. Kuda to the author, 4 July 2007. Barbara Grier read the manuscript but never considered adding a novel of that length to the Naiad list.

53. Barbara Grier to JHF, 7 August 1976, Foster Correspondence, GMC, SFPL.

54. Grier and McBride to JHF, 21 June 1976, Foster Correspondence, GMC, SFPL.

55. JHF to Valerie Taylor, 28 January 1975, MKA; JHF to Valerie Taylor, 23. January 1977, *VTWP #1*; "Publisher's Note," *A Woman Appeared to Me* (Naiad Press, 1976), i.

56. Gayle Rubin, introduction to Renée Vivien, *A Woman Appeared to Me*, translated by Jeannette H. Foster, iii–iv.

57. JHF to Anyda Marchant, 13 December 1976, MKA.

58. JHF to Coletta Reid, 22 September 1975, Diana Press File, June L. Mazer Lesbian Archives.

CHAPTER 10

1. JHF to Karla Jay, 20 April 1977, KJP.

2. Arrangements for the visit, which occurred on 14 June 1977, are discussed in Barbara Grier to JHF, 25 May 1977, Foster Correspondence, GMC, SFPL.

3. Tee Corinne, e-mail message to the author, 30 May 2005.

4. Valerie Taylor, "A Personal Appreciation, Homage to a Sister," *Chicago Gay Crusader* (October 1974), 3; JHF to Valerie Taylor, 18 June 1976, *VTWP#1*.

5. The quotations, in order, are from JHF to Karla Jay, 17 January 1976, 22 April 1976, 28 August 1977, KJP.

6. JHF to Karla Jay, 17 January 1976, KJP. The governor of Arkansas signed this bill into law on March 17, 1977.

7. JHF to Valerie Taylor, 16 March 1976 and 4 February 1977, *VTWP #1*; JHF to B. Grier, 22 November 1976, Foster Correspondence, GMC, SFPL. By late summer 1977 Jeannette had adjusted to four roommates. See Hazel Toliver to Grier, 8 August 1977, Toliver Correspondence, GMC, SFPL.

8. JHF to Karla Jay, 17 January 1976, KJP; JHF to Valerie Taylor, 19 April 1976, *VTWP#1*; JHF to Anyda Marchant, 16 May 1976, MKA; JHF to B. Grier, 30 December 1976, Foster Correspondence, GMC, SFPL.

9. Press Release, ALA Social Responsibilities Round Table, Task Force on Gay Liberation, 9 July 1974, sent to the author by Barbara Gittings; JHF to Barbara Grier, [26] April [1977], Foster Correspondence, GMC, SFPL; "Jeannette Howard Foster," *Booklist* (1 March 1977): 996; Karla Jay, "Lesbianism from the Bible On," MS 5 (July 1976): 21.

10. JHF to Karla Jay, 21 June 1975, KJP.

11. Karla Jay and Allen Young, eds., Out of the Closets: Voices of Gay Liberation (Douglas Books, 1972); Jay and Young, eds., *After You're Out: Personal Experiences of Gay Men and Lesbian Women* (Quick Fox, 1975).

12. JHF to Karla Jay, 9 August 1975, KJP.

13. JHF to Karla Jay, 7 July 1975, KJP.

14. JHF to Karla Jay, 12 February 1977, 20 April 1977, KJP.

15. The quote is from JHF to Karla Jay, 17 January 1976, KJP. Other details are from JHF to Anyda Marchant, 16 May 1976, MKA; JHF to Barbara Grier, 7 September 1977, Foster Correspondence, GMC, SFPL. Foster took great delight in ordering a book of lesbian photos from Publishers' Clearing House, seeing it as a sign of changing times. See JHF to Barbara Grier, 8 January 1977, Foster Correspondence, GMC, SFPL.

16. JHF to Valerie Taylor, 7 November 1974, MKA.

17. Barbara Grier to JHF, 19 September 1977, Foster Correspondence, GMC, SFPL.

18. JHF to Valerie Taylor, 22 April 1976 and JHF to V. Taylor, 15 September 1977, *VTWP #1*.

19. The reference to Claudia Scott is in JHF to Taylor, 7 November 1974, MKA; the reference to Pope is in JHF to Taylor, 10 December 1977, VTWP #1. The Penelope Pope Letters, 1976–1989, Collection No. 7643, are at the Division of Rare and Manuscript Collections, Cornell University Library, Ithaca, New York.

20. Miriam Tompkins died in 1954, Clara Louise Thompson in 1963, Edna Grace Taylor and Jennie Gregory in 1978. Lenore Ward outlived Jeannette, dying in 1988. Jeannette may also have corresponded with Adelia Butcher Lund, who died 20 August 1975 in Miami, Florida. See "Mrs. Adelia Lund," [obituary]," *Ashville Citizen*, 21 August 1975, 6B. Foster discussed her correspondents in JHF to Taylor, 7 November 1974, MKA.

21. Foster was captivated by Phillipa, the main character in *Latecomer*, "coming of purely New England stock myself and sharing many of her characteristics, though not all her inhibitions." See JHF to Sarah Aldridge, 25 August 1974, MKA. Foster discussed one of her former students in JHF to Valerie Taylor, 18 January 1977, VTWP #1.

22. JHF to Barbara Grier, 3 Feb 1975, Foster Correspondence, GMC, SFPL; JHF to Taylor, Christmas [1975] and 22 April 1976, VTWP #1. For more on postal censorship, see John D'Emilio, *Sexual Politics, Sexual Communities*, 2nd ed. (Chicago: University of Chicago Press, 1983), 47.

23. The reference to syphilis appears in Press Release, 9 July 1974, ALA Social Responsibilities Round Table, Task Force on Gay Liberation; to "stripped naked" is in JHF Oral History, 5 June 1975, KJP; to herstory in JHF to J.N. Katz, 29 January 19[77], JNKPs; and to the younger generation in JHF to Valerie Taylor, 7 November 1974, MKA.

24. JHF to B. Grier, 13 January 1977, 7 February 1977 and 31 March 1977, Foster Correspondence, GMC, SFPL.

25. Hazel Toliver to Valerie Taylor, 12 October 1982, VTWP #1.

26. Sexuality Survey, Lesbian Questionnaire, Karla Jay Papers, Lesbian Herstory Archives, Brooklyn, New York. The survey was anonymous but Foster was the only 82-year-old to complete it. With the exception of number of loves, I have not revealed her specific answers. The results of the survey appeared in *The Gay Report: Lesbians and Gay Men Speak Out About Sexual Experiences and Lifestyles* (New York: Summit, 1977).

27. J.N. Katz to JHF, 22 Sept. 1977; JHF to J.N. Katz, 27 September 1977, 18 October 1977, 2 November 1977; J.N. Katz to JHF, 8 November 1977, 1 December 1977, JNKP.

28. JHF to V. Taylor, 19 April 1976, VTWP #1.

29. JHF to Barbara and Donna, 18 May 1977, Foster Correspondence, GMC, SFPL.

30. For a description of the vandalism, see JHF to Grier, 3 February 1975, Foster Correspondence, GMC, SFPL; for the description of Pocahontas, see Hazel Toliver to Valerie Taylor, 21 July 1978, VTWP #1; for references to Hazel and Dot joining the church, see JHF to Valerie Taylor, 4 February 1977, VTWP #1.

31. Hazel discussed the decision to change Jeannette's mailing address in Hazel Toliver to Valerie Taylor, 8 February 1979, VTWP #1 and JHF to Valerie Taylor, [10] December 1977, VTWP #1. The reference to rest homes is from JHF to Valerie Taylor, 15 September 1977, VTWP #1.

32. Hazel Toliver to J.N. Katz, 9 December 1977, 12 January 1978, 20 March 1978, 5 July 1978; J.N. Katz to Hazel Toliver, 6 February 1978, 26 June 1978, Katz Papers.

33. Barbara Grier to Karla Jay, 12 July 1977, KJP.

34. Hazel Toliver to Friends of JHF, 8 February 1979, *VTWP #1*.

35. Hazel Toliver remembered this sentiment in Hazel Toliver to Valerie Taylor, 14 February 1982 *VTWP#1*.

36. Valerie Taylor to "Dear Joan," 28 March 1980, Valerie Taylor Biographical File, Lesbian Herstory Archives, Brooklyn, New York.

37. Hazel Toliver to Valerie Taylor, 19 August 1981, *VTWP #1*; Barbara Grier to Karla Jay, 29 June 1977, KJP; JHF to Karla Jay, 15 July 1976, KJP. By July 1979 Foster's monthly nursing home fees of $715 exceeded her monthly pension by $65.

38. Hazel Toliver to Valerie Taylor, 10 February 1979, *VTWP #1*; James R. Taggart to Coletta Reid, 2 Feb. 1979, 23 Feb. 1979, 12 April 1979, 17 May 1979, Diana Press Correspondence, GMC, SFPL; Hazel Toliver to Valerie Taylor, 11 January 1980 and 10 February 1979, *VTWP #1*.

39. San Francisco Lesbian & Gay History Project to "Dear Friends," 4 March 1980, and JHF Biographical File, Lesbian Herstory Archives; Maida Tilchen, "Jeannette Howard Foster Dies," *Gay Community News* 22 August 1981, 3.

40. Valerie Taylor to Joan, 7 April 1980, Lesbian Herstory Archives; Valerie Taylor to Enid Fleishman, 16 August 1980, Enid Fleishman Letters from Valerie Taylor, 1980–1997, Collection #7651, Cornell University Library.

41. Donors are discussed Hazel Toliver to Valerie Taylor, 15 June 1981, *VTWP #1*; Valerie Taylor to Christine Pattee, 1 April 1981, Hazel Toliver to Valerie Taylor, 14 October 1980, Hazel Toliver to Valerie Taylor, 8 April 1980, *VTWP #1*.

42. Hazel Toliver to Valerie Taylor, 14 October 1980, *VTWP #1*; B. J. Bruther, e-mail to the author, 10 November 2005.

43. Hazel Toliver to Valerie Taylor, 13 April 1981, *VTWP #1*.

44. Hazel Toliver to Valerie Taylor, 8 April 1980; Hazel Toliver to Valerie Taylor, 13 July 1979, *VTWP #1*.

45. Hazel Toliver to Valerie Taylor, 11 January 1980, *VTWP #1*.

46. Hazel Toliver to Valerie Taylor, 8 April 1980, *VTWP #1*.

47. Hazel Toliver to Valerie Taylor, 14 October 1980 and 13 April 1981, *VTWP #1*.

48. Hazel Toliver to Valerie Taylor, 13 April 1981 and 13 May 1981, *VTWP #1*.

49. Hazel Toliver to Valerie Taylor, 15 June 1981, *VTWP #1*.

50. Hazel Toliver and Valerie Taylor to an unknown list of women, n.d., *VTWP #1*.

51. Hazel Toliver to Valerie Taylor, 19 August 1981, *VTWP #1*; "Mrs. Toliver" (obituary), October 1975, newspaper clipping provided by the Randolph County, Arkansas, Public Library.

52. According to Foster's will, filed in the Randolph County, Arkansas, Probate Court, she had $15,000 personal property and no real property. See Hazel Toliver to Valerie Taylor, 19 April 1983, 25 November 1981, 12 October 1982, and Hazel Toliver and Valerie Taylor to an unknown list of women, n.d., *VTWP #1*.

53. Hazel Toliver to Valerie Taylor, 13 October 1981 and 25 November 1981, *VTWP #1*.

54. JHF to Barbara Grier, 28 July 1976; Hazel Toliver to Valerie Taylor, 19 April 1983, *VTWP#1*; "Miss Ross" [obituary], *Jonesboro, Ark., Sun*, 29 April 1986, 9; "Toliver" [obituary], *Jonesboro, Ark., Sun*, 30 August 1997, 2B.

55. Hazel Toliver to Valerie Taylor, 13 October 1981, 19 August 1981, *VTWP #1*.

EPILOGUE

1. Lee Lynch e-mail to the author, 16 July 2007. Augusta Brennan appears as a character in Lynch, *Old Dyke Tales* (Tallahassee, Fla.: Naiad Press, 1984) and *Rafferty Street* (New Victoria Books, 1998).

2. Susan Wiseheart e-mail to the author, 28 July 2007; Robin Cohen e-mail to the author, 23 August 2006.

3. Bill Kelley, e-mail to the author, 20 July 2007.

4. Christine Pattee e-mail to the author, 10 November 2005; Pattee to Hazel Tolliver, 9 November 1981, *VTWP #1*.

5. Lillian Faderman: *Surpassing the Love of Men: Romantic Friendship & Love Between Women from the Renaissance to the Present* (New York: HarperCollins, 1981), 8; Bonnie Zimmerman, ed., *Lesbian Histories and Cultures: An Encyclopedia* (New York: Garland, 2000); Barbara Grier, *The Lesbian in Literature*, 3d ed. (Tallahassee: Naiad Press, 1981).

6. Maida Tilchen e-mail to the author, 24 March 2007, 23 October 2007.

7. David Pavlich, University of Chicago Archives, e-mail to the author, 19 July 2007.

8. Mary Brophy, "Gerber–Hart Library Gives Pride to Our Community," *Windy City Times*, 25 June 1987, 20.

9. MJK e-mail to the author, 15 October 2007. According to a press release for the club, the "Sewing Circle was a popular name given to various informal groups of lesbians in Hollywood during the 1920s and 1930s."

10. A third book Naiad published in 1985, *Lesbian Nuns: Breaking Silence*, became its all-time-best seller.

11. Katherine V. Forrest, e-mail to the author, 20 July 2007.

12. Jesse Monteagudo, "Sex Variant Women in Literature," *The Weekly News* (Miami, Florida), 17 April 1985; "Sex Variant Women in Literature," *New York Native*, 14–20 October 1985; Maida Tilchen, "Lustrous Litany of Lesbian Literature," *Gay Community News* 13 (October 26, 1985): 1. All are from the Naiad Press files, GMC, SFPL.

SELECTED BIBLIOGRAPHY

PRIMARY SOURCES

Archival Sources and Collections

Cornell University Library
Ithaca, New York
Enid Fleishman Letters from Valerie Taylor
Penelope Pope Letters, 1976–1989
Carl Taylor Papers
Valerie Taylor Papers

Drexel University
Philadelphia, Pennsylvania
Library School Records
President Creese Correspondence

Emory University
Atlanta, Georgia
Library School Alumni File: Jeannette Howard Foster
Library School Records

Gay, Lesbian, Bisexual, Transgender Historical Society
San Francisco, California
Phyllis Lyon and Del Martin Collection
Elsa Gidlow Papers

Gerber–Hart Library and Archives
Chicago, Illinois
Valerie Taylor Papers
Mattachine Midwest Collection

Indiana University
Bloomington, Indiana

Faculty Housing Committee Records
Jeannette Foster Personnel File
Hazel Toliver Biographical File

Kinsey Institute for Research in Sex, Gender, and Reproduction
Bloomington, Indiana
Alfred C. Kinsey Correspondence

June L. Mazer Lesbian Archives
West Hollywood, California
Diana Press files

Lesbian Herstory Archives
Brooklyn, New York
Jeannette H. Foster Biographical File
Karla Jay Papers, *The Gay Report*
Valerie Taylor Biographical File
Periodical Files
Valerie Taylor Working Papers #1. Wolf Creek, Oregon: The Estate of Valerie Taylor, 1997.

New York Public Library
New York, New York
Karla Jay Papers
    Barbara Grier Correspondence, series I, box 3
    Jeannette Howard Foster Correspondence, series I, box 3
    Jeannette Howard Foster Oral History, series V, box 32
Jonathan N. Katz Papers
    Jeannette Howard Foster Correspondence, series I, box 3
    May Sarton Papers

ONE Institute and Archives
University of Southern California
Los Angeles, California
Editorial Correspondence

Barbara Grier–Donna McBride Collection, San Francisco Public Library
San Francisco, California
Diana Press Correspondence
Jeannette Howard Foster Correspondence
Manuscripts by Others–Jeannette Howard Foster

Private Collections
Marie J. Kuda Archives, Chicago, Illinois

Alison Cope Puffer and Winslow H. Foster Family Papers, Ludington, Michigan and LaGrange, Illinois

Foster family diaries
    Carrie Burr Prouty diaries, 1891; 1902–1913
Anna Burr Foster diaries, summer 1916; summer 1917; college diary, 1921–1924
    Helen Houghton Foster diary, summer 1916
    Winslow Howard Foster diary, 1936–1938; 1939–1941
Foster family letters, 1934–1944
Foster family photograph album, circa 1869–1936
Foster family photograph album, circa 1890s–1930s
Foster family photos (loose)

Selected Newspapers and Periodicals

The Chicago Tribune
The Janesville (Wisconsin) Daily Gazette
Journal of Homosexuality
Journal of the History of Sexuality
Journal of Women's History
The Ladder
The Lesbian Tide
Mattachine Review
Mattachine Midwest Newsletter
The New York Times
ONE
Publishers Weekly
SIGNS: Journal of Women in Culture and Society

Oral Interviews

Dorothy Collins, July 27, 2005, Bloomington, Indiana
Barbara Grier and Donna McBride, December 20, 2006, Knoxville, Tennessee
Paul Gebhard, July 14, 2005, Bloomington, Indiana
Henry Remak, February 23, 2007, Bloomington, Indiana

Jeannette H. Foster Publications (in chronological order)

Foster, Jeannette H. "J. S." *The (Rockford College) Taper* 6 (Spring 1916): 17.
Foster, Jeannette H. "Narcissus, Model 1916." *The (Rockford College) Taper* 7 (Autumn 1916): 3–8.
Foster, Jeannette H. "Poem." *The (Rockford College) Taper* 7 (Midwinter 1916–1917): 14.
Foster, Jeannette H. "Parcel Post vs. Romance." *The (Rockford College) Taper* 7 (Midwinter 1916–1917): 19–20.
Foster, Jeannette H. "A Question of Discretion," *The (Rockford College) Taper* 7 (Spring 1917): 19–25.
Foster, Jeannette H. "Background." *The [Rockford College] Taper* 8 (Spring 1918):18–20.
Foster, Jeannette H., "Judgment: A Story," *The [Rockford College] Taper* 9 (October 1919): 5–7.

Foster, Jeannette H., "Literary Allusions in the Works of Margaret Fuller," MA thesis, University of Chicago, 1922.

Foster, Jeannette H. "Reminiscence." *The Hamline Review* (November 1923): 11.

Foster, Jeannette H., "Lucky Star: A Story," *Harper's Magazine* 155 (October 1927): 624–35.

Foster, Jeannette H. "An Approach to Fiction through the Characteristics of Its Readers." *The Library Quarterly* 6 (April 1936): 124–74.

Foster, Jeannette H. "More Definite Terms to Describe Types of Reading." *Bulletin of the American Library Association* 30 (August 1936): 682–4.

Foster, Jeannette H. "Open Letter to a Colleague." *The Library Journal* (November 1938): 858–9.

Oliver, Mildred, Jeannette H. Foster, and Guy R. Lyle, et al. *Guide for Students in the Use of Books and Libraries.* Yellow Springs, OH: Antioch College Library, 1933. (2d rev. ed., 1939)

Foster, Jeannette H. "Review of Replacement List of Fiction." *The Library Quarterly* 10 (January 1940): 124–5.

Foster, Jeannette H. "Review of Subject Guide to Reference Books." *College and Research Libraries* 4 (March 1943): 165–7.

Foster, Jeannette H. "Review of Exploration in Reading Patterns." *The Library Quarterly* 13 (July 1943): 270–1.

Foster, Jeannette H. "Review of Reading Interests and Needs of Negro College Freshmen Regarding Social Science Materials." *The Library Quarterly* 13 (October 1943): 353–5.

Foster, Jeannette H. "Review of Program of Instruction in Library Schools." *The Library Quarterly* 14 (July 1944): 252–3.

Foster, Jeannette H. "Review of Library in the Community." *The Library Quarterly* 15 (January 1945): 78–9.

Foster, Jeannette H. "Library School Opinion on Degrees and Curriculum," [Philadelphia: Drexel Institute of Technology], 1945.

Foster, Jeannette H. "Review of On Judging Books: In General and in Particular." *The Library Quarterly* 18 (January 1948): 69–71.

Foster, Jeannette H. *Sex Variant Women in Literature.* New York: Vantage Press, 1956.

Addison, Jan (pseud.). "Hail and Farewell." *The Ladder* 1 (September 1957): 7–11.

Addison, Jan (pseud.). "Life Class." *The Ladder* 2 (May 1958): 4–8.

Sanford, Abigail (pseud.) "Poems of Renée Vivien translated for *The Ladder*." *The Ladder* 4 (1959): 14–5.

Foster, Jeannette H. "Ann of 10,000 Words Plus." *The Ladder* 4 (August 1960): 7–9.

Addison, Jan (pseud.). "Exit Laughing." *The Ladder* 5 (February 1963): 7–10.

Addison, Jan (pseud.). "Narrow Escape." *The Ladder* (February 1963): 7–10.

Sanford, Abby (pseud.). "The Funniest Thing." *The Ladder* (August 1964): 7–10, 22–5.

Foster, Jeannette H. "The Poet Within." *The Ladder* 10 (April 1966): 11–3.

Foster, Jeannette H. "Review of The Lesbian in Literature: A Bibliography." *The Ladder* (September 1967): 17–8.

Addison, Jan. "Clyde's Hearth." *The Ladder* (December 1967): 2–6.

Farr, Hilary. "Temple of Athene." Parts 1, 2, 3, and Conclusion. *The Ladder* (December 1967): 20–8;(January 1968): 4–9, 32–40; (February–March 1968): 7–9, 20–37, 39–40; (April 1968): 22–7.

Addison, Jan (pseud.), "A Man's World," Parts 1 and 2. *The Ladder* (July 1968): 13–25; (August 1968): 31–45.

Foster, Jeannette H. "Dominance." *The Ladder* 13 (October–November 1968): 17–8.

Foster, Jeannette H. "Review of *Somerville and Ross: A Biography.*" *The Ladder* 13 (February/March 1969): 26–7.

Foster, Jeannette H. *Sex Variant Women in Literature*. Baltimore: Diana Press, 1976.

Two Women: The Poetry of Jeannette Foster and Valerie Taylor. Chicago: Womanpress, 1976.

Vivien, Renée. *A Woman Appeared to Me*. Jeannette H. Foster, trans. Tallahassee, Fla.: Naiad Press, 1976.

Foster, Jeannette H. *Sex Variant Women in Literature*. Tallahassee, Fla.: Naiad Press, 1985.

Two Women Revisited: The Poetry of Jeannette Howard Foster and Valerie Taylor. Austin: Banned Books, 1991.

Selected Secondary Sources

Aldrich, Ann. *Carol in a Thousand Cities*. New York: Fawcett/Gold Medal, 1960.

Anderson, Margaret C. *Forbidden Fires*. Tallahassee, Fla.: Naiad Press, 1996.

Boyle, T. C. *The Inner Circle*. New York: Viking, 2004.

Brisby, Erin. "College Women of the 1930s." *The Filson Club History Quarterly* 64 (January 1990): 48.

Bullough, Vern L. *Before Stonewall: Activists for Gay and Lesbian Rights in Historical Context*. New York: Haworth Press, 2002.

Carmichael, James V. Jr., ed. *Daring to Find Our Names: The Search for Lesbigay Library History*. Westport, Conn.: Greenwood Press, 1998.

Chauncey, George Jr. "From Sexual Inversion to Homosexuality: Medicine and the Changing Conceptualization of Female Deviance." *Salmagundi* 58–59 (Fall 1982–Winter 1983): 114–146.

Chauncey, George Jr. *Gay New York: Gender, Urban Culture, and the Making of the Gay Male World, 1890–1940*. New York: Basic Books, 1994.

Christenson, Cornelia V. *Kinsey: A Biography*. Bloomington: Indiana University Press, 1971.

Corinne, Tee. *Valerie Taylor: A Resource Book*. Published by the estate of Valerie Taylor, 1999.

Cott, Nancy F. *The Grounding of Modern Feminism*. New Haven, Conn.: Yale University Press, 1987.

Corley, Florence Fleming. *Higher Education for Southern Women: Four Church-Related Women's Colleges in Georgia, Agnes Scott, Shorter, Spelman, and Wesleyan, 1900–1920*. PhD thesis, Georgia State University, 1985.

Daskom, Josephine Dodge. "A Case of Interference." *Smith College Stories*. New York: Scribners, 1900.

Davis, Katharine Bement. *Factors in the Sex Life of Twenty-two Hundred Women*. New York: Harper & Brothers Publishers, 1929.

D'Emilio, John. *Sexual Politics, Sexual Communities: The Making of a Homosexual Minority in the United States, 1940–1970*. Chicago: University of Chicago Press, 1983.

D'Emilio, John. *The World Turned: Essays on Gay History, Politics, and Culture*. Durham: Duke University Press, 2002.

Doughty, Fraces. "Lesbian Biography, Biography of Lesbians," *Frontiers* 4 (Autumn 1979): 76–79.

Duberman, Martin B. *About Time: Exploring the Gay Past*. New York: Penguin Books, 1986, 1991.

Duberman, Martin, Martha Vicinus, and George Chauncey Jr., eds. *Hidden from History: Reclaiming the Gay and Lesbian Past*. New York: Penguin Books, 1989.

DuBois, Mary Constance. "Lass of the Silver Sword." *St. Nicholas Magazine* (December 1908–October 1909: 126–33, 213–20, 296–303, 401–11, 501–8, 608–14, 694–700, 789–95, 884–91, 981–7, 1074–80.

Echols, Alice. *Daring to Be Bad: Radical Feminism in America, 1967–1975*. Minneapolis: University of Minnesota Press, 1989.

Ellis, Havelock. *Studies in the Psychology of Sex, Volume 2, Sexual Inversion*, 2nd ed. Philadelphia: F. A. Davis, 1901.

English, Thomas H. *Emory University, 1915–1965: A Semicentennial History*. Atlanta, Ga.: Emory University, 1966.

Faderman, Lillian. "Lesbian Magazine Fiction in the Early Twentieth Century." *Journal of Popular Culture* 11 (1978): 800–17.

_____. *Odd Girls and Twilight Lovers, A History of Lesbian Life in Twentieth-Century America*. New York: Columbia University Press, 1991.

_____. *Surpassing the Love of Men*. New York: William Morrow and Co., Inc., 1991.

_____. *To Believe in Women: What Lesbians Have Done for America: A History*. Boston: Houghton Mifflin Company, 1999.

Faderman, Lillian and Stuart Timmons. *Gay L.A.: A History of Sexual Outlaws, Power Politics, and Lipstick Lesbians*. New York: Basic Books, 2006.

Forrest, Katherine V., ed. *Lesbian Pulp Fiction: The Sexually Intrepid World of Lesbian Paperback Novels, 1950–1965*. San Francisco: Cleis Press, 2005.

Foster, Winslow Howard. *Ancestry of Winslow Howard Foster and that of His Wife Anna Mabel (Burr) Foster*. Ludington, Mich.: The author, 1941.

Fuller, Margaret. *Woman in the Nineteenth Century*. New York: W. W. Norton, 1979 (reprint).

Gallo, Marcia M. *Different Daughters: A History of the Daughters of Bilitis and the Rise of the Lesbian Rights Movement*. New York: Carroll and Graf, 2006.

Gardner, Robert G. *On the Hill: The Story of Shorter College*. Rome, Ga.: Shorter College, 1972.

Garrison, Guy. *A Century of Library Education at Drexel University: Vignettes of Growth and Change*. Philadelphia: Drexel University College of Information Studies, 1992.

Gathorne-Hardy, Jonathan. *Kinsey: Sex the Measure of All Things*. Bloomington: Indiana University Press, 1998.

Gidlow, Elsa. *Elsa: I Come With My Songs*. San Francisco: Bootlegger Press, 1991.

Grier, Barbara. *The Lesbian in Literature*. 3rd ed. Tallahassee, Fla.: Naiad Press, 1981.

Henry, George W. *Sex Variants: A Study of Homosexual Patterns*, 2 vols. New York: Hoeber, 1941.

Hogan, Steve, and Lee Hudson, eds. *Completely Queer: The Gay and Lesbian Encyclopedia*. New York: Henry Holt and Company, 1998.

Horowitz, Helen Lefkowitz. *Alma Mater: Design and Experience in the Women's Colleges from their Nineteenth-Century Beginnings to the 1930s*. 2d ed. Amherst: University of Massachusetts Press, 1993.

Ilboorg, Caroline. *The Masks of Mary Renault: A Literary Biography*. Columbia, Mo.: University of Missouri Press, 2001.

Jay, Karla. *Tales of the Lavender Menace: A Memoir of Liberation*. New York: Basic Books, 1991.

Jay, Karla and Allen Young, eds. *Lavender Culture*. New York: New York University Press, 1978, 1994.

Johnson, David K. *The Lavender Scare: The Cold War Persecution of Gays and Lesbians in the Federal Government*. Chicago: University of Chicago Press, 2004.

Jones, Alan Lawrence. "Gaining Self-Consciousness While Losing the Movement: The American Association for Adult Education, 1926–1941. PhD dissertation. University of Wisconsin–Madison, 1991.

Jones, James H. *Alfred C. Kinsey: A Public/Private Life*. New York: W. W. Norton, 1997.

Katz, Jonathan Ned. *Gay American History: Lesbians & Gay Men in the U.S.A.* New York: Penguin Books, 1976, 1992.

Katz, Jonathan N. *Gay American History*. New York: Thomas Y. Crowell Company, 1976.

Kinsey, Alfred C., Wardell B. Pomeroy, Clyde Martin, and Paul H. Gebhard. *Sexual Behavior in the Human Female*. Philadelphia: Saunders, 1953.

Kennedy, Elizabeth Lapovsky and Madeline D. Davis. *Boots of Leather, Slippers of Gold: The History of a Lesbian Community*. New York: Penguin Books, 1994.

Klaich, Dlores. *Woman Plus Woman*. Tallahassee, Fla.: Naiad Press, 1989.

Kotzin, Miriam N. *A History of Drexel University: 1941–1963*. Philadelphia: Drexel University, 1983.

Lynch, Lee. *Old Dyke Tales*. Tallahassee, Fla.: Naiad Press, 1988.

MacKay, Anne, ed. *Wolf Girls at Vassar: Gay & Lesbian Experiences, 1930–1990*. New York: Ten Percent Publishing, 1993.

McDonald, Edward and Edward M. Hinton. *Drexel Institute of Technology, 1891–1941*. Philadelphia: Drexel Institute, 1942.

Meaker, Marijane. *Highsmith: A Romance of the 1950s*. New York: Cleis, 2003.

Meeker, Martin Dennis, Jr. *Contacts Desired: Gay and Lesbian Communications and Community, 1940s–1970s*. Chicago: University of Chicago Press, 2006.

Milford, Nancy. *Savage Beauty: The Life of Edna St. Vincent Millay*. New York: Random House, 2002.

Miller, Neil. *Out of the Past: Gay and Lesbian History from 1869 to the Present*. New York: Vintage Books/Random House, 1995.

Minton, Henry L. *Departing from Deviance: A History of Homosexual Rights and Emancipatory Science in America*. Chicago: The University of Chicago Press, 2002.

Nelson, C. Hal, ed. *Rockford College: A Retrospective Look*. Rockford, Ill.: Rockford College, 1980.

Reynolds, Michael. *The Young Hemingway*. New York: Basil Blackwell, 1986.

Richardson, John V. Jr. *The Spirit of Inquiry: The Graduate Library School at Chicago, 1921–51* (Chicago: American Library Association, 1982)

Sadler, William S. *The Physiology of Faith and Fear*. Chicago: A. C. McClurg, 1912.

Secrest, Meryle. *Between Me and Life: A Biography of Romaine Brooks*. New York: Doubleday, 1974.

Sheppard, Lydia Dixon. *The History of Shorter College*. MA thesis, Emory University, 1941.

Sibley, Agnes. *May Sarton*. New York: Twayne Publishers, 1972.

Smith-Rosenberg, Caroll. *Disorderly Conduct: Visions of Gender in Victorian America*. New York: Knopf, 1985.

Solomon, Barbara Miller. *In the Company of Educated Women*. New Haven: Yale University Press, 1985.

Stein, Marc. *City of Sisterly and Brotherly Love: Making Lesbian and Gay History in Philadelphia, 1945–1972*. Chicago: University of Chicago Press, 2000.

Streitmatter, Rodger. *Unspeakable: The Rise of the Gay and Lesbian Press in America*. Boston: Faber and Faber, 1995.

Sweetman, David. *Mary Renault: A Biography*. New York: Harcourt, Brace & Co., 1993.

Terry, Jennifer. *An American Obsession: Science, Medicine, and Homosexuality in Modern Society*. Chicago: University of Chicago Press, 1999.

Uhlan, Edward. *The Rogue of Publishers' Row*. New York: Exposition Press, 1956.

Vicinus, Martha. *Intimate Friends: Women Who Loved Women, 1778–1928*. Chicago: University of Chicago Press, 2005.

Vining, Donald. *A Gay Diary, 1933–1946*. New York: Masquerade Books, 1979.

Weiss, Andrea. *Paris Was a Woman: Portraits from the Left Bank*. San Francisco: Harper, 1995.

Wineapple, Brenda. *Genet: A Biography of Janet Flanner*. Lincoln: University of Nebraska Press, 1989.

Wood, Mary E. "'With Ready Eye': Margaret Fuller and Lesbianism in Nineteenth-Century American Literature." *American Literature* 65 (March 1993): 1–18.

Zimmerman, Bonnie. *Lesbian Histories and Cultures: An Encyclopedia*. New York: Garland Publishing, 2000.

INDEX

NOTE: Numbers in italics refer to photos.